Thirteen Enjoyable Aspects
of
Parenting Adolescents

One Pediatrician's Perspective on
Our Greatest of Gifts,
in Their Hardest of Years

Susan Shoshana Weisberg, MD

ISBN: 1439270309
ISBN-13: 9781439270301

THIRTEEN ENJOYABLE ASPECTS
OF
PARENTING ADOLESCENTS

One Pediatrician's Perspective on
Our Greatest of Gifts,
in Their Hardest of Years

B"H

to my Better Half
Melvyn Mordechai Weisberg

to Asher, Avraham, Chana, Noach, and Sarah
and to their Grandparents

to every one of my patients and their families
for the things they have taught me
for the ways they have inspired me

and for each of my patients who left early
may they rest in peace
in the Eternal Light
and may their memory
continue
to be for a Blessing

FOREWORD

● ● ●

THIRTEEN ENJOYABLE ASPECTS OF PARENTING ADOLESCENTS
ONE PEDIATRICIAN'S PERSPECTIVE
ON OUR GREATEST OF GIFTS,
IN THEIR HARDEST OF YEARS

Books on parenting adolescents are written primarily by therapists who treat troubled teens in the heat of their problems. When I read these important and insightful books, I feel like I am leading a double life. By night, I learn of barely human fireballs morphed from remnants of formerly loving offspring. By day, I see reflective young people struggling to function in a difficult world at a pivotal time in their lives.

The difference in our perspectives as authors reflects the difference in our roles in adolescents' lives. My lens is long. I am a pediatrician who has been privileged to practice medicine in the same community for over a quarter-century. Those rainbow-haired patients of mine were also mine when they sported their original Mohawks, as giggling babies with their first crop of hair. I witnessed their first inability to walk a straight line as they explored my office at a towering 24 inches in height. I see them not as a snapshot in time, but as a composite of years of love, sweat, and tears. I find them both challenged and challenging.

This book is not about behavioral algorithms for dealing with adolescents. Nor is it an appeal for any single moral or ethical mindset. It is about what the scientific, medical literature teaches us about our teenagers. It is also about insights I have gleaned from watching a kaleidoscope of unique and remarkable families face difficult years in our difficult culture. It is what a generation of medical researchers, patients, and parents have taught me. I am grateful to have been their student.

—Susan Shoshana Weisberg, MD

INTRODUCTION

● ● ●

THIRTEEN ENJOYABLE ASPECTS OF PARENTING ADOLESCENTS

Schoolchildren are taught that music is a universal language. I disagree. Though musical notes can be read and performed by international orchestras with no common tongue, heavy metal and opera don't transcend generational and cultural lines. If you want to talk timeless, it's parenting that's our common denominator. And for every generation, the screeching fingernail on that universal blackboard is adolescence.

As a young intern, fresh out of medical school, I was privileged to train under the late Dr. Ira Rosenthal, a leader in his day and one of the last of a generation of Renaissance pediatricians. Dr. Rosenthal practiced before CT scans and subspecialists. He could delineate the biochemical causes of rare metabolic diseases and in the next breath discuss constipation and toilet training, all while carrying urine to the lab to ensure its arrival. To a physician of such brilliance, commitment, and breadth of knowledge, the splintering of medicine into different subspecialties was not necessarily a good thing. Although rumors that our Department Chairman could light cigars with his eyes were an exaggeration, Dr. Rosenthal did have a way of expressing displeasure. His weapon of choice in this regard was his unique sense of humor.

"I have just met with a delegation of internists," he announced to a group of us trainees one day as we arrived early for a conference. "They want to start a new subspecialty called 'adolescent medicine'. They want to train a little in our program, and then take our patients. They want me to teach them this 'adolescent medicine' as if it can be separated from general pediatrics." "Instead," he thundered, "let me teach you pediatricians about adolescents. Here's everything you need to know. One pubic hair, and get 'em out of your practice. Send 'em to those internists and let them have 'em!"

My mentor had an unfortunate habit, much like our mothers, of always being right. Adolescents are exasperating. It's hard to know what to do with them. Doctors who take them on lightly should be careful what they wish for. Decades after Dr. Rosenthal's declaration, my medical colleagues now seem to share his attitude. The introductory editorial in a 2005 issue of Pediatric Annals devoted to adolescent medicine was titled "The Teen Years (Whew!)".[1] Two years later, the prestigious Journal of Pediatrics published an article headlined "The pediatric subspecialty of adolescent medicine— Help wanted!"[2] There are currently 16 subspecialties within the field of pediatrics. Among them, adolescent medicine ranks 15th in popularity as reflected by the number of new doctors choosing to train in it. Only "medical toxicology", with its requirement for an extensive technical chemistry background, is selected less often.[3] In 2005, the number of doctors entering training in adolescent medicine fell by over 25%.[4] On top of that, the dropout rate among those trainees who do start out in adolescent medicine is 23%.[5] "Although the adolescent population can be challenging…" the authors of one of the articles documenting this admitted. "…Our challenge is to galvanize interest…"[6]

This will take some serious effort. A physician I once met told me that when he thought of pediatrics and adolescents, only 2 words came to his mind: "general anesthesia". I have also heard of adolescent medicine specialists referred to as "psychiatrists who do pelvic exams."[7] A gynecologist friend of mine who treats many adolescents once told me "being a teenager is a disease in and of itself."

In 2006, the renowned British Medical Journal reported of a Welsh researcher who invented a "teenager repellent", a machine that emits an unpleasant high pitched shriek audible to teens but not adults. It is rumored to be in actual use in some shopping malls. In its annual contest for science that "first makes you laugh, then makes you think", Harvard University honored the invention with a special award, their "IgNOBEL" Peace Prize.[8] [9]

Raising teenagers has been likened to "nailing jello to a tree". A parent in my practice labels adolescence a "spell" that is eventually lifted. Yet another mother told me she envisions parenting her adolescents as being similar to "working in a psychiatric hospital. They are the patients, and I am the doctor. And do doctors argue with patients? No, I just work the shifts and try to stay calm." Still another mother in my practice likens parenting teenagers to playing the game "whackamo". "You just never know who's going to pop up out of which hole," she points out "I just try to keep up." In gaming terms, I think of parenting teens more in terms of a fast game of chess, or managing a long row of spinning plates.

My approach to adolescents is colored by Dr. Rosenthal's wry outlook. Humor helps cope. As I ponder adolescents, I often consider the case of a most infamous modern parent with multiple older children, Osama bin Laden. Mr. bin Laden is reported to have over 24 offspring. OF COURSE he's holed up in a cave!!! He probably doesn't even know the free world is after him. Would you come out to 2 dozen dependents clamoring for iPods and the use of your Master Card? I think all we need to do to get him out is convince him that all his children are suitably married and financially independent.

On the other end of the political spectrum is our new President Obama. How will this brilliant and accomplished leader of the free world stay humble and grounded amidst the greatest popular support in recent history? His soon-to-be adolescent daughters will take care of it, no problem. One of President Obama's predecessors, Teddy Roosevelt, was once asked about his influence over his eldest daughter. "I can be president of the United States, or I can control Alice. I can't possibly do both,"[10] he admitted helplessly.

After fathering 3 children (including twins) within 20 months, William Shakespeare later wrote in his *Winter's Tale* that "I would there was no age between 10 and 23, or that youth would sleep out the rest…"[11] Prolonged "general anesthesia".

The art world's depiction of parenting is a little less consistent. The cover of one of my medical journals once featured a reproduction of the painting "Domestic Happiness" by Lilly Martin Spencer. It portrays glowing parents, looking finely dressed and well rested, watching their baby and toddler sleep. I got out a calculator to confirm the picture was painted before the artist's children were of adolescent age, and I was only really comforted when I read that it was the painter's husband who "supervised the household, shopped, and took care of the children."[12] It has always made sense to me that impressionist painter Mary Cassatt was childless. Those cherubic children whose beautiful portraits she painted were her sister's, and our chronicle of them ends before adolescence. For reality, my favorite piece of art is a panel of 5 differently illustrated spaces subtitled "Parent-child relationships". One panel is colorful and ordered, and another is cloud-like. The one representing adolescence is a violent splash of clashing hues.

Such is the world's view of my patients. And yet after over a quarter-century as a pediatrician, it is with a heavy heart that I complete college forms for adolescent patients who were mine as newborns. There is not a one of them I don't miss. Watching each of them grow and mature has been a professional and personal experience I treasure. Every single one has taught and inspired me and enriched my life.

My favorite medical article on adolescents was published quietly in 2008 in the Journal of the American Medical Association.[13] I was initially perplexed by its topic—the rate of side effects after blood donation in 16- and 17-year-olds. Then I learned that the relevance of this issue is that while 16- and 17-year-olds comprise only 2.8% of our population, they donate 8% of our blood supply. At a cost of more adverse reactions, especially bruising and fainting, than suffered by older donors. When it was suggested in response to this data that people under 20 years of age not be allowed to donate blood, a Red Cross official wrote that the effect would be a "considerable crisis in the blood supply."[14] These little known statistics speak volumes to me. Those needle-phobic adolescent patients of mine, terrified of tetanus shots, silently pony up a huge percentage of blood donations. One of my patients, over the objections of her parents, happily underwent a painful procedure to donate her bone marrow to a social acquaintance. Another of my patients donated bone marrow to a total stranger.

How utterly kind! How completely selfless! Those blood units my patients donate are not used by their young healthy peers. They are consumed by patients decades older. In a culture that offers our youths few opportunities to meaningfully contribute, they roll up their sleeves and give us all they can, their blood.

My adolescent patients give not only blood, but sweat and time. Every spring my desk is covered with medical clearance forms for volunteer trips. Foregoing vacations, my patients use their spring and summer breaks to build homes, orphanages, medical clinics, and churches in primitive and uncomfortable conditions in all corners of the earth.

Others of my adolescent patients volunteer here at home. They leave their fanciest of houses to clean cages at animal shelters. Some of them spend every Sunday afternoon socializing with special needs children in a beautiful "Friendship Circle" program run by the wife of a Rabbi in my community. There are similar Friendship Circles springing up in many other cities. In a story that made national television, several teenagers from my practice who play football in a Catholic league recently stopped their game to allow a patient of mine with Down's syndrome to complete a touchdown and win the game. I am proud and grateful to know these players. What an admirable sporting contrast to the sexualized half-time "wardrobe-malfunctioning", alcohol-promoting spectacle we call the "Super" Bowl.

Shakespeare's wish for my patients to sleep through their rough years would deprive us of the shining flip-side of the coin these adolescents offer. As a later English author so famously wrote, the worst of times can also be the best of times. In one of the world's best known opening lines, Charles Dickens eloquently points out that the "age of wisdom,… the age of foolishness", the seasons of Light and Darkness, and times of hope and despair can all coincide.[15] Looked at in a different light, those clashing colors representing adolescence in the painting in my office can be seen as a rainbow. Some of those colors might be dark, but there is an Arab proverb that if all we have is sun, all we get is deserts.

And while those adolescent specialist doctors rightly point out that our teenagers can be "challenging", they are equally "challenged". They weather our divorces in record numbers. They are moved between new homes and schools more often than we were. Their extended families are further away than ours were. They have more homework than we had. They get less sleep than we got. They are immersed in sexual innuendo the likes of which we never dealt with. Lurking on their internet, 24/7, are the most hardened of criminal sexual predators, just a keystroke away.

One of my own children, in the throes of adolescence, once joked to me that I had a "love-hate" relationship with my offspring. "You love us… and we hate you." The child was half right. We do love our adolescents, no matter how rough the road.

This is not a "how-to" manual on raising adolescents. It's about insights and advice. Setting aside all the doom and gloom literature on adolescents and their problems, let's journey to the brighter side of these rising sons and daughters. Whatever their issues, our teenagers are our only future and our greatest legacy. I have noticed (at least) 13 enjoyable aspects of parenting adolescents. Let's explore them…

CONTENTS

● ● ●

CHAPTER 1

• • •

THIRTEEN ENJOYABLE ASPECTS OF PARENTING ADOLESCENTS

1) Adolescents are power sleepers. They do not crave parental attention at the crack of every dawn. They do not awaken Mom and Dad at 5:30 a.m. on Sunday mornings to watch cartoons. Their 3:00 a.m. meals are not family bonding events. After those exhausting early years, enjoy your sleep.

2) Adolescents have good appetites. They eat to grow. They eat to socialize. They come home from school ravenously hungry. They super-size everything, and eat cereal by the boxful. After years of agonizing over untouched vegetables, enjoy your empty cupboards.

3) Adolescents do not throw food in restaurants. They do not whine and cry loudly in stores over toys whose price exceeds average monthly mortgage payments. They do not lie down in supermarket aisles in protest over grocery choices. After years of public humiliation, enjoy your adolescent's company and companionship when you're out and about.

4) Adolescents do not eat crayons. They do not scour the floor with microscopic accuracy in search of lost small toy parts and dropped loose change to ingest or inhale. They do not insert metal objects into the single electrical outlet in the house lacking a safety cover. They do not "decorate" walls and upholstered furniture with permanent markers. Enjoy un-child-proofing your home and rediscovering those fragile family heirlooms.

5) Adolescents do not habitually vomit on our shoulders, or drool on our better clothing. They do not require or desire any assistance involving any body fluid or byproduct whatsoever. When your family reaches the outer recesses of huge airports laden with luggage, they do not suddenly need a washroom. Enjoy relinquishing responsibility for your adolescent's bodily functions.

6)   Sibling rivalry often winds down by adolescence. Adolescents do not pummel each other in cars over travel seating arrangements, or chase each other throughout their house until a head meets a sharp object. Adolescent siblings exchange unkind words, but the physical attacks and aggressive wrestling have usually fizzled out by the teenage years. After the agony of watching your offspring inflict injuries on each other that non-family members would be arrested for, enjoy the truce. Even if they are united only by a common (parental) enemy, enjoy the peace.

7)   Adolescents know how to use computers. They program cell phones with ease, and can tell the difference between an iPod and a palm pilot with their eyes closed. When complicated computer crimes threaten entire economies, the perpetrators almost always have acne. They are downloading and burning and e-mailing away while we never really learned how to eliminate commercials on our VCRs. Just as our immigrant grandparents retained their native language by using their offspring to speak English for them, use your adolescent to help navigate our new technological world. Appreciate and enjoy their special expertise.

8)   Adolescents are physically strong. They can lift heavy groceries and drag out loaded garbage cans, while using their other hand to hold the phone. Barely out of their adolescent years, we send them to war for us. Respect and enjoy their physical abilities.

9)   Adolescents are cheaper to provide health care for than their younger counterparts. Remember all those trips to the doctor for ear infections, fevers, coughs, and diarrhea–all followed by bills? Remember those expensive baby shots and check-ups? Enjoy the possibility of not exceeding your insurance deductible by Groundhog Day.

10) Adolescents are introspective and idealistic. They care deeply about social issues we've long since given up on. Could someone older in the same situation have written, as did Anne Frank, that people are really good at heart? Enjoy your adolescent's perspective and let it inspire you.

11) Adolescents bridge generations and give great joy to their grandparents, who know that the difficult years are temporary. Younger children also dearly love their adolescent older siblings and look up to them whatever their issues. Share in the wisdom of this vision of the forest through the trees, and enjoy your adolescent's potential in your family's future.

12) Adolescents keep us humble. Inflated egos are not an occupational hazard for those of us who parent teenagers. We're way over the thrill of out-bragging the newer moms in playgroup. We're just grateful if our off-spring lack parole officers and are unfamiliar with the back seat of squad cars. Enjoy your adolescent as the ultimate antidote for arrogance.

13) Adolescents need us. They need our love, our discipline, our monitoring, and our guidance, even and especially when they don't want it. Endless devotion is the essence of parenting. Having an adolescent to agonize over is a gift and a privilege (and it's never boring). Appreciate and enjoy it.

CHAPTER 2

● ● ●

DESPERATELY SEEKING SLUMBER

Enjoyable Aspect of Parenting Adolescents Number One: Adolescents are power sleepers. They do not crave parental attention at the crack of every dawn. They do not awaken Mom and Dad at 5:30 a.m. on Sunday mornings to watch cartoons. Their 3:00 a.m. meals are not family bonding events. After those exhausting early years, enjoy your sleep.

Imagine being sent to an exotic port, half way around the world, on a business trip. After settling in, you are awakened at 3:00 a.m. by your boss, calling from the home office to update you on the day's important new financial data. After reminding the boss what time it is at your end, he reminds you what time it is at his end. And so it goes every night of your trip. You face every day feeling tired and understandably grouchy. Your boss is unable or unwilling to make adjustments to your being in a different time zone.

Our adolescents, like traveling workers, exist in a different time zone. The schedules we impose on them fail to recognize this. We are like the clueless boss.

As questionable as the rest of his judgment was, even Shakespeare's Macbeth knew the value of a good night's sleep. After murdering King Duncan, one of his biggest complaints was insomnia. Lamenting on sleep lost, he declares sleep "sore labour's bath, balm of hurt minds, great nature's second course, chief nourisher in life's feast."[16]

Our insensitivity to our adolescent's need for the replenishing power of sleep is perplexing. No parent is a stranger to exhaustion. Remember those bleary eyed first months of parenting? As youth is for the young, sleep is for the childless. Unlike orca whales and dolphins, who stay awake months after the birth of their pups without known ill effects,[17] [18] new parents in my practice drag in, almost universally late for their appointments, looking starkly different than at their prenatal interviews.

They are not alone in their exhaustion. Emma Lazarus' poem on the Statue of Liberty asks for "your tired, your poor..." And here we are. According to the Centers for Disease Control and Prevention, we Americans are a sleep-deprived culture. In 2008, CDC data showed almost a third of us reporting insufficient sleep at least one day a month, and 1 in 10 of us reporting insufficient sleep every day of the month.[19] A 2005 National Sleep Foundation poll found American adults sleeping an average of only 6.9 hours per night.[20]

Burning the candle at both ends, we stay up later and get up earlier. The number of commuters leaving for work between 5: and 6:30 a.m. increased by 25% between 1990 and 2004.[21] Monitoring of our water and electricity consumption shows similar trends toward increasing use at 5:00 a.m. Over the last decade, the number of adults watching early morning television has doubled.[22]

There are ongoing studies concerning the effects of our electric "light pollution", and in animals, the data is not good. Disoriented and exhausted birds are more likely to fly into man-made structures, and turtles are thrown off course by light from beach-front developments, leading them often onto streets.[23] We are so unfamiliar with natural night skies that during one blackout in Los Angeles, some residents were frightened by what previous generations knew as "the Milky Way".[24]

Though the CDC calls our sleeplessness "an under recognized public health problem,"[25] it's hardly news to me. My medical training years overlapped with my early parenting years, and sleep deprivation dominated my existence. In the middle of one night, working in the emergency room, I came up with an idea that was a big hit with my colleagues. I proposed making sleep an Olympic Sport. Gold Medal Olympic Sleepers would enter the deepest sleep the fastest and with the lowest heart and respiratory rates. They would sleep the longest and with the least movement. We hoped for mattress and bedding company sponsorships, and eagerly awaited the time we could begin training in earnest.

In reality, Olympic Sleep Teams would be best manned by exhausted adolescents instead of their tired parents or doctors. My then 16-year-old daughter once participated in a grueling competition, in the sweltering heat, between the different bunks at her summer camp. The prize? Late wake up. She considered it worth it.

The physical growth and hormonal changes of puberty are exhausting. Adolescents need more sleep than adults,[26] and they need it on their schedule, not ours. Teenagers often get to bed late, and they have huge differences between their weekday and weekend sleep schedules. Weekday bedtimes in adolescents are delayed by homework, television, computer time, and after-school jobs. During the adolescent years, sleep time decreases by about 2 hours per night. The pattern of sleep also changes. At 10 years of age, sleep times on weekdays are the same as on weekends. For adolescents, more sleeping is done on weekends.[27] Adolescents are biologically nocturnal. This is not choice or habit. It is physical and hormonal. When girls start menstruating, their risk of insomnia triples.[28] Through no fault of their own, adolescents get tired later at night than the rest of us. When allowed to sleep in, they wake up later than we do, as well.[29] This pattern crosses cultural lines and has been found in American, European, South American, and Asian teenagers.[30] [31] [32] [33] The pattern also crosses generations, so don't quickly blame the internet. Comparing adolescent sleep diaries in 2006 to those in 1981, researchers found no difference in bed and wake times between them.[34]

School schedules take none of this into account. Over the past generation, school districts have opened schools earlier and earlier in the morning. Junior high and secondary schools starting early in turn often release students by 3:00 p.m., frequently into unsupervised homes. To have access to school sports facilities, some skating and swim teams practice as early as 5:00 a.m. Despite surveys showing almost 90% of parents favoring later school starting times, many school districts simply won't budge on this issue, citing "unalterable" bus schedules.[35] This is while they simultaneously complain about tardiness, which can also cost them lost revenue in states where funds are distributed based on attendance.[36] A school administrator in my own home town once told me that early school schedules were needed to train students for the working world. I disagree with this concept. By the time adolescents reach adulthood and hit the working world, their sleep needs have changed and matured. In the meantime, why are we sleep depriving them with schedules that conflict with their physical needs?

I do agree with school administrators, however, that there are important lessons for adolescents to learn regarding working and sleeping. Tired truck drivers have more accidents.[37] [38] Tired airport baggage screeners miss more security risks.[39] Employee sleep deprivation contributed to the Chernobyl nuclear accident, the Three Mile Island near meltdown, the loss of the Challenger space shuttle, the Comair airlines crash in 2006 that killed 49 people,[40] and the Exxon Valdez oil spill.[41] The cost of cleaning up that oil spill, by the way, has exceeded $192 million.[42] The payouts on the Comair crash were "undisclosed" but probably in the same range.

Sleep deprivation is an expensive medical issue, as well. Tired doctors make more mistakes than better rested ones.[43] [44] [45] [46] In one of the most heart-wrenching case studies I've ever read, a 38-year-old Boston woman in labor with a full term first pregnancy lost her baby and required a hysterectomy after medical errors attributed largely to a tired physician on call for 21 hours at the time of the tragedy. As part of the agreed upon malpractice settlement, the hospital sponsors an annual lectureship on patient safety.[47] Surgeons make 20% more errors in simulated procedures when tired.[48] Sleep deprived interns make 20% more serious errors in critical care units.[49] Doctors in training blame fatigue for almost half their errors.[50] Their performance after call is as impaired as if they were mildly alcohol intoxicated.[51] Exhausted doctors don't just hurt patients. They are almost twice as likely to stick themselves with contaminated needles.[52] And after they're done at the hospital, tired interns have more car accidents driving home.[53]

If doctors and other adult professionals can't tolerate sleep deprivation, why should adolescents be expected to? Schools interested in educating adolescents on working and sleeping should teach students about the need for adequate sleep instead of depriving them of it.

Patients with chronic diseases often complain that their weakness and fatigue are disabling. As a physician, I consider fatigue to be a form of pain. Captured enemy soldiers are often sleep deprived as a form of torture. Animal studies in birds and mammals show "profound deficits in neurobehavioural and physiological function" with sleep deprivation.[54] The human body doesn't do any better. Besides the discomfort of exhaustion, there are objective adverse medical effects from sleep deprivation:

1) **In the ultimate extreme, death**. Adult dogs die after about 13 days without sleep. Puppies die after only 6 days. Rats die after 13 to 21 days

of total sleep deprivation. In humans, a rare genetic disease called "fatal familial insomnia" has been reported in 24 families, with one known "sporadic" case. Patients with it have a variety of neurological symptoms and severe, untreatable insomnia. The average length of time from diagnosis to death is 18 months.[55][56]

2) Death due to sleep deprivation also occurs when tired drivers cause accidents. After just 17 hours without sleep, driving performance is as impaired as after 2 alcoholic drinks. After 28 hours, hand-eye coordination is as impaired as with legal intoxication.[57] Driving is so sensitive to sleep deprivation that immediately after the spring shift to daylight savings time, with a loss of 1 hour of sleep, the traffic accident rate increases 8%. After the fall shift back, recovering that extra hour of sleep, accident rates fall 8%.[58] Driver sleepiness is implicated as a causative factor in up to 3% of all motor vehicle crashes in the United States.[59] The National Highway Traffic Safety Administration estimates the cost of drowsy driving in America to be $12.4 billion per year, accounting for 1500 deaths and 76,000 injuries annually.[60] In 2003, the state of New Jersey passed a law making it a crime if a driver who hasn't slept in over 24 hours causes a fatal accident.[61] In accidents where a driver falls asleep at the wheel, 55% involve drivers under 25 years of age. The 2 peak time periods for the occurrence of such accidents is during the night, and during the afternoon from 2 to 4 p.m.[62] Given adolescent new drivers' inexperience behind the wheel, adding fatigue to the mix is particularly dangerous on the road.

3) Sleep deprivation can cause psychiatric symptoms, from hallucinations to hyperactivity. In 1959, a New York City radio disc jockey stayed awake for 200 hours in a glass booth in Times Square as a charity fund raiser. By the end, he had developed symptoms of paranoia and delusional thinking. He required an escort home after running away from a doctor whom he believed to be an undertaker trying to bury him alive.[63] Many years later, another disc jockey, this time from Shreveport, Louisiana, broke the world record for sleep deprivation after staying awake for 361 hours and 55 minutes. By the seventh day, he had massive hallucinations.[64]

A study of jailed young offenders found the degree of their aggression inversely correlated to the amount and quality of their sleep.[65] Other research has demonstrated a decrease in aggressive thoughts and actions in substance abusing adolescents given 6 weeks of interventions to improve their sleep.[66]

Sleep deprivation may also play a role in teenage depression and poor self-esteem. A survey of 2260 Illinois middle school students found that the better rested the student, the fewer the symptoms of depression and low self-esteem.[67] Other surveys have found an association between sleep problems and depression and the use of mental health services.[68 69] Adult night shift workers are known to have increased rates of depression.[70 71] While correlation does not prove causality, when the director of the Sleep Disorders Center at the University of Illinois normalized sleep in 13 depressed teenagers, their moods significantly improved.[72] One connection between mood and sleep may be light exposure. When college students nap after all-night studying, they are exposed to light at abnormal times. This disrupts their biological rhythms, at least one researcher has theorized. Some people's moods are very sensitive to light exposure or deprivation, which has been implicated as a cause in depressive syndromes that are seasonal in pattern.[73]

4) Sleep deprivation causes academic problems. When tired, children exhibit shorter attention spans, more learning problems, and an increase in hyperactive and aggressive behavior.[74] One researcher found that sleep restriction to 6½ hours per night for a single week caused children to have higher scores on the rating scales used to diagnose ADD and ADHD.[75 76] A similar study published later randomly divided children into 2 groups, one assured adequate sleep and the other sleep-deprived. Unaware of which group a student had been assigned to, teachers were able to correctly figure it out by observing the children's academic performance and behavior.[77] Compared to children without known attentional problems, children diagnosed with ADHD have increased rates of disordered sleep patterns.[78 79] Children with poor sleep habits also have more behavioral problems and lower scores on tests of memory and social competency.[80] Students with disordered sleep due to snoring problems have lowered IQ and attention test scores that show improvement when the snoring is medically treated. [81 82 83] Anxiety and sleep problems are strongly paired, though it is unclear to me which is the symptom and which is the underlying disease.[84]

5) Sleep deprivation impairs athletic and gross motor functioning. Traveling baseball teams perform less well when they head east, losing time. Analyzing Monday night football data, sleep researchers found that east coast teams lose more often, and by more points, than their west coast competitors. The reason may be that the games, regardless of location, all start at 9:00 p.m. Eastern Standard Time. For west coast players, that means 6:00 p.m. their time, further from bedtime and closer to the time of peak physical performance in the biological clock. A survey of Olympic athletes found that none listed their peak performance times as before 9:00 a.m. or after 9:00 p.m.[85] Fatigue matters.

Injuries, both in and out of sports, are more common after sleep deprivation. In one study, boys between 1 and 14 years of age had higher rates of injury the day after getting less than 10 hours of sleep. For both genders, there was a correlation between injury risk and being awake for at least 8 hours beforehand.[86] Over 2300 years ago, Sun Tzu warned warriors, in his classic The Art of War, to avoid fatigue in battle. His advice is timeless.

6) Teens with sleep problems have a higher rate of substance abuse.[87] Whether this is cause or effect is unknown.

7) Sleep deprivation impairs the immune system. Mothers of young children who reported "rarely or never" feeling well rested were over 2½ times more likely than better rested parents to suffer respiratory illnesses and infections.[88] A study of 42 men deprived of just part of one night's sleep found significantly less immune cells in their blood the next day.[89] Another study that restricted sleep in people before giving them flu shots found that the tired recipients had less than half the blood antibody response 10 days later compared to better-rested counterparts. Particularly striking was the fact that the shot recipients in that study were deprived of sleep only prior to immunization. They had 10 days after vaccination to rest before those blood levels were measured.[90]

8) Sleep deprivation affects the heart and circulatory system. A Harvard study found that compared to those who slept 8 hours per night, nurses who slept only 6 hours at night had an 18% increased risk of having a heart attack. Nurses who slept 5 or less hours per night had a 39% increased risk.[91] Doctors working extended overnight shifts have been found to have increased blood levels of proteins related to vascular inflammation and atherosclerosis.[92] Research published in 2008 found less coronary artery calcification in people who slept longer, and much greater rates of calcification in people sleeping less than 4 hours per night.[93] When our time clocks are pushed forward to daylight saving time in the spring, there is an increase in heart attacks for the first 3 weeks of the new schedule.[94] Adding to the cardiac risks of sleep deprivation are the effects that coffee and caffeine have on the heart when exhausted people use these stimulants to help stay awake.[95]

As for blood pressure, data published by the American Heart Association in 2006 showed over double the rate of hypertension in people getting 5 or fewer hours of sleep per night.[96] [97]

9) Sleep deprivation may have neurological consequences. Sleep deprivation the night before EEG tests for seizures has been used to increase their diagnostic yield by uncovering more abnormal findings in children with epilepsy.[98] One-fifth of children with occasional headaches have sleep problems. Two-thirds of children with daily headaches have sleep issues. Patients suffering with daily, chronic headaches are over 6 times more likely to have sleep problems than children with only infrequent migraines.[99]

10) Sleep deprivation may have a connection to diabetes. A University of Chicago study found a difference in blood sugar responses to meals in men after they were sleep deprived. Also, their insulin release and blood sugar clearance was 40% slower after sleep deprivation. Their elevated blood sugar levels were similar to those seen in pre-diabetic patients. Longer term, the Harvard study of nurses' health found an increased risk of diabetes in women with abnormal sleep patterns.[100] Research on patients with known "type 2" diabetes found lowered blood sugar control with less sleep.[101] Similar results were found in overweight children sleeping less than 6 hours per night.[102]

11) Sleep deprivation may increase the risk of cancer. A Danish study found that women who worked at night had a 50% greater risk of breast cancer than better-rested peers.[103] In 2007, the International Agency for Research on Cancer, a division of the World Health Organization, added overnight shift work as a probable carcinogen, citing links for both breast cancer in women and prostate cancer in men.[104]

12) Sleep deprivation contributes to obesity.[105] People who sleep less have increased appetites. A study from Eastern Virginia found that overweight patients slept an average of almost 2 hours less per night than thinner counterparts. Another study, this time from California, also found an inverse relationship between average nightly sleep duration and body weight. These researchers went a step further and identified a possible explanation. They measured levels of "ghrelin" and "leptin", two hormones involved in appetite regulation. Lack of sleep affected levels of both hormones toward favoring food intake. A University of Chicago study had similar findings.[106] As the connection between less sleep and increased weight is confirmed by more and more data,[107] most weight loss programs now recommend adequate sleep for successful dieting. Of particular concern for children and adolescents is a study with 32 years of follow-up that found increases in later obesity after sleep restriction earlier in life.[108]

Dr. Mary Carskadon, a sleep researcher, put it pretty bluntly when she said: "kids' circadian cycles are already hammered by their biology. Add to that the ridiculously early school start times across much of the country, and sleep gets squeezed right out of their schedules."[109] The result is exhausted, sleep-deprived adolescents. In one survey, 18% of teenagers reported falling asleep in class 4 or more times per week.[110] Our adolescents are so tired that one expert called them "among the sleepiest people in the world, rivaling narcoleptics…" He cautioned doctors against mistakenly diagnosing them with chronic fatigue syndrome. He termed it a "blind flash of the obvious" to explain why they struggle to get to school, and said that their sleep patterns mimic the jet lag that would result from cross country travel every few days.[111]

Our adolescents have a biological, physical need for more sleep, on a different schedule, than adults or children. Compared to younger children, adolescents release melatonin, a chemical marker for sleep readiness, a full hour later. Though one study found American 10th graders getting an average of 6.8 hours of sleep per night,[112] researchers from Stanford University have established that adolescents need an average of 9.25 hours of sleep per night to maximize their alertness.[113] [114] The sleep deprivation teens so often suffer causes a variety of harmful consequences. Helping our teenagers sleep and feel better is a goal we can and should accomplish. Let's explore some ways:

1) Let's work with our schools to alter class schedules to match adolescent's biological sleep needs. In 1994, the Minnesota Medical Association wrote letters to the state's 450 school districts urging later school day starting times for adolescents. Parents supporting the move notified school board members by telephone—at 5:30 a.m. when their children had to get up to get to school on time with the schedule then in existence.[115] In 1997, Minneapolis public schools responded and moved school starting times 2 hours later for middle schools and one hour later for high schools. "They come to school better rested", reported one principal. "They're more alert. And they participate more actively in classroom activities."[116] Some schools in Kentucky and Maryland have also delayed their starting times. There is data showing that increased sleep improves academic performance from middle school through college.[117] Also, when high school starting times were rolled back just 1 hour in one Kentucky county, teen car crashes there fell by 16.5%.[118] [119] The authors of a text-book on sleep and psychiatric disorders published in 2008 devoted a full chapter to documenting the mounting evidence that delayed school start times help adolescents in multiple, measurable ways.[120] The National Sleep Foundation estimates that over the past decade, over 80 American school districts have rolled back starting times.[121]

Another positive outcome of later school schedules occurs at the other end of the day. Teenagers on early school schedules often get home by 3:00 p.m., only to be left there unsupervised by working parents. A very significant portion of sexual encounters in adolescents occur during that afternoon period between school dismissal and parent's arrival home. When late start means later dismissal, afternoon unsupervised time may be diminished.

2) Let's work with our schools to reduce homework. The National Education Association and the National Parent Teacher Association recommend a maximum of 70 minutes of homework per night for 7th graders, and 2 hours per night for high school seniors. The amount of time my patients routinely spend per night on assignments far exceeds these guidelines. A University of Michigan survey documented an increase in homework time of over 50% between 1981 and 2007. The benefits of this increased work have not been demonstrated. The nation of Japan cut homework in the 1990s, and there are movements to accomplish the same here. Three recently published books on this topic, *The Case Against Homework*,[122] *The Homework Myth*,[123] and *Closing the Book on Homework*,[124] should be required late evening reading for school administrators.

3) Encourage tired teenagers to nap. Studies by NASA and the Federal Aviation Administration show that pilot performance improves after cockpit naps of just 40 minutes.[125] A European study found that people who took half hour or longer naps, 3 or more times a week, lowered their death rate from heart attacks by over a third.[126] And a survey conducted by the Greek Pediatric Society found that adolescents practicing the custom of siesta, or mid-day napping, report significantly less daytime sleepiness.[127]

4) Limit driving privileges for fatigued adolescent drivers. Make adequate sleep a requirement for use of the family car. Just as "friends don't let friends drive drunk", "family doesn't let family drive tired". The United State's CDC formally declared November 5-11, 2007 as "Drowsy Driving Prevention Week".[128] Celebrate it 52 weeks a year in your home.

5) **Minimize television viewing to lessen sleep problems in adolescents.** Teenagers who watch 3 or more hours of television per day have an increased risk of sleep problems. When adolescents in one study kept television viewing to less than an hour a day, their risk for developing sleep problems fell significantly.[129] Children monitored after computer game playing were found to have less "slow wave" sleep, and they demonstrated declines in verbal memory.[130] Researchers in Finland have even found that "passive exposure" to television is associated with sleep problems. In the presence of adults watching television, children themselves not actively watching still suffer sleep disturbances.[131] Most sleep therapy experts recommend against having televisions in bedrooms. Limiting total daily television time might also help adolescents become better rested.

6) **Be mindful of caffeine's side effects.** Caffeine is the most widely used stimulant on the planet. A survey of middle school students found caffeine consumption to be greatest from Wednesday through Saturday. The researchers who published that study theorized that students used caffeine as the school week dragged on to counteract the exhaustion from their increasing sleep debt. In turn, however, the caffeine seemed to cause poorer quality sleep.[132] The same effect was found in a later study of schoolchildren in 6th through 10th grade. Adolescents with high caffeine intakes had double the rate of sleep problems and were twice as likely to be tired in the mornings.[133] It might be helpful for teens with sleep problems to limit their caffeine intake.

7) **Alcohol use in teenagers is associated with difficulty awakening in mornings, and with falling asleep more often in school classes.** This is only one of many reasons for adolescents to abstain from underage alcohol consumption.[134]

There is an old Yiddish saying that "little children don't let you sleep; bigger children don't let you rest." True enough, but let's consider this glass half full. If nothing else, adolescents know how to sleep, and their tiredness is not laziness. They are not using sleep to avoid us or be defiant. They are not future work world drop-outs. They are biologically in need of more sleep than we allow them to get. Well-rested adolescents are better students and safer drivers. Helping teenagers get more sleep is not an exercise in indulgence or a reinforcement of irresponsibility. It is an act of compassion and understanding. Let this physical, medical issue be common ground instead of room for conflict in dealing with your teenager.

CHAPTER 3

● ● ●

LIFE IN THE FOOD LANE

Enjoyable Aspect of Parenting Adolescents Number Two: Adolescents have good appetites. They eat to grow. They eat to socialize. They come home from school ravenously hungry. They supersize everything, and eat cereal by the boxful. After years of agonizing over untouched vegetables, enjoy your empty cupboards.

There was once a zoo having problems with mother birds rejecting their young. Baby birds were being thrown out of their nests. The problem was solved when only mother birds were allowed to feed their offspring. It seems that when the baby birds were being fed and filled up by human zoo workers, they weren't hungry when they were re-united with their feathered mothers. Feeling already satisfied, they didn't look up and "gape" open their mouths like normal baby birds. Their mothers interpreted this as unhealthy, and by instinct rejected them and redirected their energies to babies who seemed, hungry, healthy, and more likely to survive. Mother cats are also known for rejecting the poorest feeders in their litters. Weak little "runt" kittens are offered no help feeding and are sometimes even killed and eaten themselves.

As I practice pediatrics, I often think of those rejected baby birds and runt kittens. We humans have every bit as much instinct in our feeding relationships. At the Fifth International Congress on Twin Studies in 1987, a researcher from the Cranfield Institute in England presented a study that found mothers of twins more likely to favor the heavier of their babies. The bigger the difference in the twins' sizes, the more likely it was for there to be a preference.[135]

The parents of "fussy" young eaters feel confused and rejected. In their families, feeding and nutrition are issues that can lead to bitter conflict and intense power struggles. I once witnessed two parents, both Ivy League educated professionals, have an argument over baby food. In the heat of the battle, it's easy to forget that toddlers are happiest using their new-found motor skills to search for uncovered electrical outlets and unsecured stairways. They're too busy to sit and eat, and when they do, the volume they need is proportionate to their little size.

It is our instinct to feed our young. It is our pleasure to see them accept and enjoy our efforts. Feeding dominates our earliest interactions with our newborns. And for babies, sucking is a reflex that ends in a lot more than a simple swallow. Infants are more likely to open their eyes while feeding than at other times. This makes feeding a social and bonding event, as well as a nutritional one. As we age, does anything really change? Can you imagine a social life without food? We have breakfast meetings and dinner dates. We "do" lunch, not just eat it. And then there are teas, coffee clutches, and brunches. "Breaking bread" makes for a lot more than crumbs.

Our feeding relationships with our teenagers are no less important than our feeding relationships with our toddlers. There is a growing body of medical literature on the effects of "family dining."

A study of 4746 Minnesota adolescents found that those who ate together often with their families had lower rates of tobacco, alcohol, and marijuana use, fewer symptoms of depression, less suicide attempts, and higher grade point averages.[136] That study was careful to factor out "family connectedness" and differences in family income and makeup. Data from another study, involving 99,462 students in 213 different American cities, yielded similar findings. It found the rates of all high risk behaviors from drug, alcohol, and tobacco use to violent activities to eating disorders, inversely related to the frequency of family meals.[137] Yet another study, from Harvard, showed that girls who ate family dinner at home every night were less likely to try alcohol or to binge drink.[138] Columbia University's National Center on Addiction and Substance Abuse has also studied this issue. Their data was dramatic. Compared to frequent family diners, they found that adolescents eating family dinners only infrequently had triple the rates of marijuana, alcohol, and illegal drug use. They were also twice as likely to do poorly in school.[139] Over a 5 year period, longer term data from yet another study found family meals offering continued, long term protection from tobacco, alcohol, and marijuana use.[140] And on another issue, adolescent girls who eat more family meals have lowered rates of eating disorders.[141]

One last study on communal eating involved German students at a boarding school. Half the students were assigned to eat breakfast every day in a group setting with their peers. The others went to class on an empty stomach. The breakfast eaters had better moods, attention spans, concentration, alertness, and memory.[142]

Some commentators on family dining issues have even further reaching ideas about family meals. In *The Civility solution; What to Do When People are Rude[143]*, writer P. M. Forni defines the place where ethical behavior starts as none other than "the dinner table". That author considers manners a primer for moral philosophy. In a 2005 Wall Street Journal editorial titled "Much Depends on Dinner", a busy Law Review publisher and father of two young children ruminates on missing dinner with them most nights, pointing out that dinner is like a "formal poem" with a fixed pace that can't be "hastened by technology or e-mailed as an attachment to our kitchens." He calls dinner "a substantial part of our children's lives."[144] A church pastor once wrote an editorial in Newsweek magazine about a weekly dinner a group of church members organized. The diverse group has dined together for over a year, and amidst social upheaval and economic challenges, she described the meals as "our last best hope."[145]

As a pediatrician, I find data on family meals and commentaries regarding their significance both striking and profoundly important. Yet little is written about this in my medical journals. Instead, the current medical research focuses on other nutritional issues.

Though parents often agonize over picky eaters, the main nutritional risk our children and adolescents face is not inadequate food intake. It is iron-deficiency anemia. Up to 9% of toddlers and 11% of adolescent girls are iron deficient.[146] Overweight children are at increased risk of anemia, as are infants 9 to 12 months of age and adolescent girls.[147] Anemic children have lower math scores,[148] and they may be more susceptible to infection[149]. Neurologically, they may be at greater risk for fever seizures when very young,[150] and they are often restless. One study found lower iron levels in children with ADD compared to those without it.[151] When English researchers gave iron to adolescent girls with low but not anemic iron levels, their verbal learning and memory skills improved.[152] A similar study from Israel found better mood, concentration ability, and energy levels in girls given iron.[153] In one well documented case, a 3-year-old diagnosed with ADD and hyperactivity was found to have a very low blood iron level. After 8 months of treatment with iron, his behavior improved to the point where he was no longer considered to have behavioral problems.[154] Foods containing iron include red meats, spinach, eggs, prunes, beans, molasses, wheat germ, and the many iron fortified cereals. In young children, iron absorption is increased by orange and apple juices, and decreased by cow's milk and tea.[155] [156] [157]

It is also easy for adolescents to short themselves on calcium and vitamin D. This is a serious problem as about 40% of our adult bone mass is accumulated during the 4 years of the adolescent growth spurt.[158] [159] Puberty is a time of massive bone growth, and both calcium and vitamin D are needed to sustain it. When researchers checked blood vitamin D levels in 300 adolescents, 10% had borderline low levels, 25% had levels in the low range, and 5% had levels considered very low. Those with low levels exercised less and drank a third less milk than their peers with normal vitamin D levels.[160] A second, similar study found even greater deficiency rates, with seasonal variation and lower levels in fall and winter when there is less exposure to the sunlight needed for the body to maximize the formation of vitamin D.[161] A third study found only 30% of adolescents consuming the recommended amount of calcium per day.[162] [163] Yet another study, of inner city adolescent girls, found 73% of them to be vitamin D deficient, 17% of them severely so. [164] There is a case report from 2006 where a 17-year-old boy from inner-city New York, known to eat mostly "junk food", developed seizures and suffered 2 broken legs. His problems were traced to calcium deficiency.[165]

Remedying adolescent's poor calcium and vitamin D status involves dietary changes. Dairy products and some juices are vitamin D fortified, and good sources of calcium include dairy products, tofu, broccoli, collards, spinach, cod liver oil, some fish especially sardines and salmon, and fortified juices. Calcium absorption is inhibited by high-phosphorus foods (especially soda), caffeine, alcohol, and cigarette smoking.[166] [167] Sunlight increases the formation of vitamin D in the skin, and exercise helps utilize calcium and incorporate it into bone. In one study involving gymnasts, however, extreme exercise was too much of a good thing and blocked the benefit of calcium supplements.[168] An alternative approach, which did demonstrate success in increasing bone density, was a program encouraging increases in dietary intakes of calcium and vitamin D coupled with moderate exercise.[169]

Adolescents with eating disorders and low vitamin D levels have been found to have weakened bones and even resultant fractures.[170] Thinning of the bones has also been seen in Asian vegetarians.[171]

About 6% of adolescents classify themselves as vegetarians. Most of them will consume milk and eggs, but about 1 in 200 adolescents are "vegans", excluding even those foods. One-half to three-quarters of adolescent vegetarians are girls.[172] Vegetarians have lower cholesterol levels, lower blood pressures, lower body weights, and less heart disease.[173] They consume less fast food, sugar sweetened soda, and fruit drinks, but take in more diet soda and caffeine.[174] [175] Well and good, but there is another side to vegetarianism in adolescents. Many of them use it as a weight control method, and their rates of eating disorders are high. Compared to their meat eating peers, adolescent vegetarians are twice as likely to be frequent dieters, 4 times as likely to admit to intentional vomiting, and 8 times more likely to use laxatives to purge.[176] [177]

There are also nutritional deficiencies of concern in vegetarians. Those who exclude dairy products are at risk for inadequate calcium intake. To make matters worse, calcium absorption is inhibited by the "oxalate" chemicals in spinach, beet greens, Swiss chard, and chocolate; and the "phytate" chemicals in whole grains, legumes, nuts, and seeds.[178] Good sources of calcium for vegetarians who exclude milk include calcium fortified soy foods, tofu, calcium fortified juices, dried figs, sesame tahini, collard, turnip greens, broccoli, molasses, beans, legumes, figs, almonds, and Chinese cabbage.[179] Vitamin D is also an issue when dairy intake is excluded. Fortunately, many soy and rice milks are now supplemented with vitamin D, and it is also "self-made" by the body with exposure to sunlight. Iron is another issue for vegetarians. The type of iron in plants is absorbed less well than iron from meat.

Most worrisome to me as a physician, though, is vitamin B-12 deficiency in vegetarians. Vitamin B-12 is only available from animal products. Vegetarians who exclude eggs and dairy foods can only get vitamin B-12 from specially fortified cereals, soy or rice milks, or vitamin supplement pills.[180] Deficiency of vitamin B-12 (also named "cobalamin") can cause a special type of anemia and a variety of neurological problems.[181] There are at least 4 documented cases of breast fed babies of vegan mothers who suffered B-12 deficiency with neurological symptoms, weakness, growth failure, and anemia.[182] [183] One 10 month old boy had to be admitted to an intensive care unit in a coma from the problem, and was found to have atrophy of his brain. He was left developmentally delayed.[184] Also horrifying were 2 case reports in The New England Journal of Medicine that described vegans who became **irreversibly, permanently blind** from vitamin B-12 deficiency.[185] [186] Vegetarian adolescents need careful monitoring for eating disorders and nutritional deficiencies, and supplementation with iron, calcium, vitamin D, and vitamin B-12 may be a good idea. Vegetarian adolescents who exclude eggs and dairy foods warrant supervision by a nutritionist or physician with special expertise in nutrition.

Whether people eating full diets need vitamin supplement pills is a matter of debate. Elderly Canadians given multivitamin pills had fewer sick days and better immune system function in one study,[187] but no advantage was found in a larger study of Americans published the next year.[188] Similarly, in the 1980s, a small English study showed increases in IQ in children given vitamins. Soon thereafter a larger study found no benefit.[189] A study published in 2007 combined the results of 68 different trials involving over 232,000 people. The data showed no benefit from the use of "antioxidant" supplements including beta carotene, selenium, or vitamins A, C, or E. Even worse, some analyses of the data showed the supplements actually increasing death rates.[190] Long term high dose "megavitamin" use has not been proven to prevent asthma, ADD, or hyperactivity. There is conflicting evidence as to whether high dose vitamin C helps when taken during viral upper respiratory infections.[191] [192] There is consistent evidence that children born to mothers who took prenatal vitamins have lower rates of nervous system and spinal cord birth defects, and there is also data showing that they may also have a lower risk of some childhood cancers.[193]

Good medical literature generally supports vitamin supplementation only for people at special risk of nutritional deficiency, including pregnant women.[194] [195] [196] [197] Doctor's reluctance to recommend vitamin supplements for everyone may be based on the fact that overdoses of them, especially iron and vitamins A, D, E, and K, are especially dangerous. Such overdoses can cause a variety of problems including increased pressure in the brain, bone pain, impairment of blood clotting, and liver damage.[198] [199] [200] [201] But given adolescent's documented rates of iron, calcium, and vitamin D deficiencies and their high rates of eating disorders and vegetarian diets, all in the face of the massive demands of pubertal growth, I don't think it's unreasonable to give teenagers a daily multivitamin supplement containing iron.

Just when children finally do mature and learn how to eat, we change our tune and worry about them getting overweight. During puberty, adolescents gain half their adult weight, but only a fifth of their adult height. Girls gain twice as much body fat as boys during this period.[202] Body composition studies of girls show that they reach their peak accumulation of body fat at 13½ years of age. They do not reach their peak height for a full 4 years later.[203] In other words, adolescents "bulk" up at the start of puberty, with their height catching up to their weight later on. This is normal, but often alarming to parents primed to fear obesity.

It is true that obesity is on the rise. The obesity rate in American 12- to 17-year-olds tripled between 1976 and 2000.[204] Among Western nations the United States, Ireland, Greece, and Portugal lead the pack in obesity rates.[205] Internationally, from China to Northern Africa, the rest of the world is catching up.[206] But while obesity is on the rise, it's also not a suddenly new issue. It was described as early as the 17th century, and the January, 1865 issue of the Harper's Weekly magazine featured advice on weight loss.[207] I have a paper in my files from 1987, yellowed with age, titled "Increasing Pediatric Obesity in the United States."[208] And for all our adult assumptions on the emotional consequences of overweight, a 2005 study found that "adolescents with above normal body mass did not report poorer emotional, school, or social functioning."[209] Overall, there are only 4 aspects of obesity that I believe the medical literature makes consistently clear:

1) Obesity has a huge genetic component. A study of 540 adult Danish adoptees published in 1986 confirmed earlier twin studies and found a weight correlation between adoptees and biological but not adoptive parents. The authors concluded that "family environment alone has no apparent effect"[210] on weight. Another study published the same year compared weights within pairs of identical versus fraternal twins. Correlation was much greater within the genetically identical sets.[211] Yet another study of twins, this time twins reared apart, yielded the same conclusion: "the childhood environment has little or no influence."[212] Looking at this issue from a different direction, researchers in Canada housed and overfed 12 pairs of identical twins for about 3 months. Given the exact same calories, the amount of weight gained ranged from 9½ to 30 pounds. The variation in amount of weight gained was much greater between than within twin pairs, the explanation for which is "genetic factors".[213] An editorial in the New England Journal of Medicine published in 1990 reviewing the topic of the genetics and obesity ran under the headline "Destiny Rides Again…"[214] Decades of research confirms the major influence of genetics in weight and obesity. Complex, new research involving the hormone protein "leptin" and the genes for its receptors use bigger words and bigger budgets to repeatedly just confirm the same concept.[215] Over a century ago, in 1892, the father and dean of American medicine Dr. William Osler pointed out that the "tendency to…obesity is often hereditary." In 1905, a strain of obese yellow lab mice was identified, providing an animal model for hereditary obesity. A hundred years and a lot of research dollars later, this concept remains only repeatedly confirmed. Obesity is largely a genetic, inherited problem.[216] The environmental, non-genetic component of obesity may be socially influenced. An article published in the New England Journal of Medicine found clustering of obesity in social networks. People with overweight friends, especially of the same gender, were 57% more likely than others to become obese themselves over time.[217]

2) Obesity has many medical complications, and it's expensive in terms of health care dollars. It's been big news lately in the lay press, with stories about our needs for larger airline and toilet seats and oversized coffins.[218] Higher body weights are associated with increased rates of heart disease, high blood cholesterol, high blood pressure, stroke, diabetes, sleep apnea, gout, arthritis, and some types of cancer.[219][220] Obesity complicates and slows recovery from ankle and other injuries, and it also is a risk factor for hip and ankle fractures, knee dislocations, and many other leg and hip problems.[221] Overweight people have shorter life spans[222][223][224][225][226] by from 5 to 20 years,[227] and in the United States alone, about 300,000 deaths a year are attributed to obesity.[228] Babies born to obese mothers have more birth defects, from heart problems to cleft lips and palates, among others.[229][230] In economic terms, it has been estimated that almost 7% of all American health care dollars are spent on obesity-related causes[231] As far back as 1986 the estimated cost of overweight was thought to be over $39 billion.[232] In 1999 alone, Americans spent $321 million on prescription medicines to treat obesity.[233] The hospital costs of obesity-related diseases in youths quadrupled between 1979 1999, to over $127 million annually.[234] In 2006, the projected cost of obesity was $49 billion for every 4 million children born in the United States.[235]

3) Obesity can have emotional associations. Some adolescents demonstrate self-confidence and resiliency about being overweight. On the other hand, fewer obese girls attend college.[236] Others suffer from teasing and bullying,[237] lower quality of life with less self-esteem, and depression.[238][239] It is possible, however, that the link between depression and obesity may be the other way around. Weight gain is a known symptom of depression. Instead of being depressed because they are overweight, our obese adolescents may be gaining weight because they are depressed. A British study found correlations between a variety of adverse childhood experiences, including physical abuse and neglect, and the later development of obesity.[240] Multiple studies have documented an association between the presence of depressive symptoms and anxiety during childhood and the later development of obesity.[241] [242] Adolescents considering themselves to be at the lower end of the social spectrum have higher rates of obesity. Being popular is protective against weight gain.[243]

4) Medicine has not yet found an effective treatment for obesity. There are now over 1000 diet books on the market in the United States.[244] Between 30 and 50 billion dollars a year is spent on diet foods and weight loss remedies.[245] Here's what the medical literature concludes about the success of all these efforts:

> —"…for many adolescents, dieting to control weight is not only ineffective, it may actually promote weight gain." (Drs. A. Field and a group of physicians from Harvard, whose research showed dieting in teenagers was often associated with binge eating and weight gain.)[246]

> —"The large community-based trials…demonstrated that targeting individual behavior was ineffective in reducing the prevalence of…obesity" (Dr. David Williamson from the Centers for Disease Control, in an editorial in the New England Journal of Medicine on "The Prevention of Obesity")[247]

> —"…a dismal history…" (Dr. R. Goldbloom, in a commentary on Dr. Field's article and dieting in general)[248]

> —"…usually disheartening." (The Medical Letter)[249]

> —"…not impressive. Compliance decreases with time, and weight is regained. Repeated cycles are common." (Canadian Dr. Claude Bouchard in an editorial in the New England Journal of Medicine)[250]

> —"…abysmal; 1/3 to 2/3 of …[lost] weight is regained within 1 year and nearly all is regained within 5 years." (Drs. Manson, Colditz, and Stampfer in an editorial in the Journal of the American Medical Association)[251]

> —"No current treatment for obesity reliably sustains weight loss…" (Drs. Leibel, Rosenbaum, and Hirsch publishing in The New England Journal of Medicine)[252]

—"The task is enormous, the long-term results are still dismal, and the cure rate is still zero. It is not a curable disease." (Dr. A. Frank in the Journal of the American Medical Association, whose point was that although many obese people can lose weight, they still have a metabolic "basic physiologic abnormality".)[253]

—"Most overweight individuals can successfully lose some of the weight, but the majority regain that weight within 5 years." (Drs. Jack and Susan Yanovski, publishing in the Journal of the American Medical Association.) [254]

—"...many people cannot lose weight no matter how hard they try, and promptly regain whatever they do lose." (Drs. J. Kassirer and M. Angell in an editorial in the New England Journal of Medicine)[255]

–"a troubling challenge" (Dr. M. A. Kenke in a review of a book on obesity in the New England Journal of Medicine)[256]

–"regrettably...spectacularly unsuccessful" (Drs. M.B.E. Livingston and K.L. Rennie commenting on the success of preventing and treating childhood obesity in a textbook on the topic)[257]

A review of the medical literature on obesity in children and adolescents was published in 2006. The authors identified 1310 articles published on the topic between 1975 and 2003. Only 8 of them involved studies that met strict scientific standards for validity. It was concluded that it is "not possible to evaluate the effectiveness of dietary treatment for childhood obesity..."[258]

One solidly scientific study was sponsored by the American National Institutes of Health at a cost of $20 million. Over an 8 year time period with intense school interventions, there was no change in body fat in the children studied. [259] A similar study involving over 4000 children from 4 different states yielded the same results.[260] Yet another similar study, this time from Australia, again showed no success in treating obesity with intense school interventions. According to the investigators, the study was "both costly and ineffective".[261]

Intense school programs in Dutch and French schools have shown modest effects in controlling weight gain, but the studies were short term.[262] [263] Another school based strategy showing modest success in improving fitness and decreasing body fat involved an intense year-long program, but at follow-up the changes had promptly reversed over summer vacation.[264] Yet another school's success was also "not sustained" at follow-up.[265]

Despite these disappointments, there are glimmers of hope on the horizon. Two good studies have found that reducing television viewing time reduces the obesity rate.[266] A program that was student-led, pairing children together in a "buddy" program, lessened weight gain rates in one Canadian elementary school.[267] Daily weighing has been shown to maintain weight loss,[268] and one physician has also reported weight loss success with weekly meetings with weighing.[269] Comparing different types of weight loss diets, a New England Journal of Medicine article found that as long as total calories were decreased, any regimen could be effective. There was no advantage to eliminating specifically any type of nutrient like carbohydrates; all that mattered was the total calorie count.[270]

The modest successes in these few programs have been achieved by implementing a few simple changes. To integrate these principles into your own household:

A) **Get rid of your "obesity machines", also known as televisions**.[271] Television viewing and the presence of a television set in a child's bedroom increases the risk of being overweight in school aged children and even in preschoolers.[272] [273] [274] [275] [276] [277] [278] [279] In one study, children watching 5 or more hours of television per day were over 8 times more likely to be obese than children watching up to 2 hours per day.[280] Television viewing is associated with more snacking, less physical activity, and taste preferences for high calorie foods seen in commercials.[281] In response, Britain has banned the advertising of "junk" food on television before 9:00 p.m.[282] In America, the Kraft company voluntarily stopped advertisements aimed at children under 12 years of age in 2005. [283] When television viewing is decreased, or when televisions are activated by stationary bicycles hooked up to them, children lose weight.[284] [285] [286] "Active" screen time with "X-box" gaming units has likewise been shown to burn off calories.[287] [288]

B) **Increase physical activity**.[289] [290] [291] But be aware that this alone won't reduce weight. It takes 2 hours of walking, for example, to burn off the calories in one regular soda.[292] Also be aware that for children, increasing physical activity may mean making compromises regarding safety concerns. Over worries about liability, some American towns have banned diving boards in public pools. Some also prohibit sledding on public property, and even running at recess in public schools.[293]

C) **Cut the sugar-sweetened drinks**. Soft drinks constitute the greatest source of added sugar in adolescent's diets. There is a correlation between the intake of sugar-sweetened drinks and obesity.[294] [295] [296] In England, a school program that educated students on the adverse effects of carbonated drinks reduced the obesity rate.[297] In 2004, the American Academy of Pediatrics issued a policy statement recommending the elimination of soft drinks in schools.[298] A study published two years later found this simple intervention modestly effective in promoting weight loss in overweight adolescents.[299]

D) **Eat at home, decreasing exposure to fast food and restaurant meals**. Restaurant food is fattening, with 60% more calories than homemade meals.[300] To make matters worse, serving sizes are increasing. Average plate sizes in restaurants, for instance, have gone from 10½ to 12 inches. Marketing research has found that consumers who wouldn't buy 2 small fries will buy 1 supersized portion, equal in volume to a double smaller order.[301] In 1955, a quarter of our food budget was spent at restaurants; in 1999, it was almost half. On the average day, over 40% of Americans eat at a restaurant, and 30% of children eat fast food. [302] On days when they are offered fast food, adolescents and children eat more total calories.[303] [304] A study that calculated the ratio of population to fast food restaurants found that the more such eating establishments per square mile and per local resident, the higher the obesity rate.[305] Back at home, adolescents who regularly eat breakfast before leaving for the day have lower rates of weight gain.[306]

E) **Encourage "mindful" eating**. College students take less food in cafeterias without trays.[307] People using larger bowls and spoons eat more.[308] Be aware of the calories in different foods. Be aware that we eat more when we eat quickly, when we dine in groups, when we have more food choices, or when we exchange used for clean plates during meals.[309]

F) **Encourage good sleep habits**. There are many, many studies linking sleep deprivation to weight gain.[310] One study found children getting less than 9 hours' sleep per night to have almost 5 times the obesity rate compared to children sleeping 11 or more hours per night.[311]

G) **Be a good example**. There is a correlation between the amount of TV parents and children watch.[312] In many other dimensions as well, what we do is more important than what we say. In a study looking at mother-daughter eating habits, it was found that girls were more influenced by what they saw their mothers eat than by what they heard their mothers verbally advise.[313]

For obesity prevention in younger siblings of adolescents, there are also some measures that can be taken. First, breastfeed babies as long as possible. Children breastfed a year or longer have obesity rates less than 1/5 the rate in children never breastfed.[314 315 316 317 318 319 320] For infants breastfed less long, the association seems valid but less clear cut.[321 322] Smoking during pregnancy may also increase obesity rates in offspring, though the association hasn't been well studied.[323] Requiring young children to "clean their plates" is associated them requesting larger portions later.[324] Other feeding styles that affect children's risks of obesity include extreme concern about infant weight by mothers,[325 326] and coaxing to encourage eating in children who refuse food.[327 328]

There is ongoing research on drugs to treat obesity, and there is even a vaccine against the hunger hormone "ghrelin" that is being tested in rats.[329] But considering all the data on the effectiveness of different weight loss strategies, an editorial in the Journal of Pediatrics published in 2007 declared that at this point, "surgery…is the only intervention that has been shown to provide sustained weight loss."[330] The number of people under 20 years of age opting for such surgery tripled between 1996 and 2002,[331] but of great concern to me in these addiction prone adolescents is that such surgery increases the effect of alcohol. There are reports of weight loss surgery patients having increased rates of alcoholism afterwards.[332]

As a physician, I am required to be able to establish the effectiveness of any intervention, medication, or therapy I recommend or prescribe. This is as it should be. It is the basis of "evidence based" medicine. I must also balance the side effects of anything I recommend against the intended benefit.

Applying this standard to weight loss advice, I can't in good conscience offer much of it. The United States Task Force on Community Preventive Services agrees, and formally declares that there is "insufficient evidence" to recommend school interventions.[333] Other people, however, eagerly jump onto this slippery slope. There is a growing movement for schools to encourage "healthy eating" and weigh students. In 2003, Arkansas passed a state law requiring schools to weigh children every year. This ignores the advice of the federal Task Force, which pointed out "the stigma attached to overweight" makes this issue "a difficult concern" raising "ethical concerns". [334] It also ignores the advice of every single eating disorder organization.

Like those eating disorder experts, I am vehemently opposed to weighing children in school. This is because I have seen the dark side of dieting. I have witnessed an adolescent die of anorexia. And I have seen an adolescent left severely impaired by side effects from an over-the-counter, totally legal, "natural" diet drug.

When I meet families who are angered by my refusal to recommend unproven (and they all are) ways to make children lose weight, I remind them that the only known effective way for vulnerable children and adolescents to lose weight is to give them an eating disorder. Horrifyingly, anorexic and bullemic patients do indeed lose weight.

Weight loss attempts can cause harm and death. They can also be counterproductive, contributing to the very problem they are trying to resolve. A 3-year Harvard study of 15,000 children between 9 and 14 years of age found that frequent dieting was associated with binge eating and with more weight gain in dieters than in nondieters. [335] For younger children, denying food also often backfires. When children's access to foods is restricted, it only increases the probability that those foods will be eaten when available. [336] When left to play in a room full of toys and snacks immediately after a full meal, 4-year-olds from families with complete snack food restriction ate by far the most. [337] Five-year-old girls with mothers who actively control their food intakes ate more for lunch after high calorie drinks than peers whose mothers didn't worry as much about weight. [338] The more feeding control a mother reports, the more her child eats in experimental, laboratory meals. [339]

For people who can successfully diet, many enter a cycle of regain and subsequent dieting. Whether this "weight cycling" is harmful is debatable. [340] The famous "Framingham Heart Study", with over 30 years' data on residents of Framingham, Massachusetts, showed increased death and heart disease rates in people with large weight fluctuations. [341] In animal research studies involving pigs and rats, weight cycling increases rates of high blood pressure, heart arrhythmias, and degenerative heart changes. Weight fluctuation has also been correlated with increased rates of obesity. [342] [343]

Sometimes dieting goes from bad to even worse. At least 58 people died from liquid protein diets introduced in 1976 and 1977. The very low calorie "Cambridge Diet" of the early 1980s killed 6 people.[344] The earliest prescription drugs for obesity were amphetamines, which were highly addictive. After they fell out of favor, they were followed by amphetamine-related medicines with similar effects on appetite but less nervous system stimulation. In 1959, FDA approval was granted to the first such prescription drug "phentermine". The next one, "fenfluramine", was approved in 1973. Its mirror image "dexfenfluramine" was approved in 1996, after 10 years' use in 65 other countries.[345] [346] In 1992, a flurry of articles suggested that the combination of fenfluramine and phentermine, called "fen-phen" was effective for the long term treatment of obesity. Although the combination was never FDA approved, over the next 3 years its use increased by a factor of almost 20 fold.[347] By 1997, over 14 million prescriptions for the paired drugs had been dispensed in America. The same year, however, fenfluramine and dexfenfluramine were taken off the market when it was found they caused heart valve problems[348] [349] [350] and a severe form of lung failure called "pulmonary hypertension" which kills half its victims.[351] One 29-year-old woman died of pulmonary hypertension 8 months after taking only 23 days of fen-phen.[352] Another victim of dieting, a 44-year-old man, lost several fingers when dexfenfluramine caused artery spasm and poor circulation in his hand.[353] Fenfluramine and dexfenfluramine are also known to cause damage to some brain cells in rats and monkeys.[354]

Non-prescription weight loss remedies can be just as dangerous. The worst are "ephedra" and "ephedrine", also called "herbal fen-phen" or "ma huang". Ephedra is an herb. Ephedrine is a chemical in the ephedra herb. In the United States, ephedra was technically a legal "dietary supplement" until banned by the FDA in 2004.[355] Law suits from manufacturers followed, with no final resolution on the issue.[356] While prescription and over-the-counter medicines in the United States must be reviewed for safety and effectiveness by the FDA, that agency only gets involved with "dietary supplements" after they have been shown to be "a significant or unreasonable risk".[357] [358] While manufacturers of "dietary supplements" cannot claim that their product treats a disease, they are allowed to claim that their product lowers the risk of a disease in a population.[359]

Ephedra weight loss products used to be widely available in health food stores, and adolescents (and adults) often believe that because a product is "herbal" or "natural", it is safe. Wrong!!! Arsenic, lead, tobacco, and cocaine are also "natural". No matter what it's called, a "dietary supplement" isn't one unless we'd put it in our 3rd graders lunches. Ephedra is amphetamine-like in action. Between 1994 and 1998, the FDA received over 800 reports of harm from ephedra, from high blood pressure to heart attacks to death.[360] Between 1997 and 1999, there were 140 such reports, involving 10 strokes, 7 seizures, 10 deaths, and 13 cases of residual permanent disability.[361]

As a physician, it is disappointing to me that for so long my vulnerable adolescent patients could innocently buy ephedra products in "health" food stores, misled into believing that because they are "natural" they are safe. Many prescription drugs come from plants and "natural sources", and they are not exempted from FDA scrutiny because of it. The heart failure drug digoxin, for example, comes from the foxglove plant. It is so toxic that I once saw a patient almost die over a decimal point error in its dosage. Penicillin comes from a "natural" mold, and people have died from allergic reactions to it. Adolescents should all be warned of the dangers of ephedra, which is still obtainable on the internet.

The most common form of death by dieting, however, comes in the form of eating disorders. In 1983, singer Karen Carpenter died of complications from anorexia. In 2006, Brazilian model Ana Carolina Reston was lost to the same disease. The death rate in women with anorexia is 12 times higher than in the general population.[362] Only half of patients with eating disorders recover fully. About 1 in 3 recovers partially, and 1 in 5 never even improves.[363] The death rate from eating disorders is from 5 to 24%, making it the most deadly of all psychiatric illnesses,[364 365 366 367 368] and more dangerous than many cancers. As a medical student, I saw a debilitated adolescent with anorexia die from an infection that otherwise should never have threatened her. In my medical practice, I have 4 parents who lost siblings to complications of eating disorders. Such deaths from eating disorders are often misleadingly attributed to the medical final event instead of the underlying real culprit, making most people unaware of how deadly eating disorders really are. The tragic and controversial case of the Florida woman whose feeding tube was removed in 2005 was a typical example. Most press stories reported the cause of her condition as a "heart attack". More detailed stories revealed that her heart had stopped due to an electrolyte imbalance from an eating disorder. Depleted of potassium, her heart rhythm became abnormal and the heart muscle went into a spasm. Unable to get blood pumped to it, her brain was deprived of oxygen.[369]

In a review article on eating disorders in the New England Journal of Medicine, the authors termed their physical and psychological consequences "grave".[370] Complications of eating disorders include:[371]

1) **Stunting of height**, without complete "catch-up" growth even if the eating disorder is successfully treated. This is a particularly distressing issue for boys, whose eating disorder rates are on the rise,[372] [373] [374] and whose cases are often severe and complicated.[375]

2) **Loss of brain tissue**. MRI studies on patients with eating disorders show loss of both grey and white matter brain tissue, with corresponding increases in spinal fluid volume and fluid spaces within the head.[376] [377] [378] A small follow-up study of recovered anorectics showed an "irreversible component" to their brain damage, with "persistent grey matter volume deficits".[379]

3) **Thinning of the bones and osteoporosis**, not necessarily reversible.[380] In one study, abnormal bone densities were found in over half of anorectic girls.[381] There was a report in England of 5 patients with anorexia who had vertebral collapse, usually seen only in elderly people.[382] In a study in the United States of 20 women with eating disorders, half had significantly decreased bone mineral density, and 2 had fractures, including a 34-year-old with a broken hip.[383] In another study, bone thinning was seen in girls who had been anorectic for only 6 months.[384]

4) **Cardiac problems**, including abnormalities of heart rhythm,[385] changes in heart muscle[386] and heart valves,[387] and blood pressure instability. Most deaths from eating disorders are caused by cardiac complications of these diseases.[388]

5) **Immune system weakness**, with susceptibility to infection. Patients with anorexia have thinning of the bone marrow, where blood cells are made.[389] One in 5 is anemic. One in 5 also has low levels of white blood cells, which are the cells that mount immune responses.[390] [391] As a medical student, I saw a young anorectic girl die of "Pneumocystis" pneumonia. This dangerous type of pneumonia is usually seen only in patients with disseminated cancer or AIDS.

6) **Problems with the gastrointestinal tract**, including inflammation of the pancreas,[392] signs of liver inflammation,[393] narrowing of the stomach outlet, and rupture or sudden swelling of the stomach. The stomach

swelling often occurs during recovery and re-feeding. It is particularly dangerous and can result in shock and sudden death. Early descriptions of this tragic phenomenon were published after World War II, when liberated concentration camp survivors often died after finally being given full meals.[394]

7) Starvation and deficiencies of minerals and vitamins. Low potassium levels cause heart rhythm problems and are the most common cause of death in anorexia nervosa.[395] Low phosphate levels can also cause heart rhythm disturbances.[396] Zinc deficiency can cause hair loss, severe sloughing and blistering of the skin, altered taste sensations, and mood changes.[397] [398]

8) Infertility and irregular menstrual periods. One study found that 1 in 12 women being treated at infertility clinics have an eating disorder. Women with eating disorders who do conceive and make it through pregnancy have smaller babies with lower "Apgar" scores. They also have more problems breast feeding their infants.[399]

9) Damage to the body and intestinal tract from vomiting. Patients with eating disorders and vomiting have been known to puncture their esophagus, irritate their vocal cords causing hoarseness, swell their salivary glands, and erode the enamel off their teeth. There have also been cases where surgery has been required to remove toothbrushes accidentally swallowed while being used to induce vomiting.[400] [401] [402] [403]

10) The **suicide rate** in people with eating disorders is higher than the suicide rate in the general population.[404]

11) If all this weren't enough, eating disorders can also be complicated by **still more issues**, including thyroid problems, kidney problems, and even eye problems. One disturbing aspect of the complications of eating disorders is that the presence of many of them does not correlate with the severity of weight loss.[405] Eating disorders can also co-exist with other addictions, including exercise addiction.[406]

Eating disorders are not new. They've been known to exist since the 14th century.[407] One of the earliest written accounts of anorexia was published by English physician Dr. Richard Morton in 1689. He referred to it as "nervous consumption".[408] By 1873 it had been described in both England

and France, in both girls and boys, and a Dr. W. W. Gull had coined the term "anorexia nervosa".[409] [410]

So while we didn't invent eating disorders, we have taken them to new rates. This may be because we are a nation obsessed with looks and weight. Our mass media both reflects and influences our attitudes about these issues. Researchers who looked back over 33 years' worth of 5 different women's magazines found 2 main trends. Over time, models shown in the magazine ads became thinner and thinner. At the same time, the magazines featured more and more articles on losing weight. Another study found that almost a quarter of the ads in Spanish women's magazines, mostly aimed at adolescent girls, "encouraged weight loss".[411] Since 1922, the body mass of Miss America winners has consistently fallen. Over the last 30 years, most Miss America's weights place them within the range of "undernutrition" according to two researchers from the Johns Hopkins School of Public Health. More than 10 million viewers watch the Miss America Pageant each year.[412] Another study documented that when first exposed to Western television, Fijian adolescent girls had dramatic increases in their rates of body dissatisfaction and disordered eating. [413] [414] Back in the states, a Harvard study of 7000 girls found that trying to look like females on TV, in movies, or in magazines was correlated with a risk of self-purging at least monthly.[415] A survey of American girls in 5th through 12th grade found a direct correlation between the frequency of their reading women's magazines and dieting. Half the girls reported wanting to lose weight because of magazine pictures, and 69% acknowledged that the pictures influenced their idea of ideal body shapes.[416] Another study found an increased risk of eating disorders in girls who either read women's magazines frequently, or listened to the radio often.[417]

To make matters worse, if our girls put down their magazines to play with dolls, they may very well pick up a Barbie doll. Barbie's proportions do not conform to human anatomy. To have Barbie's shape, the average woman would have to be 2 feet taller with a 5 inch larger chest, a 3 inch longer neck, and a 6 inch smaller waist. To grasp the magnitude of Barbie's influence, be aware that in America we have 10 times more Barbie dolls than children. As of 1996, over 800 million Barbies had been sold here, with annual revenues of over $1 billion.[418] [419]

If our girls put down their magazines and their Barbies, they might turn next to the internet. There they will find "pro-anorexia" web sites and chat rooms with advice on ways to purge and restrict eating. In 2001, the Yahoo!

company shut down some such sites, enforcing their service agreement prohibiting "harmful, threatening, and abusive" messages.[420]

When our children log off the internet, put away the Barbies, and close the magazines, we're still not home free. There is an unfortunate link between sports and eating disorders, too. Some studies in the 1980s suggested that lean runners performed better. Other studies have confirmed that coaches wield significant influence over adolescents' eating habits and use of "dietary supplements".[421] In a study that compared the weight perceptions of academic versus ballet teachers, it was found that while academic teachers underestimated students' weights, the ballet teachers erred in the other direction. The dance teachers inaccurately perceived their students as heavier than they really were, opening the door for justifying weight loss.[422] Up to a quarter of female gymnasts use self-induced vomiting to control their weight.[423] Male wrestlers often lose weight before matches to be paired with smaller opponents. In one survey, a third of Wisconsin high school wrestlers admitted to bulimic behaviors.[424] A similar study of college wrestlers in Indiana found that 82% had fasted for over a day, 16% had used diuretics (water pills), and 9% had made themselves vomit at least once per week.[425] From one-third to two-thirds of female college sports participants use vomiting, laxatives, diet pills, or diuretics to control their weight.[426][427] Between 1960 and 1992 the average weight of US Olympic women gymnasts decreased 19 pounds, and their height decreased 5 inches.[428] Small size is considered an advantage in ballet, gymnastics, and figure skating.[429]

The concept of "pleasantly plump" is history. If there ever was an "anorecti-genic" culture, we are it. Our children are inundated by influences encouraging eating disorders. And unfortunately, they are getting the message. As about a third of our world's population suffers malnourishment and hunger in undeveloped countries, our adolescents are starving themselves on purpose. About 1 out of every 200 American adolescent girls has anorexia.[430] Up to 1 in 10 young Americans has a problem with self-induced vomiting.[431][432] A 1985 survey of 10th graders in Northern California documented that 1 in 7 had tried self-induced vomiting or other purging methods.[433] A national survey published in 2000 found that 1 in 7 adolescent girls had tried self-purging, as had 1 in 14 boys. Almost half of the girls had tried dieting, as had a fifth of the boys.[434] In 1990, the Centers for Disease Control surveyed over 11,000 high school students in all 50 states, the District of Columbia, Puerto Rico, and the Virgin Islands. One in 5 girls and 1 in 20 boys had tried diet pills.

One in 7 girls and 1 in 30 boys had made themselves vomit to try to lose weight.[435]

Almost half of adolescent boys report being unhappy with their weight, and a third don't like their shape.[436] Another survey found two-thirds of adolescent girls "preoccupied with weight".[437] At the same time 2 large government studies found a quarter of Americans obese,[438] two-thirds of us considered ourselves overweight.[439] In 2002, a survey of adolescents from Minnesota found that two-thirds of average weight girls wanted to weigh less.[440] Only half of girls and a quarter of boys who consider themselves overweight actually are.[441] Among underweight adolescent girls in another survey, half described themselves as extremely fearful about getting overweight, and a third were preoccupied with body fat.[442]

Most alarming of all is how worried our younger children are about their weight. A survey of 4th to 6th graders in Cincinnati found that half wanted to be thinner, and a third had actually tried to lose weight.[443] Half of the children participating in that study were younger than 9 ½ years old. Another survey of 9- to 11-year-olds revealed that almost 1 in 5 had tried dieting.[444] Even more disturbing was a study from Maryland, published in 1996, that found 40% of 9- and 10-year-old girls trying to lose weight.[445] Among 8-year-old children from North Dakota, 38% wish they were thinner.[446] Sadly, one-seventh of the children in the Cincinnati study answered "yes" when asked if they thought their friends would like them more if they were thinner.[447] There have been children as young as 7 years of age diagnosed with anorexia.[448] In my own medical practice, I have personally witnessed a trend where younger and younger children are uncomfortable being weighed. It is not uncommon for girls visiting me for kindergarten exams to make self-conscious comments at the scale. I no longer allow nurses in my office to weight my patients. Instead, I do it myself as an opportunity to assess them for eating disorders.

Risk factors for the development of eating disorders include: being a high achiever in a competitive school, having a perfectionist type personality, frequently reading girls' magazines or listening to the radio, having a substance abuse problem, having a family history of eating disorders, living with only 1 parent, or being a wrestler, gymnast, figure skater, or dancer.[449] [450] [451] [452] [453] Diabetic girls also have a higher rate of eating disorders.[454] Adolescents who correctly perceive that their mothers want them thinner are more likely to be frequent dieters.[455] And adolescents who received teasing or negative comments about their weight from family members are also more likely to exhibit symptoms of eating disorders.[456] [457] [458]

Eating disorders can be hard for families to diagnose. Most people with bulimia have normal weights.[459] Eating alone is a common tip off for problems.[460] Screening questions often asked by doctors include:[461] [462]

"Are you unsatisfied with your eating patterns?"
"Do you ever eat in secret?"
"Do you make yourself sick because you feel overly full?"
"Do you worry you have lost control over how much you eat?"
"Have you recently lost over 14 pounds in a 3 month period?"
"Do you think you are fat when others say you are thin?"
"Do you think food is dominating your life?"

If the answer to any of the above questions is "yes", seriously consider the possibility that your adolescent has an eating disorder. If you do have a teenager with such a problem, be aware that other issues often accompany eating disorders, including higher rates of tobacco, alcohol, marijuana, and other illicit drug use.[463] [464] The common denominator here is that these all represent different forms of addictions. Adolescents are particularly vulnerable to developing addictions of all types, and eating disorders can be looked at as addictions to weight loss.

Let's review what all the medical literature cited above teaches us about obesity and eating disorders in adolescents:

1) "70% of the variability in human body weight may be accounted for by genetic factors"[465]

2) Only about a quarter of obesity in adults begins during childhood or adolescence.[466]

3) The adolescent surge in body weight precedes the height growth spurt, temporarily giving them proportions that make them seem heavy.

4) No individual diet plan has been shown to be successful.

5) Dieting can be medically dangerous.

6) Adolescents are particularly vulnerable to developing eating disorders.

7) The death rate from eating disorders is staggering—up to 20% in some studies. Such deaths are often mischaracterized, and they are rarely publicized. Eating disorders have the highest death rate of any psychiatric disease, making them more deadly than many cancers.

8) For those who are not killed by eating disorders, the recovery rate is not great. Up to half of patients with anorexia never completely recover.[467]

Putting all this together, there is only one sensible recommendation about how to handle the agonizing issue of weight in adolescents: **BE CAREFUL!!** Consider simply allowing adolescents to live out their awkward years, with the assurance that their bodies are not yet final products. Be wary of the high risk sports for eating disorders, which for girls share the common thread of wearing tight-fitting, revealing clothing. Encourage adolescents to dress modestly. Thinner girls could do a real kindness for their heavier sister peers if they also dressed less revealingly, helping set a standard that didn't emphasize body differences. Watch your words. In one study one of the major determinants of 9- and 10-year-old girls trying to lose weight was a "mother telling her she was too fat."[468] Do not try to conceal weight loss requests in terms of "healthy eating". Adolescents will see right through it. A survey of 10- to 12-year-olds found they described someone who ate healthy foods as "thin".[469] In the absence of severe medical issues like high blood pressure, diabetes, or orthopedic problems, letting adolescents wait and diet when they are adults may avoid the development of eating disorders.

Remember where the road paved with good intentions leads? Many schools still weigh students, and many also still have mixed-gender swimming classes. How many adults would want to be weighed at their workplaces? How many adults would want to stand immodestly in a wet swim suit next to their co-workers? The official position of the National Association of Anorexia Nervosa and Associated Disorders is that weight and body measurement testing in such a "public setting can be humiliating" and "may foster inappropriate responses, comparisons and teasing."[470]

Obesity and heart disease prevention programs are now involving schools. Yet there are few studies addressing whether such programs might increase eating disorder rates. One involved 8-year-old children in a low risk setting.[471] Other research looked at 480 middle school girls in 10 different schools, and had likewise favorable results. In two related studies, girls exposed to a program promoting healthful nutrition, increased physical activity, and a limitation of television viewing had lower rates of purging or using diet pills.[472] [473] Still another study directly promoting a relaxed attitude toward weight and shape concerns using the internet also lowered eating disordered behaviors, this time in college students.[474] These studies are only a start,[475] however, run by experts and carefully monitored.

Weight control in children and adolescents is a slippery slope leading to thin ice. Anyone who enters this treacherous territory must be mindful that how adolescents perceive their weight is more important than their actual weight. Independent of their poundage, high schoolers who believe themselves to be of abnormal weight have an increased likelihood of suicidal behavior.[476] "Normal" weights in growing adolescents, however, are a wide and changing range.

Perhaps our adolescents might find it easier to accept their own varying bodies if we were more accepting of our own. As we staple our stomachs, botox our faces, and liposuction our abdomens we set an unnatural standard for our children to aspire to. As we surround them with airbrushed visions of "perfection" on screen and in print, we accustom them to an unrealistic standard of existence.

A Rabbi I greatly respect once shared the story of a special piece of advice his father-in-law offered after his marriage. His new wife's soft spoken father, also a Rabbi, called them back out of their car as they were about to drive away after their wedding. He had something important say to his daughter. It was simply "always have the meals ready on time." As is so often the case, the elders of our faiths quietly get it.

Decades later, secular medical research has confirmed the senior Rabbi's advice. My favorite articles on adolescents and eating are those that have established the protective effects of family meals. Multiple studies have confirmed that for adolescents, a greater frequency of family meals correlates with lower rates of tobacco, alcohol, and marijuana use, less depression, less rates of suicidal thoughts and attempts, lower rates of eating disorders, and higher grade point averages.[477] In other words, the more a family eats together, the better their adolescents fare. As parents agonize over obesity and eating disorders, how about making these results our mantra? Your adolescent will be chowing down dormitory food all too soon. Their place at your table will be an empty chair before you know it. In the meantime, enjoy their healthy appetites. Maybe the way to their hearts really is through their stomachs.

CHAPTER 4

• • •

GETTING TO NO YOU:
FEAR, GUILT AND FAITH,
AND OTHER USEFUL PARENTING TOOLS

Enjoyable Aspect of Parenting Adolescents Number Three: Adolescents do not throw food in restaurants. They do not whine and cry loudly in stores over toys whose price exceeds average monthly mortgage payments. They do not lie down in supermarket aisles in protest over grocery choices. After years of public humiliation, enjoy your adolescent's company and companionship when you're out and about.

Imagine moving to the upscale community of your dreams, in the intellectual and social circle you've always longed to join. Imagine living right next door to your favorite entertainer, author, or philosopher. Then imagine having to be accompanied everywhere in that neighborhood by a loud and oddly dressed escort prone to offensive and inappropriate jokes and public nose-picking.

As our adolescents navigate their brave, new world this is exactly how they feel about us. Just when our offspring finally behave better in public, they don't want to be seen there with us. This is normal. They are biologically programmed with this attitude. It's the opposite of the stranger anxiety in toddlers that pulls them back to us just as they are first able to crawl and walk away toward danger. Without forces the other direction, how would our adolescents ever separate from us and pursue their own identity?

Anyone doubtful of the neurological, biological basis of our adolescent's feelings about us should consider the case of a family in my own medical practice. There are two children in this family. Both are beautiful souls housed in bodies exhibiting severe autism. One has limited speech, and the other is nonverbal. As their mother puts it "they certainly don't understand the social structure of society." Nor is any of their behavior "based on their psychological understanding of family or authority dynamics." Yet both of these much loved boys exhibited adolescent rebellion. One often physically pushed his mother away. The other found a new favorite phrase: "Mommy go 'way!"

Teenagers find us inherently socially distasteful. Adults who fail to accept this principle will simply never understand them. No amount of botox or liposuction will ever render us less repulsive to our children, and our attempts to sexualize our appearance and dress their age only disgusts them more. This is a painful universal truth. We are no "cooler" than our parents. As for other painful universal truths: 1) our mothers were right about almost everything and 2) the life cycle applies to us, too.

Adolescents are inherently sullen, moody, and short-tempered. A physician I once met told me that when he thought of adolescents, only two words came to mind—"general anesthesia". Short of that, but along the same lines, I recommend Lamaze. Almost all expectant mothers dutifully drag to Lamaze classes, reluctant spouses in tow. Almost all of them tell me, newborn in hand, that it was of little, if any, help. The physics of birthing put a limit on what any breathing technique can accomplish. I have spent the better part of my career contemplating a use for all this training. As my patients aged, it dawned on me! When Junior hits puberty, start breathing. Inhale, focus on the important issues, and exhale. If you speak, anything you say can and will be used against you, anyway. So pick your battles and for everything else, however unpleasant, just breathe.

If you can pull this off you may very well find that it's just what your adolescent needs. We are a proactive generation. Ask any teacher or school administrator about us "in-your-face" parents. I once heard a hospital chaplain speak of his helplessness and frustration when called to the Emergency Room one day to counsel a family who had just lost their young child in a car accident. The family was of a different ethnicity and faith, and worshiped in a different language. "I couldn't even pray with them", the chaplain said. "I just stood there." And in the blur of that family's darkest nightmare, that's the light they remembered. They later thanked the chaplain for his compassion and strength and for just being there in their most awful of hours. In our hurry to do and fix, we have forgotten the power of simple presence. As John Milton so famously wrote, "They also serve who only stand and wait."[478] Sometimes, on your adolescent's behalf, "don't just do something; stand there".

After years of preventing toddlers from annihilating each other in sandboxes using complex time-out protocols, shifting gears to parental non-intervention is no easy task. On several occasions, I have seen early parenting compared to puppy training. Dr. Wendy Mogul, the author of the insightful book *The Blessing of a Skinned Knee*, was the first person I ever heard draw this parallel. Years later, the editor-in-chief of a pediatrics journal, a professor at the prestigious Johns Hopkins University School of Medicine, wrote an editorial on this issue, titled "Puppies and Children: Some Similarities."[479]

For the record, comparing humans and animals is not an analogy I am easily drawn to. Please note I do not ever refer to children or adolescents as "kids". Technically, "kids" are young goats or antelopes. My precious and complex patients are nothing of the sort.

That said, there are indeed some overlapping dimensions to rearing puppies and toddlers. Both tasks require consistency and detachment. Results are largely predictable, and cause and effect are often not far apart. These parallels end at adolescence. Teenagers are not at all like puppies. They are more like cats. They are not overtly affectionate or obedient. They like to sleep. But as any cat "owner" (myself included) will affirm, there is much about them to love.

Cats and dogs, however different, at least offer consistency within their species from generation to generation. Lassie's issues as a puppy were no different than Toto's. Dorothy's Toto was no less loyal than Orphan Annie's Sandy. Hemingway's cats were no less independent than mine.

Our adolescent's behavioral issues, however, shift over time, reflecting our changing culture. This is most painfully evident in what they say to and about us. I am unaware of any society, at any historical time, in any place on earth, where children have ever been allowed to speak to their parents the way ours do.

Our offspring's ambivalence about us is not new or unique. We were no better than our children in our feelings about the generation ahead of us, but we didn't verbalize it. And for everybody involved, that was for the best. "Zip it" was not a fashion statement in our youth. It was a survival skill.

But unfortunately for us, and for our children, we have thrown out verbal restraint. It is as foreign to our offspring as 8-track tapes or correctible typewriter ribbons. Remember the concepts of "thinking it but not saying it" and "keeping it to yourself"? Silence is no longer golden. We shun any such "repression". We have talk shows, talk radio, and talk therapy.

In allowing our children to "speak their mind" we have rendered them unlikable by many standards. In doing so, we have failed them. "Free" speech can have a heavy price tag. Our children are no worse in their thought processes than we were, but as they speak their mind publicly, they become desensitized to its ugliness. One strategy for combating verbal abuse from teens is to video or audio tape them and make them listen to themselves at calmer times. They are often shocked. Without verbal restraint, our adolescents cannot put their best foot forward. Squeaky wheels don't always get greased. Sometimes they get ignored and avoided when people around them learn to cover their ears. Today's teenagers don't lack goodness. They lack parents with the common sense to teach them to "zip it".

Verbal restraint is not all we parents have thrown away. In a single generation, we have discarded two of parenting's most tried and true behavioral management tools—fear and guilt. Without fear, there is no discipline. Without guilt, there is no conscience.

The fear I refer to here is not the rage and terror variety. This is no appeal for physical abuse, which doesn't lead to fear, anyway. It leads to desensitization and resignation. Tragically abused children end up helplessly passive. The fear we lack is the type that acknowledges that our conduct can and should have consequences. Would we pay as much income tax if we weren't afraid of being audited? Would we drive the speed limit if we weren't afraid of getting a ticket? There is no shame in this. It is human nature. We are not inherently good, we are inherently capable of being good after fighting off our other inclinations.

This conflict is as old as life itself. It's the kicking in utero between Jacob and Esau. It's the "light" and the "darkness", the "day" and "night" created in Genesis. Worried about "self-esteem" and "self-confidence", many parents consider it a positive accomplishment for their children to believe they are "good". Labeling a child "good" is as destructive as labeling them "bad". Neither one will know what to do with their other half. When parents worry about their children's "fragile" egos, they become afraid of them as well, and reverse roles. Most of us were taught that the obviously scared one is whom the dog bites. Children lash out at timid parents, as well. They need us to guide them, not fear them. Parents afraid of their offspring become unable to say, simply and firmly, "no". We have a popular book titled *Getting to Yes*.[480] Our generation of parents needs to get to "no". In physically active children, the "fearless" ones get injured. In the bigger game of life, "fearless" is a recipe for trouble.

One of my favorite cartoons, by artist Mike Smith,[481] depicts "then" and "now" pictures of the same schoolboy on a bench outside a door, obviously awaiting discipline. On the "then" picture, the title on the door is "Principal's Office". The "now" door is a "District Attorney's Office". As our fearless children spin more and more out of control, we reach further out for help. Our school hallways are now patrolled by over 17,000 police officers.[482] Over the decades of my career, one change I've observed firsthand is an increasing overlap between law enforcement and medical professionals in child advocacy team work. In dealing with increasingly complex problems, often involving minors as both victim and accused, law enforcement expertise is invaluable. While their help is much appreciated, if there was ever a culture clash between professions, law enforcement and pediatrics is it. We pediatricians delight in our privilege of caring for scrumptious beautiful babies, and our workdays often include a healthy round of peek-a-boo. Law enforcement professionals do not play patty cake, nor do they consider it impressive to be able to name all 7 dwarfs (Bashful, Happy, Grumpy, Sleepy, Sneezy, Dopey, and Doc). Law enforcement people are often physically large, and they are usually armed. They use words like "perpetrator" and "incarcerate". They apply the term "situation" in expansive and creative ways to refer, equally calmly, to scenarios ranging from fender-benders to mass murder. They even have scary first names, like "Sergeant" and "Commander". I once heard a nationally renowned child abuse expert physician explain that the reason he allowed the law enforcement members of his team to chair his regional meetings was because "they have guns." Without even trying, law enforcement professionals intimidate many of us pediatricians, but not our patients. Over and over again I am often told of community youth officers being spoken to by youngsters with increasingly bold, blatant disrespect.

On the flip side of the coin, tough tongues are often accompanied by tender ears. Over and over, I find that mouths that spout filth are attached to ears that perceive only hurt. Adolescents, I am convinced, process all they are told quite literally. They lack any social filter. For those of us who use humor to cope, this can be a disaster. Sarcasm is taken at face value by teenagers. And in defense of adolescents, all humor has a sliver of truth in it. Think of all we say as being recorded in writing in another language, to be read to our children by a translator who knows nothing of us. Speak accordingly. Imagine your joke about nominating your teenagers as poster children for Planned Parenthood being read by a humorless government official from another culture. This is how adolescents hear it. There is an old saying that if you argue with a fool, no one can tell the difference. The same is true with children. When we argue with teenagers, we appear equally immature. When we take their comments personally, we have lost perspective. And when we respond in kind, we underestimate their sensitivity.

Parents object to being spoken to disrespectfully. I have never, however, heard a parent complain of not being feared. Yet fear and respect are overlapping spheres, and if we want our children to respect us and our rules, they must also fear us.

And what type of role models are we in the fear, respect, and rule following departments? In 2006, an athletic league of 13 private elementary schools in Illinois cancelled its volleyball and basketball finals due to unacceptable parental behavior.[483] Near my home there is a speed limit sign that says "strictly enforced" on it. I've seen others that warn of "zero tolerance". Shouldn't a simple number be enough? How do we speak of our children's teachers and school administrators? What do we say about the traffic officer who asks us to move our car out of the no parking zone before we've gotten our coffee to go? And what do we say about ourselves? There was a New York Times best seller book about women's feelings about, among other things, "work, motherhood, and marriage." It was titled *The Bitch in the House*. Its counterpart publication about men was *The Bastard on the Couch*. If we even lightly publicly refer to ourselves this way, how do we expect our children to speak to us?

One of the most profound explorations of the meaning of life was written by King Solomon in the Book of Ecclesiastes. It contains many famous verses. "Everything has its season, and there is a time for everything under the heaven" was used as lyrics by the Byrds singing group in their 1960s hit song. Hemingway paraphrased "and the sun rises and then sun sets—then to its place it rushes; there it rises again." in a title to one of his novels. The often quoted "there is nothing new under the sun" comes from the Book of Ecclesiastes, as does the original, Biblical version of "you can't take it with you"– man "can salvage nothing from his labor to take with him". So how does King Solomon, believed by some to be the wisest man in history, climax and end his masterpiece? What final piece of advice does he leave mankind? "The sum of the matter, when all has been considered: Fear G-d and keep His commandments, for that is man's whole duty. For G-d will judge every deed—even everything hidden—whether good or evil."[484] If this ultimate wisest of guys recommends fear, let's reintroduce it into childrearing and put it into good use.

From an alternative point of view, referring to our "inner enemy", it was Englishman Sir Francis Bacon who first wrote, in the 1600s, that "Nothing is to be feared but fear itself." In 1933, President Franklin D. Roosevelt repeated and paraphrased this quote most famously in his first inaugural speech, in discussing the dire economic depression of the day, but it was Sir Francis Bacon who originated this often mis-attributed phrase. Of note, Sir Francis Bacon had precisely zero children. His child rearing credentials are likewise non-existent. In children, fear is nothing to be afraid of. It's a lack thereof that gets our offspring into much of their trouble. To be safe, and to be law-abiding, our children need a good dose of "healthy fear" instilled in them.

Closely related to fear are shame and humiliation. Used carefully and with love they, too, have a place in child rearing. There is a company in Michigan that test marketed a bumper sticker for cars driven by teens. It had a web site and toll free number to report dangerous driving. I have seen similar solicitations on trucks manned by professional drivers. Yet the inventor of the teen driving surveillance system found it a tough sell. "Parents don't want to offend their kids by making them drive with the stickers," he said. [485] In Oklahoma, in a move that sparked great controversy, the mother of a 14-year-old made her daughter publicly display a sign reading "I don't do my homework and I act up in school." While some onlookers were so upset they called the police, a newspaper article regarding the incident noted that immediately afterwards the teen's attendance was "perfect" and her behavior improved. "I won't talk back," this adolescent pledged. The mother in that case stayed with her daughter during her punishment. A picture of them showed her lovingly embracing her child. Explaining her motives she said "I felt I owed it to my child to at least try."[486] The word "discipline" has its roots in Latin terms connoting the positive attributes of education and learning. We confuse it with simple punishment in error, and we avoid it at great cost.

Humiliation also works as a threat. I have seen verbal abuse near cease when parents have audio taped teenage rants and threatened to share them with other adults. When replayed at a neutral time for the offender, some honest adolescents have even expressed remorse for their speech.

Fear and guilt go hand in hand, and we dumped them in the same hand basket leading to the most infamous of places. Guilt is a natural byproduct of introspection, and without the self-assessment that leads to it, there can be no growth or self-improvement. "Guilty conscience" is a redundant term, and the anticipation of guilt is a powerful deterrent. Previous generations put this natural recourse to good use, and so should we.

In doing so, of course, we must be careful to use guilt and fear in only appropriate amounts. As with other almost other remedies, there is a dose-related therapeutic range, above which is toxicity. Oxygen deprivation causes death within minutes. Oxygen overdosage, we learned tragically, causes blindness in newborns. Vitamin D deprivation causes rickets. Vitamin D overdosage can cause kidney damage. A perfect dose of the drug digoxin can control heart failure. A little too much can cause arrhythmias and death. So it is with fear and guilt. Too little causes cultural chaos. Too much can be paralyzing and emotionally damaging. Both extremes are disabling.

In his 2005 book *"If Only; How to Turn Regret into Opportunity"*, University of Illinois psychology professor and researcher Neal Roese writes of the positive virtues of regret. He explains that it can make people wiser, and inspire them toward corrective action or help them make better choices in the future.[487] Another researcher, from Virginia, has found that people who feel guilty show more empathy towards others. They are better at working out conflicts and have generally healthier interpersonal relationships, as well. Yet another psychologist, from the University of Iowa, conducted a study where toddlers were led to believe they had damaged something expensive. It was found that children who were uncomfortable with their perception of having done something wrong showed greater restraint later.[488]

Part of guilt's unpopularity is its association with religion. We are a functionally secular culture. We knew where to head after that awful September 11th, but within a month we'd been there and done that. It has been shown that Americans spend more time in shopping centers than in church.[489] Teenagers spend so much time in malls that as of 2007, almost

50 had formal curfews banning unsupervised adolescents during certain hours.[490]

An insightful author and physician specializing in substance abuse calls this "Spiritual Deficiency Syndrome". Nationally famous for his work in chemical dependency, Dr. Abraham Twerski traces much of our children's discontent to a lack of faith, a force he terms "vitamins for the spirit". He differentiates happiness, the pursuit of which is guaranteed in our constitution, from pleasure, and warns that the pursuit of pleasure can turn toward drugs and alcohol in the absence of spirituality and its joy. "Teenagers see the world as a difficult place…Show them what it its like to be spiritual and to be happy with spirituality," he advises.[491]

A few years ago a hospital where I am on staff sponsored a committee to address the issue of helping physicians find "Meaning in Medicine". Our group consisted of all types of doctors, including a family physician, an emergency medicine specialist, a psychiatrist, one of the hospital's top administrators, and the hospital chaplain. We were Catholics, Protestants, and Jews and we even had a Hindu Priest. We met and discussed coping with the frustrations and stresses of practicing medicine. The number one tool we all used was our faith. Each faith took us different directions with different forces, but it was faith that was sustaining us through difficult careers. Our meetings had topics like guilt, anger, and humility. Sound a little like parenting?

Faith is yet another child rearing tool we have pitched. In Hebrew, the word "child" shares the same root word as "to build". And buildings need foundations. In every dimension, childrearing is life's ultimate challenge. It will hurt you in places you didn't even know you had. And no political or social system alone is adequate to navigate its deep and murky waters.

In giving up fear, guilt, and faith we have thrown away some of parenting's best tools. We erred. In other words, we were human. Maybe one of the reasons we gave up old parenting methods is because we face so many new parenting issues. Internet pornography and ubiquitous drug availability were not problems Grandma wrestled with.

The most powerful parenting tool of all, however, we have not abandoned. That is love. Without love, there is no influence. The essence of parenting is infinite devotion and endless love, and I witness it every day in my pediatric practice. Whatever our faults, we are loving parents. Maybe we confuse indulgence with love, maybe we confuse over-protectiveness with love, and maybe we confuse permissiveness with love, but our hearts are in the right place. And I believe that in their hearts, our children know it. If for no other reason than being in this life together, and even though they find us socially repulsive, enjoy your adolescent.

CHAPTER 5

● ● ●

JOINT PAIN

Enjoyable Aspect of Parenting Adolescents Number Four: Adolescents do not eat crayons. They do not scour the floor with microscopic accuracy in search of lost small toy parts and dropped loose change to ingest or inhale. They do not insert metal objects into the single electrical outlet in the house lacking a safety cover. They do not "decorate" walls and upholstered furniture with permanent markers. Enjoy un-childproofing your home and rediscovering those fragile family heirlooms.

The good news is that after toddlerhood, our homes are physically safer places for children. The bad news is that dangers we agonize over while covering electrical outlets and moving bleach to high ground pale in comparison to what we face in protecting our adolescents.

Our offspring face a different world than did our ancestors. Imagine starting a brave, new culture with several dozen families, all from different backgrounds. With great respect, the nation's elders combine the best concepts of our generation. An attitude of universalism and inclusiveness is encouraged. Divisive faiths are melded into a shared acknowledgement of a Higher Power. Interpersonal relationships are pleasant and based on simple kindness. An emphasis on the enjoyment of life as a way to honor it is a prominent ideal. You discover a friend who shares your passion for enjoying life. You learn new things together and experience great fun. Even though many in the community have befriended your pal at different times, your friend is rejected and shunned. Your friend is cocaine.

In many ways, we are that brave, new culture. We emphasize pleasure as a way of enjoying life. And when we are not enjoying life, we often address it "chemically". Our teenagers are immersed in a "pharmaculture". They are surrounded by drug use, both illicit and prescription. Look at our architecture. Where there used to be fast food restaurants on every corner, there are now pharmacies. My office list of local pharmacies has expanded exponentially over the last two decades. While at those pharmacies, my patients can purchase a perfume named "Addict", and an energy drink named "Cocaine".[492] We Americans comprise 5% of the world population, yet we use 60% of the world's drugs.[493] Our children are following our example. One in 7 high school seniors reports abusing a prescription or over-the-counter drug in the past year. One in 10 has illicitly used Vicodin.[494] A survey of college students found 20% admitting to the illicit use of prescription drugs at sometime during their lives.[495] Seventy percent of them get their prescription drugs from a friend or relative. Ritalin is inhaled or injected. Attention-deficit disorder, "ADD" drugs are used before tests as "academic steroids."[496] Girls who are legitimately prescribed ADD medicines are more likely than boys to divert them to friends, usually girlfriends. Up to a quarter of them admit to giving some of their medication away. Sadly, 10% of medication redistributers shared them with their parents.[497]

The increasing abuse of prescription drugs has paralleled our increasing exposure to direct-to-consumer advertising sponsored by pharmaceutical manufacturers. Expenditures for such ads increased from $1.8 billion in 1999 to $4.2 billion in 2004.[498]

Pharmaceutical companies are not the only ones saturating our environment with ads. Alcohol companies spent over $590 million on magazine advertising in 2001 and 2002. Many of their ads reached our children. In 2002, compared to people 21 years of age and older, underage adolescents were exposed to 45% more beer and ale ads, 12% more distilled spirits ads, and 65% more low-alcohol "refresher" ads.[499] More subtle promotion comes in the form of "alcohol-branded" merchandise, mostly tee shirts or headwear, bearing company logos. One out of five American adolescents owns such paraphernalia, and only a quarter of these items are purchased at stores. The rest are give-aways, often from friends or family. Ownership of such logo-branded clothing or products is associated with increased rates of initiation of alcohol use in adolescents.[500] The promotional costs of these items are well worth it to alcohol manufacturers. In 2006, it was estimated that the alcoholic beverage industry rung up $22.5 billion in sales to underage drinkers, about 18% of their total revenue. Adult pathological drinking brought them another $25.8 billion.[501]

Marketing illicit drugs is much cheaper. They get free endorsement in subtle ways. I saw both the late actor Rodney Dangerfield and athlete

Dennis Rodman refer to using "just pot" when interviewed on a conservative television talk show, without challenge. Newsweek magazine quoted one 2004 presidential candidate's wife as saying that when she raised her boys she told them never to do cocaine, but as for other drugs, if they used them "tell me, because I want to know what it was like."[502]

By 13 years of age, 28% of American children have had an alcoholic drink and 10% have tried marijuana.[503] A national survey of high schoolers conducted by the Centers for Disease Control in 2003 showed that 45% of the students had used alcohol in the previous month. Forty percent had used marijuana, 22% within a month before the survey. One in 11 had tried cocaine, and 1 in 25 had used it within the preceding month. One in 30 had tried heroin. One out of every 31 had illegally self-injected a drug at least once, and 1 in 8 had inhaled either glue or an aerosol spray. One in 16 had taken a steroid pill or shot without a doctor's prescription. One in 13 had used methamphetamines at least once, and one in 9 had tried ecstasy.[504] This data is particularly disturbing in light of adolescents' vulnerability to peer pressure. I have seen drug addiction compared to communicable diseases. Just as infections spread from person to person, drug users recruit new ones as well, continuing the cycle.

Once recruited, new drug users don't have to go far for advice on fine-tuning their new habits. The internet hosts many sites that offer advice on the use of psychoactive drugs. Several actually sell drug-related products. When a dozen adolescents in substance abuse programs were interviewed on their use of the internet, only one stopped using drugs after consulting web sites. Ten reported initiating drug use after surfing the web. One was motivated to start using a filter for his marijuana, another changed the route of administration of his drugs, and one other increased his use of drugs.[505] Children can use the web to order illegal drugs, or they can use sites to learn how to make their own illegal drugs. There are internet sites that offer formulas for ecstasy and methamphetamines. There are also sites that give reviews and ratings of rave parties.[506 507]

Our attempts to stem this tide of pro-drug influence are feeble. In 2004, the American Presidential administration released news videos of adverse effects of drug use in adolescents. The tapes were distributed by the Office of National Drug Control Policy and broadcast by about 300 television stations to 22 million households. In response, our Government Accounting Office claimed they violated federal laws and constituted "covert propaganda". They objected to the drug control office failing to disclose its role in producing and distributing the videos.[508]

Many adolescents receive equally mixed messages at home. I often meet parents who calmly assure me their children thankfully have no substance abuse issues. In the next breath they elaborate that their adolescents are, of course, "experimenting", but "only with pot". Or they are, naturally, "partying but just with alcohol." Such parents consider "experimentation" with drugs and alcohol a "normal" adolescent phase. A modern rite of passage. A common stage between childhood and responsible adulthood, regrettable but often inevitable.

This attitude is utter nonsense. *"Just pot"* and *"only experimenting"* are 2 of the most dangerous word combinations in the English language.

Data presented at the 2003 annual meeting of the American Psychiatric Association showed physical changes in brain cells in a variety of animal species given Ecstasy that were evident for at least 7 years after exposure. There was ulceration of the brain cells that regulate serotonin. Serotonin is a brain chemical whose imbalance is believed to be involved in psychiatric disease, especially depression. Damage to the serotonin brain regulatory system could theoretically have serious psychiatric consequences.[509] Special brain scans of former methamphetamine users, some drug free for months, show persistent changes in dopamine metabolism.[510] Dopamine is another brain chemical involved in mood, and it also affects learning and movement. Parkinson's disease, commonly seen in older adults, involves changes in brain cells that involve dopamine. Yet another study showed that a single dose of cocaine changed brain cell connections in such a way as to render them more responsive to future stimulation.[511] Such escalations in responsiveness can help set the stage for further use.

Immature nervous systems are not only vulnerable to the development of addictions. They are also uniquely vulnerable to the consequences of addiction. Babies exposed to alcohol before birth often have physical and developmental disabilities. Exposure to cocaine before birth leaves children more likely to have behavioral problems, including distractibility.[512] Similar behavioral changes are also seen in animals exposed to cocaine before birth.[513] In humans, children exposed to cocaine before birth have lower IQs 9 years later.[514] At 10 years of age, such children have lower functioning in some verbal, visual, and motor skills, and they also have identifiable changes on specialized brain scans.[515] [516] They are often found to have smaller overall head sizes, as well.[517] Through 10 year of age, it has also been found that children exposed to cocaine before birth still have slower growth rates.[518]

Babies exposed to marijuana before birth exhibit poorer sleep patterns and increased levels of excitability.[519] At 3 years of age, children who were prenataly exposed to marijuana still demonstrate more night wakenings.[520] Animal studies show that offspring exposed to marijuana before birth have fewer brain cells, more learning problems, and higher levels of emotional reactivity than unexposed peers.[521] It is unclear whether the rate of crib death is increased by prenatal drug use. Some studies have found increased SIDS rates in infants born to mothers who use cocaine, heroin, and amphetamines. One study, published in 2001, also found increased SIDS rates in infants whose fathers used marijuana around the time when their baby was conceived.[522]

The developing adolescent brain may also be anatomically, physically changed by alcohol exposure. Animals at the equivalent age of adolescence show inflammation, cell death, and neurochemical changes in the brain from alcohol exposure. Early data is suggesting that teenagers who use alcohol end up with smaller sized hippocampal areas in their brains.[523] There are specialists in adolescent research who believe that alcohol use may cause a permanent loss of intellectual ability.[524] When researchers from Duke University did MRI scans on children who started using marijuana before 17 years of age, they found them to have smaller brains and less gray matter than non-users. The early marijuana users were also physically smaller in height and weight. The growth retardation from marijuana may be related to the drug's known effects on pituitary hormones.[525] A study from the Netherlands, published in 2007, investigated the long term results of short term ecstasy use. Three years after taking an average of 3 tablets total, short term, low-dose ecstasy users still scored poorer on tests of verbal recall and recognition compared to those who had never tried the drug.[526]

There are other short and long term physical, medical consequences of drug and alcohol use, as well. Adolescents have had heart attacks, complete with ECG changes, from cocaine and marijuana use.[527] In the first hour after taking it, cocaine increases the risk of heart attacks by a factor of 24 times. Chronic cocaine users have heart attacks 7 times more often than non-users. Substance abusers who mix cocaine with alcohol increase their risk of sudden death by a factor of 20 times.[528] Sudden death is also strongly associated with inhalant abuse. One study found that 1 in 5 victims of sudden death from inhalants had no history of previous inhalant abuse. It is believed they died with their first, single use.[529] Such victims are often quite young, because the use of inhalants peaks between 7th and 9th grade.[530]

Cocaine can cause serious physical damage, especially to the nose and mouth. A picture in the New England Journal of Medicine published in 2007 shows a huge gaping hole in the roof of one user's mouth extending all the way up to the inside of his nose.[531] Another picture published in the same journal in 2006 showed a cocaine user's hand, discolored from the blockage of blood flow from a blood clot. Amputation of the thumb was required.[532]

Alcohol causes liver damage, and the country with the highest rate of cirrhosis of the liver, France, is also the nation with the lowest legal drinking age, 16.[533] Cocaine can also cause liver damage, and a hepatitis-type illness, by disseminating little blood clots that clog small liver vessels.[534]

People under the influence of hallucinogens can appear like they are suffering from schizophrenia. I personally saw a patient in an emergency room once whose life was saved by onlookers who prevented her from "trying to fly" from a high balcony in a crowded mall. Visual loss has been known to occur when hallucinating people, their pupils dilated from drug use, have purposefully stared into the sun.[535] According to CDC data, poisoning is second only to car accidents in causing accidental deaths in Americans, and the vast majority of such poisonings in adolescents and adults are from substance abuse involving illegal or prescription drugs.[536] In 2005, unusual problems after heroin use occurred in 5 American states. It was found the heroin was contaminated with a local anesthetic and a veterinary animal stimulant.[537] Methadone boiled in an aluminum pot was found to be the cause of seizures and severe aluminum toxicity in one user.[538] The byproducts of crystal methamphetamine and ingredients used in its production are so toxic that they pose danger to inhabitants of other apartments in buildings housing "meth" labs. Residues trapped in carpeting, vents, and wallboards have been shown to remain there for more than 6 months after production in a building is stopped.[539] In my own medical practice, I once got a frantic call from a mother when a methamphetamine production lab was discovered in the dorm of a major Midwestern state university, 3 floors below where her daughter was living. The entire dormitory was evacuated, and professional hazardous materials teams detoxified it.

Given that the toxic effects of drugs are usually dose-related, the study documenting intellectual deficits 3 years after 3 ecstasy tablets is nothing less than horrifying. Considering that increased dosages lead to increased toxicity, it is likewise of great concern that marijuana plants have been selectively bred to render them up to 15 times more potent over the past 20 years.[540] The addictive potential of marijuana is also increased by its now frequent contamination with other illicit drugs.

Studies from both Sweden and New Zealand published in 2002 showed that marijuana users have an increased risk of subsequently developing schizophrenia. The New Zealand study found a stronger effect with earlier use. Danish data describing marijuana induced psychosis found that people at increased genetic risk for schizophrenia had over double the rate of psychotic reactions to marijuana use.[541] A review of 35 studies addressing the issue of whether this is cause or effect concluded that marijuana did increase the risk of developing a psychotic illness later in life.[542]

The connection may be that marijuana increases the release of dopamine in a certain pathway in the brain called the mesolimbic pathway. The mesolimbic pathway is exactly where a relationship between increased dopamine and mental illness has been suggested.[543] [544] Chronic psychotic psychiatric diseases have also been linked to LSD, PCP, and amphetamine use.[545] Daily marijuana use in young women has been associated with a 5-fold increase in depression and anxiety. British researchers have found that weekly marijuana use by teenagers doubles the rate for later problems with depression and anxiety.[546] Similar data correlating early marijuana use with increased rates of depression and anxiety has been found in studies from America,[547] Britain, and Australia.[548] In the American study, adults who first used marijuana before 12 years of age had double the rate of later serious mental illness. Australian researchers found triple the rate of depression in frequent marijuana users who first tried it before 15 years of age.

Whether marijuana has a "gateway" effect in leading to other drug use has been a topic of much debate. Correlation does not always prove causality, but adolescents who use marijuana are 104 times more likely to use cocaine versus those who never smoked it.[549] Also, a study published in 2003 found that twins who had smoked marijuana by 17 years of age had a 2.5 higher risk of other drug use or alcohol dependence than their never marijuana using co-twin.[550] Marijuana is used 4 times as often by methamphetamine abusers than by non-abusers. Illicit stimulant users are twice as likely as non-users to smoke marijuana.[551]

Many people mistakenly underestimate the addictive potential of marijuana. It is estimated that 3 million Americans are addicted to marijuana in that they report at least 3 of the following 6 problems: needing more marijuana or noticing diminished effects from the same amount; using more marijuana than previously; wanting or not being able to cut down on marijuana use; spending a lot of time getting, using or recovering from marijuana; missing work or social events to use marijuana; or continuing to use marijuana despite problems with it.[552] In 2006, Cambridge University published a book titled *Cannabis Dependence*. Their research found that about 10% of people who use marijuana become addicted to it at some point. Among people seeking treatment for addiction, 1 in 6 lists marijuana as their main problem.[553] Marijuana ruins marriages, careers, and lives.

Marijuana use is associated with lower educational accomplishment,[554] lower work productivity,[555] and increased risks of motor vehicle accidents.[556] Much of the reason why may be that impairment in thinking skills and short-term memory persist for up to 15 days after marijuana use. Very heavy use leaves abusers with poorer memory, psychomotor speed, manual dexterity, and thinking skills after even 28 days of abstinence.[557] [558]

Marijuana use is also associated with increased rates of many physical illnesses, including heart and lung disease,[559] [560] and it is associated with higher rates of lung, head, and neck cancers.[561] [562] Marijuana smoke is 5 times as damaging to lungs as cigarette smoke, with much higher tar and carbon monoxide concentrations than tobacco.[563] A case report of a 27-year-old man who died of metastatic lung cancer revealed a lifetime use of marijuana that started at 3 years of age, peaking at 11 years of age. His doctors blamed his death on the tar in his marijuana, which they estimated exposed him to the equivalent of 80 to 100 years of tobacco use by his mid twenties.[564] Marijuana smoking has also been associated with sudden ruptures of the outer lining of the lungs. At one hospital alone there were 3 adolescent boys in 5 years who suffered brain strokes thought to be due to marijuana. Two of them died.[565]

An increased risk of many infectious diseases is yet another accompaniment to marijuana use. Marijuana leaves have been cultured and shown to harbor a number of germs including funguses, and smoking it increases exposures to these infectious agents. There have been reports of marijuana users developing severe problems with sinusitis from fungal germs,[566] [567] [568] [569] and smoking marijuana greatly increases gum loss and periodontal disease.[570] In irritating the mouth and throat, marijuana use may render these areas more susceptible to infection. Marijuana use also increases the risk of meningococcal meningitis in high school students. This is the most violent form of spinal meningitis, killing up to 20% of its victims, usually within the first 24 hours, and leaving almost a third permanently injured, often from multiple amputations after shock impairs their circulation.[571]

Marijuana smokers' vulnerability to infection may be a reflection of a newly reported side effect of marijuana, an actual alteration of the immune system. Italian researchers have found a direct correlation between increased lifetime marijuana use and decreased functioning of the blood immune system by several different measures. They called the effect "marked" and suggested that it might "increase the susceptibility and promote the progression of infectious diseases and tumors…"[572] Considering the fact that drugs and alcohol lessen sexual inhibitions, this impairment of the immune system from marijuana is a real concern as our rate of heterosexually transmitted AIDS cases increases. CDC data published in 2004 revealed that in the United States, 35% of all new HIV cases are heterosexually transmitted.[573] An association between methamphetamine use and an increase in unsafe sexual practices and HIV transmission has already been published.[574] [575] [576] Included in the immune system are cells that have antitumor activity. In suppressing them, marijuana leaves people more susceptible to cancer. As marijuana smoke contains about 50% more carcinogens than cigarettes, this is cause for concern.[577]

Adolescents who use alcohol, the substance best known for decreasing sexual inhibitions, have more than double the amount of unplanned and unprotected sex compared to their peers.[578] In an era when half of our new AIDS cases occur in people under 25 years of age, most often through heterosexual sex, this is particularly worrisome.[579] Young alcohol users and "experimenters" are also more likely than non-drinkers to have alcohol and other substance abuse problems in middle and high school.[580] Binge and heavy drinkers have higher rates of depression,[581] and they have increased risks of committing or being victimized by virtually all types of violent behavior.[582] In 2001, we lost 4500 Americans younger than 21 years of age to alcohol-related deaths.[583] On our college campuses, drinking contributes to an estimated 1700 deaths, 599,000 injuries, and 97,000 sexual assaults or date rapes per year. One in 10 college students admits to having damaged property under the influence of alcohol.[584] Arrests for alcohol-related behavior on college campuses have increased by 21% over the past few years.[585] The state of Wisconsin has enacted stronger laws against alcohol-related rapes, now allowing prosecutors to argue in court that women may be incapable of consenting to sex while intoxicated.[586]

Making matters even worse, a quarter of drinking college students now use alcohol together with "energy drinks". Sales of energy drinks hit $3 billion in 2006, the same year over 500 new brands of them were introduced, including one named "Cocaine".[587] When mixed with these caffeine and sugar laden products, alcohol becomes more toxic. In combating the sedative effects of alcohol that used to send intoxicated teens back to their dorm beds to sleep it off, energy drinks keep college students awake and ready for more. College students who mix alcohol with energy drinks drink more per outing, and they drink more often. Combining forces, students who take in both energy drinks and alcohol have higher rates of being sexually assaulted, being sexual predators themselves, or being injured while under the influence.[588]

Yet another dangerous combination occurs when unknowing adolescent girls are given alcohol spiked with "club" drugs like ecstasy. These "date rape" drugs are clear, odorless, tasteless, and undetectable on most hospital toxicology screens. They are dangerous alone, but even more deadly when the depressant effects of alcohol are added to the mix.[589]

In turning our daughters into sexual assault victims, alcohol turns our sons into rapists. And it transforms normally careful children into killers when they drive drunk or under the influence of illicit drugs. Thirty percent of teenagers killed in car crashes are intoxicated.[590] After a single marijuana cigarette, adult pilots had measurably impaired performance 24 hours later, though only one study participant reported being aware of it.[591] Adults who drive drunk are 11 times more likely than sober drivers to have a fatal car accident. Teenagers who drive drunk are much more impaired—they are 52 times more likely to have a fatal crash.[592] Near my own hometown, there have been several recent tragedies involving adolescents who drove drunk. One high school student killed his best friend, and another left his friend permanently paralyzed. These young people are known within my community to be kind individuals from loving families. They carry a staggering burden.

They also both served time in correctional institutions over these tragedies. In some such cases, parents have been hit with civil lawsuits over their children's driving misconduct. Substance abusing adolescents subject themselves to arrest, incarceration, and serious legal trouble. I once read an article about lawyers whose whole professional specialty is "spring break". They are busiest between noon and 2:00 p.m., when vacationing students start calling from jail. Our adolescents keep these practitioners quite busy.[593] In one particularly heart wrenching criminal case, in 2006 a Pennsylvania police chief arrested his own son. High on cocaine, the boy had robbed a bank.[594] When our children's academic records are accompanied by criminal records, they may find their later access to some professions and jobs restricted.

As both perpetrators and victims, substance abusing adolescents interface with a violent world. In Germany in 2008, there was an outbreak of severe lead poisoning, some cases with serious aftereffects, in marijuana users. It was traced to the deliberate contamination of the drug with lead to make it weigh more. The additional profit was estimated to be $1500 per kilogram.[595] In 2006, a teenager from a relatively crime-free suburb near my home was shot to death during a drug transaction involving marijuana. The boy had been a standout swim team member at his high school. He was shot in the head and his body was left in his car in a suburban parking lot. His murderer was also a teenager at the time. A trauma unit director once told me that the injuries drug dealers inflict on each other during turf wars were worse than anything he'd seen as a medic in Viet Nam. In 1989, there was a report of 13 children from 12 to 19 years of age seen in a Washington hospital that year with gun shot wounds to the legs, some of whom required major vascular/reconstructive surgery. The children were recruited drug dealers who were not performing as expected.[596] In New York City a few years later there was a series of cases of a new type of facial trauma also traced to punishments for bad drug deals. It involved a cutting of the mouth from the corner up across the face in a "half smile" pattern almost up to the ear.[597] A colostomy nurse once also told me of a cluster of patients she'd cared for with gunshot wounds up the rectum, also inflicted as part of drug dealing.

Are the perpetrators of such viciousness who we want our adolescents associating with? Is their violent world what we want our children supporting? The widow of a brutally murdered DEA agent once announced that she blamed her husband's death not only on those directly involved, but also on the huge numbers of suburbanite American "recreational" drug users who keep the drug industry in business. She was right. Anyone purchasing illicit drugs supports the entire network that supplies it. I also once saw a Mexican governmental official implore America for help in cleaning up drug cartel violence in his country. He pointed out that much of his nation's trouble and heartache can be traced to its northern neighbor's demand for drugs. Since 2006, about 15,000 Mexicans have been killed in drug cartel violence. One of them was 30-year-old Navy Petty Officer Melquisedet Angulo, who died in a battle that left a major drug lord dead in December, 2009. They day after Officer Angulo's funeral, where he was hailed a hero by the Mexican government, drug hit men killed his mother, sister, brother and aunt.[598] Sharing the responsibility for this horror are the consumers that keep the drug business alive. Our adolescent drug users are an integral part of that industry's customer base.

People who purchase alcohol for underage drinkers are also partners in pain. A quarter of adolescents over 13 years old report that their own parents have supplied them with alcohol. One in 5 teens has attended parties where alcohol was provided by friend's parents. Older siblings are another major source of alcohol for young teens. Across all age groups, girls are more likely than boys to be obtainers of alcohol. As more passive participants in underage drinking, many parents fail to secure alcohol in their homes. A third of teens report it easy to divert alcohol at home without their parent's knowledge. Forty percent find it easy to sneak alcohol from friend's parents.[599] [600]

Are these parents aware that our children are 6.5 times more likely to die from underage drinking than from illegal drug use?[601] Alcohol kills more of our teenagers than all other drugs combined. Overall, underage drinking in general leads to almost 5000 deaths per year.[602] Alcohol use increases the rates of injury from driving, walking, swimming, and boating. People who begin drinking prior to age 21 are more likely to be hurt while under the influence of alcohol,[603] and problem drinking in adolescence extends to an increased risk of problem drinking during early adulthood.[604] Compared to people who delay alcohol use until after 21 years of age, those who begin drinking prior to 14 years of age are 5 times more likely to be alcohol dependent later on.[605] [606] They are also 7 times more likely to be in an alcohol-related car accident, and 10 times more likely to experience alcohol-related violence during their lives.[607] Also of note, younger adolescents, especially girls, are more easily intoxicated than older drinkers. In one study, it took just 3 drinks in 2 hours for boys up to 13 and girls up to 17 years of age to spike blood alcohol levels over the legal limit for intoxication.[608]

If all this wasn't horrifying enough, here are a few more facts. After factoring out multiple issues including a history of sadness or abuse, young adolescents who use alcohol are more likely to be depressed, suicidal, or violent than non-drinking peers.[609] [610] Across all ethnic groups, girls who develop early are more likely to initiate sex early and in turn to have earlier and more pregnancies. Researchers found that the connection is mediated by the earlier use of alcohol by these earlier developing girls.[611] High school students who binge drink have poorer grades, higher rates of sexual activity, and higher rates of tobacco and illicit drug use.[612]

Is this what we want for our precious children? "Only alcohol?" "Just pot?" "Just partying?" One poll showed that 1 in 4 American parents of teenagers believe their children should be able to drink at home with parents present.[613] [614] A third of teenagers and almost half of 17-year-olds report having attended parties where parents are present when adolescents use marijuana, cocaine, ecstasy, or alcohol.[615] Do these parents believe that drug and alcohol use, once endorsed by them, will be restricted to home? Do they believe their home provides immunity to addiction? Is Russian Roulette safer when you play it in your own living room? When it comes to drugs, alcohol and adolescents, ignorance is not bliss. Parents who underestimate the devastation that underage drinking can cause should read *Smashed; Story of a Drunken Girlhood*, by Koren Zailckas.[616]

The reason our teenagers have so much trouble with alcohol is that adolescents are uniquely vulnerable to the development of addictions. Over 40% of children who start using alcohol before age 14 develop alcohol dependence, versus 10% who don't drink until over age 20.[617] Teenagers' propensity to dependency extends beyond alcohol to virtually all types of addictive traps. Eighty-two percent of tobacco addicts started smoking before age 18, but almost no smokers start over age 25.[618] While the overall rate of dependence for people who try marijuana is 9%[619], for adolescents who try it before age 16 the rate is 21%.[620] The addiction rate for those who try cocaine is 17%, and for heroin its 23%.[621] In Scotland, where 13% of adolescents between16 and 19 years of age have tried cocaine, this addiction rate can be only be expected to have profound, prolonged consequences for the entire generation.[622]

There are people for whom one single drug exposure is permanently addictive. The particular vulnerability of adolescents to addiction may have a biological basis. Special MRI's that show neural activity in addition to brain anatomy show different activity in different brain parts in adolescents versus adults. Compared to adults, adolescents shown stressful images demonstrate less activity in the frontal lobe (the home of more rational, logical thought and action) and more activity in the amygdala (a part of the brain "limbic" system that involves more emotional reactions).[623] Other research has shown continuous growth of a part of the brain called the anterior cingulate gyrus through about age 21.[624] The anterior cingulate gyrus is responsible for inhibition. "That's why when you mature, your ability to say 'no' is increased" according to Dr. Nora Volkow, who was appointed director of the National Institute on Drug Abuse in 2003.[625] Dr. Volkow's counterpart at the National Institute of Alcohol Abuse and Alcoholism, Dr. Daniel Hommer, is also researching the biological basis of adolescents' high risk for the development of addictions. Dr. Hommer's work focuses on an area of the brain called the "nucleus accumbens", which involves motivation and responsiveness to rewards. Brain scans of adolescents being paid to complete simple tasks show much less activation in this region compared to young adults. Dr. Hommer explained that "my guess is that this is developmental… Adolescents have much less involvement in motivation—it's not fully developed."[626] What did show stimulation of the nucleus accumbens area was another study that scanned adolescents' brains as they were shown beer and liquor advertisements.[627] When paired, these findings support a theory of addiction called the "reward deficit" theory. The idea is that since adolescents get less pleasure from everyday tasks and accomplishments, they are more tempted to turn to drugs and alcohol.

In a positive light, these findings can be taken to mean that there is a real pay off to stopping our adolescents from using drugs and alcohol during their young, vulnerable years. Instead of delaying the inevitable, we may be actually permanently preventing substance abuse by getting adolescents safely to a point in their lives when they can think more rationally, say "no" more easily, and find pleasure in other, safer pursuits. As for how to accomplish this, here's a few principles:

1) **Supervision and parental involvement really do matter**. A study published in 2004 found that adolescents whose parents had anti-smoking rules were less likely to use tobacco.[628] A later study, from Massachusetts, found that adolescents in homes with total smoking bans were more likely than those from more permissive homes to develop anti-smoking attitudes.[629] New Hampshire and Vermont families with carefully monitored children's television and movie watching and prohibition of R-rated films have lower rates of both adolescent tobacco and alcohol use.[630] Interventions that increase parental monitoring of adolescents have been found to decrease not only smoking, but also marijuana and other illicit drug use, as well.[631] A high-risk behavior prevention program for inner-city

African American boys that involved parents likewise significantly helped with drug use.[632] A similar program involving rural, Midwest public schools had similarly successful effects on preventing methamphetamine use, with sustained protective effects 5 years later.[633] In an American Academy of Pediatrics publication based on data from northern California high schools, it was suggested that "high levels of parental monitoring do in fact discourage both boys and girls from beginning to use drugs."[634] For adolescents in Colombia, where illegal drugs are easily available, one study found that the single element that cancelled out other risk factors for marijuana use was "a close parent-child bond".[635] Closer to home, a survey of adolescents from Georgia "demonstrated a consistent pattern of health risk behaviors…associated with less perceived parental monitoring."[636] In that study, adolescents from homes with less parental monitoring had over double the rate of frequent marijuana use than peers from more supervised homes.[637] In 2005 a study was published that followed a group of children born in the 1980s. Families with the least parental involvement and the most coercive discipline methods had the highest rates of marijuana use.[638]

Study after study echoes these results. A paper published in 2001 reviewed the medical literature in this area and cited 39 different references. The authors concluded that there is a definite association between the amount of parental monitoring and interaction and adolescent involvement in drug and alcohol use, high-risk driving, and juvenile delinquency.[639]

Knowing where your children are, by the way, is a start, but it does not ensure supervision. Adolescents at one end of a large suburban home with a busy adult multitasking on the internet and telephone at the other end of the home are functionally unsupervised. Adolescents need close, interactional supervision.

Disappointingly, the schools to which we give both our precious children and our hard-earned tax money get failing grades themselves in the supervision department. When surveyed by the CDC, 22.3% of American high school students report having been offered, sold, or given an illegal drug by someone on school property during the prior year. Within a single month prior to being asked, 4.5% of American high schoolers have used marijuana on school property, and 4.1% drank alcohol there.[640] One study also found that 28% of schools allow staff to smoke indoors, and 83% allow staff and students to smoke outdoors but on school property. Girls 13 years of age in that study were almost 5 times more likely to smoke daily if they attended schools where they saw staff smoking.[641]

Parents also influence by example, and that influence is particularly strong during adolescence. Children living in homes with parental substance abuse develop the problem themselves much more often than children without such exposure, possibly largely due to genetic susceptibility. However, the effect is much more pronounced when the exposure to parental substance abuse occurs during the adolescent years. About 30% of children exposed before 12 years of age develop chemical dependency. After 13 years of age, over half of such children become addicted.[642] Parent, heal thyself. It is not too late for it to have a positive effect on children's risks of substance abuse, even in the face of genetic susceptibility.

2) Access matters. Physicians who abuse prescription drugs often initiate their use when they are first able to write prescriptions and "when they become more readily available in the workplace."[643] One survey of 500 practicing physicians found that in the previous year, a quarter of them had self-prescribed a psychoactive drug and 1 in 10 had used one "recreationally."[644] Anesthesiologists, who have the greatest day-to-day access to controlled substances, have one of the highest rates of physician addiction,[645] and after treatment, their relapse rate upon re-entry to their drug-filled work place is up to 66%.[646] Physicians overall have a very high suicide rate; 40% higher than average for men, and 130% higher than average for women. Doctors who commit suicide often do it with drugs from their own offices, poisons close at hand.

Drug availability influences patients as well as their doctors. In Australia, the enactment of a law making it easier to obtain barbiturates was followed by an increase in suicides involving them.[647] It is no coincidence that inhalant abuse is common among grade school children. Inhalants are legal, inexpensive, and the easiest to obtain of all illicitly used substances. The simple cough medicine dextromethorphan, also relatively cheap and readily available, is one of the most commonly abused over-the-counter drugs.

The increase in abuse of prescription and over-the-counter drugs parallels the increase in their doctor recommended presence in our homes. Over the past decade, we physicians have been taught to more aggressively address patient's pain, and at the same time new and better drugs to treat it have become available. Between 1992 and 2002, the number of prescriptions for hydrocodone and oxycodone increased by 380%.[648] There was a corresponding even larger increase in the rate of abuse of these drugs, by 618%,[649] and in turn, an increase in deaths from overdoses of such medications. In West Virginia, between 1999 and 2004, 93% of deaths from unintentional medication overdose involved prescription painkillers.[650] In 2002, 1 in 13 adolescents admitted to using pain medications illicitly.[651]

It is no surprise that adolescents are sensitive to the challenge of drug and alcohol availability, especially when it's combined with peer pressure. After factoring out the effects of parental monitoring, one study showed that having substance abusing friends increased the chance adolescents would begin using drugs themselves. Adding in high levels of parental supervision did not overcome the effects of peer relationships.[652] A study conducted by the World Health Organization involving 31 different nations, mostly European and North American, found a correlation between the frequency of evening outings with friends and the use of marijuana.[653] Adolescents are best kept away from drug and alcohol using peers.

As to which adolescents are drug users, don't count on outer appearances to be a helpful guide. I have given medical care to maximally pierced, ill-groomed adolescents who remind me, when asked, that they'd never take drugs because it would impair the precise coordination they need to skateboard down whole staircases. Alternatively, most of the substance abusing patients on the inpatient adolescent psychiatric units where I'm on staff look absolutely "clean cut". They often also have fine academic records. The profile of the drug addicted adolescent as unkempt with poor grades is not always accurate.

3) Enabling matters. No other culture and no other generation of parents have ever allowed teenagers the autonomy we give suburban American adolescents. Consider the Brazilian Indian tribes of the Upper Xingu. A book published by the Harvard University Press describes how they handle adolescents. "When they reach puberty, boys and girls remain in seclusion inside the hut for prolonged periods, which can amount to 1 to 2 years for males…receiving a lot of food and being introduced to the handicrafts and oral traditions of the tribe. At the end of the period, when the adolescent comes back to the community life, his physical and muscular condition are remarkably improved."[654] Substance abuse and delinquent behavior are not problems in traditional Upper Xingu families. Compare and contrast this with our treatment of our most vulnerable, pubertal offspring. We give them cars, car insurance, cell phones, charge cards, cash, and privacy. More teens than ever in our suburbs have both their own bedrooms and their own bathrooms, which they often consider private and "off limits" to other family members. All this is fertile ground for substance abuse. No adolescent is entitled to these privileges, and no adolescent domain should ever be exempt from parental searches.

The ultimate in enabling occurs when adults directly provide drugs and alcohol to minors. A quarter of teens report being supplied with alcohol by their own parents.[655] Almost 30% get it from an older sibling. Parents who participate in supplying alcohol to minors risk not only those minors' well being, but their own, as well. In 2002, a Virginia mother was sentenced to 27 months in jail for supplying alcohol for her son's 16th birthday party. The party was an overnight event, with guests turning in their car keys and agreeing not to leave until morning.[656] Near my own hometown, 2 parents who allowed minors to drink in their basement were tried and convicted of felonies after 2 of their guests were killed in a car accident shortly after leaving. We have a local "Parents Who Host, Lose the Most" campaign, and a special police underage drinking party tip line.

4) Knowledge helps. Be mindful of the risk factors for substance use and dependency. Children with predispositions to addiction should be particularly monitored. Risk factors for early onset drinking include: parental discord or divorce, substance abuse in the home, genetic predisposition to addiction, the presence of a psychiatrically ill person in the home, a history of physical or sexual abuse, a history of domestic violence in the home, smoking, underage sibling drinking, peer drinking, positive attitudes toward alcohol, possession or willingness to use alcohol promotional items, or a past history of having conduct problems or depression.[657 658 659 660 661 662 663] Although generally considered positive attributes, yet another predictor of teen alcohol use is higher social self-esteem in girls and higher athletic self-esteem in boys.[664] Last but not least, simply being a college student is one of the best predictors of alcohol abuse. One study found 44% of college students reporting binge drinking within the previous 2 weeks.[665] Students are most vulnerable when they first arrive on campus.[666]

Diagnosing alcohol addiction in teenagers is sometimes difficult. One set of questions thought to be helpful are: 1) Have you ever ridden in a car driven by someone under the influence of alcohol or drugs? 2) Do you use alcohol to relax or fit in better? 3) Do you drink when alone? 4) Have your friends ever told you to cut down on alcohol use? 5) Do you ever forget things while under the influence? Or, 6) Have you ever gotten into trouble while intoxicated?[667]

Protective factors against underage drinking include eating family dinner often or having high levels of religious involvement, supportive parents, or an affectionate temperament.[668]

While filling out college health papers for a patient of mine a few years ago, I came across a campus housing request form. On it was a printed option for a "substance free dormitory". I have seen it on other college forms since. Are we this helpless? Do our colleges deal with other illegal activities by segregation? Are there rape-free dorms, or murder-free dorms?

We are not that helpless. There are ways to address adolescent addiction:

1) Increase the price of alcohol by taxing it. Cost and consumption are inversely related for alcohol. It has been calculated that increasing alcohol costs by 10% would reduce binge drinking by 8% and decrease severe child abuse by 2%.[669] [670]

2) Get the law on your side. Stricter enforcement of the minimum legal drinking age in one college town was found to decrease drinking in students there by 20%.[671] Parents have a right and responsibility to demand that the universities that we entrust our precious children to aggressively address drug and alcohol abuse.

3) Get rid of promotional merchandise encouraging alcohol use. This includes hats, tee shirts, water bottles, key chains, and anything else they can get their logo on. These materials endorse alcohol use, and their possession has been associated with early drinking in adolescents.[672]

4) Attend to psychiatric problems that increase the risk of substance abuse, including conduct disorders and depression.[673] [674] [675]

5) Increase the number of family meals eaten in your household.[676] [677]

6) Minimize exposure to movies and advertising that promote alcohol. Marketing works. The alcoholic beverage industry spends fortunes getting name recognition via direct advertising and sponsorship of sporting events only because it increases sales. Good data shows that media exposure to alcohol consumption contributes to teen drinking.[678] [679] [680]

7) Put your money where your mouth is. More adolescents are killed by substance abuse than by cancer. Rally for research on this deadly problem. Support legislation to address underage drinking. Be enthusiastic about having your hard earned tax dollars used to support "Recovery High Schools". Such schools are expensive, but needed. As of 2006, there were only 22 such schools nationwide in the United States.[681]

Last, but not least, if we are going to ever decrease the number of our adolescents living in those non-substance-free dormitories, we are going to have to do some national soul searching as to why our children want to be there. Dr. Abraham Twerski, a leading expert in chemical dependency, points out that we have come to confuse our national commitment to the pursuit of happiness with the pursuit of pleasure. "Doing good is not the same as feeling good," he points out. Dr. Twerski traces much of the void in our children's lives to our secularism. He calls faith "vitamins for the spirit". He warns that the pursuit of pleasure in place of happiness can turn toward drugs and alcohol in the absence of spirituality and its joy. "Teenagers see the world as a difficult place…Show them what it its like to be spiritual and to be happy with spirituality," he advises.[682] It is no coincidence that our most successful substance abuse program, Alcoholics Anonymous, has a strong spiritual component and emphasizes submission to a Higher Power. The successful Interval Brotherhood Home is run by a priest, Father Sam Ciccolini. Since 1970, he has helped over 8000 chemically-dependent people break free. The relapse rate in his graduates is lower than the national average. Why? It's because of the "spirit", he says. Faith is both his tool and his message.[683] In Puerto Rico, 75% of drug treatment programs are faith based. In 2003, the government there voted to declare drug dependence a spiritual and social problem instead of a simple mental health issue.[684]

Personally, I believe that much of our adolescents' attraction to drugs is rooted in simple boredom. Author Barrett Seaman, who wrote a book on underage drinking named *Binge*, insightfully points out that the rise of drinking on college campuses parallels the trend of grade inflation, whereby students are rewarded for less work with better grades. Outside the classroom, our children also work less than other generations. This leaves them with both a void in their schedules, and a void in their lives. Affluence has deprived our children of one of life's greatest satisfactions— the comfort of jobs well done. Coming from smaller families, our children don't have many siblings to help care for. Nor do our children tend to our homes. Summer in the suburbs means streets clogged with landscaping trucks. No generation has ever hired so much cleaning help. Idle hands really are the devil's playground, and boredom is fertile ground for trouble.

There is also a moral and ethical aspect to substance abuse. Our children's bodies are not all their own. Their physical selves house beautiful souls, given to them by a Higher Power. Harming those bodies with alcohol and drugs is disrespectful to both the One who created them, and to those of us who have worked so hard to nurture our gift through the sleepless nights of infancy and the accident prone years of toddlerhood. It declares that the natural world G-d gave us is not enough to keep them satisfied. It reminds me of the story of a man who challenges the Almighty, claiming he can also create life. "I start with dirt…" he explains. "No you don't", G-d thunders, "Make your own dirt!" We can't even make our own dirt. So how is the awesome spectrum of life and nature around us not enough to hold our attention?

A young teenager I am privileged to know told me she was able to immediately stop her drug use after her mother tragically and suddenly died. "It made me look completely differently at life" she told me. "When I saw how fragile life is, I had to ask myself, 'What am I doing?'" With most people of our generation living longer, are we lulled into thinking we have years to waste? Previous generations faced their "mid-life" crisis point, a time for reflection on our mortality, in young adulthood instead of at menopause. Our parents and grandparents also had much more exposure to death, with extended family members usually dying at home instead of hospitals. Perhaps this heightened awareness of the life cycle left them less willing to take risks. The brilliant 20th century physicist Richard Feynman wrote that he gave up alcohol when he realized it interfered with his most pleasurable activity—thinking. Our adolescents would benefit from seriously contemplating these alternative perspectives.

As a pediatrician, it is as painful for me to diagnose a substance abuse problem as it is to uncover a malignancy. They can be equally life-threatening, and equally tragic for families. Parenting is not always a cause and effect endeavor. I have seen loving, attentive parents suffer unspeakable agony watching their children battle addiction, often ending years later with a funeral. No parent would ever accept a little cancer, or a slight pregnancy as OK. Let's have the same attitude toward illicit drug use and underage drinking. There is no such thing as "experimentation" with anything addictive that obliterates self-control.

Adolescents using illicit drugs are drug users, not drug "experimenters". They risk their lives and their future. They devastate families emotionally and financially. They support a violent, murderous drug industry. If you find any room for tolerance or neutrality here, or if you believe illicit drug use to be any kind of normal or acceptable developmental phase, or if you think those law enforcement people and school administrators with zero tolerance for illicit drugs and underage drinking are unfair or unkind, you're wrong. Sometimes simply wrong. Sometimes disastrously wrong. Sometimes dead wrong.

CHAPTER 6

• • •

NOT SO SWEET SEXTEEN

Enjoyable Aspect of Parenting Adolescents Number Five: Adolescents do not habitually vomit on our shoulders, or drool on our better clothing. They do not require or desire any assistance involving any body fluid or byproduct whatsoever. When your family reaches the outer recesses of huge airports laden with luggage, they do not suddenly need a washroom. Enjoy relinquishing responsibility for your adolescent's bodily functions.

There is a story of a young student who uses foul language in school. Having failed to resolve the problem with a variety of disciplinary approaches, the school principal finally calls the child's parents. The father is horrified by his child's conduct. Hurt and distraught, he unleashes a string of obscenities describing his disappointment.

As we address our children's sexual activities, we are that distraught parent. My term for the prevalence of sexual activity in our adolescents is simply "cause and effect."

Over the long haul of childhood, environmental forces steer our offsprings' choices more than it might seem in the short run.

There is a family of accomplished musicians in my medical practice. Three generations play string instruments with great skill. It is a beautiful thing to see and hear. How was this accomplished? Early on, the children heard classical music. They were treated to concerts. With a gentle, positive tone, opportunities were presented and instruments were provided. Other families I have worked with are particularly athletic. Their children enjoy watching games with their parents, and can recite sports statistics in detail. Their house is the one with the basketball net above the garage and the bat and ball in the grass. Within a few years, they are in my office for sports physicals, with batches of forms from a variety of school teams. In the art world, parental influence on life choices is likewise nothing new. The impressionist painter Pissarro had 6 children who survived to adulthood. Five mirrored his passion and became artists.[685] Other 19th century painters included brothers Rembrandt and Rubens Peale, whose father's career encouragement started with their given names.[686]

Our generation's cultural pastime is no longer art. It is sex. And our children bear witness. After growing up immersed in sexual imagery and innuendo, what do our adolescents do when newly in charge of their bodies? By their 13th birthday, 7% of American children have already had sexual intercourse.[687] A survey of 9th graders found that 19% reported having already had oral sex, and another 31% reported they intended to have it within the next 6 months. As for vaginal sex, 13% of 14-year-olds had already had it, and another 26% plan to have it within 6 months.[688] Overall, 48% of American high school students have had sexual intercourse[689] [690], a third them, when asked, within the previous 3 months. By the time they graduate, 20% have had 4 or more sexual partners.[691] During college, one study found an average of 10 "hook up" partners per student, involving genital physical contact, oral sex, or intercourse. Interview data showed that college students reported that hook ups were more likely to involve "genital touching" than "meaningful conversation". One researcher called this the new "campus norm".[692]

How has this been encouraged? Look around. We have perfumes named "Total Seduction", and television shows named "Sex and the City", and stage plays named "The Vagina Chronicles", and songs that serenade us with lyrics like "your body is a wonderland." There was once a large bakery near my home with trucks and billboards proclaiming them "Good in Bread". An ad for a popular TV show at a bus stop in my area asks "Going Home to Watch 'Sex' with Friends?" Sexually suggestive ads try to sell us everything from cars to bathroom faucets. When arriving at the University of Iowa, one of my own children was presented, in a "welcoming" packet for new students distributed at the bookstore, with a doorknob tag advertising cold remedies made by the Procter and Gamble Company. On one side it said "Getting better in bed", and the reverse announced "I like to do it in the morning". Even parenting magazines join in. *Parents* magazine in 2005 featured a short article on "Home Remedies for Great Sex".[693] *Child* magazine ran a feature on "Sex, Romance, & the New Dad."[694] The same month, *Parenting* magazine gave advice in their "Smart Solutions" column on how to solve one readers' problem of not having "sex as much as we used to." Suggestions included "sex during Saturday morning cartoons can still be good sex."[695] A popular book for adolescents, released in movie form in 2005, is *The Sisterhood of the Traveling Pants*. The book deals sensitively with many issues facing today's young teens in a creative way, tying 4 girl's lives together as they share a pair of pants. Rule Number 4 regarding use of the pants, however, is "You must never let a boy take off the Pants (although you may take them off yourself in his presence)."[696] Another children's book titled *My Life in the 7th Grade* describes a bathroom conversation between 2 characters regarding condoms.[697]

As we sexualize our environment we shorten our children's precious few years of innocence. It is a theft that cannot be repaid.

Two-thirds of television programs involve sexual content, and 1 in 7 portrays sexual intercourse, either depicted or strongly implied.[698] Programs most watched by our teenagers are even more sexually explicit. Eighty-three percent of television shows whose audience is predominantly adolescent contain sexual content, with an average of 6.7 scenes involving sexual content every hour. One in 5 of such scenes in shows with mostly teen viewers overtly or implicitly portray sexual intercourse.[699] [700] [701] The average American adolescent views almost 14,000 sexual references per year, only 165 of which deal with birth control, self-control, abstinence, pregnancy risk, or STDs. A third of "family hour" shows include sexual references. Soap operas, now popular on college campuses, contain about 3 acts of sexual intercourse per hour, only 25% of which involve married partners.[702]

And that's just the drama shows. When watching the news at dinnertime, between commercials for erectile dysfunction drugs, our children grow up hearing stories about sexual misconduct by politicians of each party, at every level of government. Lately, it's "Governors Gone Wild". In becoming such shameful public role models, elected officials fail not only themselves and their own families, but my impressionable patients, as well. In 2005, one Midwestern state governor referred to "testicular virility" in responding, on the air, to a television reporter's question. Of note, that governor has young children. When they reach adolescence, he may have a different perspective on public references to genitalia. The author of the traveling pants book also has 2 "young" sons. When they are young teenagers, will she want girls taking off their pants in front of her boys?

A national study of 12- to 17-year-olds found that those at the upper end of sexual television viewing time had double the risk of having intercourse in the next year when compared to those at the extreme lower end of the curve.[703] They were also twice as likely to experience a pregnancy or father a child before age 20.[704] Exposure to talk about sex without actual depiction of sexual acts had the same effect.[705] Another study of previously not sexually active adolescents under 16 years of age found that poorly supervised television watching of 2 or more hours per day increased their probability of initiating sexual activity the next year by a third.[706] As for films, research on adolescent girls found that the 30% who had been exposed to X-rated movies had less healthful sexual practices and increased likelihoods of having more sexual partners and more intercourse than non-exposed peers.[707] Exposure to explicit music lyrics considered "degrading" was also found to increase the rates of sexual intercourse and other sexual activity in another study that followed teens a full 3 years.[708]

If there is any one single study that sums up how sexualized our American culture is, it is one that looked at the rates of sexual activity in immigrant and migrant children. Not surprisingly, the degree of assimilation into American culture has actually been found to be predictive of an earlier onset of sexual intercourse for Hispanic teenagers. Spanish only speaking teens living in the United States are two-thirds less likely to have had sex compared to English only speaking counterparts.[709]

Exposure is only one part of the equation that contributes to our adolescent's rates of sexual activity. After surrounding them with sexually suggestive influences, we offer our children little advice on the ethics and morality of sexual behavior. We show them only the gas pedal and not the brake. In driver's education, we teach our adolescents the rules of the road and insist on supervised training before we allow them behind the wheel. As for sex education, we give our adolescents cars to drive to prom, on unsupervised dates, with our daughters in strapless low-cut dresses, with few if any instructions on what we find sexually acceptable. In a great act of bravery, sparking criticism, school officials Brother Kenneth Hoagland and Reverend Philip Eichner cancelled the senior prom at their school in 2005 because it had become an "alcohol-sex-drugs…orgy".[710] In doing so, they demonstrated rare moral leadership. While other schools impishly try breathalyzing raucous dance attendees, knowing full well what the post test night will involve for those who pass, Brother Hoagland and Reverend Eichner stood up and became the role models our adolescents really need.

In setting sexual limits, religiously observant families have it easy. Their guidelines are defined and straightforward. Fundamentalist faiths prohibit physical contact before marriage. Families who find sexual activity outside marriage acceptable also owe it to their offspring to define specifically when, where, and how such contact fits into their moral structure. While doing so they should remember that children are masters at spotting ambiguity and merciless about tolerating hypocrisy. If sex with "significant others" is OK, how do we define such partners? Adolescent girls, in particular, often mistake lust for love. "Serial monogamy" could theoretically involve a new "monogamous" partner every week. If sex at age 18 is OK, why not at age 17, and right on down? Condoning sexual activity in adolescents is a slippery slope leading to thin ice.

Parents also need to remember that actions speak louder than words. With our high divorce rate, many adolescents have single parents who are themselves dating. Teenagers who stumble across evidence of their parents having intimate dating relationships are given a powerful message.

Thankfully, parental influence cuts the other way, too. Adolescent sexual behavior can be altered by our attitude, monitoring, and family dynamics. One large study published in 2000 looked at ages of sexual initiation in children in over 3300 families. For adolescents with warm and close mother-child relationships, maternal disapproval of early sexual intercourse was associated with less and later sexual activity.[711] In another study, children with high levels of parental monitoring and greater communication about sexual risks had less, later, and lower rates of high risk sexual activity.[712] Researchers publishing in 2006 documented that over a full year, children of parents strongly opposed to adolescent sexual activity initiated it only half as often as peers who did not sense parental disapproval.[713] Yet another large, national study found that adolescents who classified their parents as strongly opposed to their having sex had 40% fewer sexually transmitted diseases.[714] [715] Factoring out all other variables, still other data has shown parental disapproval of adolescent sexual intercourse to lower the risk of STDs in offspring a full 6 years later.[716] The extended disapproval of faith-based systems is also protective against sexual activity in adolescents. Studies have found students attending parochial schools to have lower rates of sexually transmitted diseases,[717] and a recently completed survey of 572 girls 13 to 21 years of age has confirmed previous studies showing that high levels of religious belief correlated with later and less sexual activity with fewer lifetime partners.[718]

Also influencing adolescents' sexual activity is simple opportunity. "Home alone" for teenagers is X-rated. Sexual intercourse in high schoolers tends to occur between 3:30 and 6:00 p.m., the "latchkey" hours.[719] A study that looked specifically at this issue found that adolescents home alone after school were 2½ times more likely to have sexual intercourse than those with adults on the premises.[720] Less parental monitoring has been demonstrated to correlate with higher rates of sexually transmitted diseases,[721][722] and high levels of physical parental supervision have been shown to lower the rates of sexually transmitted diseases in adolescents. Note the emphasis here on actual, tangible, parental physical presence. High levels of "perceived parental communication" with close verbal relationships and comfort in discussing sexual matters had no protective effect in one study that addressed the issue.[723] Researchers in charge of an HIV prevention program found adolescents with "infrequent" parental monitoring to have twice the rate of sexually transmitted diseases compared to those who are watched more carefully.[724] Teens who work more than 20 hours per week, minimizing their "leisure time", have lower rates of sexually transmitted diseases.[725] As for unemployed adolescents, a study published in 2002 found that boys unsupervised more than 5 hours per week after school had double the number of gonorrhea and Chlamydia infections compared to those alone less than 5 hours weekly. That same study also found a correlation between unsupervised time at home and more sexual activity and higher numbers of lifetime sexual partners. A full 91% of participants in that study reported "a home setting" as the place where their most recent sexual act had taken place. Over a third of those sexual encounters occurred between 3:00 and 6:00 p.m.[726] Another study addressing adolescent's attitudes toward sexual intercourse found significantly less intention to have sex in teens who families practiced careful and successful parental monitoring.[727] The inverse relationship between higher levels of parental monitoring and lower rates of sexual and other high risk activities is documented over and over in the medical literature.[728][729][730][731] Parental monitoring has been proven protective across different cultures, countries, and ethnicities.[732][733][734][735][736][737]

The ultimate in unsupervised is the college dormitory. In housing our older adolescents in "coed" dorms, we leave them alone in bedrooms. The result? "Hook ups", defined not only by the sexual contact they involve, but also by a lack of any expectation of an accompanying deeper relationship. One author who visited several college campuses while writing a novel described it as a "sexual carnival".[738] College professor Donna Freitas, who has taught courses on sexuality at Boston University, reports dorm parties where students role play whores and pimps.[739]

The problem with this is that "casual sex" is anything but. Professor Freitas, after conducting a survey of 2500 college students from a variety of schools nationwide, found that 41% of students who "hook up" are "profoundly upset about their behavior". In describing their experiences, her students used words like "dirty", "empty", and "regretful".[740] There is an emotional and physical toll to our adolescents' sexual activities. Compared to peers who delay sexual intercourse, sexually active teenagers have much higher rates of depression and suicide attempts.[741] [742] [743] [744] One study showed increased rates of depression proportionate to the increased numbers of partners for sexually active teens.[745]

The psychological disaster that adolescent sex can be hits our daughters particularly hard. One study found sexually active girls 6.3 times more likely to attempt suicide than sexually active boys.[746] Seventy percent of adolescent girls sexually active before age 16 report that they wished they had waited longer. As for why they didn't, reasons for first intercourse are "to please the partner" for 20% of girls.[747] Low self-esteem has been associated with loss of virginity in young girls, but not in boys.[748]

Part of our daughter's problems with sexual activity may be their disappointment when they discover that one of the most painful and pessimistic theories regarding relationships may unfortunately be true. As the old saying goes, "women use sex to get love; men use love to get sex". In 2005, researchers published a study that investigated sexual risk taking in relationships. They compared risk taking by partners acquainted beforehand to risks taken in new relationships deemed "romantic" from the start. Their data showed that girls, but not boys, were less likely to discuss STDs or contraception in new, exclusively "romantic" relationships. In commenting on their data, the authors pointed out that the medical literature shows "that female adolescents tend to romanticize relationships while male adolescents emphasize sexual aspects." Girls, they pointed out, "tend to connect sexual activity with greater levels of commitment..."[749]

In other words, our most educated girls in the history of the planet are still confusing sex with love. A 5-year study in Baltimore looked at the accuracy of teenagers beliefs about their sexual partner's other sexual involvement. Boys in that study showed a tendency to overestimate their girlfriend's having other concurrent relationships. For girls, it was the opposite. Two-thirds of boyfriends whom girls thought were monogamous actually had other, simultaneous relationships.[750] The official AIDS prevention slogan of Uganda, used in some American educational programs, is "No Glove, No Love". This advice might be more accurate if it dropped the reference to "love". For our relationship lost generation, Tina Turner's sentiment that "What's Love Got To Do With It?" seems more relevant.

Even more damaging is that for many girls, sexual activity is not even a choice. Reasons for first intercourse in girls having it prior to age 16 include "my partner forced me" in 15% of cases. A quarter of girls say they "did not wish to engage" in sex at such an early age.[751] Overall, 9% of American high schoolers report having been physically forced to have sexual intercourse when they did not want to.[752] In 2 separate studies, another 40% of adolescent girls reported having submitting to "unwanted sex" to avoid angering their partner.[753 754] Between the ages of 14 to 23, a quarter of urban women report experiencing verbal or physical sexual coercion within the past year by a date or acquaintance.[755] One college survey found 15% of female college students reporting sexual violence during their undergraduate years, and 20% reporting previous sexual victimization. Perpetrators were equally likely to be partners, friends, or acquaintances.[756] Among high school girls, 17% report being intentionally physically hurt by a date in the previous year. The risk was increased for girls who were sexually active.[757] Among adolescent girls reporting unwanted sexual experiences, 26% of them in one study had never previously divulged the experience.[758] Another study found the average time between the occurrence and disclosure of such unwanted sexual experiences to be an average of 2.3 years.[759]

Sexual assault in adolescents sometimes involves the use of "date rape drugs", that are odorless and colorless and easily dissolved in drinks. Girls should open their own drink cans and accept drinks in glasses only directly from restaurant or bar servers, not from other patrons. They should also never leave drinks unattended.

Girls are not the only victims of partner violence. Seven percent of boys report suffering sexual violence during college.[760] Sixteen percent of boys report having at least one unwanted sexual experience during childhood or adolescence.[761]

There are gender differences in both the rates of victimization, and the rate of perpetration, of violence. One study found that for "minor" aggression in dating relationships, including shoving, grabbing, and slapping partners, Spanish adolescent girls were 4 times more likely than boys to be aggressors. For more severe acts, boys were the perpetrators more than twice as often as girls.[762] A separate American study echoed these findings. It likewise found females 4 times more likely to perpetrate physically aggressive conduct.[763]

For sexual assault, the roles reverse. Less than 1% of adolescent girls admit to sexual perpetration. Six percent of pre-college aged boys disclose having been sexual perpetrators, as do 2% of male college students.[764] This is important data for employers of babysitters. While the vast majority of babysitters are female, over three quarters of sexual assaults on children by babysitters are perpetrated by boys. Almost half of babysitter sex offenders are under 18 years of age.[765]

Yet another form of adolescent sexual victimization, sometimes fatal, is self-inflicted. It is called "autoerotic asphyxiation" and involves self-choking with belts, ropes, sheets, or clothing in conjunction, often, with masturbation. It has been nicknamed the "good kid's game" because the adolescents who try it are often those who forgo alcohol and drugs. They believe this to be a "safe high". Tell tale signs include bloodshot eyes, disorientation after time alone, the wearing of high necked clothes to hide marks and bruises, and headaches. Although deaths due to the choking game are often mislabeled as suicides, the CDC attributed 82 fatalities to it in the United States between 1995 and 2007. The average age of death was 13 years of age, and 86% of those who died were boys.[766]

For victims of pressured or forced sex, there is a terrible emotional toll. Girls who have suffered such experiences are more likely to consider and attempt suicide,[767] [768] have more and unprotected subsequent intercourse, have more sexually transmitted diseases including HIV,[769] [770] be pregnant more often, use tobacco and marijuana,[771] develop bulimia,[772] have problems with later sexual functioning,[773] or engage in physical fighting. Boys who are pressured or forced into sexual behavior are more likely to consider and attempt suicide, have more and unprotected subsequent intercourse, have more subsequent male and female sexual partners, be involved in more pregnancies, use tobacco, have problems with later sexual functioning, and display bulimic and laxative purging behaviors.[774] And when intimate partner relationships turn physically abusive, involved adolescent girls display more illicit drug use, antisocial behavior, depression, and suicidal behavior.[775]

As a glimmer of hope in these sad statistics, data from one study showed a substantial lowering of the suicide risk in teen survivors of childhood sexual abuse by strong family connectedness, teacher or other adult caring, or school safety.[776] Hopefully these factors can be emphasized and extrapolated to cushion the trauma of adolescent sexual abuse by force as well.

Whatever the circumstances of conception, abortions can also carry a heavy emotional price for adolescents. Just as recurrent anxiety attacks often coincide with anniversaries of deaths or tragedies in patients' lives, there have been reports of "anniversary depression" with physical symptoms[777] and even suicide attempts in adolescents on the due date of pregnancies that were aborted.[778] Follow-up studies have shown increased rates of anxiety and depression among women whose pregnancies ended in abortion compared to those whose ended in miscarriage.[779] One study found a 65% increased risk of scoring "high risk" for depression on psychological evaluations in women 8 years after abortions, as compared to similar women whose then pregnancy ended in a birth.[780] Another study found increases in depression and anxiety in subsequently pregnant women with histories of abortion.[781]

The Centers for Disease and Control, in 2006, launched a campaign to address dating violence. Their program is named "Choose Respect" and involves a variety of educational materials and a web site (www.chooserespect.org). April in America, the CDC also tells us, is officially our "National Sexually Transmitted Disease Awareness Month."[782] Both these campaigns are aimed at adolescents. There are good reasons why.

Every year, 1 in 4 sexually active American teenagers is diagnosed with a sexually transmitted disease.[783] Adolescents have a higher rate of STDs than any other age group.[784 785] Although youths represent only 25% of the sexually active population in America, they acquire half of the STD's.[786] Such infections, and unplanned pregnancies, are more common in adolescents who initiate sex at younger ages.[787] Young girls in particular are biologically more susceptible to STD's than adults, because their immature cervix has a thinner layer of protective cells. Girls just maturing have a single layer of "columnar" type cells in their cervix, where as older women have multilayers of "squamous" cells. To make matters worse, one researcher found lower levels of protective antibodies in the vaginal tissues of adolescent girls compared to adult women.[788]

In the United States, half of new HIV infections occur in young people between the ages of 13 and 24. Two-thirds of HIV infections in youths are sexually acquired. Half the girls at a Bronx HIV clinic reported only one sexual partner, and three-quarters of the female HIV patients there were unaware that any partner had put them at risk.[789] There are several factors that put these unsuspecting girls in harm's way. First, about 280,000 Americans with HIV don't know it.[790 791] Only 22% of sexually active high schoolers get HIV tested, and only half of adolescent or young adult HIV infected people are aware of it. They may honestly not know they are exposing partners.[792] Other people with HIV know it yet ignore it. A follow-up of adolescents born with HIV yielded disturbing results. When 16 sexually active teenagers with HIV since birth were interviewed, 7 said they had never disclosed their status to any partner. Only 10 used condoms all the time. Two said they had never used condoms.[793] In a larger study, combining results from 268 articles published between 1990 through 1994, reviewers found that young people consider condoms "stigmatizing", and that they assess partner's disease risks using unreliable indicators, like appearance.[794]

One other sexually transmitted disease, pelvic inflammatory disease, or "PID", is 10 times more common in 15-year-old girls than in 24-year-old women. One in 5 women with PID is left with later infertility from scarring of their fallopian tubes, and 1 in 10 suffers dangerous ectopic, tubal pregnancies because of it.[795 796 797 798] One of the most common causes of PID is Chlamydia, an often silent infector. In most women and half of men, Chlamydia causes no symptoms. In 40% of women, however, Chlamydia explodes into PID, leaving them at risk for future infertility. When John Hopkins University introduced a home testing kit for adolescents that could be ordered over the internet, 10% of the kits returned were positive for Chlamydia, and 1% showed gonorrhea.[799] Compared to tests taken from formal, pelvic exams, researchers have found the home collected tests very accurate.[800] For boys, urine tests can be accurate for diagnosing Chlamydia in place of the older, uncomfortable method of swabbing the inside of their urethra.[801]

Despite demonstrating good objective knowledge of the issues involved, one study showed that less than 40% of adolescent boys used condoms at their first intercourse.[802] Over a third failed to use condoms at their most recent sexual intercourse, per data from another study from the Centers for Disease Control.[803 804] And despite public educational efforts, the number of teens using condoms did not change between 2003 and 2007. Tallying not only the rate of condom use, but also the technical correctness of their use, one study found only 16% of adolescents using condoms both consistently and properly.[805]

Many adolescents respond to the dangers of sexual intercourse by favoring oral sex. This is false security. STDs, including hepatitis[806] [807] and HIV, can be passed via oral sex. The risk of HIV transmission from oral sex is estimated to be from one-tenth to two-thirds the risk from vaginal or anal sex.[808] Up to 8% of HIV infections in gay men are acquired through oral sex.[809] The herpes virus type 1, usually associated with facial "cold sores", is now an increasing cause of genital herpes, especially in college students.[810] Mouth and throat cancers caused by STDs are also on the rise. Over the past 30 years, there has been an almost doubling of mouth cancer caused by human papillomaviruses, the same sexually transmitted germ that causes cervical cancer in women.[811] [812] [813] Emotionally, one survey found girls who engaged in oral sex more likely to feel bad about themselves and "used".[814]

There is no such thing as "safe sex". There is "less dangerous sex", but never "safe sex". No form of birth control is 100% effective, and every act of vaginal sexual intercourse involves a risk of pregnancy. All physical sexual contact likewise involves the possibility of HIV and STD transmission, and condom use reduces but does not eliminate that risk. In 2000, the NIH assembled a panel of 28 medical experts to discuss the "Scientific Evidence on Condom Effectiveness for STD Prevention." After a 2 day debate and workshop, they reported that if used 100% of the time, condoms decreased HIV transmission by about 85%.[815] [816] Some experts believe that condoms reduce the risk of other STDs by only about 60%.[817] [818] [819]

A study that investigated the validity of self-reported condom use published in 2009 found that a third of teen girls claiming to have used condoms during sexual intercourse in the previous 2 weeks had evidence of sperm in vaginal samples. The authors of that study concluded that either condoms had not been used, or they were not used properly.[820] A third possibility is that they were used, as well as possible, and that they just didn't work as a barrier. We know that condoms make for poor birth control. The Planned Parenthood organization quotes a rate of 2 pregnancies per year for every 100 women whose partners use condoms perfectly at every single sexual encounter. The rate is 15 pregnancies per year for every 100 women whose partners don't always use condoms properly.[821]

Let's now do some math. The average sperm, not counting its 50-micron long tail, has a head of 4 microns in diameter. The AIDS virus has a diameter of 0.1 microns. Calculating the volume of their mass, a sperm cell is 63,800 times larger than an AIDS virus. This is very roughly the difference between the size of a single grape and a watermelon. If sperm are that good at penetrating condoms, why would we trust them to be great at holding back AIDS viruses? It is true that sperm have the advantage of a propellant tail, but the waves they create could sweep along viruses, too.

One of the physicians on that NIH panel reporting on condom effectiveness correctly pointed out that "in all areas *except* adolescent sexuality, pediatricians always strive for risk elimination rather than risk reduction."[822] Unfortunately for our children, he is right. There is a real double standard here. We doctors aren't speaking about adolescent sexual activity in the same terms we use to characterize other activities that threaten our patient's well being. If anything else that half of high schoolers did was associated with increased risks of depression, suicide, impaired future fertility, and death from AIDS, wouldn't we be "all over it"? Yet this is not the case with adolescent sexual activity.

We are strangely silent, I believe, because we physicians are taught to be non-judgmental. We do not wish to offend or cause hurt. If there is anything that best reflects our unwillingness to "just say no" and refuse to endorse adolescent sexual activity, it is the name of the physician author of the only book I have ever read that bluntly describes the dangers inherent in teens having sex. The author's name, as listed on the cover, is "Anonymous, MD". The book is titled *Unprotected*, and its author, a college health service doctor, feared professional and personal recrimination if he or she revealed their name. I believe every parent should read this book, and I hope author "Anonymous" someday feels safe enough professionally to speak his or her message openly.

That 15% HIV risk left over with condom use is unacceptable to me in my medical practice. I wouldn't consider an 85% reduction in cocaine use OK. I wouldn't be satisfied with an 85% reduction in dangerous driving behaviors. Parents who agree with me need to communicate that to their children and supervise and safeguard them accordingly. Parents who disagree need to disclose and define their own risk tolerance to their children. Educational efforts may be more effective than expected. A study of sexual risk taking behaviors found that after the announcement of basketball player "Magic" Johnson's HIV infection, fewer patients in one clinic had "one-night" stands or 3 or more partners.[823] Closer to home, another study, published in the journal Pediatrics in 2006 documented that "one of the strongest protective factors against early sexual behavior was clear parental communication about sex."[824]

Yet for all the sexually innuendo surrounding us, are we really speaking about sexuality to our children? A few years back, a vaccine was licensed in the United States that protects against a disease spread exclusively by penetrating vaginal sexual intercourse. Knowing my interest in vaccine medicine (I published a book on the topic, titled *Factcines*) many acquaintances approached me to ask about the shot. In discussing their daughter's risk for infection, I asked them all "Is your daughter having penetrating vaginal sexual intercourse?" Some were confident their children were not, but as for the rest, not a single parent ever answered "yes". Not one. Almost all said either "she has a boyfriend" or "she's going to college." Despite myriads of evidence that they most certainly are sexually active, not a single parent of any teenage girl I met was able to state clearly or precisely that their daughter was having sexual intercourse. While we glide through American life unfazed by slews of commercials for erectile dysfunction drugs around us, we are unable to discuss sex in technical, accurate terms in reference to our children. Mouthing our mantra of "safe sex" with total comfort, we are unable to define with certainty our moral and ethical limits of physical contact and teach it to our offspring.

Our children are hungry to fill this void. College professor Donna Freitas wrote an interesting article in The Wall Street Journal describing her experiences teaching a class on sexuality at Boston University. She was surprised to find her students "fascinated" by Wendy Shalit's book *A Return to Modesty*, which gives a conservative, faith-based perspective on sexuality. Her pupils were likewise fascinated by evangelical dating manuals like *I Kissed Dating Goodbye*, by Joshua Harris, and Lauren Winner's *Real Sex*. Professor Freitas discovered that her class "seemed shocked" but "reacted as if these authors describe a wonderful fantasy land." Our "young people are longing for the kinds of guidelines and rituals for dating that religion can offer," wrote Ms. Freitas.[825]

Our silence on sexual issues is dangerous. Do parents and school administrators really believe that HIV bypasses high school and college campuses? Do families who don't agree with strict fundamentalist prohibitions believe their confused adolescents aren't entitled to defined, alternative boundaries and guidelines? Whatever our different faiths and religious observance levels, most of us parents of young adolescents do not want our daughters following Rule #4 in the "traveling pants" book advising them that they may take off their pants "yourself" in the presence of a boy. Nor do we agree with the song lyrics proclaiming our adolescents' bodies to be "wonderlands". Our children's bodies are not public wonderlands to be lightly "hooked up" with at colleges we work hard to entrust them to. They are wondrous creations housing souls capable of better uses of health and strength. They are vulnerable bodies, best protected by privacy and modesty, our culture's most unexplored territory.

However unpleasant the statistics, there is a silver lining among them. Never forget the 2½-fold reduction in sexual activity rates for adolescents with adults at home after school, or the delays in sexual initiation with close monitoring, communication, warm and close mother-child relationships, and parental disapproval of sexual activity. We still make a difference. Even if our interaction is rejected and all we can offer is our presence, we are still needed. Enjoy the accomplishment of having gotten your adolescent this far. Trade diaper duty for guard duty with pride and purpose, and use your spare time to ask school administrators, advertising executives, children's authors, and entertainment industry writers to join in and help out.

CHAPTER 7

• • •

SIBLING RIVALRY AND OTHER
REDUNDANT CONCEPTS

Enjoyable Aspect of Parenting Adolescents Number Six: Sibling rivalry often winds down by adolescence. Adolescents do not pummel each other in cars over travel seating arrangements, or chase each other throughout their house until a head meets a sharp object. Adolescent siblings exchange unkind words, but the physical attacks and aggressive wrestling have usually fizzled out by the teenage years. After the agony of watching your offspring inflict injuries on each other that non-family members would be arrested for, enjoy the truce. Even if they are united only by a common (parental) enemy, enjoy the peace.

After working your way through school and earning an MBA, imagine getting a solid job with potential for advancement within the company. After investing many years working your way up the corporate ladder, however, the business owner brings in his college drop-out son to be groomed for the executive position you were hoping for. You are assigned to train him. Then you asked to allot him half your office, and finally you are informed he will also share your salary. You are outraged, but your boss tells you to be nicer to your little brother.

Parents often see their children through rose-colored glasses. Siblings view each other through equally distorted lenses that often focus only on faults. The most classic example of this comes to us early on in the Bible. In Genesis we are told that our patriarch Jacob dearly loved his son Joseph, ignoring his unfortunate habit of tattling on his brothers. Soon thereafter in the Bible come the chronicles of Joseph's being sold into slavery by those brothers.

An article published in 2009 in one of my medical journals addressed the long term psychological consequences in families of deceased infants.

Interviewing surviving siblings, many of them expressed guilt. It was also documented, however, that "several siblings felt gratitude rather than guilt, glad they were spared sharing a bedroom or even that the family had more financial resources to direct toward them."[826] While initially shocking, these comments are admirably honest.

Such feelings are instinctive. In the animal world, unborn baby sand sharks eat each other in utero.[827] Similarly, as one of their first acts, newly hatched cuckoo birds eject other eggs from their nests. After almost 3 decades as a pediatrician, this strikes me as only efficient. Why drag things on? Let 'em get it over with.

"Sibling rivalry" is as old and as universal as the Bible and nature itself. It is the most redundant term in the English language. Here is a list of my close favorite runners up for ultimate redundancy:

Human Error
Conflicted Adolescent
Women's Intuition
Difficult Child
Defiant Toddler
Tired Mother
Working Mother
Dog Bite
Cat Scratch
Dead Goldfish

Here's a list, also, of the opposite of redundant. My favorite oxymorons, inherently contradictory terms:

Family Vacation
White Grout
Minor Procedure
Casual Sex
Safe Sex
Easy Delivery
Easy Baby
Permanent Address
Parenting Expert
Significant Other
Reality Show

Here's yet another list of words. These terms have no relevance to our human condition on earth, and should be banished from meaningful conversation:

Fair
Closure
Permanent

My extensive medical library and journal article collection contains virtually nothing regarding sibling rivalry. In my slender "siblings" file is a lonely 2006 article from the Wall Street Journal titled "Sibling Rivalries" that discusses the complexities of passing businesses down to adult children. It uses words like "touchy" and "resent" and "tricky".[828] And that's in reference to adult siblings. Overall, I find this dearth of advice regarding sibling rivalry comforting instead of frustrating. It's a testament to truth in publishing. Even those know-it-all "experts" who can toilet-train in a day, teach napping to still-wet newborns, and calm defiant toddlers in a single chapter don't go near sibling rivalry. They know better.

Alternatively, there is a small body of medical literature on the medical benefits of having siblings. The absence of siblings has been associated with high blood pressure,[829][830] higher risks of asthma and allergies,[831] higher rates of multiple sclerosis,[832] and worse cases of mononucleosis.[833] People from larger families have lower rates of asthma, hay fever, and eczema.[834] Later children from larger families also have lower rates of some types of lymphoma and leukemia and type I diabetes.[835] Part of the help conferred by siblings may be a result of the additional mess created by multiple children. Dirtier homes, with more floor dust, have also been associated with lower rates of asthma in children who live there.[836]

Psychologically, only children have "reduced sociability" and increased needs for social support.[837][838] A study from Finland found higher rates of both behavioral problems and "probable psychiatric disturbance" among only children.[839] One of my favorite child therapists went formally on record about the benefits of sibling conflict in a local newspaper interview titled "Sibling Rivalry Not All Bad". She pointed out that sibling rivalry prepares children for life as a "first experiment in competitive living".[840]

So perhaps fortunately, I personally cured sibling rivalry only once in my parenting career. My oldest two children had just both acquired cats at the local shelter. The felines fought. This, I brainstormed, was a

Harvard-pediatrician Dr. Brazelton "teachable" moment. I embraced opportunity. "You love your pets, just like I love you. Doesn't it hurt to see them fight? That's how it hurts your parents when you fight." I analogized. "Wouldn't it feel great if everybody in our house could be buddies?" There was silence. I basked in my reign as a Master Clinician and Parent Supreme. Within minutes, my time was up and my children were arguing about whose cat had started it…

My children's conduct has strong historical precedent. Sibling discord traces its origins back to the Bible's first murder, where Cain killed his brother Abel. Before giving birth, Isaac's wife Rebecca felt twins Jacob and Esau "agitated within her",[841] struggling in utero. Jacob's sons in turn sold their brother Joseph into slavery only as a compromise measure. Their first plan was to kill him.

In all 5 of Moses' Bible Books, there are only 3 sets of siblings who lacked for sibling rivalry. Let's start with friends and brothers Aaron and Moses. Yes, they got along famously, but Aaron got to watch Moses sent down a river in a basket. And when he came back, Moses brought with the audible voice of G-d Himself. Next consider Simon and Levy. Their compatibility enabled them to collaborate on plundering an entire city on behalf of their sister. And then there were Joseph's boys, Menashe and Ephraim. They got along, but their dad was the Viceroy of Egypt and the Bill Gates of his day. They had servants galore picking up after them, and they didn't have to divvy up the better toys. Brotherly love is so rare, it is taught, that the ancient Holy Temple in Jerusalem was built at the site where 2 brothers met in the night while traveling to help each other. If this was the building site requirement, I doubt there were a lot of other real estate choices.

Short of tubal ligations after first deliveries, we will simply never do any better with sibling rivalry than sand sharks. When hopelessly-optimistic acquaintances ask me for advice on this issue, I find the best way to silence them is to simply ask how they got along with their own siblings.

For consolation, though, let's rationalize. There are advantages to sibling rivalry. Socially, it's good training for life outside the nest. Siblings are brutally honest, and they give us a social awareness that outsiders are too polite to provide. Siblings let us know our shortcomings, and self-improvement starts with self-awareness. "Only" children are known for being socially challenged, sensitive, and easily hurt. Maybe "no pain no gain." A study from Northern Finland found the highest rate of psychiatric and behavioral problems in children without siblings. The lowest rate occurred in children from families with 11 to 19 children.[842]

Siblings also offer physical, medical advantages. The more infant sibling exposures a person has during his or her first 6 years of life, the less their risk of multiple sclerosis later in life.[843] As infants, children with greater numbers of older siblings have lower rates of eczema while young.[844] Recall also that people from larger families have lower rates of asthma, hay fever, and eczema,[845] and that the younger of many siblings have lower rates of some types of lymphoma, some leukemias, and type I diabetes.[846]

When all else fails, one family took sibling rivalry to the Olympics. Sisters Sada and Emily Jacobson are world experts in saber, a form of fencing that made its Olympic debut in 2004. "We fight all the time." said Sada in an interview.[847]

Twenty years after the cat crisis, after my older children had both moved out, they got together for dinner one night just for fun. My initial reaction was outrage. I'd spent two agonizing decades of my life listening to them fight, and they were capable of getting along? Who knew?

And so it goes within my patients' families. I have several sets of siblings in my practice who attend the same college. I have received many phone calls where one was calling on the other's behalf, asking for advice on how to nurse their former rival through a variety of illnesses. I also have a patient who sponsored a charity drive at his high school to fund research on a disease his sister suffers.

Even Joseph and family made peace in the end. Just 8 chapters in the Bible after being sold into slavery by his brothers, Joseph and his siblings reunite in joyful weeping. Joseph's new found connections provide food for the clan and allow them to continue on with development of monotheism.

There is a medical joke that pokes fun at different doctors. It is the story of 3 physicians on a hunting trip. A flock of geese flies over. The surgeon kills with a single, perfect shot. The family practitioner showers the sky with bullets, explaining "I wasn't sure where to shoot, so I thought I'd try all directions." The pediatrician just stands there and watches the ducks go by. Why? "I knew if I waited long enough they'd go away." That's where I'm at with sibling rivalry. I can't fix it, but it eventually calms down. When it does, enjoy the peace.

CHAPTER 8

• • •

WINNER TECHS ALL

Enjoyable Aspect of Parenting Adolescents Number Seven: Adolescents know how to use computers. They program cell phones with ease, and can tell the difference between and iPod and a palm pilot with their eyes closed. When complicated computer crimes threaten entire economies, the perpetrators almost always have acne. They are downloading and burning and e-mailing away while we never really learned how to eliminate commercials on our VCRs. Just as our immigrant grandparents retained their native language by using their offspring to speak English for them, use your adolescent to help navigate our new technological world. Appreciate and enjoy their special expertise.

If intergalactic travelers ever visit planet earth to study human life, they will find us gazing quietly at screens. They will find screens in every home and workplace, above grocery check-out lines, and at gas pumps. They will see us gazing quietly, transfixed at our screens first thing in the morning and last thing at night, day in and day out. Our visitors will note that a disproportionate number of our screen-gazers are young. This may be perplexing to our space travelers. On other planets, it is the elders who spend the most time worshiping their deities.

In the beginning, the real G-d gave us our human brains, a complex array of 100 billion neurons designed to process information and store memories. We found it insufficient. We invented the textbook. Socrates was horrified. His objections were recorded by Plato in *Phaedrus*. Plato quoted his mentor protesting that reliance on the written, as opposed to oral tradition, would "create forgetfulness in the learners' souls, because they will not use their memories".[848] Centuries later, we combined written script with mass oral communication, inventing the radio. In 1936, the American Journal of Psychiatry published an article terming it an "invader of privacy" with "many a disturbing influence", causing a "puzzling change" in behavior and leaving parents "bewildered…frightened, and helpless."[849]

And so it goes. We are not the first generation of parents struggling to keep up with change. On the other hand, we do suffer one unique new addition to our woes. Mother Socrates, I am sure, had no trouble figuring out how to crack a book. Our grandparents spun those radio dials with ease, however new-fangled they were. The learning curve on our new gadgets is longer and higher. We may be the first parents who are literally unable to work what we fear.

I once ran across an article written by the Chief of Child Psychiatry at the prestigious Massachusetts General Hospital. This accomplished physician is also a professor at Harvard Medical School. At the end of his article, he gave credit to his teenage son for fixing the computer so he could finish the project.[850] As the entire government of China tries to limit use of the internet and squelch dissent, teams of "hacktivists", many of them teenagers, creatively circumvent their efforts.[851] Movie piracy via DVD copying, which has cost Hollywood billions in lost revenue, was first accomplished by a computer program written by a then 15-year-old Norwegian boy who won a school prize for the project before being indicted by the government.[852]

If practice makes perfect, our adolescents should be good at using technology. A study by the Kaiser Family Foundation found that counting all technologies including television, DVDs, videos, music, the internet, and computer and video games the average American child has 8 ½ hours of exposure per day.[853]

All this started with TV. Television made its debut at the at the New York World's Fair in 1939, where RCA (Radio Corporation of America) president David Sarnoff declared it "an art which shines like a torch of hope in a troubled world."[854]. In 1941, the FCC authorized the start of commercial television transmission, and regularly scheduled television programming started in the United States in 1947. By 1955, three-quarters of American homes had a television. It took the radio twice as long to make it into so many households, and it took the car 52 years to get that popular. Telephones took 67 years to infiltrate our homes to such a degree,[855] but by 1995, more American families had televisions than phones.[856] A decade later, it was found that American homes contain more televisions than either toilets or people.[857]

By the time children in the United States graduate high school, they have spent more time viewing television than attending school,[858] and they will have seen almost a million ads.[859] By 70 years of age, the average American has spent the equivalent of 7 to 10 years watching television.[860][861]

There is much less data on screen time associated with computer use. This may be because research interests lag behind new realities. The internet was only invented in the 1960s, and it was initially military and university based. In October, 1969, it crashed on the letter "G" in the very first "LOGIN" by UCLA developers. The first e-mail program was invented in 1972, and more widespread e-mail capability as we know it wasn't developed until 1982. The word "cyberspace" was coined in 1984, and "internet surfing" was added to our language in 1992. Also in 1984 the domain name system was introduced, and 1000 host sites were on the internet. In 1990, the "www." system was begun, but by 1994, less than 20% of Americans used the internet. In 1995 "America on Line" was started. By 2006 there were 92,000,000 web sites on the internet. In 2003, "MySpace" was started, followed by "Facebook" in 2004 and "YouTube" in 2005. "Twittering" was created in 2006. Not counting those twitters, it has been estimated that in 2008, there were 210 billion e-mails sent every day, at a rate of 2 million per second. The first video and computer games were developed in the 1960s, at MIT and Stanford, but the first to achieve widespread commercial success was "Pacman", introduced in 1980. "Super Mario Brothers" hit the market in 1985.

A 2007 study found most adolescents spending 3 hours per week on their computers,[862] but another study released in 2009 put the average amount of time spent on the internet at 17 hours per week, with "heavy" users logging in an average of 42 hours weekly. The data in that study was not stratified by age, but it was noted that "internet use increases as age decreases."[863]

Despite all the time we spend together, we have a complex relationship with our TV, internet, and video game past times. How do we both loathe and love them? Let us count the whys:

1) **Television promotes obesity and poor eating habits**. Adolescents who watch more TV eat less fruits and vegetables.[864] Obesity rates are lowest in children watching less than an hour of television per day, and highest in those whose daily viewing time exceeds 4 hours.[865] One study

demonstrated an extra 170 calorie intake for every hour of television watched.[866] Over the long term, another study calculated a 2% increase in obesity rates for every hour of TV watched per day.[867] Analyzing 120 studies on the topic, the Institute of Medicine deemed TV advertising a contributor to high calorie, low nutrient diets in children.[868] Most food-related ads directed toward children focus on reinforcing brand recognition via associations with media characters.[869]

Other negative physical effects of technology and media exposure include reduced increases in bone mass growth during pre-adolescence in heavy TV viewers,[870] carpal tunnel syndrome, upper back pain and stiffness with upward displacement of the scapula bone in avid video game players,[871] and a rare thigh rash with hyperpigmentation traced to infrared radiation from propping laptops on the legs while in use.[872]

On a positive note, media influences can be redirected. In 2006, the cable network Nickelodeon decided to put SpongeBob and Dora the Explorer on packages of healthful foods, including vegetables and fruit.[873] In addition, there are now video games that involve physical movement and activity. They have been shown to effectively burn calories in both children and adults.[874]

2) Television viewing may contribute to the development of ADD and ADHD. A study published in 2004 found that early and more TV exposure correlated with more attention problems at 7 years of age.[875] Two other studies reached similar conclusions. One found an increased risk of subsequent attention problems in youths who watched 3 or more hours of TV per day. They also noted an increase in poor grades, poor homework completion, and negative attitudes toward school starting at 1 hour per day of television exposure.[876] In another study, there was a correlation between the amount of television viewing between 5 and 11 years of age and the rate of attention problems at 13 to 15 years old.[877]

Two other studies headed different directions. One found an association between later attention problems and entertainment TV viewing before 3 years of age. There was no adverse effect from watching educational television prior to 3 years of age, or from any type TV exposure at ages 4 to 5 years old.[878] Last but not least, in a triumph for couch potatoes everywhere, separate researchers found the relationship between TV exposure and ADHD symptoms to be "close to zero and not statistically significant."[879]

3) Aside from whether or not it contributes to the development of ADD and ADHD, media exposure may affect intellectual growth and achievement, sometimes for the better, sometimes not. Audible television noise in homes is associated with less awareness of adult human speech, and fewer attempts at speech in exposed children, according to a study that had children 2 to 48 months of age wear digital recorders.[880] Reading scores in children 6 to 7 years of age were found by other researchers to be decreased in children with more television viewing before 3 years of age, but increased in children who watched more TV between 3 and 5 years of age.[881] In another study, 3rd graders with bedroom televisions had lower academic test scores, but those with home computers had higher scores.[882] Teens with bedroom televisions likewise have poorer school performance.[883] When considering content as well, exposure to adult subject matter media was associated with poorer school performance when watched on school days.[884] Overall, by 26 years of age, one study found more cumulative television viewing throughout childhood and adolescence to correlate with poorer educational achievement and lower overall well-being.[885]

Game time also impacts negatively on academic achievement, more so for boys. Of the one-third of adolescents who play video games, 80% are boys, and they clock in an average of 1 hour per school day at their gaming consoles. Compared to non-playing peers, gamers spend 30% less time reading and 34% less time doing homework.[886]

Surveys also find adults reporting less reading time for books and periodicals as their technology use increases.[887] Preschoolers exposed to more television are read to less often.[888] In one study, parents were able to name their children's favorite television show more often than they were able to name their favorite book.[889] Hence a recent book titled *How to Talk About Books You Haven't Read* [890], by a literature professor from Paris, and another named *Education's End*, by a Yale professor.[891]

From another perspective, parents distraught about the so called demise of reading should recall that internet use involves reading, as does the increasingly popular "Kindle". In 2006, a Florida middle school made national news when students and teachers there wore cards with book titles they were reading on necklaces. The result was "mass book chats" and runs on the library.[892] Our tech-savvy teens still enjoy a good read. And when they put down the books to do homework, there are plenty of online sites that offer a variety of tutoring services. One site requiring paid subscription, Cosmeo, works with actual curriculum standards from every state. There are also many educational products designed for computer use, like MathMedia's line of educational materials to "unlock the mystery of math" that were invaluable in my own family. Children with special learning needs or attention issues can pace themselves online in ways not possible with group classroom instruction.

4) Television, movies, and social networking sites promote risk taking. The relative risk of physical injury with fractures, burns, and bruises increases with each hour per day of average television viewing.[893] One physician published 3 reports of children severely injured while imitating stunts performed by motorcyclist Evel Knievel.[894]

In a survey of 50 "G" or "PG" rated movies released between 1995 and 1997, only 27% of car occupants wore seat belts, and only 6% of bicycle riders wore helmets.[895] Between 2000 and 2004, the seat belt usage rate was even worse at 15%, but helmet use was better at 39% for motorcycle riders and 24% for bicycle riders. In crash scenes, only 11% of unbelted or helmet-free characters were depicted suffering injuries.[896] In the 100 top American films of 1994, 90% of violent actions resulted in no depicted injury.[897] Any physician working in emergency medicine in the 1980s (myself included) will recall suturing the foreheads of intoxicated patients who attempted to crush cans on their faces in imitation of a popular movie scene.

On the internet, 54% of adolescent MySpace profiles divulge information self-documenting risky behavior. In one survey, 25% referenced sexual activity, 41% reported illegal substance use, and 14% mentioned violence.[898]

It is a small ray of hope, but a study published on the very next page after that MySpace survey found greatly reduced rates of references to risky behavior 3 months after a single physician e-mail to profilers documenting such activity.[899]

5) Time spent on technology makes for less and lower quality sleep. Teenagers who watch 3 or more hours of television per day have an increased risk of sleep problems. When adolescents in one study kept television viewing to less than 1 hour a day, their risk for developing sleep problems fell significantly.[900] Another study found that through 4th grade, the amount of television viewing and the presence of a TV in the bedroom correlates with the frequency of sleep problems.[901] Most sleep therapy experts recommend a ban on televisions in bedrooms, and a limit to total daily television time. A study of adolescent sleep habits found that teens who electronically multitask in the evening often simultaneously drink caffeinated beverages, and end up getting less sleep overall. Nighttime technology users were most likely to report falling asleep during school.[902]

The days when TV programming ended at midnight are long gone, but some screen savers on computers can be set to provide "white noise", like fish tank bubbles, that block out background influences preventing sleep. Otherwise, "lights out" may also have to mean "computers off".

6) Television viewing is associated with several psychological problems. The insomnia and television connection is not just a matter of competing time slots. There also the issue of television program content. Television-induced nightmares have been reported in up to 9% of children, up to once a week.[903] In a survey of parents of kindergarten through 6th graders, 37% reported their children had been frightened or upset by something on TV in the previous year.[904] For young adolescents in 3rd through 8th grade, one survey found a direct relationship between the amount of daily television viewing and symptoms of anxiety, depression, and post-traumatic stress.[905][906] Scottish children 4 to 12 years of age who had high levels of media time, combined with low physical activity, had increased levels of "psychological distress".[907] In a study involving follow-up of adolescents who were not initially depressed, those with the highest television and media exposure were more likely to be depressed 7 years later.[908]

Between 1937 and 1999, every single childrens' movie released to theaters depicted at least 1 act of violence. In 2000, every single animated G-rated video on the market depicted violence. Two-thirds portrayed resultant injuries, half of which were fatal.[909] About 60% of television programs have violent content,[910] and one study found an average of 20 acts of violence per film in the top PG-13 rated movies of 1994.[911] By 18 years of age, the average American child has seen television depictions of 16,000 murders and 200,000 acts of violence.[912][913] Adding insult to injury, a review of musical video television channels found African Americans falsely overrepresented on them as both aggressors and victims.[914] Even non-violent programs involve exposure to violence. During the 1996 and 1998 Major League Baseball Playoffs, two-thirds of commercials depicted violence.[915]

On the brighter side, the anonymity of the internet provides a safe haven for people to access mental health advice. According to one survey, a quarter of adolescents have used the internet to look up information about depression.[916] As a comfort measure, one set of pediatricians even found that watching cartoons on TV was more soothing to children being stuck for blood than being caressed by their mothers.[917]

7) The same violent television content that gives children bad dreams also contributes to bad conduct. Higher television viewing times have been associated with higher rates of aggressive and bullying behavior.[918] In Canada, a researcher compared behavior in primary school children before and after the introduction of television into a small community in 1973. There were significant increases in both verbal and physical aggression after TV came to town.[919] [920] For both adults and children, for children of different ages, and for children in different cultures, playing violent video games is also associated with later physically aggressive behavior.[921] The American Academy of Pediatrics writes that "more than 1000 scientific studies and reviews conclude that significant exposure to media violence increases the risk of aggressive behavior in certain children and adolescents…"[922] In one study, children classified as bullies in grade school had watched over 50% more television than non-bullies at 4 years of age.[923] According to one researcher, media exposure is particularly encouraging of aggressiveness in girls, not by changing their nature, but by removing their inhibitions.[924]

Adults, also, lose social inhibitions online. An article in a national newspaper in 2005 carried the title: "E-mail can make divorce worse", and gave examples of the escalation that technology can cause in human conflict. One warring couple's e-mails were termed "venomous" and another divorcee explained that it was easier to say "unimaginably hateful things" via e-mail than on the phone or in person. When children intercept such communications, they have been known to post them online or create web sites chronicling family problems.[925]

Some bullying that starts on the net stays on the net. "Cyberbullying", or electronic bullying is perpetrated via internet posting, chat room comments, e-mail, instant messaging, or texting. In a survey of 6th through 8th graders at 6 different schools, 11% reported being bullied within the previous few months. Half did not know the perpetrator's identity. Seven percent of students surveyed were both bullies and bully victims, and 4% were perpetrators only.[926] Another study found that a third of those harassed online were chronically cyberbullied.[927] Data presented at the Society for Adolescent Research in 2008 put the rate of electronic bullying much higher. Researchers in Florida found 40% of middle schoolers reporting cybervictimization within the past 6 months.[928] Tragically, one 13-year-old Missouri girl lost her life to suicide in 2006 after extreme cyberbullying, as it turns out from an adult masquerading as an adolescent.

The connection between technology use and aggressive behavior may be mediated by physical brain changes. A study presented at the Radiological Society of North America found special "functional" MRI studies of adolescent video gamers showing decreased activation in the brain area controlling inhibition, and increased activity in the "amygdala", which mediates emotion.[929] Previous work by the same researcher demonstrated MRI brain changes in adolescents who watch violent media that mimicked the same brain changes seen in disruptive, behaviorally disordered peers. [930]

In the reverse, when researchers randomly assigned some children to media reduction interventions, their rates of verbal aggression and aggressive behavior, per peer reports, decreased.[931]

Putting the internet to good use, there are many sites advising children and schools on how to handle bullying. As for video games, they also have a bright side. Video game skill correlates with laparoscopic surgical skill, and video games have been suggested as a training tool for new surgeons.[932] Researchers have also demonstrated that video gaming can improve vision, especially peripheral vision.[933] Still others claim that video games are complex, healthy forms of delayed gratification.[934]

8) Television promotes sexual promiscuity. Two-thirds of television programs involve sexual content, and 1 in 7 portrays sexual intercourse, either depicted or strongly implied. [935] The average American adolescent views almost 14,000 sexual references per year, only 165 of which deal with birth control, self-control, abstinence, pregnancy risk, or STDs. A third of "family hour" shows include sexual references. Soap operas, now popular at college campuses, contain about 3 acts of sexual intercourse per hour, only 25% of which involve married partners.[936] A study of 12- to 17-year-olds found that those at the upper end of sexual television viewing time had double the risk of having intercourse in the next year when compared to those at the extreme lower end of the curve. Exposure to talk about sex without actual depiction of sexual acts had the same effect.[937] Other studies have confirmed the correlation between TV viewing and increased risk of sexual initiation.[938] [939] A study published in 2008 documented that teens exposed to the highest levels of television sexual content were twice as likely to father or birth a child within 3 years compared to peers with the least exposure.[940] Location counts, too. Another survey found teenagers with TV equipped bedrooms more likely to smoke, use alcohol, and be sexually active than peers without them.[941]

On the internet, much sexual activity is in the form of "cybersex", often involving communication with vivid sexual imagery and language and masturbation. It is available on computers and now also on broadband cell phones. One foreign cell phone company even offers a "virtual girlfriend".[942] Middle school boys in particular are extremely susceptible to addiction to cybersex. They need to know that as they outgrow their years as legal minors, they can be charged with child pornography for having pictures of near peers on their computers or phones.

Still other sexual exposure on the internet is unintentional. Almost half of adolescent internet users report online exposure to pornography within the past year. Two-thirds of that exposure was unwanted, and occurred via keystroke or search errors or file-sharing.[943]

9) Our mass media promotes tobacco, alcohol, and illicit drug use. In 2004, the same year we spent $543 million in tobacco prevention programs, 78% of American middle school students reported seeing actors smoking on television or in movies. One study that looked at movie smoking found an association between adolescent smoking initiation and exposure to both positive and negative characters.[944] Besides that influence, the tobacco industry spends $39 per American,[945] a total of about 12.5 billion dollars annually, in direct advertising and promotion.[946] And, it's paying off. Youngsters who watch 5 or more hours of TV per day are 6 times more likely to start smoking than those whose daily viewing time is less than 2 hours.[947] Of the 200 top movies rented for home viewing during 1996 and 1997, all but 4 showed substance abuse, and 22% depicted actual illicit drugs. In the top 1000 most popular songs of the same years, 27% made reference to alcohol, illicit drugs, or tobacco.[948] In 2005, a third of the most popular songs had explicit references to illicit substance use, exposing the average adolescent to 84 references to explicit substance abuse every day.[949]

At these rates, adolescents receive 30,000 musical references to substance abuse annually.[950] Teenagers also view 2000 beer commercials in the average TV viewing year.[951][952] In a survey in one Maryland suburb, children correctly identified more brands of beer than names of American presidents.[953][954] In another study, of California high schoolers, greater levels of television and music video viewing hours were associated with earlier onset of alcohol use.[955]

This situation is not hopeless. In Sweden and in other countries where television beer and wine ads are banned, per capita consumption has dropped by as much as 20%.[956] Music like the song "*Wasted*" may also counter lyrics favoring substance use. The internet can be put to good use, too. Teens increasingly turn to the internet for tobacco cessation advice, many of them accessing "GottaQuit.com".[957] In yet another turn for the better, Ms. Tyra Banks and Mr. Ken Mok, producers of "America's Next Top Model", banned smoking in contestant housing in 2008. They also committed to taping a photo shoot with an anti-smoking message.[958]

10) Television promotes consumerism and materialism, targeting our children with advertising. Recall that television is basically one big marketing tool. As the story goes, there was once a very successful traveling salesman. He would charm his way into the living rooms of people's homes and share amazing stories of his travels, travails, and adventures. Between stories, the salesman would ply his wares to spellbound customers who hardly noticed his sales pitches. One day, one of the salesman's stories offended a homeowner. More such offensive stories followed, and it was clear the man was a terrible influence on the young children in the home. The father and mother of the house angrily escorted the salesman out, but their children beckoned him back, plugged him in, and simply changed the channel.

As early as a year of age, babies shown videos of actresses' reactions to toys mimicked the same reaction when presented with the same plaything.[959] Third grader's requests for advertised products is directly associated with the amount of their screen exposure time.[960] A 2004 Task Force of the American Psychological Association deemed children younger than 8 years of age specifically prone to accepting advertised messages without critical evaluation.[961] In 2006, the American Academy of Pediatrics called children "cognitively and psychologically defenseless against advertising."[962] Despite a conclusion by our Federal Trade Commission in the 1970s that advertising to children less than 6 years of age is "unfair and deceptive", we Americans have not yet banned advertising to our youngest of consumers. Instead, we exploit their weakness with $12 billion per year in advertising aimed specifically at children.[963] In contrast, Greece, Denmark, and Belgium restrict advertising directed at children. Sweden and Norway forbid ads aimed at anyone younger than 12 years of age.[964] We have yet to follow suit, and are actually headed the other direction. In 2006, McDonald's Happy Meals gave out toy Hummers. The brand also launched a children's web site with games and printable coloring pages. Online in the virtual "Whyville", children can purchase Toyotas.[965] On college campuses, after Nielson TV ratings included students in its system, advertisers branched out with TV-themed parties and promotional give-aways.[966]

11) Television and movies promote distorted body images. Vulnerable adolescents are very sensitive to what they see in the media. Their self-image and body image are greatly affected by the visual images they are exposed to.[967] In Fiji, a study of teenaged girls demonstrated dramatic increases in rates of eating disorders after the introduction there of American television shows.[968] Distorted body images follow increases in all types of media and magazine exposure, and adding a way to the will, the internet is full of pro-anorexia sites offering tips on purging and weight loss.

12) Technology use is addictive. A 2007 article on "internet addiction" found most adolescents spending 3 hours per week on their computers. Teens defined as addicted, at the upper level of internet use, spent 11 hours per week on their computers.[969] Internet addiction is more common in boys, and it seems to be more common in China.[970] The Communist Youth League there considers over 2 million of its 18.3 million teenagers addicted to internet use. Most computer-addicted Chinese teens are boys, and the Chinese government has blamed the problem on a "lack of diversions".[971] They have ordered game developers to add software to their product that docks players points after several hours of uninterrupted play.[972] Back in the States, a University of Iowa study found from 1 in 145 to 1 in 333 Americans internet-addicted.[973]

Gambling in particular thrives on the internet. Gambling has been referred to as a "silent" addiction, because it has no physical clues like dilated pupils or tell-tale breath. It has been estimated that up to 2 million youths have a gambling problem, and at McGill University in Montreal there is even a Centre for Young Gambling Problems and High-Risk Behaviors. According to the Harvard Medical School Division on Addictions, people who begin gambling as children are 4 to 6 times more likely to become compulsive, problem gamblers than those who avoid it until adulthood.[974] The internet is fertile ground for gamblers, so much so that in 2001, the American Psychiatric Association issued a health advisory warning regarding internet gambling addiction. That same year, computerized gambling was thought to involve $2.3 billion. Many online game sites targeting children and teens, at the height of their addiction vulnerable years, have easy, direct links to gambling sites.[975]

Like gambling, pornography viewing can also be an addiction, and the internet provides access to it like no generation has ever had. One in 7 adolescent internet users admit to intentionally visiting an X-rated web site during the previous year. Slightly more admit to downloading images from file sharing programs, many of which are pornographic.[976]

Tragically, computer gaming use took a horrific turn after Hurricane Ike in 2008. Associated power outages required the use of generators. There were 37 cases of carbon monoxide poisoning from those gasoline powered generators, more than half of which were traced to the use of them to run video games. One child involved died at the scene.[977]

13) Screen time diminishes family time and changes our social lives. One study found that between 2005 and 2008, American family time fell by almost a third. Children who view violent programs spend less time with friends, one survey found.[978] Video gamers, on the other hand, spent no less time with family and friends compared to non-playing peers.[979] Time spent watching television, even with family, is associated with less overall time spent in other activities with parents and siblings.[980] Women surveyed in another research project felt ignored "sometimes" or "often" as other family members spent more time on the internet. While television, at least, can be watched socially, the internet is a solitary activity. At the keyboard end, that is. Online, 1 in 7 internet users report being part of an online community.[981] In 2007, more than half the members of online communities declared those internet social connections as important to them as their offline social circle.[982] One in 3 American children reports having friends they have never actually met in person.[983]

On a more positive note, online communications are a life line to patients of mine with rare or chronic diseases. They are a real medical benefit as well when patients share therapeutic success and failure experiences. A survey of psoriasis sufferers found half reporting "improvement in their quality of life" associated with participation in online psoriasis support groups. The authors publishing that data recommended "physician engagement" within these communities to even further enhance their value.[984]

There are many reasons families involve media in the lives of their children. Sadly, one is the perceived safety risks of being outside instead of indoors in front of the television. In a national study of preschool children, the amount of time children watched TV was inversely related to how safe their mothers believed their neighborhood was.[985]

Unfortunately, however, our children's virtual neighborhood is no save haven from street crime. One survey of 1500 regular internet users between 10 and 17 years of age revealed that in a years' time, 1 in 5 had received unwanted sexual solicitations via the internet.[986] A third of solicitations were received in chat rooms, and 43% through instant messaging.[987] Teenagers participating in chat rooms or communicating online with people unknown to them were most likely to be solicited. Ninety percent of the incidents went unreported, partly because 2/3 of parents and 3/4 of the children involved did not know how or where to seek help. Over 2/3 of the solicitations went directly to children's home computers. One in 10 was accompanied by a request for a physical meeting, and 1 in 50 involved direct telephone contact.[988] [989]

Paving the way for this is our own children's naiveté online. When 1500 internet users between 10 and 17 years of age were asked about their online conduct in the previous year, 55% admitted to having posted personal information on the web. A quarter had electronically forwarded private, personal information. A third included people known to them only online in their buddy lists, and 43% met people online through the internet only. One in 20 talked about sex with someone known to them only online.[990]

"Pornography helped drive the early adoption of new technologies such as the VCR and the internet,"[991] a Wall Street Journal article once pointed out. They got it started, and they keep it running. Internet child pornography is estimated to be a $20 billion per year industry, involving 3.5 million images.[992]

As an integral part of the internet, pornography lurks behind every keystroke. It is now available for download even to cell phones. And even when not sought after, it's an honest typing error away. A quarter of adolescents who use the internet report at least 1 unwanted sexual exposure in the previous year. One in 6 unwanted contacts with internet sexual imagery occurs due to misspelled site searches. Another 1 in 6 is mistakenly reached via a link to another web site.[993]

Trouble in cyber city doesn't end with sex. The internet also hosts many sites that offer advice on the use of psychoactive drugs, some of them selling drug-related products. When a dozen adolescents in substance abuse programs were interviewed on their use of the internet, only one stopped using drugs after consulting web sites. Ten reported initiating drug use after surfing the web. One was motivated to start using a filter for his marijuana, another changed the route of administration of his drugs, and one other increased his drug use.[994] Children can use the web to order illegal drugs, or they can use sites to learn how to make their own illegal drugs. There are internet sites that offer formulas for ecstasy and methamphetamines. There are also sites that give reviews and ratings of rave parties, and others that offer advice on minimizing risks at such parties while failing to condemn them.[995] [996]

The internet is a virtual cookbook of recipes for trouble. No school or public library would ever stock books on such topics, but in a keystroke on the web our children can learn how to refine their anorexia and bulimic behaviors, commit suicide or murder, or design computer viruses, all in the privacy of our own homes.[997] The internet is also a tool for high tech cheating. There are web sites offering term papers, and teenagers have hacked into school computers to steal answers and change grades.

The dark side of the internet involves big trouble and complex solutions. Television shows or movies that undermine families' values can be effectively dealt with by parents. Access to these unnecessary evils can be restricted or even eliminated. The problem is definable, and the cure is straightforward. This is not the case with other technologies.

The internet is 24/7 and never boring. It's easily and increasingly accessible. And, it pairs anonymity with unaccountability. If there was ever a recipe for trouble, this is it. And as with all other avenues for adolescent downfall, it is addictable.

The addictiveness of technology may have more to do with the victim than the medium. As with all other addictions, adolescents are particularly vulnerable. There may be a physical, biological basis to this. Special brain MRIs that show neural activity in addition to brain anatomy show different activity in different brain parts in adolescents versus adults. Compared to adults, adolescents shown stressful images demonstrate less activity in the frontal lobe (the home of more rational, logical thought and action) and more activity in the amygdala (a part of the brain "limbic" system that involves more emotional reactions).[998] Other research has shown continuous growth of a part of the brain called the anterior cingulate gyrus through about age 21.[999] The anterior cyngulate gyrus is responsible for inhibition.

Still more studies on the biological basis of adolescent's high risk for addiction focus on an area of the brain called the "nucleus accumbens", which involves motivation and responsiveness to rewards. Brain scans of adolescents being paid to complete simple, mundane tasks show much less activation in this region compared to young adults.[1000] When adolescent's brains are scanned as they watched beer and liquor ads, however, there is good stimulation of the nucleus accumbens area.[1001] Together, these findings support a theory of addiction called the "reward deficit" theory. The idea is that since adolescents get less pleasure from everyday tasks and accomplishments, they are more tempted to turn to other forms of stimulation.

During a symposium on addictive diseases, one psychotherapist challenged those of us who work with children to ask all adolescents open ended questions about internet and chat room involvement. She said we would be "startled" and "amazed". Another speaker recalled that while "we used to think that…drugs and alcohol…broke down defenses…" he now considers the internet the "greatest disinhibitor for adolescents."[1002]

On the brighter side, we parents are not helpless against negative media and online influences. If we don't wish to remove televisions from our homes, we can at least move them out of our children's bedrooms. Recall that the presence of television in adolescent bedrooms is associated with poorer school performance, less physical activity, fewer family meals, and worse dietary habits.[1003] We can also set an example by reducing our own television viewing. There is a correlation between the amount of television parents and children watch.[1004] [1005] There is a "TV Allowance Device" marketed by a company named Mindmaster that gives weekly electronic allowances to children via their own personal code. It also allows block out times for restricting television viewing during meal and homework times. Text messages and chat room comments can also be monitored. I personally wish all parents could be provided instant e-mail copies of any communications generated or received by their children. This would fight fire with fire, using technology to reign in technology. Perhaps it would decrease cyberbullying.

In investigating links between television and behavior problems, one study thankfully found that for preschoolers, the detrimental effects of previous television exposure could be negated by later limits. Prior TV use that was reduced by kindergarten was not associated with behavioral problems.[1006] Another study documented the effectiveness of parental restrictions on television use. Parents in that study who used "restrictive mediation" had the children with the least media exposure. Those who chose not to address the issue had offspring with the greatest TV exposure.[1007]

There is a book extolling the potential positive effects of television in children's lives titled *The Elephant in the Living Room: Make Television Work for Your Kids*.[1008] The authors of that book are investigators who have conducted much research on the topic of media influence on children. The Wall Street Journal also once featured an article on "Fun for the Whole Family,

Really". It suggested watching classic movies with children as an antidote to our "trashy pop culture".[1009]

Outside the home, the National Center for Missing and Exploited Children and a new Financial Coalition Against Child Pornography has been working to shut off online payments to web sites selling illegal images. They have involved credit card companies and law enforcement agencies.[1010]

In schools, boards are addressing cyberbullying with new codes of conduct, but in many ways their hands are tied. "School administrators need to understand that their authority stops at the schoolhouse door" a legal director for the American Civil Liberties Union declared in discussing the issue. Another lawyer, for the National School Boards Association, advises administrators to warn parents that their "district is limited in its ability to discipline". Private schools have more power, and Father Kieran McHugh of the Catholic Pope John XXIII High School in New York banned the use of MySpace by his students. He also monitors the site, and contacts parents when postings from his students are found.[1011] Another approach to cyberbullying, taken by a Jewish youth group, also made national news. The North American Federation of Temple Youth printed unkind postings off of social networking sites and papered the walls of an auditorium with them. The students found it shocking to see themselves and their friends portrayed so negatively on real paper. In discussing the problem of painful cyber postings, psychology professor Gregory Hall, who teaches a "Cyber-psychology" course, points out that "social norms are the last thing to develop". He calls this the "Wild West Syndrome".[1012]

Part of the punishment for some students who broke into the computer system at a high school near my office was that they had to explain to teachers and administrators how they had done it. As masters of the media and modem, our adolescents wrestle with issues we never had to face. Our children were not born requesting high speed DSL and unlimited cable access. It was imposed upon them and not demanded by them. And while we may despair over our adolescents reaching out to internet chat rooms, have we given them many alternatives? In our physical "community", how many of us can name everyone our block?

Our dream of better living through technology has been a nightmare for our children in many ways. Our media images distort reality in every dimension, with consequences. What a leap our children must make if they are ever to enjoy the slow satisfaction of gardening when they download by the nanosecond. After interrupting their shows with commercials every few minutes and changing skits equally often on Sesame Street, why do we refer to a short attention span as a "deficit" and "disorder"? Our children are quick change artists because we have taught them to be.

Our media world affects our future as well as existing families. Most of us would like to acquire grandchildren via children-in-law, after family weddings, and when our children are at medically-safe reproductive ages. We get no help in this ultimate quest from the media. The music world long ago gave up on marriage. A survey of the Billboard Top 50 the week of Valentine's Day in 2007 found no references to marriage. In 1939, "Two Sleepy People" was about husband and wife, and Frank Sinatra's "Love and Marriage" was a later hit.[1013] Perhaps this is because "Mr. and Mrs. Is the Name", a popular 1935 title song for a movie of the same name, is often no longer the case in our homes.

On television, "Married with Children" is the "blessed" union our children see. So-called "stars" are photographed with bouncing, beautiful babies born to quickly thin mothers at advanced ages, and we are not privy to whether or not assisted reproduction or donor eggs were involved. If all this can be overcome and our children still wish to marry, they face yet another challenge. After immersing them in media images of cosmetically surgically-altered and air-brushed physical perfection, is it any surprise our young adults have trouble settling on a spouse? After tearing themselves away from their televisions, what a disappointment our adolescents must feel if they see an average, honest face. What a compromise they must feel when they date a normal looking person. High cheekbones are more photogenic than high morals or good hearts. And when every crime is solved and every family problem resolved a single show, how are our children supposed to understand real marriage in real time? Good marriages are long journeys and quiet novels, not sitcoms. They are intangible but real entities with an existence of their own, separate from the spouses in them. Much of their fulfillment comes simply from the accomplishment of sustaining them. Trying to make a media representation of marriage is like trying to take a picture of a smell, and maybe we would be better off if we didn't even try.

For better or worse, in sickness and in health, our media and technology are here to stay. In the Bible, the hotspot for finding spouses was the water well. It worked for Jacob and Rachel, and it worked for Isaac and Rebecca.

Moses also met Tzippora when she was drawing water for sheep. We will soon have children whose grandparents met online. It will be shocking to those grandchildren that we elders grew up without internet access.

As we fumble through our new technological maze of a culture, enjoy any assistance you can get from our adolescent masters of the modem. Admire their expertise, keeping in mind that the void between their emotional maturity and computer mastery is dark and dangerous territory. Many of our "advances" are wolves in sheep's clothing, and much of our new hard drives are filled with old, hard truths.

CHAPTER 9

● ● ●

TRAUMA QUEENS

Enjoyable Aspect of Parenting Adolescents Number Eight: Adolescents are physically strong. They can lift heavy groceries and drag out loaded garbage cans while using their other hand to hold the phone. They can jog and bicycle distances we can hardly drive. Barely out of their adolescent years, they go to war for us. Respect and enjoy their physical abilities.

A king once decided to identify and honor the community in his land that kept its children the safest. Records were checked, and the town with lowest number of accidents was determined. The king traveled to the town to bestow his Safety Award in person, but he was surprised to see no children at his Special Royal Ceremony, or anywhere else. The town had no playgrounds or sports fields, and no toys were visible in any common courtyards. The king demanded to see the town's children, but he was informed they were never allowed outside.

The king had every right to pitch a royal fit. Exercise offers children a variety of benefits besides physical fitness. It is effective therapy for depression.[1014] [1015] It improves emotional wellbeing in adolescents and it lowers rates of fatigue, psychological symptoms, suicidal behavior,[1016] and physical complaints.[1017] In one study, mental and physical quality of life was improved in women who were randomly assigned to exercise.[1018] Students who participate in interscholastic sports have lower rates of tobacco use and addiction.[1019] [1020] Compared to sedentary peers, active teens are less likely to have low self-esteem, and they are more likely to have higher grades.[1021]

Yet with every form of physical activity comes risk. Adding in the immaturity and impulsivity of adolescence makes for exponentially more risk.

Adolescents are both physically strong and head-strong. Their strength is their weakness. In peak form, we lose them to overconfidence and risk taking. The death rate for adolescents 15 to 19 years of age is over qua-druple the rate for children 10 years younger. Every year, about 25,000 American families suffer the ultimate of bereavements in losing a child. Over half of those tragedies involve adolescents. Three-quarters of these losses are sudden, from accidents, homicide, or suicide.[1022] Ten times as many are caused by trauma than cancer.[1023]

The leading cause of death for older adolescents in the United States is motor vehicle accidents. About 5500 American teens die in car crashes every year. Two-thirds of them are the drivers of the cars involved, and one-third are passengers.[1024] At 16 years of age, new drivers are 20 times more likely to have accidents than the average, older driver.[1025] Between 16 and 19 years of age, teenagers account for only 3% of all miles driven, yet they are involved in 15% of accidents involving fatalities.[1026] More American teens have been killed in car crashes than in all our wars combined.[1027] And for every adolescent killed in a car accident, there are about 100 other, non-fatal injuries, including many involving the brain and spinal cord that are permanently disabling.[1028] Passengers of teen drivers have twice the fatality rate as those driven by people over 25 years of age.[1029] About half of fatal accidents involving teenagers occur after dark, especially on Friday and Saturday nights.[1030] The dollar costs of all this are staggering. In 2003, motor vehicle accidents involving teenagers cost $2 billion in hospital charges alone.[1031]

Much of teenager's driving troubles are related to simple inexperi-ence, but there are other factors, too. Younger drivers between 18 and 24 years of age involved in fatal accidents are more likely to be intoxicated than older drivers. Driving risks increase at lower blood alcohol levels for younger versus older drivers, and to a greater degree across all levels of intoxication.[1032] Another risk factor for accidents involving teen drivers is the presence of passengers. Although only 10% of teens in 1 study viewed having peer passengers as dangerous,[1033] the relative risk of a driving fatality increases with each additional passenger transported. It is raised even more when the passengers are male or teenagers themselves.[1034] [1035] Teenaged passengers with adult drivers wear seat belts less often than the driver, and teens riding with a peer driver wear them less than half the time.[1036] In 2001, only 22% of 16-year-olds killed in car crashes were wearing seat belts.[1037] In the CDC's 2003 Youth Risk Behavior Surveillance, 18% of high schoolers had "rarely or never worn seat belts" when a passenger. Within the prior 30 days, 12% of those same students had driven after drinking alcohol, and 30% had ridden with a driver who had been drinking.[1038] In a study of fatal accidents in Colorado, 16-year-old drivers involved were more likely than older drivers to have been speeding, charged with a traffic violation or reckless driving, or have a crash with loss of control in a single vehicle, rollover, or run-off-the-road type accident.[1039] Last but not least, our teenagers' characteristic exhaustion may contribute to their poor driving. Sleepiness is a factor in almost half of fatal accidents.[1040]

For reasons unknown, adolescent drivers are also more likely than others to be the victims of road rage. Perhaps their inexperienced, awkward driving maneuvers are misinterpreted by others. Over half of teen drivers report being the victims of mild road rage in the past year. Girls were as likely as boys to be the targets of severe road rage.[1041]

If all of the above weren't enough, it is even more disappointing that within 6 months of being licensed, teen drivers who took driver's education classes have the same accident rates as those who didn't.[1042] Nevertheless, there is still room for hope here. It mostly comes in the form of a system called "graduated driver's licensing". This eliminates the "all or nothing" aspect of teen driving privileges, and transitions new drivers into their responsibility. It's the "training wheels" of the car world. The American Academy of Pediatrics has published a "model bill" for a 3-tiered system that involves 1) a learner's permit at age 15 with driving only under adult supervision; 2) a provisional license next, after a road test and no violations during the permit time, with limited privileges and a requirement for adult accompaniment between 10:00 p.m. and 6:00 a.m.; and 3) full licensure at 18 with a violation-free past record.[1043] Also included in such plans are a zero tolerance for alcohol use, nighttime driving curfews, restrictions on the transport of passengers, and strict requirements for seat belt use by passengers.[1044] As of 2002, 37 American states and the District of Colombia had graduated driver's licensing programs. The results have been dramatic. In Michigan, within 2 years the accident rate in 16-year-olds fell by 25%.[1045] In North Carolina, results were even more pronounced. Fatal crashes decreased by 57%, daytime accidents decreased 20%, and nighttime accidents fell 43%.[1046] Data published in 2006 showed an overall reduction of 20% in fatal crash rates for 16-year-old drivers under the jurisdiction of graduated driver's licensing laws.[1047]

Within our homes, there is even more we can do. Well before driving age, our children watch us role model driving. Take this into account when you choose how fast to drive when in a hurry. Think out loud when children drive with us, explaining difficult driving decisions as they are being made. Most difficult for them to learn is how to predict the actions of other drivers, which is fairly abstract but possible with experience and observation. There are driving simulation computer programs, and even driving monitoring and tracking systems for cars that record acceleration, braking, and distances traveled.[1048] Teens should be warned not to drive distracted with cell phone use and car radio manipulation on the road, but having a cell phone with them allows teens to call for rides home when facing unsafe driver alternatives. Disappointingly, however, while 56% of parents in one study believed their teens would call them for transportation home from a party where they had been drinking, only 13% of their children said they would.[1049] Families need agreed upon plans for such situations, sometimes involving predetermined "code words" that signify the problem to avoid embarrassment in front of peers.

Despite the loss of one American every 30 minutes to an alcohol-related crash,[1050] our offspring are surrounded by social acceptance of alcohol use. Adolescents' exposure to alcohol advertising increased 38% between 2001 and 2007, and alcohol ads are often particularly clever and humorous. Given their cost, they should be. The alcohol industry spent $923 million on television ads alone in 2007.[1051] Alcohol ads dominate sports programming, and there is now a country song about alcohol written in the first person, on an album named "Time Well Wasted" with lyrics like "I can make anybody pretty" and "I can make white people dance." It points out that "I helped Hemingway write". It fails to mention how many people it sends to their graves. A more accurate musical rendition of what alcohol does is the "Simple Plan" group video named "Untitled" about the anguish of a teen drunk driver who kills someone and has to live with it. Have your children watch it.

Parents also help by refusing to tolerate speeding. We all need to be constantly aware that everything we do faster, we do more dangerously. This is true for bike riding and skate boarding, where teens may recall wiping out at younger ages when going too fast. Runners trip more easily than walkers. And fast drivers lose control easier than more conservative ones. By definition, accidents happen by accident. Speeding, on the other hand, is a decision. Insist that your children choose the speed limit. When all else fails, parents also need to remember that in most states they have the right to unilaterally revoke their children's drivers licenses.[1052] Parents also possess the power of the pocketbook. Few teens work to arm themselves with cars, gas, and insurance. We are their enablers. Money talks, though in a language most parents of our generation don't speak.

There are some interesting perspectives on the reasons for our children's dangerous driving. One PhD physicist, Leonard Evans, has published a book blaming our high driving fatality rate on our emphasis on mechanical improvements in cars. He claims that in focusing on safer vehicles and better road design, we have neglected personal responsibility. While we were looking the other way, Britain, Canada, and Australia achieved reductions in fatalities, that had we matched, would have saved 200,000 American lives between 1979 and 2002.[1053] A study that investigated the driving-related attitudes as well as conduct of adolescents published in 2009 yielded some unexpected and disturbing results. Compared to older drivers, younger drivers acknowledged a higher awareness of the negative risks of dangerous driving. However, those same young drivers admitted stronger motives for bad behavior behind the wheel. They cited risky driving as a way to seek excitement, let off steam, gain prestige, and demonstrate confidence. Their higher perception of risk was associated with a greater self-reported frequency of riskier behaviors.[1054] Similarly, perhaps as a self-fulfilling prophecy, another study showed that adolescents with a belief they would die soon participated more often in high risk activities.[1055]

If risk emphasis doesn't prevent dangerous driving, and if Professor Evans is correct that we need to focus on personal responsibility, then what our adolescents need is an emphasis on the morality of driving. In 2007, the Vatican declared driving a moral issue, and released a set of "Ten Commandments" for drivers. Pope Benedict XVI cited the Biblical commandment not to kill, and addressed road rage and the use of cars for sinful activities. The unique document urged motorists to pray when behind the wheel, and to act kindly toward accident victims and their families. Cardinal Renato Martino called negligent driving a challenge for society and the church.[1056]

Worldwide, about 1,200,000 people die every year in motor vehicle accidents. Another 50,000,000 are injured. The rates are highest outside the United States, especially in developing nations.[1057] Part of American teenagers' rites of passage now often involves international travel, often for school organized "spring break" vacations. These are potential disasters.

Pedestrian and car accidents are just one of many possible risks in these situations. First and foremost, the medical care in almost all other countries is no where near the quality we enjoy here. Just because the hotel has marble floors and decorator appointments and a "doctor" on call doesn't make for good medical care. Almost nowhere else in the universe does that doctor have the hospital and subspecialist backup I enjoy practicing medicine here in the United States. Transport back to medical safety uses precious time and decreases the survival rate and recovery potential from many illnesses and injuries. With the advent of international cell phones over the past several years, I now often speak to patients in foreign countries. At the fanciest of resorts, I am consistently uncomfortable with the medical care I hear of. I had a patient with a major head wound from a diving accident simply sutured with no neck immobilization or attempts to rule out a spinal fracture. I have had numerous vomiting infants offered injections considered contra-indicated in America.

A 2005 article in The Pediatric Infectious Disease Journal, a prestigious and well-respected publication, documented "poor standards of care" with frequent contamination of intravenous solutions in the neonatal intensive care unit of a Mexican general hospital.[1058] In Africa, it was reported in the New England Journal of Medicine, "it is common for hospitals to own only a handful of injection sets, which tend to be reused without sterilization… it is a poorly kept secret that such reuse is common."[1059] In Uganda, the rate of HIV in inpatients at some hospitals is over 50%.[1060] In a Libyan hospital based HIV outbreak, the biggest risk factor was having received intravenous treatment.[1061] There has also been a hospital based HIV outbreak in a pediatric ward in Moscow. Death rates from injuries are higher in developing countries, as well. Some of the data demonstrating this is derived from Peace Corps worker tragedies.[1062] [1063] While I admire physicians who function without the medical equipment, subspecialist help, and tertiary care hospitals I am privileged to have here, I want better for my patients.

Other safety concerns with international travel involve risks of assault and criminal victimization. In 2006, kidnapping became a problem in Bolivia, where victims were taken by people dressed in fake police uniforms. Some were raped, and others were murdered. Central and South American nations also have problems with armed robberies of tourists.[1064]

There is also the issue of alcohol use in teenagers out of the country. Many cruises and vacation locations are chosen because of a lack of drinking age limits. Drugs and casual sex abound. Public safety laws in most countries are far behind ours, affecting issues from food safety to fire prevention measures and the likelihood of smoke alarms and indoor sprinklers in hotels. Law enforcement is much less funded and less sophisticated than we are used to, and the transport and emergency medical teams we take for granted may simply not exist at the spa.

On domestic "spring break" vacations, we need to evaluate and redefine acceptable conduct and tolerable risk. A television "Dateline" exposé from 2002 on the issue was quite revealing, as was an article in Family Circle from March, 2003 about "Kids Gone Crazy; What Really Happens on Spring Break" that one high school principal in my hometown distributed to parents.[1065] Another American magazine, Good Housekeeping, conducted an online survey of mothers whose children had gone on spring break trips. Here is what their children confessed to them after their travels: 24% used illegal drugs, 68% drank alcohol despite being underage, 35% had sexual intercourse, 80% went out without adults, and 61% stayed out past curfew or snuck out. The physician founder of a chain of hospitals in Mexico reports that every year someone who's drunk or drugged there dives from their hotel balcony into the pool, with tragic consequences. "Every year, some kid goes home paralyzed," he says. "Every single year."[1066]

Yet another venue that abounds with unsafe teenage behavior is the college dorm. College students consume more alcohol than non-college attending peers.[1067] A third of college students qualify for a diagnosis of alcohol abuse based on their conduct in the previous year, and 1 in 17 meets the standard for chronic alcohol dependence.[1068] I have seen college housing registration forms that allow students to request "substance free" rooming. In my medical practice, one of the most frequent discomforts I hear from returning college students is dorm room unavailability while their roommates "entertain" members of the opposite sex. One large University I am aware of has local law enforcement officers patrol dorm halls for obvious intoxication and drug use. There are other solutions to these problems, all starting with a commitment from college administrators to decreasing our children's risks while we entrust them to their first "home away from home". Most students do not fund their educations through income earned cutting grass and delivering newspapers. They are at college on our hard-earned money, giving us power no matter what their age. Both our children and the universities that depend on their attendance need to know that dorm living is not an essential part of the life cycle, and the provision of such is not a required part of parenting.

All student housing should be "substance free", and campuses need to make policies that restrict alcohol use and prevent its abuse. One particularly vigilant mother in my medical practice purchased a breatha-lyzer apparatus and tests her teens on arrival home. High schools often use breath analyzer tests at extra curricular events, and some are now using them during the school day as well.[1069] Colleges could prohibit intoxication on campus and enforce it the same way, if parents and school officials could agree on the issue. Universities could also require the live-in presence of adult faculty members on every dorm wing in addition to student liaisons. Such personnel should be CPR certified and trained in the recognition of substance and alcohol abuse and dependency. It should not take tragedies followed by expensive lawsuits to raise college administrator's conscious-ness in this area. If they merit the privilege of housing our precious and vulnerable adolescents, it should be a natural consequence of their heartfelt concern for our children's well being.

The medical risks of "casual" sex and multiple partners could also be minimized by decreasing alcohol intoxication on campus, and by limiting opportunities for privacy and co-ed visitation. One of the lowest budget pornographic tapes ever made, "Girls Gone Wild: College Girls Exposed", was filmed by crews who simply walked onto college campuses with cameras and consent forms for students of age. I read an interview of a production team member who described how easy it was to record explicit sexual activity of all types, on the spot, day or night. It is inevitable that such behavior will result in some of our college student offspring contract-ing sexually transmitted diseases, including both HIV and infections that can decrease future fertility in girls. Single gender housing with restricted visitation can be approached as a medical instead of moral issue.

Another way to minimize the risks of adolescent's activities is to redirect their energies to pursuits like sports. For teenagers especially, idle hands really are the devil's playground. A study of public high school students in Kentucky found student athletes less depressed and less likely to use cigarettes or marijuana than non-participating peers.[1070] In a larger national study, young female athletes were less likely to be substance abusers or sexually active than more sedentary girls.[1071] Yet another large survey found less tobacco, alcohol, and illegal drug use and less sexual activity and violence in high school sports team members of both genders.[1072] In a 2001 study, physical activity was also found to be associated with fewer feelings of sadness and suicidal behaviors.[1073] An article published in 2004 took things a step further. They used sports teams as a vehicle to promote health education on disordered eating, substance abuse, and other health issues, with good results. Participating athletes used less diet pills and illegal sports supplement drugs, and they reported less new sexual activity and fewer dangerous driving habits.[1074]

The good news is that adolescents benefit in a variety of ways from physical activity. The bad news is that they're getting less and less of it. A study published in the New England Journal of Medicine in 2002 found "substantial declines in physical activity during adolescence in girls...beginning as early as the age of 10 years."[1075] The CDC's 2003 national survey of high schoolers also found falling rates of physical activity in both genders between their freshman and senior year.[1076] Another study attributed this to the low probability of an adolescent continuing to participate in the same activity for 4 full years.[1077] Team drop-outs often fail to replace one organized sport with another. The numbers of students walking and bicycling to school also falls over grade levels. In middle school, 13.5% of children get there on their own, versus 7.7% in high school. Higher parental educational levels were associated with lower rates of walking or bicycling.[1078]

In addition to not having to navigate themselves between home and school, our children have few physical responsibilities at either end. We have dissociated work and exercise. Landscaping trucks clog our suburban streets all summer while our adolescents are inside logged onto their computers. At home there are cleaning ladies, and at school there are janitorial staffs.

In Japan, this is not the case. Japanese students clean their own schools, bathrooms and all, from 1st grade through high school.[1079] In Hungary, there is a "Children's Railway" serving the outskirts of Budapest, run by 10- to 14-year-olds in uniform. Children staff ticket windows, manage track switches, plan schedules, and monitor signal lights. One youth worker described it as "like a job, but fun." One adult supervisor on the train reports that his grandson, a rail worker, "doesn't behave himself at home," but at work "greets me properly."[1080]

Physical work is healthy and satisfying for adolescents, and it should be encouraged. On the other hand, young workers need special training and careful protection. Teen employees suffer more injuries on the job than their adult counterparts.[1081] Because many adolescents work in the restaurant industry, many of these injuries include cuts and burns.[1082] Other injuries involve toxic exposures. One poison control center documented toxic risks to adolescent workers in the form of exposures to cleaning compounds, paints, solvents, hydrocarbons, and bleaches. Common locations of exposures included food services, car shops, and retail stores.[1083] On construction sites, one study found 84% of teen workers performing at least 1 task prohibited by labor laws.[1084] Across all work sites, another survey found half of teens performing prohibited tasks, including using dangerous equipment and selling alcohol.[1085] Overall, about 100 adolescents die on the job in America every year. The most dangerous occupation in America is "unskilled labor", and having not completed their education, our adolescents are by definition just that. One study that looked at adolescents compensated for job-related accidents found almost half such injuries to be permanently disabling.[1086] Safety rules for teen workers can be accessed on the internet at youthrules.dol.gov and osha.gov/SLTC/youth/summerjobs.[1087]

Besides accidental injury, intentional assault on the job is also a real risk for adolescents. In one survey, a third of employed teenagers reported having experienced some form of workplace violence. Ten percent report being physically attacked (31% by customers and 29% by co-workers), 25% were verbally threatened (55% by customers), and 10% were sexually harassed (44% by co-workers and 34% by customers).[1088] Teens working with cash, or alone in stores, are at particular risk for robbery.

Other adolescents toil outside the formal work world, as caregivers within their own families. A study conducted by the Administration on Aging, part of the United States Department of Health and Human Services, found that over a million children 8 to 18 years of age help out with ill or disabled relatives. Half say the task consumes a significant part of their time, and a quarter shoulder the job without help from other family members. As our generation of late childbearers ages, it is probable that even more of our teens, with older parents, will need to help out as care givers. Like their adult counterparts, adolescent care givers deserve our recognition and admiration. They also need our support and help. And it doesn't seem they are getting it. Child caregivers have higher rates of anxiety and depression than peers.[1089] [1090]

Our adolescents are at risk not only at work, but also at play. There is a dark side to our adolescents' sports participation. The Olympic motto of *"Citius, Altius, Fortius"* which is Latin for "faster, higher, stronger", is an ideal adopted by too many of our teenaged sports participants. In the 1990s, 2 female gymnasts on the American Olympic team died of sports-related medical problems, one from an eating disorder and another from a spinal trauma from a vaulting injury.[1091]

Exercise can become an addiction, especially for eating disordered teens. Aside from the gratification of weight loss, there is also the well known "runners high". Physicians have even proposed formal definitions for "exercise dependence".[1092]

Adolescents are particularly prone to unrealistic hopes and expectations regarding athletics. One survey revealed that 50% of boys and 20% of girls thought they "definitely" or "probably" had a chance of becoming professional athletes, and 52% of boys and 20% of girls thought they would "definitely" or "probably" receive an athletic scholarship to college.[1093] For a more realistic guide to college sports, try consulting *Put Me in Coach: A Parent's Guide to Winning the Game of College Recruiting*, by Laurie A. Richter.[1094]

Adolescent athletes who can't keep up often turn to performance enhancing drugs, also often referred to as "ergogenic aids". Their interest is fueled by the media. One study found that boys who read men's magazines and fashion, health, and fitness magazines were twice as likely as others to use supplements to try to improve their physique or performance. Girls most likely to use supplements were those wanting to look like female media "stars".[1095] In 2003, a survey sponsored by the Blue Cross and Blue Shield Association estimated that over a million American 12- to 17-year-olds have used such supplements.[1096] Performance enhancing substances include: [1097 1098 1099 1100 1101 1102 1103 1104 1105]

1) **Steroids,** also called "roids" or "anabolic-androgenic" steroids in medical circles, are actually synthetic derivatives of testosterone. Steroids are controlled substances. It is a felony to obtain them without a doctor's prescription. They are particularly dangerous drugs with many side effects including testicular atrophy, impotence, baldness, acne, irreversible breast tissue growth in boys, irreversible masculinization in girls, high blood pressure, increased cholesterol levels, heart muscle damage, liver damage, liver tumors, long term increased risks of liver cancer, early growth stoppage with irreversible closure of bone growth centers, gastric irritation and upset, weakening of tendons, weakening of the immune system, and psychiatric effects including dependency.

Steroids come in both oral and injectable forms. They are often abused in cycles of 6 to 12 weeks followed by drug-free hiatus periods. During active phases of use, steroids are often used in different combinations. This is called "stacking".[1106] One steroid, tetrahydrogestrinone, or "THG" is a new, FDA unapproved drug that is reportedly undetectable in urine. Some steroids abused by athletes are made for veterinarian use. By the time they finish high school, from 5% to 11% of boys report having used steroids.[1107] Because of their masculinizing properties, steroids used to be primarily a male sports issue. Unfortunately, this is no longer the case. A study published in 2007 documented 5.3% of high school girls admitting to ongoing or previous steroid use.[1108] Other data, from the CDC, put the rate of steroid use in young adolescents at 7.6% for boys, and 5.7% for girls.[1109] [1110]

Symptoms of steroid use can include extreme mood swings, aggressive behavior, worsening acne, high blood pressure, or unusual skin streaking. Sudden withdrawal can cause extreme fatigue, sudden loss of muscle mass, and depression. Injection sites can look red, and they can become infected. There is one case where a bodybuilder suffered a severe "MRSA" staph infection from a steroid shot.[1111]

Steroids have a strong association with aggression. Nazi soldiers took steroids in World War II to increase aggressiveness.[1112] [1113] Alarmingly, in animal studies, the effects of steroids can outlast their presence in the body. Hamsters given steroids in 1 study were 10 times as aggressive as untreated cage mates, and after stopping the steroids, injected hamsters stayed aggressive a length of time equivalent to half their adolescence. Autopsies revealed physical brain changes, with an increase in neuro-transmitter chemicals in the "hypothalamus", which regulates social behavior.[1114]

2) DHEA and Androstenedione are closely related steroid precursors that are marketed as "dietary supplements". Normally, they are produced in human adrenal glands and testicles and then converted to other hormones in the body. In 1996, the FDA banned the medical use of DHEA, declaring it to have no legitimate therapeutic indications. In 1998, however, professional baseball player Mark McGwire hit a record 70 home runs, and publicly credited androstenedione with helping. By 1999, sales had increased 5 fold among young people.[1115] DHEA and androstenedione are banned by the International Olympic Committee, the National Collegiate Athletic Association, and the National Hockey and Football Leagues, among others. Unfortunately, however, they were not made into controlled substances by the Anabolic Steroid Control Act of 2004. Toxicity and side effects are as for regular steroids.

3) Creatine, an amino acid derivative, is normally made by the human liver, kidney, and pancreas. It is also ingested from meat and fish. It is sold over-the-counter as a "dietary supplement" in powder, liquid, tablet, and gum forms. There are conflicting data as to whether creatine helps athletic performance. This supplement stresses the kidneys like a large protein load, and has been reported to cause renal failure in patients with underlying, pre-existing kidney problems. Other adverse effects include muscle cramping, dizziness, weakness, nausea, diarrhea, and fluid retention with weight gain.

4) **Stimulants** used to enhance sports performance include caffeine, amphetamines, and ephedra. These substances can cause heart rhythm problems and place athletes at greater risk of dehydration and heat stroke. Allied soldiers were given amphetamines during World War II to increase alertness and endurance. It was found that they would march longer despite painful foot blisters when on amphetamines.[1116] [1117]

5) **Erythropoietin**, brand named "Epogen", is a synthetic form of the human hormone that stimulates blood cell production. It is used for some forms of severe anemia. Some endurance sports athletes use it believing it will help them carry more oxygen. It is dangerous because high blood counts are associated with increased risks of stroke, seizures, heart attack, and blood clots of all types. These risks escalate even more when combined with dehydration, which can easily occur during sports participation.[1118] [1119]

Some athletes have been known to cut to the quick and go directly to **blood transfusion** to increase their blood counts. This is commonly called "blood doping". In 1985, amidst a regional blood shortage, 7 out of 24 members of the U.S. Olympic cycling team admitted to taking blood transfusions in a motel room.[1120]

6) **Human growth hormone** is an injectable, prescription product intended for use in children with documented deficiencies of it and extreme short stature. Human growth hormone is a very expensive drug, and its use would hopefully be limited by its high cost, but as early as 1992 almost a third of adolescent boys reported knowing someone who was abusing it.[1121] In 2001, one of every 29 college athletes was using growth hormone.[1122] [1123] Among its side effects is an irreversible change in appearance from bony overgrowth in the face. The use of growth hormone in non-deficient people may also increase their risks of cancer and diabetes, and it can worsen exercise capacity, tissue swelling, and joint pain.[1124] Healthy mice given growth hormone have shorter life spans.[1125] [1126]

7) **Human chorionic gonadotropin**, called "hCG", is an injectable hormone from the female placenta used to treat some forms of infertility in

girls, and some forms of genital underdevelopment in males. It is also sometimes used as an alternative to surgery in prepubertal boys when "undescended" testicles are located up in the abdomen instead of down in the scrotum. Unfortunately, hCG has recently been reported to be a popular drug of abuse for athletes seeking performance enhancement. This is because hCG stimulates the production of the male sex hormone androgen, which is a steroid. The side effects of hCG are the same as for steroids taken directly.

8) Clenbuterol, a stimulant with additional tissue growth stimulating properties, is marketed only for use in horses with airway obstruction. It has also been used illicitly by athletes thinking it will increase their body mass. This oral drug has serious side effects including tremor, cardiac stimulation, low blood potassium, and other electrolyte imbalances.[1127]

9) Sodium Bicarbonate is taken by some athletes before intense sports activity. They believe it will delay fatigue by decreasing acid build up in muscles. It hasn't been shown to do that, but it does slow the excretion of some other drugs, increasing their possible toxicities, and it can cause diarrhea and cramps.

10) Some athletes and bodybuilders are using combination products that include the **"date rape" drugs** gamma hydroxybutyric acid (GHB), gamma butyrolactone (GBL), and 1,4 butanediol (BD). They exist in both powder and liquid form. Athletic abusers of these drugs believe that during the deep sleep they induce, growth hormone is released. Date rape drugs are particularly dangerous. They were initially developed as anesthetics but deemed too risky. They have no proven athletic benefits. They are also highly addictive. Withdrawal symptoms can be striking and can include tremor, vomiting, psychosis, and insomnia. A third of patients withdrawing from GHB require physical restraint, and death from swelling of the lungs has also been reported in people withdrawing from GHB. Milder withdrawal symptoms can last up to half a year, and include anxiety and memory problems. [1128]

11) Although it does not enhance physical ability, weight loss to qualify for competition against smaller opponents gives truly heavier players an advantage. Before weigh-ins, athletes sometimes use **diuretics**, especially "lasix", to induce fast weight loss. This drug can cause dehydration and blood electrolyte imbalances.[1129]

Some of the above substances may be purchased legally. They are also heavily advertised in sports and fitness and men's magazines. "Dietary supplements" bypass the regulations and strict testing required of declared pharmaceutical products. In 2006, Congress passed revisions to the 1994 Dietary Supplement Health and Education Act allowing the FDA some power to remove dangerous such products from the market. It also requires reporting of serious adverse events.[1130]

Some sudden deaths in high school athletes are caused by these supplements, often via disturbances of electrolyte balance or heart rhythm. Other sudden deaths occur when the physical stress of exertion unmasks or exacerbates underlying medical issues. Sudden deaths in athletes are 5 times more common in boys than girls, and greater in college versus high school players. Less common causes include muscle inflammation and break down with sickle cell trait, severe allergic reactions to exercise, or asthma flares. Sudden rupture of the spleen can also be fatal. This often follows mononucleosis, usually within 21 days after the first onset of symptoms, but it can also occur much later, even 7 weeks later. The spleen does not have to be enlarged on physical exam to rupture with mono.[1131] [1132]

Overall, three-quarters of sudden deaths in athletes are due to heart conditions, including ruptured heart large vessel aneurysms in Marfan's syndrome, abnormalities of the coronary arteries, early and severe atherosclerosis, heart arrhythmias, or an inborn overgrowth of the heart muscle.[1133] [1134] [1135] In only 6% of cases are these heart problems known about in advance.[1136]

Marfan's syndrome is best known in associated with basketball players. This is because people with Marfan's syndrome are particularly tall and thin and often very flexible. Other clues to diagnosis include the ability to overlap the thumb and little finger when wrapped around the other wrist, and a fingertip-to-fingertip extended arm span ("wing span") that is much longer than the body height. Some people with Marfan's syndrome have large, floppy ears, a bluish hue to the whites of their eyes, nearsightedness, misalignment of the eye lens, and flat faces with narrow jaws and dental crowding. They also have increased rates of scoliosis, or curvature of the spine.

Marfan's syndrome is most dangerously associated with heart problems. There is often floppiness of the valve between the left upper and lower heart chambers, called "mitral valve prolapse", and there is also often weakening with stretching of the bottom of the aorta artery. Tearing or rupture of the dilated aorta can cause sudden death during strenuous sports activities. Both of these heart problems can be seen on echocardiograms, which are ultrasounds of the heart. About 1 in every 40,000 people has Marfan's syndrome. It is inherited in a dominant way, that is, it is passed on from just one affected parent, but about a third of cases are spontaneous and occur with no known previously existing genetic source.

People with **abnormal coronary arteries** sometimes have a history of chest pain and fainting with exertion. Athletes with premature atherosclerosis can also have a history of chest pain, but they usually falsely attribute it to more innocent causes like heartburn or muscle spasm.

Heart arrhythmias, especially one named "prolonged QT syndrome" can cause sudden death. Sometimes there is a history of sudden deaths in relatives, and sometimes there is also a history of fainting or palpitations. Some arrhythmias can be diagnosed on regular ECG tracings, but others occur only intermittently and are lucky to be picked up on 24 hour or longer recordings. Chest trauma, usually from baseball hits, can cause arrhythmias and sudden death with no known risk factors. This tragedy is called "commotio cordis". The risk of it may be lessened by using softer "safety" baseballs and wearing chest protectors,[1137] [1138] although one study found commercially available such protectors of little benefit for juvenile pigs tested while wearing them.[1139]

Other sudden deaths in athletes are traced to a problem where there is abnormal overgrowth of the heart muscle. This condition has many names, including **"hypertrophic cardiomyopathy"** abbreviated **"HCM"**, **"asymmetric septal hypertrophy"**, or **"idiopathic hypertrophic subaortic stenosis"**, abbreviated **"IHSS"**. The problem is often totally asymptomatic, but other times there are heart murmurs or a history weakness, fatigue, shortness of breath, palpitations, dizziness, fainting, or chest pain. Like Marfan's syndrome, IHSS is inherited in a dominant way, from just one affected parent.

There is great controversy about the wisdom of widespread echocardiography screening for the conditions associated with sudden death in sports participants. The heart is a muscle, and athletes who train will increase its size and power. This can result in findings on screening ECGs and echocardiograms that can cause false diagnoses.[1140] [1141] [1142] [1143] In Italy, a national program for screening athletes with ECGs before sports participation was instituted in 1982. The rates of sudden cardiac deaths in screened athletes subsequently fell by 89%.[1144] In Japan, schoolchildren routinely receive ECGs to detect congenital heart problems, and the International Olympic Committee recommends ECGs every 2 years for competitors. There is also some ongoing research on the use of a blood test for "B type natriuretic peptide" as a marker for HCM. The substance is released by heart muscle when it is stressed by pressure or overload.[1145]

All sports participants should have thorough physical exams. Beyond that, most physicians would recommend additional cardiac testing for athletes who have a medical history of fainting, palpitations, chest pain, dizziness, or exercise intolerance; or a family history of sudden death, Marfan's syndrome, or HCM.

More widespread "routine" testing is a policy decision for public health experts, and it is not without pitfalls. Accurate diagnoses may not prevent all tragedies. False diagnoses can result in unhealthy cessation of exercise and future denials for medical insurance, which can in turn limit other medical care.

Yet another medical problem than can rear its head with sports participation is seizures. Fast breathing, or hyperventilation, can set off convulsions in susceptible people. Patients are often asked to breathe deep and fast during EEG tests to increase their yield. Exercise can also lower blood sugar. There have been reports of joggers suffering seizures, uncovering a variety of underlying diagnoses.[1146] Still other adolescent athletes have headaches with or immediately following exercise. The problem is more common in girls, affecting 30% in one study, especially those with a history of problems with migraines.[1147] Contagious skin infections, especially from "MRSA" type staph germs[1148] and herpes viruses are a special risk for participants in contact sports, especially wrestlers and football players. There is even a "herpes gladiatorum" named for how it is acquired.

In addition to its associations with medical diseases, sports participation carries with it, of course, risks of injury. There are overuse syndromes, stress fractures, and injuries including fatalities. Repeated concussions and head trauma can cause brain damage, with often subtle but permanent consequences. Every sport has its characteristic risks, from "tennis elbow" to "pitcher's elbow" to "little league shoulder" to "bowling plexopathy"[1149] to "swimmer's ear" to "water ski colon".[1150]

Knee injuries are a special problem for teen athletes. Tears of the "ACL" ("Anterior Cruciate Ligament") and the meniscal cartilages are especially common in active adolescents, and they often occur together. In 1972, America's Title IX Legislation guaranteed equal access to sports for both genders at high schools and colleges receiving federal funds, and girls' sports participation increased exponentially. In turn, it was accompanied by a 1000-fold increase in ACL injuries in women, who are up to 6 times more prone than boys to suffer them. Most ACL tears occur without physical contact, during cutting and pivoting maneuvers. The ACL stabilizes the knee and holds the shin bone in line with the thigh bone. When the ACL tears, the knee often "gives out". Besides the immediate damage ACL tears inflict, half of people suffering them develop arthritis 10 to 20 years later if they are not treated.

Meniscal tears are often associated with a "pop" and a locking of the knee, followed by swelling. The 2 knee menisci (medial and lateral) are firm cushions between the thigh and shin bones that act as shock absorbers. Meniscal tears more often involve contact sports, especially football.[1151] [1152]

Every year, up to 18% of high school athletes suffer significant injuries. The risk of sports injuries increases with the age and size of players.[1153] It is also greater with higher family income and advanced educational levels of parents.[1154] Besides the physical damage involved, there is significant emotional trauma to sports injury. In 1994, sports medicine specialists from the Mayo Clinic described 5 injured athletes who became suicidal after sports injury. Each situation involved prior athletic success, serious injury followed by incomplete recovery, and replacement by teammates.[1155] Brain concussion is also often associated with depressed mood.[1156]

In assessing the risks of adolescent physical activity, it is important to remember that dance and cheerleading are themselves strenuous sports. Most dance injuries occur in younger dancers, especially ballet dancers. Almost half are attributed to overuse.[1157] Over half of catastrophic sports injuries in women occur in cheerleaders. Pyramiding and "flying" (at heights 6 to 20 feet) are the most dangerous cheerleading activities. Efforts are underway to improve the safety of cheerleading by declaring it an official sport and instituting universal guidelines for practice and exhibition. Pyramiding can be made safer if participants simply wear tight fitting clothing that will not get caught under their hands while they are balancing in formation.[1158] [1159]

Catastrophic injuries like fatal head trauma and paralyzing neck fractures can occur in any sport, but for boys, football is most often involved.[1160] This association may overestimate the danger of the sport, because it is also the one with the most participants. In 1990, there were 1,300,000 American high school and 75,000 college football players.

In reality, adolescents face danger in virtually every sports arena. Ice hockey, gymnastics, and wrestling[1161] have all been associated with disabling injury and death.[1162] Skiing-related injuries killed 128 adults and 21 children in Colorado between 1980 and 2001.[1163] Horseback riding is so dangerous that it is associated with more injuries, per unit time, than either motorcycling or auto racing.[1164] Soccer injuries are on the rise, and when players collide, there are no helmets for head protection. After football, soccer is the next most likely sport to cause concussions. [1165] Injury rates for cheerleading are also increasing as it involves more gymnastics maneuvers, higher pyramiding, and more extreme catapults, and it is the only sport where the concussion rate is higher in practice than during performances.[1166] Some sports have instituted new rules and helmet requirements that have helped with injury rates, but for bicycling, which accounts for 90% of preventable head injuries,[1167] teenaged cyclists have the lowest rate of helmet use. One study of California college student regular bike riders revealed that only 5% of them wore a helmet.[1168]

Swimming, usually considered a safe sport, also carries risk for adolescents. Teenagers 15 to 19 years of age have the 2nd highest drowning rate of any age group, with a higher rate than 5- to 14-year-olds. Adolescent drowning victims almost always die in outdoor bodies of water instead of pools. Alcohol is a factor in 13% of these drownings, and although 75% are witnessed, teens are less likely than younger children to receive bystander CPR.[1169]

Recent medical literature highlighting the dangers of concussions in young athletes is cause for great concern.[1170] New research emphasizes that a concussion does not necessarily, or usually, involve full-blown unconsciousness. Concussions are defined as head trauma induced alterations in mental status. They can involve a lack of recall of the injury, loss of awareness, dizziness, loss of balance, blurred vision, a sensation of 'seeing stars', nausea or vomiting, severe headache, confusion, or a feeling of 'being in a fog'. Although 63% of sports-related concussions occur in football, [1171] ice hockey play is actually associated with a higher incidence of concussion, accounting for 12% of such injuries despite a much lower number of participants. Concussions occur more often in game play than in practice, and are 6 times more likely to happen in formal, organized sports compared to simple leisure play.[1172]

Every year, 10% of college and 20% of high school football players suffer concussions. Younger players are more susceptible. Yet 80% of concussions go unreported, either because they are not recognized, or because the athlete involved does not want them noticed.[1173] Reasons for player reluctance to report such injuries include not wanting to leave play or practice, not wanting to let teammates down, or most often, not believing the concussion was serious.[1174] Even willing-to-report players can fail to call attention to concussions when they honestly don't know what hit them. A study of professional Canadian football players found that of those experiencing concussions, only 19% were aware of it.[1175]

Unfortunately, it is a serious error to take any concussion lightly. Returning to play before full recovery sends athletes back in while still impaired, with delayed reaction times and sometimes slightly less coordination and balance. This sets them up for re-injury, or "second impact" syndrome.[1176] [1177] Having suffered a previous concussion after head trauma is a risk factor for subsequent such reactions to impact, especially within the first 10 days after initial injury.[1178] Players who lose consciousness with concussions are particularly vulnerable, by a factor of 6 times, to subsequent concussions.[1179] Just how long the vulnerable period is for second impact syndrome is a matter of debate, and it may vary between individuals.

When convulsions follow concussion, if brief and self-limited they are not predictive of future epilepsy.[1180] The news is not as good for other neurological consequences of concussions. Concussions impair the brain's ability to process information. The reduction in brain functioning is greater and longer after subsequent than first concussions, leaving repeatedly injured players in need of longer recovery time-outs.[1181] Repeated concussions over months or years can cause cumulative loss of brain function.[1182] Neuropsychological testing of college football players found that those with repeated concussions had "reduced cognitive performance" similar to people with diagnosed learning disabilities.[1183] A similar study demonstrated that compared to athletes in track and swimming who are not exposed to head trauma, amateur soccer plays scored lower on tests of attention, memory, and planning abilities.[1184] [1185] There have been autopsies of deceased young athletes with histories of multiple concussions and later cognitive and psychiatric problems. Horrifyingly, brain changes in these cases are similar to those seen in Alzheimer disease.[1186][1187]

Repeat head injuries in close succession, hours to weeks later, are more likely to be catastrophic or fatal than isolated event injuries.[1188][1189][1190] In analyzing such tragedies in high school and college football players, where the outcome was death or permanent neurologic deficit, it was found that in 59% of cases there were previous histories of head injury, 71% in the same season. Over a third of the athletes with previous injury were playing with still present residual neurological symptoms. One in 10 of the catastrophic injuries occurred after cumulative minor injuries as opposed to sudden, severe identifiable events. Of those permanently disabled or fatally injured players, 98% were high school as opposed to college students. Tragic injuries were 3.5 times more likely to occur in play than practice. Early return to play after previous injury, and the use of poorly fitting, refurbished, or defective helmets were all associated with catastrophic injury. Neck fractures accompanied head injury in 2% of these tragedies.[1191]

Often causing confusion as to whether or not neck injury is present in student athletes is the occurrence of "stingers" or "burners" in football players. Stinger injuries are extremely common in football players. They involve sensations of burning, stinging, numbness, or tingling down the arm into the fingers, and they are thought to be due to stretching or irritation of nerves. Sometimes there is associated arm weakness, but there is only rarely neck pain or stiffness. Stinger episodes usually resolve in minutes, and afflicted athletes often shake their arms for relief. When stinger symptoms are prolonged or atypical or when they involve neck pain or stiffness, the possibility of neck injury must be considered and acted upon.

To minimize injury, sports helmets should be carefully fitted, preferably by certified athletic trainers. When coaches or others perform helmet fitting, errors occur in up to 25% of cases.[1192] To minimize heat stroke, there is a new helmet that checks wearer's temperatures and radio transmits them every 10 seconds to a PDA on the sidelines. Since 1995, the deaths of 39 American football players, mostly high schoolers, have been caused by heat stroke.[1193]

To avoid the ultimate tragedy these scenarios can end in, adolescent athletes should be aware of the early symptoms of heat stroke. They should know they often do not include a sensation of feeling hot, but rather a feeling of confusion and dizziness. They should also be taught to recognize and report any and all concussions. Return to play should be delayed until full recovery, and all error should be on the side of caution. Teenaged sports participants who suffer repeated concussions, even subtle and widely spaced, also need to be aware that they may be permanently harming themselves by continuing to play. Athletes with repeated histories of concussions in response to head trauma need to seriously consider redirecting their participation to alternative, non-contact sports.

The regulation of college sports dates back to 1905, when then President Teddy Roosevelt threatened to ban football nationwide after 18 deaths resulted from maneuvers such as launching ball-carrying players over touchdown lines. In response, the National Collegiate Athletic Association was born. Their supervision reformed college sports in the early 1900s, a time when the Journal of the American Medical Association published an editorial fuming that "little good can be claimed for football..."[1194] With the pressures of televised college sports, and with half of division I-A football players requiring surgery for injuries from college competition,[1195] and with a graduation rate of only 63% among college team players,[1196] the NCAA still has work to do.

Insult is added to injury when sports "accidents" aren't. Inappropriate aggression is a real problem in adolescent athletics. Like pornography, sports violence is hard to define but easy to recognize. And now that so many spectators have video cameras, the problem is being increasingly and graphically documented. There is very little medical literature on this subject, and most of what is published deals with ice hockey. One article has pointed out that mandating hockey head and facial protective equipment eliminated eye, face, and dental injuries but was "problematically linked with an increase in catastrophic spinal injuries."[1197] The studies' authors theorized that wearing protective equipment gives athletes a false sense of security and allows officials to be more lenient as well. Feeling immune to injury, "the net result has been an increase in illegal and injurious behaviors..."[1198] A similar phenomenon occurred in football in the 1950s. When the plastic football helmet replaced the weaker leather one at about that time, the sport became more brutal. The number of neck injuries tripled, and deaths from spinal injuries doubled.[1199] False security was also evident in a survey of student hockey players. Ominously, 24% believed that spinal cord injury was not possible with their protective equipment, and 45% felt the same way regarding brain injury.[1200]

Clearly this is an area where more research is needed, regarding not only players, but also parents, coaches, and referees as well.[1201] In the meantime, many of us pediatricians make advice on this topic a mandatory lecture for potential perpetrators during sports physicals. I also remind my patients that I consider the inability to avoid violent conduct a disability that can warrant the withdrawal of my clearance to continue sports participation. Parents can and should make the same threat. When we fail to identify and control the perpetrators of sports violence, we share in the responsibility for the injuries they inflict. Not every player aggressively struck down gets up again, and when their assailants mature they become lifelong victims themselves, of their own consciences.

Adolescents also perpetrate violence off the playing field. It starts at young ages with bullying. From 20% to 30%[1202] of school children are victims, perpetrators, or simultaneous victim-perpetrators of bullying. They are not the only ones harmed by it. There is now also recognition of the negative effects of bullying on "bystanders" who are simply witnesses. Victimized children and adolescents have higher rates of depression, anxiety, suicidal thoughts, poor self-worth, and low self-esteem, and they are less willing to participate in physical activity.[1203] Bullied diabetic children have worse glucose control and lower adherence to treatment plans.[1204] Bullies have higher rates of delinquency, substance abuse, and psychiatric illness. All involved have higher rates of sleep problems, poor appetite, headache, backache, and abdominal pain.[1205] Among young adolescents, one study found bully perpetrators psychologically strong and in high social standing among peers. Victims were emotionally distressed and socially excluded.[1206] Most bullying occurs at school, but is unwitnessed by authority figures.[1207] In early grades, girls are bullies more often than boys, but the gender ratio reverses by middle school.[1208] [1209] Early, severe bully perpetrators often remain violent throughout life. One study found greatly increased felony conviction rates at 24 years of age in previous bullies. [1210] [1211] Many school based interventions have been found to reduce bullying levels, but antibullying measures need to be continued to sustain their effectiveness.[1212] [1213]

Our youngsters abuse each other not only through bullying in school, but also through domestic violence in dating relationships. The CDC has published data showing that in the previous 18 months, 12% of 7th through 12th graders report having experienced physical dating violence. Another 20% report they have experienced psychological victimization. Girls who are victimized while dating are more likely than others to become abused women during adulthood, and they also have higher rates of substance abuse, risky sexual behavior, eating disorders, and suicidal thoughts and attempts.[1214] Over half of teen date rapes occur in apartments or homes, twice as often in the boy's home than in the girl's. Depression is both an outcome and a risk factor for partner violence. Girls with depressive symptoms have a 24% increased chance of moderate to severe partner victimization.[1215]

Prevention of dating violence involves encouraging teens not to be alone with partners, and to end relationships where there has been **H**urt, **I**nsults, **T**hreats, or **S**creaming. Adolescents should also be educated to look out for early warning signs in potentially abusive partners: extreme jealousy, controlling behavior, quick involvement, unpredictable mood swings, alcohol and drug use, explosive anger, the use of force during arguments, hypersensitivity, belief in rigid sex roles, cruelty to animals or children, a history of violence toward other partners, threats of violence, a tendency to isolate partners from their friends and family, and a tendency to blame others for problems.[1216] Dating teens should always have cell phones and a way out if they ever feel uncomfortable.

As both victims and perpetrators, our adolescents are exposed to ever expanding levels of violence in their lives. Homicide is the 2nd leading cause of death in American teenaged boys.[1217] For every adolescent killed, another 41 are hospitalized and 1100 more are treated in emergency rooms for violence-related injury.[1218] Teen homicide rates are higher than the rates for Americans in any other age group. In the United States, youths 12 to 19 years of age experience triple the number of rapes and physical assaults, and twice as many robberies as older Americans.[1219] Between 1984 and 1993, the number of adolescent homicide victims in the United States increased by over 150%.[1220] During the same period, the rate of homicides committed by youths increased by 172%.[1221] Between 1983 and 1993, arrests of adolescents increased 90% for murder, 78% for aggravated assault, and 63% for robbery.[1222]

Some blame the rise of gangs and harder drugs, combined with greater handgun access, for these sad statistics. Others blame increasing exposure to media and video game violence for inciting young viewers. In one study, participation in the power sports of boxing, wrestling, martial arts, and weight lifting were associated with increased levels of aggressive and antisocial behavior outside those sports activities.[1223] In another study, intention to use violence in adolescents was associated with illicit drug use, previous exposure to violence, and a lower frequency of religious service attendance.[1224]

Actual fight-related injuries are more common in teenagers who have been violent in the past, or who have witnessed or experienced violence themselves. Girls who report previous victimization are over twice as likely as others to behave violently themselves.[1225] Girls are more likely than boys to fight in retaliation to previous events, and both genders often cite "teasing" and "being disrespected" as motivation for conflict.[1226] For boys, illicit drug use increases the chances of subsequent fight-related injury, and for girls, the risk is higher with depression. For both, higher grades and better general health are associated with lower violence risks.[1227] Up to half of American middle schoolers report having been in a physical fight.[1228] Another study found that among middle school students, 5% of boys and almost 1% of girls have carried a gun to school, and 20% of boys and 8% of girls have taken a knife or club.[1229] The better news is that according to CDC data, between 1991 and 2003, adolescent weapon carrying and physical fighting decreased, though 5% of students still reported missing school because of safety concerns.[1230]

There are far ranging consequences to our adolescent's exposure to violence. In one study, adolescents with high exposures to violence were more likely than others to self-rate their overall health as poor.[1231] Other data found students with exposure to violence exhibiting significantly more physical symptoms of stress, and expressing increased feelings of fear, anger, sadness, and frustration.[1232] In yet another study, anger was the dominant emotion present after trauma.[1233]

There is ongoing study and debate about how to address adolescent violence, and the emergence of some reasons for hope. A study published in 2008 assigned assault injured teens in an emergency department to a mentored 6 session problem solving curriculum with supporting home visits by a health educator. Results were favorable.[1234] Other investigators have had some success with a violence prevention website.[1235] Schools have instituted effective antibullying programs, and a system to teach anger control and stress-related coping skills is being tried in New Orleans.[1236] A doctor's office-based intervention involving psychosocial screening and parental educational support has been shown to decrease aggressive behavior in children 7 to 15 years of age.[1237] And back at home, a study investigating family influences on adolescent behavior found less physical fighting in youths whose parents disapproved of the use of violence.[1238]

For teenaged perpetrators of violent crimes, there is controversy as to how to help. An NIH panel recently warned that group detention centers, boot camps, and "tough" programs may actually worsen the problem.[1239] [1240] A better option seems to be therapeutic foster care for violent adolescents involving placement in homes with specially trained parent supervisors.[1241]

In the famous words of heavyweight boxer Bob Fitzsimmons, "the bigger they are, the harder they fall." Respect your adolescent's strength, and muster all of yours to help them harness it. Time will teach them that "healthy fear" is a redundancy, and that the greatest form of strength is restraint. In the meantime, make saving them from themselves your highest priority, with every trick in your parenting book and with every fiber of your being. And in every fiber of your adolescent's being, make sure they know that when it's our beloved big children who fall, they don't go down alone.

CHAPTER 10

• • •

ADOLESCENT HEALTH SCARE ISSUES

Enjoyable Aspect of Parenting Adolescents Number Nine: Adolescents are cheaper to provide health care for than their younger counterparts. Remember all those trips to the doctor for ear infections, fevers, coughs, and diarrhea—all followed by bills? Remember those expensive baby shots and check-ups? Enjoy the possibility of not exceeding your insurance deductible by Groundhog Day.

Imagine moving into a new house and discovering that your builder used the wrong blueprints. Some rooms are larger than you wished. Others are smaller than intended. Some doors and windows are not where you wanted them, and the light switches are awkwardly positioned. When the lights flicker, you fear the electrical wiring was done wrong as well, perhaps dangerously so. Your builder has retired and moved away, and having already signed on your mortgage and moved in, you try to make the best of your situation. Yet sometimes it is frustrating that your neighbor's house seems to have been precisely, perfectly constructed.

Adolescents' bodies are their new homes. Usually not at all the size or style they wished for, and often uncomfortable. Teenagers start puberty with one body and end it with another. They experience upheaval in every physical, hormonal, and emotional human dimension. They are thrust into autopilot at a high speed on a hard road. Most of them suffer this in silence.

Though they comprise 15% of our American population, adolescents make only 9% of doctor's visits.[1242] When we physicians do see them, it is usually under duress. Clutching sports participation forms requiring our signature, teenagers populate medical waiting rooms as squirming, nervous masses of self-consciousness. They are decidedly uninterested in hearing about newly-licensed vaccines or recent advances in the prevention of atherosclerosis. Their goal in showing up at our office is to exit same as quickly as possible after a minimum of probing, physical or verbal. One doctor appropriately titled an essay on these awkward encounters "A Mutual Anxiety".[1243]

The medical issues that are most frightening to adolescents are the ones they least wish to discuss. When I examine my reticent and reluctant adolescent patients, sometimes the best consolation I can offer them is simple affirmation. Decades older than my patients and at the other end of the life cycle, I would rather stay there and die sooner than trade ages with them. This is a truth they can relate to.

During the tumult of adolescence, our children acquire 20% of their adult height and 50% of their adult weight. Internal organs and soft tissues increase in size, and blood volume expands. Bones remodel and increase their mass by 45%.[1244]

Heralding all this, the first sign of puberty that I notice in children is heightened body awareness. When that preoccupation is combined with the stress inherent to change and the physical demands of growth, the result is a recipe for discomfort. Mind and body connect, and adolescents end up with more than their fair share of physical symptoms. "Conversion reactions", where mental conflicts manifest as physical complaints, are more common during puberty.[1245] One study found an occurrence of 2 or more physical symptoms in the previous 6 months in 44% of adolescent girls and 28% of adolescent boys.[1246] Another survey of American 6th through 10th grade girls found that more than once per week, 29% had headaches, 21% had stomachaches, 24% had back pain, and 31% had morning fatigue.[1247]

When surveyed over a 4 to 6 month interval, almost a third of adolescents in one study reported feeling fatigued at one time or another, and not just in the morning. Half of those affected reported feeling fatigued over the entire study time period.[1248] When another set of researchers asked adolescents if they suffered from severe fatigue, 1 in 5 girls and 1 in 15 boys said yes. Over 2/3 of those affected had been suffering for over a month.[1249]

These statistics mirror the large number of exhausted adolescents I see in my own medical practice. Fatigue is a form of pain that should be acknowledged and empathized with. The fatigue that adolescents so often suffer can be truly disabling.

Teenagers also often suffer from headaches. In survey of 7900 middle school students, 1 of every 42 girls and 1 in 125 boys reported having 15 or more headaches per month. Over half of adolescents with chronic headaches considered them a hindrance to learning. Twenty percent of those headache sufferers overused medication in trying to treat them. [1250]

To treat their various ailments, up to 75% of adolescents self-medicate without checking with adults. As many of 20% of them take aspirin, which can cause Reye's syndrome, with swelling of the brain, liver failure, coma, and death. For stomach pain, 11% take ibuprofen and 13% take aspirin, both of which cause stomach irritation.[1251] Adolescents need guidance in choosing over-the-counter medicines, and they should be taught to never take aspirin or "salicylate"-containing products throughout young adulthood.

Besides the physical discomfort of adolescence, some of the stress of puberty comes from its unpredictability. Adolescents (and their parents) are intensely curious about how tall they will end up. There are a few formulas for making such predictions, none of which is completely reliable. Just for the record, here are the best known methods for estimating ultimate adult height:

1) take the height at age 2 years and double it,

2) average the height in inches of both biological parents, then add 2 inches for boys and subtract 2 inches for girls, or

3) multiply the height in inches at 3 years of age by 1.29 and add 16.6 for girls and 21.6 for boys.[1252]

Some of these calculations may be confounded by changes in population growth patterns between generations. Between 1973 and 1992, for instance, the average height of schoolchildren increased by over ½ inch. This was accompanied by a decrease in the number of very short children and an increase in the number of very tall children at the extreme ends of growth curves. These changes were most evident during early adolescence, and may best reflect a trend toward earlier growth spurts.[1253] When immigrant children are studied, the change over these decades is even more dramatic. A study of American immigrant children of Chinese, Asian, Hispanic, and Filipino ethnicity showed catch-up growth and increased growth velocities that often outpaced longer resident counterparts.[1254]

As the realities of final adult height move from calculator predictions to actual end size, parents often agonize over short stature. It is true that since 1900, 19 of our 28 presidential elections have been won by the taller candidate. Maybe that's why early suggestions as to what to title our national leader included "His Serene Highness" and "His Elective Highness". Between 1789 and 1988, only 2 American presidents were shorter than our national average.[1255] [1256]

On the other hand, there are some down sides to tall stature. General Napoleon Bonaparte deliberately placed tall men in the front lines in wartime, a practice that some believe contributes to French short stature.[1257] And at 6'4", isn't it harder for Osama bin Laden to blend in and hide out? There is also some data suggesting that taller people, especially men, have more cancer. Researchers from the National Cancer Institute found less malignancy of all types, and particularly less colorectal cancer, in shorter men. For their shorter female counterparts the correlation between cancer and stature was weaker, but shorter women had less breast and colorectal cancer, as well. [1258]

As for the psychosocial effects of short stature, multiple studies have addressed the issue, with similar results. University of Indiana researchers found "few significant differences…on measures of psychosocial and intellectual functioning" when they compared people referred to their medical center for short stature to the general population.[1259] In another survey, shorter European children were found no different than taller peers in self-esteem, conduct, emotional behavior, or IQ.[1260] A study published in 2004 compared short New York 6th to 12th graders with taller peers. There was "minimal detectable impact on peer perceptions of social behavior, friendship, or acceptance."[1261] Yet another researcher interviewed short children and their parents. Although 2/3 of the parents believed their offspring had been "adversely affected" by their stature, answers to behavioral questionnaires by those same parents and the children's teachers placed the youths "well within the normal range for psychological well-being."[1262] And while short children report bullying at about twice the rate as average height peers, the offending bullies are more likely to be short themselves.[1263]

In 2003, the American FDA first approved a brand of growth hormone for use in children with simple short stature. Analyses of 10 studies showed that 5 years' of 6 to 7 injections per week with the drug, at an annual cost of about $20,000, yields an average total height gain of 1.6 to 2.4 inches.[1264] Later calculations confirmed a cost of $52,000 per inch of height from growth hormone shots. It has been estimated that if all American children below the 3rd growth percentile were treated with growth hormone, the bill would be about $40 billion.[1265] [1266]

Aside from increasing their stature, it is unclear what growth hormone accomplishes for its recipients. In a New England Journal of Medicine review on the use of growth hormone for short stature, a pediatric endocrinologist pointed out that in limited studies, the treatment "has not demonstrably improved measures of quality of life for children." She concluded that "… the purported psychological benefits of achieving a taller stature are of questionable merit."[1267]

At the other extreme, tall girls were of concern for previous generations. In the 1940s, fast-growing girls from tall families were treated with hormones. This is now rarely done, and there are those who believe that growth hormone therapy may likewise lose its popularity. In commenting on the issue, a 6'3" tall woman physician wrote that manipulating height "medicalized even the most basic of genetically-acquired traits". [1268]

Parents and adolescents often agonize not only over physical growth, but also over the timing of pubertal development, as well. Girls usually develop first, starting their growth spurt at about 10 years of age. Boys start a little over 2 years later. Girls hit their maximum growth rate at about 12 and finish growing at about 16. Boys max out their growth rate at 14, and continue to grow for about 4 more years. Girls grow 2 ½ to 4 ½ inches a year during puberty, and boys shoot up 3 to 5 inches annually during their adolescence.[1269] It is believed that over 90% of the influence on the timing of puberty is genetically determined.[1270]

Sexual development in girls usually begins between 8 to 13 years of age. The first sign is breast development at an average of about 10 ½ years of age. Small "breast buds" under the nipple slowly enlarge, often at different rates on different sides. Breast development is not considered delayed until there is a total lack of any breast budding by age 13. Breast growth takes about 3 years to complete. The growth of pubic hair usually follows the start of breast budding within a few months. It takes about 2 to 3 years to reach the final, adult pattern. The development of underarm hair is less predictable, and its course is not very helpful in defining normal versus abnormal pubertal patterns. Menstruation usually starts 1½ to 2 years after breast budding, between 10 to 15 years of age. The interval between the 2 events is variable, however, and can span even 4 years.[1271]

The average age of the first menstrual period has fallen over the past 150 years, but seems to have leveled off in the past few decades. In 1830 in Norway, for instance, periods began at an average 18 years of age.[1272] At this point, most pediatricians don't consider sexual development in girls abnormal unless there are no pubertal changes whatsoever by age 14, or no menstruation by age 16, or no menstrual periods within 2 years of final, complete breast development. One of the most frequent causes of delayed or interrupted menstruation is eating disorders.[1273]

At the other end of the spectrum, the development of secondary sexual characteristics is not considered abnormally early unless breast or pubic hair development starts before age 7 in Caucasian girls or before age 6 in girls of African American heritage.[1274] Of note, early development can be stimulated by estrogen hormone products or medicines, including even estrogen- or placenta-containing hair products.[1275]

Psychologically, early development has negative effects on girls. Those who menstruate prior to 11 years of age have more behavioral problems and lower educational levels, thought to be due to earlier initiation of sexual activity.[1276] [1277]

Girls complete their skeletal development, closing up their bone growth plates, after menstruation starts. Those who develop and start menstruation late, often with a family history of delayed development, often continue growing into their late teen years. At whatever age they begin, menstrual periods often occur without ovulation for the first 6 to 12 months. They are typically irregular and unpredictable during this time. As ovulation begins, menses often get heavier and more uncomfortable. By the end of high school, 70% of girls surveyed reported using over-the-counter medicines for cramping during the previous 3 months.[1278] Girls who begin menstruating later also often take longer to ovulate and establish regular cycles. In general, it takes about 6 years after starting to menstruate for a predictable cycle length to define itself.[1279]

Just about the time they finally establish regular menstrual cycles, adolescents often leave for college. When living with other girls in close housing there, "pheromones" secreted by women often wreak havoc on their periods. These undetectable hormones work to make women in close proximity menstruate simultaneously. If new roommates start off 2 weeks apart in their cycles, they can both be thrown off schedule for several months as their cycle times try to synchronize.[1280] [1281]

Another common cause of irregular periods in both adolescent and adult women is "polycystic ovary syndrome". Considered a hormonal problem, but without a clear diagnostic test, polycystic ovary syndrome involves by definition enlarged, cyst-filled ovaries, best documented by ultrasound exam. Along with this comes irregular menstrual periods with infrequent or absent ovulation, acne, obesity, and increased hairiness. Polycystic ovary syndrome also often includes an unusual rash, called "acanthosis nigricans", which classically occurs in skin fold areas, usually on the neck, and appears as a dark, velvety thickening of the skin.

Up to 5 to 10% of women are believed to have some degree of polycystic ovary syndrome. If often runs in families. Over a third of mothers and sisters of women diagnosed with polycystic ovary syndrome also have it. There is no single, definitive test for polycystic ovary syndrome, and diagnosing it is not always easy or straightforward. The diagnosis is made by the presence of classic characteristics on physical exam, by ultrasound of the ovaries revealing multiple cysts, or also sometimes by lab tests demonstrating elevated levels of "androgen hormones". Blood tests are often also done to rule out other conditions that can mimic polycystic ovary syndrome. Treatment involves weight control, regulation of periods, and sometimes the use of medications to minimize symptoms from the excess of androgen hormones. Preventing the future insulin resistance, diabetes, high blood pressure, and extra cardiovascular risk that can accompany this syndrome is high priority, and when women with polycystic ovary syndrome are ready to start families they often need help with fertility.[1282] [1283]

Sexual development in boys starts with enlargement of the testicles between 9 and 14 years of age, usually at about age 12. Boys' height growth spurts don't begin until a year or more afterwards, and they continue to get taller longer, often through the teen years and even into the early 20s for late starters.[1284] Shortly after the start of genital organ enlargement in boys, pubic hair development begins. Deepening of the voice and growth of underarm and facial hair follow, but not always in sequence. During puberty, the testicles increase by 7 to 10 times in volume, and the penis increases by 3 to 4 times in length.[1285] The average age for the start of sperm production is 13½. The development of signs of puberty in boys younger than 9 years of age is considered abnormal,[1286] as is the absence of development by age 14. While late developing boys usually simply continue to grow more years, one study suggested that boys who start extremely late may not always attain their maximal, catch-up height.[1287] As they approach 14 years of age, boys lacking any pubertal development warrant a medical evaluation.

As boys produce larger amounts of testosterone during puberty, they also secrete small amounts of estrogen. Early on, this hormonal surge can cause breast development and enlargement, usually asymmetrically and often with tenderness. This "gynecomastia" occurs in 70% of boys[1288] and usually resolves on its own within 6 to12 months. Although normal, this pubertal gynecomastia is typically very alarming to adolescent boys. Real breast development and enlargement is striking and longer lasting. Boys with true, marked breast development are often simply taller and heavier than normal, but in up to 1/3 of cases there are a variety of different underlying medical causes.[1289] Marijuana use can stimulate gynecomastia, as can the use of topical lavender or tea tree oils.[1290] Boys with prolonged, large breast growth deserve a medical workup, but the 70% of boys with normal gynecomastia need simple reassurance.

Other issues in adolescent male health provide less cause for optimism. Testicular cancer is the most common malignancy in men between 15 and 34 years of age. All boys should be taught to regularly perform testicular self-examination. Somehow this message is not getting through, however. In one survey of Ohio teenage boys, half were unaware of the reasons for genital examination, and the same number did not use testicular protection during sports. Over 99% answered incorrectly when asked about symptoms of serious testicular conditions.[1291]

Yet another byproduct of adolescent hormonal surges, shared by both genders, is **acne**. Over 85% of teenagers are afflicted with it. In Western, industrialized societies, that is. In a study of Kitavan Islanders of Papua, New Guinea and Ache hunter gatherers of Paraguay, not a single case of acne could be found.[1292] Back in the West, 30% to 40% of teenagers say that their acne makes them feel "frustrated, embarrassed, anxious, or lacking in self-confidence."[1293] The emotional toll of acne has been reported to comparable to that resulting from many chronic diseases including diabetes, asthma, arthritis, and seizures. Patients with severe acne seen at university medical centers are more likely than others to be depressed, withdrawn, anxious, angry, and unemployed. Americans spend $100 million a year on over-the-counter acne products, and $1 billion a year on acne in total.[1294] There are a variety of oral and topical medicines to treat acne, and no single, agreed-upon regimen. In my own medical practice, I try to maximize the use of topical medicines before turning to oral drugs, but other physicians choose differently. There are many different acne remedies, but most boil down to a relatively few common ingredients that fall in to 5 basic categories:

1) topical antibacterials

2) topical drying agents that break up or prevent acne plugs

3) oral antibiotics

4) for girls, some birth control pills, and another hormone

5) strong systemic oral therapy with Accutane, a vitamin A derivative

Here is a rundown on the most commonly used acne remedies within each of these categories:[1295] [1296] [1297] [1298] [1299] [1300] [1301] [1302] [1303] [1304] [1305] [1306] [1307] [1308]

1) Topical antibacterials: **Benzoyl peroxide** is the oldest and best known member of this group. It is a topical antibacterial oxidizer that directly kills some acne causing germs. It also dries skin and may suppress oil production and break up plugs in pores. Resistance to benzoyl peroxide has not been reported in the bacteria associated with acne. It is an ingredient in many over-the-counter and prescription washes, gels, lotions, emulsions, and creams in strengths from 2.5% to 10%. Up to 10% of people are sensitive to benzoyl peroxide, and it can bleach-stain clothing. Most doctors start with lower concentrations, especially in people with very fair or easily irritated complexions. Topical forms of the antibiotics **erythromycin or clindamycin** can be prescribed either alone, or in combination-products with 5% benzoyl peroxide. **Azeleic acid** is yet another antimicrobial agent, sometimes used in cream form for acne. It has mild bleaching power. It may be less effective than other topical antibacterial medicines, but it also seems less irritating. The other infrequently used topical antibacterial is a sulfa antibiotic derivative named **sulfacetamide**.

2) Topical drying agents that break up or prevent acne plugs include mostly vitamin A derivatives called "retinoids". These medicines were first introduced in the 1970s, and come in a variety of strengths and many different formulations, including creams, gels, lotions, and even microemulsions. Retinoid topical agents include **tretinoin, adapalene**, and **tazarotene**. When treatment with these medicines is begun, things sometimes seem to get worse before they get better. This is because early, previously invisible acne can be inflamed from the drug action. Besides retinoids, other medicines with similar actions are the **salicylic acid and sulfur products** sold in many over-the-counter preparations. Some of these smell bad, but they can be useful for people whose skin is too sensitive for retinoids.

3) **Oral antibiotics** used to treat acne include **tetracycline** (which can cause nausea, and must be taken on an empty stomach), **doxycycline** (which can cause rashes with sun exposure), **minocycline** (which can pigment the mouth and teeth, cause inflammation of the liver and joints, and mimic lupus), **erythromycin** (which can cause nausea), **ampicillin** (a penicillin drug) and **trimethoprim-sulfamethoxazole** (which, as a sulfa drug, can cause rashes with sun exposure and rare, but horrible and sometimes fatal, sensitivity reactions). All these medicines can also cause allergic reactions.

4) **Hormonal acne treatments**, an option only for girls, include both **estrogen-containing birth control pills**, and, rarely, another hormone called **spironolactone** given together with them. Birth control pills increase the risk of blood clots, especially in smokers or people with sickle-cell disease and many other underlying conditions. Spironolactone can disrupt the menstrual cycle and cause breast tenderness.

5) The ultimate acne treatment is **oral isotretinoin**, a derivative of vitamin A and well known by its brand name, "Accutane". This very effective but last-line therapy attacks acne via many different mechanisms. It also has many side effects, the most frightening of which is birth defects of the heart, brain, and ears in infants born to mothers who took it while pregnant. Such tragedies have even affected babies exposed in utero to only a single dose. Other side effects of oral isotretinoin include inflammation of the liver; increased cholesterol levels; abnormal night vision; dryness of the eye, mouth, skin, and nasal tissues; joint and back pain; and symptoms of brain tumors. After treatment with isotretinoin, 40% of patients stay acne free, 40% relapse but only mildly, and 20% require retreatment. Although medications and mental health are always of concern in adolescents, one small study involving 12- to 19-year-olds treated with oral isotretinoin found them to actually have a decrease in depressive symptoms associated with the therapy.[1309]

Other forms of acne therapy include steroid injections, chemical peels, dermabrasion, narrow-band blue light exposure, and pulse-dye laser treatments. Herbal approaches involve calendula tea compresses, green bean tea washes, or the use of tea tree oil, aloe vera, burdock, witch hazel, lemon juice, or apple cider vinegar. Still other home remedies for acne include the application of fluoride toothpaste (not gel) or sugar onto individual acne spots, or the use of oatmeal or egg white masks over the whole face. In very severe, sudden fulminant acne flares, sometimes short courses of oral steroids are used to abort the attack.[1310] For milder acne, the one scientific study on the subject found that simple face washing twice a day significantly improved acne more than single daily washing. It is unclear if washing even more often is harmful or not.[1311] Also unclear is extent to which diet affects acne. Thankfully, chocolate was cleared as a culprit in 1969,[1312] but there is some data associating acne with dairy, especially skim milk intake.[1313] [1314] It has also been suggested that acne may be due to our highly glycemic, carbohydrate-rich western diet.[1315]

As is the case for short stature, there may be medical advantages to acne. Using data from men who attended Glasgow University between 1948 and 1968, British researchers found that former students with a history of acne had a lower risk of dying from all causes except prostate cancer. While the rate of prostate cancer was slightly increased in former acne sufferers, the risk of heart disease was much lower.[1316]

Besides acne, another infectious disease synonymous with adolescence is "mono", or **"mononucleosis"**. This syndrome was first described in the Russian medical literature in 1885.[1317] In full bloom, mono involves swollen glands, extreme exhaustion, a horrible sore throat covered with pus, fevers, and an enlarged spleen and liver. Most cases are caused by the "Epstein-Barr" virus, but up to 15% of cases are caused by a variety of other germs, including syphilis, toxoplasmosis, cat-scratch disease, herpes viruses, or cytomegalovirus, also known as "CMV".[1318]

Just as not all mono is caused by the Epstein-Barr virus, not all Epstein-Barr infections result in mono. Most Epstein-Barr infections actually have few or no symptoms. In populations with more crowded living conditions, young toddlers and children are infected with mono at very young ages, and they weather it better than Westerners who catch it later. In Hong Kong, for instance, the peak age for mono is between 2 to 4 years of age, and the disease is generally mild. By 10 years of age, almost 100% of Chinese children show blood immunity to the Epstein-Barr virus. In Africa, by 21 months of age, 78% in infants have already had their Epstein-Barr virus infections, but in one study not a single young such child could be found with any history consistent with what we consider mono.[1319] A British study found increased rates of mono in people who had lived in tropical countries, in girls, and in people with greater numbers of siblings. They also found evidence that besides being spread by household contact, mono can be a sexually transmitted infection. College students who always used condoms when having intercourse, and those with fewer sexual partners, had lower rates of mono than students with more partners.[1320]

Mono is a slow-moving illness. The incubation period after known exposure is 2 to 7 weeks. Most symptomatic cases in adolescents last for 3 to 4 weeks, but rarely symptoms drag on for up to 6 months.[1321] [1322] Although mono is usually more miserable than dangerous, it has its complications. The most feared is rupture of the spleen, which can occur in up to 1 in 1000 mono cases.[1323] Only 17% of splenic ruptures are spontaneous. Most occur after mild trauma during the middle of the illness.[1324] This is why many physicians keep patients with mono out of contact sports for a minimum of 4 to 6 weeks.[1325] Another worrisome complication of mono is airway obstruction from massively swollen tonsils. Whether steroids help prevent this is a matter of debate.[1326] Though one study found only 8% of mono patients qualifying for steroid treatment based on the severity of their airway swelling, 45% of mono sufferers are prescribed them.[1327] There is also debate about using antiviral medicines to treat mono. Early studies failed to demonstrate any benefits from treating mono with antiviral drugs.[1328] More recent data, from a small study with no placebo group, showed a possible benefit.[1329]

Neurological complications of mono include severe headache, facial "Bell's" palsy, temporary paralysis, and inflammation of the brain. Ten to 15% of mono cases are associated with inflammation of the liver, and 1 in 20 adolescents with the infection have yellow jaundice. Mono "hepatitis" also causes nausea, vomiting, and abdominal pain. Anemia and inflammation of the heart and other organs has also been reported in association with mono. Longer term, there may be an association between mono and multiple sclerosis. Although by 40 years of age 96% of adults show blood evidence of having had mono, people with multiple sclerosis have higher than average blood antibody levels against the Epstein-Barr virus. Those few people who show no blood antibody evidence of having had mono have a several-fold lower chance of developing multiple sclerosis than former mono sufferers.[1330] [1331] [1332]

The mono blood tests we doctors perform in our offices are notoriously inaccurate, with "false negatives" occurring in up to 15% of adolescents who really have the infection.[1333] A more accurate test for mono, unfortunately, is to administer amoxicillin, ampicillin, or other penicillin derivative antibiotics to anyone infected with it. **Nobody knows why, but the combination of mono infection and amoxicillin, ampicillin, or penicillin drugs results**

in a body rash 90% to 100% of the time. Patients are then mistakenly believed to be allergic to these medications. This is a well-documented but little known phenomenon.[1334] [1335] [1336] [1337] To avoid an uncomfortable rash, and to prevent being mistakenly labeled with a drug allergy, patients known or suspected to have mono should not take amoxicillin, ampicillin, or other penicillin antibiotics.

In addition to acne and mono, adolescents face many other infectious disease threats during their teenage years. Some infections are complications of "cosmetic" procedures, including tattooing, piercing, or plastic surgeries. Some of these procedure-associated infections are due to immunization targeted diseases, including hepatitis B and tetanus. Still other infections that adolescents suffer, most notably meningococcal meningitis, hepatitis A, whooping cough, and the sexually transmitted cervical cancer-causing human papillomavirus, also have corresponding vaccines that target them.

While previous generations of adolescents considered themselves past the shot years, times have changed. New CDC guidelines now recommend several vaccines for teenagers. For a detailed discussion of adolescent and childhood vaccines, side effects, and controversies complete with references for all data presented, please see my book *Factcines,* published in 2008 and available at Amazon.com. For now, here is a quick review of adolescent immunization issues:

Tetanus "booster" shots are recommended 5 years after the pre-kindergarten booster. Thereafter, no more than 10 years should elapse between subsequent doses throughout adulthood. Tetanus germs are all around us. We are unfamiliar with the disease only because most Americans are immunized against it. But immunity wears off over time. Teenagers and young adults often fall behind on getting tetanus booster shots, sometimes with disastrous consequences. Half of tetanus cases in 2003 in America occurred in people between 25 and 29 years of age. One of the 130 tetanus cases reported in the United States between 1998 and 2000 followed a tattooing procedure. Worldwide, tetanus is still a major killer. In 2000, the World Health Organization reported about 230,000 deaths from tetanus in 58 different nations.

Tetanus shots are given in combination with **diphtheria** vaccine. Like tetanus, diphtheria is a disease we Americans are unfamiliar with only because most everyone here is immunized against it. Diphtheria works by lodging in the throat and secreting a circulating toxin that damages all types of body tissues. Back at its base in the throat, infectious debris often dislodges in the airway and asphyxiates its victims. Some people quietly harbor diphtheria germs without getting ill, and vaccination does not eliminate such carriers. This maintains an ongoing reservoir of infection for when immunization levels fall. When there was a vaccine shortage in Russia and the Ukraine during the 1990s, over 5000 people died in resulting epidemics. Historically, before immunization against diphtheria was begun in the 1930s, diphtheria was the most common killer of toddlers in the industrial world. In some American cities, over a thousand children were lost to it every year.

Another past killer of American children was **pertussis, or whooping cough**. In the early 1900s, pertussis was the leading cause of death from infectious disease in children. In 1923, over 9200 children died of pertussis in the United States. As of 2004, it was estimated that the disease still killed 300,000 people worldwide, mostly in nations without vaccination programs. In America, disease rates fell after widespread immunization of infants was begun in the 1940s. Over time, however, it became apparent that vaccine immunity wears off during adolescence, and in 2005, whooping cough boosters were added to the diphtheria-tetanus combination booster shot given to adults. While pertussis in teenagers is in no way as dangerous as in infants, adolescents with the disease serve as a dangerous reservoir of whooping cough germs that can be passed to newborns or incompletely immunized older babies.

Shockingly, the most deadly disease of the early 1900s was neither whooping cough nor diphtheria. It was **influenza**. The worldwide "Spanish flu" pandemic of 1918-19 killed 20-25 million people. More Americans and Europeans died from Spanish flu than from World War I. One Alaskan village lost 85% of its residents to influenza within 5 days. What was particularly striking about that Spanish flu was that those most likely to be killed by it were strong young adults. In 2006, the CDC expanded previous recommendations and called for annual influenza immunizations for all children between 6 months and 18 years of age. When the 2009 swine flu reared its head, public health authorities' initial fears about its potential for trouble were fueled by deaths from the new strain that, while rare, occurred disproportionately among relatively young people. With its capacity to so quickly infect and fan out, influenza is a particular concern for students living in crowded dormitories.

In addition to the newly recommended adolescent flu shot, and the newly-licensed adolescent whooping cough vaccine, yet another new immunization now recommended for all adolescents is the **meningococcal meningitis** vaccine. Meningococcal meningitis is the most violent form of "spinal" meningitis, often killing its victims in hours. Because it can cause severe shock, survivors are often left multiple amputees from not being able to maintain perfusion of body tissues while ill. The director of the nonprofit National Meningitis Association that promotes awareness of the meningococcal meningitis vaccine is Ms. Lynn Bozof, who lost her college student son Evan to the disease after 26 days of illness and amputation of all 4 of his limbs. His case, so tragic, is not unusual. An older form of the meningococcal meningitis vaccine was previously recommended mostly for international travelers or beginning college students only, not because it was a dangerous shot, but because it was only partially protective. In 2005, however, a newer meningococcal vaccine was FDA approved that combines parts of killed meningitis germs with proteins that render the paired product much more stimulating to the immune system. This "conjugate" type vaccine is stronger and longer lasting, and it eliminates the silent carriage in the throat that helps meningitis germs get around. It is approved and recommended for all children over 11 years of age. Adolescence is a time of increased risk for meningococcal meningitis, possibly because of the crowded living conditions that exist in overnight camps and college dorms. Proven risk factors for high schoolers who get meningococcal meningitis include attending crowded dances or social events, and the use of tobacco or marijuana.

The very newest adolescent immunization is the **human papillomavirus, or "HPV"** vaccine, first licensed in the United States in 2006. It is also often referred to simply as the "cervical cancer vaccine". This is because over 99.7% of cervical cancer cases have been traced to HPV infection acquired via vaginal sexual intercourse. In 2005, cervical cancer killed 290,000 women worldwide, including 3710 Americans. Throat, penile, and anal cancer, as well as genital warts, can also be caused by HPV. Of the over 100 known human HPV strains, 2 cause 70% of cervical cancers. Both of the licensed HPV vaccines target those strains, and one also combats 2 additional strains that cause genital warts. HPV vaccination is given as a series of 3 shots over 6 months, and it is recommended for all girls over 11 years of age. There is debate as to whether it should also be given to boys to protect both them and their sexual partners.

Besides HPV, the hepatitis viruses are also sexually transmitted. **Hepatitis A** is usually referred to as "food-borne" hepatitis, because it is often passed in tainted food, especially in foreign countries. In reality, however, hepatitis A germs are spread in a variety of ways besides through food, including via sexual contact. The hepatitis A virus is a particularly hearty germ. It is capable of surviving over 30 minutes at 130 degrees, and for several years frozen at -94 degrees. Hepatitis A kills up to 1 in 333 people who become ill with it. Infections can drag on for several months, and they can then relapse. The hepatitis A vaccine was first licensed in the United States in 1995, and it is now recommended for all American children as a two-dose series. Although it is currently being incorporated into the toddler vaccine schedule, adolescents who missed it are also being immunized.

The other common form of **hepatitis, type B**, is known as "blood" borne hepatitis. It is passed via contaminated needles and also by household and sexual contact. Besides being immediately dangerous as an acute infection, often with liver failure, hepatitis B also kills people by causing liver cancer, especially in people who are infected with it early in life. One in 7 people who gets hepatitis B as an adolescent or young adult is eventually killed by it, either in the form of immediate or chronic liver failure, or from liver cancer later on. Since 1997, it has been recommended that all American infants be hepatitis B vaccinated in a series of 3 doses, and most states require it for school attendance. Unimmunized adolescents are at particular risk for acquiring hepatitis B as a consequence of their high risk behaviors, including intravenous drug use, sexual activity, or improperly conducted, unsterile tattooing or piercing procedures.

The medical complications of tattooing and piercing are a particular issue for our current generation of adolescents. Today's teenagers get more tattoos and pierces, in more places, than ever before. Among adults between 18 and 50 years of age, 24% have tattoos and 14% have body pierces.[1338] Up to 51% of undergraduate students now have body pierces, and 23% have tattoos. Female students are more likely to be pierced than males. Both genders are tattooed equally, but male athletes are more likely to be tattooed than nonathlete boys. Eighteen percent of pierces get removed, as do 4% of tattoos.[1339]

Though certainly gaining in popularity, piercing and tattooing are not entirely new phenomenon. Previous generations of Alaskan Eskimos and Aleuts used stones, bones, and ivory to pierce their children, a practice that was discouraged by European Christian missionaries. [1340]

As for the safety of more modern such procedures, the news is not good. One in three adolescents reports knowing someone who suffered a complication from body piercing.[1341] A study published in 2003 looked at 35 American body piercing establishments. Only 31of the 35 practitioners on duty had training, for a median of 15 days. Eight of them inadequately reprocessed piercing guns, and 4 inadequately reprocessed forceps or guiding equipment. Nineteen performed extra cleaning of equipment after using it on a customer known to have hepatitis.[1342] Another survey of 14 shopping mall kiosks offering piercing revealed that most use antiseptics inactive against typical causes of piercing infections.[1343] Perhaps best reflecting the general lack of safety in these facilities is the requirement by the American Association of Blood Banks that people with new pierces or tattoos wait a full year before donating blood.

Piercing and tattooing have been associated with the transmission of hepatitis, syphilis, HIV, papillomavirus, tuberculosis, tetanus, methicillin resistant staph "MRSA", and even gangrene and leprosy.[1344 1345 1346 1347] One study researching 626 new cases of hepatitis C ended up attributing 41% of them to commercial tattooing.[1348] A separate study blamed a third of hepatitis C cases on tattooing.[1349] In addition to the risks of infectious disease, tattooing can involve complications from the chemicals in the coloring agents used. The FDA reports that over 50 different colors are used in tattooing, from a variety of sources. Some are metallic salts, others are organic dyes. The metallic ingredients in some eyelid tattoos have been associated with tissue trauma from the magnetic forces involved when MRI's are done on people with them.[1350] Other tattoo recipients have been known to have problems with "sarcoid" bumps at the site.[1351]

Hepatitis C is passed not only by piercing procedures, but also by shared body jewelry used in piercing sites.[1352] Additional complications of 51 tongue piercings in one study included 13 cases of chipped teeth, 4 cases of injury to the gums, and 8 cases of increased salivation, as well as 2 infections.[1353] There is a report of a woman who almost died of an infection around her heart caused by a meningitis germ spread by a tongue pierce,[1354] and brain abscesses have also been reported after tongue piercing. One woman's tongue pierce caused severe facial nerve pain described as "electrical shock" like.[1355] Cartilage ear pierces are likewise particularly prone to infection and complication, including the type of severe scarring and disfigurement usually associated with boxing injuries.[1356 1357 1358 1359 1360 1361] Many cartilage infections are caused by a germ named "pseudomonas", which can be particularly difficult to treat.

One follow-up survey of body-pierced college students found that 37% of men and 22% of women later allow their pierces to close.[1362] Up to 20% of adults with tattoos have also considered having them removed,[1363] but erasing tattoos is not so easy. It seems that currently the best way to remove tattoos is to use pulsed lasers to rupture the tattoo ink particles and the skin cells harboring them. The process involves multiple treatments and is not cheap or perfect. Skin scarring or discoloration can result.[1364] Temporary henna tattoos are often irritating to skin, especially when the black dye p-Phenylenediamine "PPD" is added to make the tattoo last longer. PPD reactions can be severe and long lasting. In the 1930s, when PPD dyes were used to color eyelashes, there were reports of blindness and possibly 1 death from the chemical. Vacationing children often receive PPD containing henna temporary tattoos in other countries, and they are also often applied at fairs and amusement parks within the United States.[1365] A new, safer temporary tattoo ink is now being marketed by a New Jersey company. Their "Freedom-2" ink looks like permanent, colorful ink but it can be removed with a single laser treatment. [1366]

Yet another association with adolescent body piercing and tattoos to be aware of is their correlation with high risk behaviors. Adolescents with tattoos and/or body piercings are more likely to have participated in disordered eating, drug use, sexual activity, violent behaviors, and suicide attempts.[1367] [1368]

Piercing and tattooing are not all our adolescents do to alter their bodies. Increasing numbers of them are turning to plastic surgery, as well. In one suburban American high school, 2/3 of high school juniors reported knowing someone who had undergone cosmetic surgery.[1369] In 2003, surgeon members of the American Society of Plastic Surgeons performed 326,000 cosmetic procedures on teenagers. These procedures included 52,000 nose reshapings, 3200 liposuctions, and 7600 breast enlargement or reductions.[1370]

These statistics do not include procedures performed by physicians and surgeons from other specialties. Most gastric bypass and banding weight loss surgeries, for example, are performed by general or "bariatric" surgeons. The risks of weight loss surgery in still-growing teenagers are largely unknown. One consideration is the limited absorption of vitamins after such procedures, including vitamin D and calcium. This is of particular concern because up to 60% of bone mass is acquired during adolescence. As one review on the topic concluded, the long-term effectiveness of weight loss surgery in adolescents is "uncertain, and the need for further research is crucial."[1371]

Our adolescent girls are also undergoing more breast reduction and enlargement surgeries. Of great concern to me as a pediatrician is the effect these procedures have on the future breast feeding abilities of adolescents who undergo them. An article published in 2006, funded by a company that makes breast pumps for nursing mothers, documented some new findings regarding breast anatomy. New research has found that women have fewer milk ducts than previously believed, and that special sinuses previously thought to hold milk don't really exist. It was also just recently discovered that fat and milk gland tissue are more mixed together than we used to think. This means that it is very likely that in removing fat, some milk glands are going to be lost, as well. It also means that any lost glands, as part of a fewer number than formerly thought to exist, represent more of the available milk producing tissue than previously believed.[1372]

Less invasive than surgery, piercing, or tattooing, but also with long-term consequences, is skin tanning. Body conscious adolescents frequently participate in indoor tanning, often at salons. One in ten children 12 to 18 years of age reports having used a tanning bed in the previous year.[1373] A quarter of Caucasian American girls use tanning facilities 3 or more times while teenagers.[1374] On one Midwestern college campus, almost half of students reported using tanning lamps during the preceding year. This is despite 90% of those users admitting to knowledge that sun exposure causes skin cancer and premature aging.[1375]

The World Health Organization has formally recommended against tanning by any means for anyone younger than 18 year of age. They have also called for banning untrained personnel from working at tanning salons.[1376] And for good reason. Tanning can be dangerous in both the short and long run. One survey of emergency physicians found that almost half reported having treated patients for skin burns from tanning, 58% acquired at commercial tanning facilities. A quarter of injured patients had second-degree burns, and 59% had eye injuries, including corneal and retinal injury.[1377] When undercover investigators visited 54 commercial tanning facilities in California, not a single one complied with all safety regulations and recommendations. Only 3 of the facilities complied with recommendations regarding maximal light frequency limits. Over 57% were willing to violate parental consent rules.[1378]

Besides injuries from heat and light, there is another danger adolescents face when they tan. As is the case with so many other activities that put them at risk of harm, tanning can become an addiction for teenagers. Many frequent tanners in one study reported difficulty stopping. Tanners who started at younger ages, and those who found that tanning improved their mood, had the hardest time quitting.[1379] In another study, researchers evaluated beach-goers sunbathing in Texas. A quarter of them fulfilled the formal psychiatric diagnostic criteria used to define having a dependency to tanning.[1380]

Given the dangers and addictability of tanning, it is disappointing that one study found half of Colorado high school newspapers carrying advertisements for commercial tanning facilities, often with offers for unlimited tanning.[1381] State regulations intended to curb teen tanning are of unclear effectiveness. A phone survey study of tanning establishments in 4 states with youth access regulations found only about 2/3 of those facilities in compliance with rules denying tanning to potential customers under restricted ages.[1382] Later researchers found no difference in underage tanning rates between states with versus without regulations.[1383]

On a more positive note, the 2 factors that have been consistently effective in discouraging teen tanning are parental attitude and role modeling. In one study, the single best predictor of adolescent indoor tanning behavior was the perception of whether or not parents would allow it.[1384] Other data showed that teenagers participating in indoor tanning were much more likely than non-tanners to have a parent who tanned indoors.[1385 1386]

Parental attitude has much the same influence on adolescent smoking as it does on tanning. In one study highlighting the incredible power of parenting, teenagers who perceived both parents to strongly disapprove of smoking were less than half as likely as peers with more lenient parents to become smokers. That study found the influence of parental attitude to be just as strong a deterrent even when those disapproving parents were themselves smokers. And to complete the total coup that this data represents, parental disapproval of smoking trumped even the affects of peer smoking.[1387] Parental influence is likewise reflected in data showing that the more meals a family eats together, the lower the smoking rates in their adolescent girls.[1388] When eating out, laws restricting smoking in restaurants seem to also lower tobacco use in adolescents. One study found significantly lower rates of long-term, established smoking among youths from towns with strong restaurant anti-smoking regulations.[1389]

Smoking bans in homes have also been found to decrease rates of regular smoking, even in households where parents smoke.[1390] In school, students who participate in interscholastic sports have lower smoking rates,[1391] as did students who in one study participated in peer activities designed to counter the environmental influences encouraging smoking.[1392]

Unfortunately for parental smokers, other studies on inter-generational smoking have found role modeling to be more powerful in its effect on adolescent smoking. Multiple researchers have demonstrated a direct correlation between tobacco use in parents and children.[1393 1394 1395] And unfortunately for friends of smokers, still another study found that socializing with smoking peers greatly increases rates of smoking initiation for adolescents.[1396]

Outside the home, parents who disapprove of smoking have a powerful adversary. In 2003, tobacco companies spent about $15.1 billion on advertising and product promotions, more than double what was spent in 1998.[1397] This is in addition to the free advertising that exists in the form of smoking by actors in movies and television shows. A quarter of G-rated movies include depictions of smoking, as do 44% of PG and 77% of PG-13 movies[1398] and a large percentage of movie trailers.[1399] Multiple studies correlate greater media exposure to smokers with greater smoking initiation rates. [1400 1401 1402 1403 1404] The influence of exposure to movie smoking holds true even when the smoking character is a negative figure and not the film hero. One study found that for adolescents of lowest risk-taking behavior tendencies, viewing negative characters smoking was an even stronger influence encouraging smoking than seeing "good guys" smoke.[1405]

In American middle schools, 1 in 13 students report using tobacco.[1406] In high school, 20% of students are current cigarette smokers.[1407 1408] On college campuses, almost half of students report having used some tobacco product within the previous year.[1409] In 2004, Philip Morris USA sold 187.1 billion cigarettes. And they only have half the market in America.[1410] It has been estimated that over a lifetime of tobacco use, the expense of buying cigarettes equals the cost of buying a house.[1411]

All this is despite Centers for Disease Control data associating tobacco use with 443,000 deaths, 5.1 million of years of potential life lost, and $97 billion in lost productivity each year in the United States alone.[1412] Worldwide, the World Health Organization reports that smoking kills 5,400,000 people annually.[1413] Smoking kills more than twice as many people as AIDS, alcohol, car accidents, drug use, and suicide combined.[1414] This is through increased rates of many cancers including lung, mouth, stomach, colon, pancreas, kidney, bladder, cervical and more, and through chronic emphysema lung disease, and through increased coronary artery disease. It is also in addition to the increased rates of cataracts, hearing loss, dental disease, and increased facial wrinkling and aging that smoking causes. One study found male British smokers dying an average of 10 years earlier than non-smoking peers.[1415] Another study, from India, found a loss of 6 years of life for male smokers, and 8 years for women smokers.[1416]

What fuels these cigarette sales is, of course, simple addiction. To attract new smokers, tobacco companies lower the menthol content of cigarettes, which renders the product more acceptable for new smokers.[1417] Then, between 1998 and 2004, manufacturers increased the nicotine content of cigarettes by 10%, making them more addictive.[1418] Finally, as is the case with all other addictable activities, adolescents are uniquely susceptible to falling prey to dependency. One study found 10% of adolescent smokers losing the power to stop within 2 days of first trying tobacco. Another 25% were addicted within 30 days of their first cigarette.[1419] Among adult smokers, 82% started before 18 years of age. Almost no adult smokers report having first started after 25 years of age.[1420] A study that looked at lifetime tobacco use found that the adult smokers using the most tobacco were those who started smoking younger. In that study, men who started smoking before 14 years of age were twice as likely as those who started later to smoke 41 or more cigarettes per day.[1421]

Adolescents are unaware of their susceptibility to addiction. A third of preteens in one survey believed they could smoke without becoming addicted.[1422] Many adolescent smokers also mistakenly believe that alternative forms of tobacco are safer than cigarettes. They shun cigarettes in favor of cigars, chewing tobacco, and "hookah" or "water" pipes, also called "narghile" or "shisha". Hookah pipes consist of a water bowl, pipe, hose, mouthpiece, and head filled with sweetened or flavored tobacco. They have been in widespread use, mostly in India and the Middle East, for over 400 years, and they are now surging in popularity internationally. In the United States, a study published in 2008 found 20% of students on one college campus acknowledging hookah pipe use within the preceding month.[1423] A 2009 study documented hookah pipe use in 10% of high schoolers.[1424]

These alternative tobacco forms are false security. Hookah pipes deliver tobacco that is less irritating than cigarettes, making it only easier to get addicted to. The smoke from water pipes has high concentrations of tar, nicotine, carbon monoxide, and heavy metals, sometimes higher concentrations than in cigarette smoke. To make matters worse, alcohol and psychoactive drugs are often added to the tobacco in hookah pipes.[1425] Smokeless tobacco is likewise dangerous, delivering a high and concentrated dose of nicotine to the mouth. Chewing tobacco is associated with increased risks of mouth, esophageal, and pancreatic cancer and possibly lung cancer, as well. In India, half of oral cancers are attributed to smokeless tobacco use.[1426] Both hookah pipe smokers and smokeless tobacco chewers are more likely to eventually also become cigarette smokers.

When they do, access to cigarettes is no problem. Every published study that has investigated the issue has found adolescents able to purchase cigarettes on the internet easily and cheaply using either charge cards or money orders. State laws attempting to limit these sales have been feebly unable to curb them. One study found a "zero compliance" with California laws aimed at preventing internet tobacco sales to minors.[1427] [1428] [1429] In-person at the checkout counter, FDA surveys of retail stores have found a 26.6% rate of sales of cigarettes to minors.[1430]

Still in their teen years, 60% of smokers report adverse health effects from smoking including fatigue, cough, and diminished exercise capacity and endurance. The 70% of student smokers who have tried to quit also report withdrawal symptoms including nicotine craving, anxiety, and difficulty concentrating.[1431] Younger smokers who try to quit have a lower success rate than adults.[1432] If their barrier is guilt about the fate of tobacco farmers, it has been suggested we make them aware that new uses for tobacco plants are being developed. They include genetically engineering the plants to produce proteins for potential AIDS vaccines, collagen for drug delivery systems, or pollutant absorbers for environmental clean up.[1433]

If adolescents fail to heed our anti-tobacco messages, possibly it is because they literally can't hear us. While hearing loss used to be a grandparent issue, it is now a concern for our teens as well. The culprit here is loud music. For reference, be aware that human speech occurs at a noise level of about 55-66 decibels. Also be aware that decibels are logarithmic mathematical units, like the scales used for earthquakes, so that a little increase is a big difference. Here in the United States, Occupational Safety and Health Administration regulations require employers to provide hearing protection for workers exposed to noise over 90 decibels in loudness. There are those who advocate for interventions at lower levels, as serious hearing loss can occur with exposures between 85 and 90 decibels.[1434] When researchers attended 3 concerts involving 3 different musical genres, average noise levels were 99.8 decibels, and sound reached as high as 125.6 decibels. These levels exceed those allowed by all American public health rules. When formal "audiogram" hearing tests were done on attendees after those concerts, 64% of those who went without earplugs showed temporary hearing loss. Among concert goers who did wear earplugs, 25% also demonstrated hearing changes afterwards.[1435]

The news regarding recorded music listening is not much better. Most adolescents in one study admitted to often playing their MP3 players at maximum volume. The output level from those music players exceeds those capable of causing hearing loss.[1436] The public health impact of MP3 players is huge. In 2005, 28% of our American population owned one.[1437] The National Institute on Deafness and Other Communication Disorders has developed a "Noisy Planet" campaign to try to promote hearing protection for teenagers. Their interactive web site is: http:// noisyplanet.nidcd.nih.gov. [1438] Our national health goals in the United States, as set forth by our Department of Health and Human Services, include the reduction in hearing loss in adolescents and children caused by excess noise. France has set a 100 decibel limit on the output from iPods, and there have been lawsuits in America related to hearing loss in consumers, but it will remain to be seen what formal action, if any, our government will take to meet its goal of protecting our children's hearing.[1439] An internet based consensus of experts has recommended many strategies for preserving adolescents' hearing, including the manufacture of safer music listening devices and public health campaigns to increase awareness of the dangers of loud music.[1440] If their advice is ignored, our adolescents will be replacing their earpieces with hearing aids in very short order.

Most other medical issues in adolescents involve the field of **teen mental health**, a term some people find inherently contradictory. A 2009 Institute of Medicine report called on the White House to create a new entity to coordinate and implement efforts to improve the mental health of young Americans. It has been estimated that 14% to 20% of young Americans suffer emotional disorders, costing us an estimated $247 billion.[1441] In 2006, when the National College Health Association surveyed over 23,000 students at a variety of different American colleges and universities, their results were disturbing. Over half of students reported feeling hopeless at least once in the past year. Forty percent had felt depressed enough during the prior year to have difficulty functioning, and 10% had seriously considered suicide.[1442]

Suicide is the second leading cause of death in college students, and the third most common cause of death in younger adolescents. On university campuses in the United States, there are 1100 suicides and 24,000 attempts every year.[1443] Among younger adolescents 15 to 19 years of age, 11% of deaths are from suicide.[1444] Warning signs include previous suicide attempts or threats, preoccupation with death, antisocial conduct patterns, family stress, depression, extreme and impulsive behavioral tendencies, disturbed interpersonal relationships, previous sexual abuse, or a family history of suicide.[1445 1446 1447 1448] Over 90% of people who commit suicide have pre-existing psychiatric problems, mostly depression,[1449] and boys diagnosed with psychiatric problems before 8 years of age are more likely to later complete or seriously attempt suicide.[1450] Youths whose sexual orientation is bisexual or homosexual also have greatly increased suicide risks.[1451] Girls attempt suicide twice as often as boys, but boys complete it 6 times more often than girls.[1452] Girls are most likely to commit suicide via hanging or suffocation. Boys are most likely to use guns. [1453] Adolescents who live in homes with firearms, whether or not they are kept unloaded or locked up, have higher suicide rates.[1454 1455] Clusters of suicides have occurred after media coverage of completed suicides, with the numbers of additional deaths proportional to the intensity and amount of media attention.[1456] Depression, also, can be contagious. One study has found adolescents with depressed friends more likely to themselves develop depressive symptoms.[1457] Although the rates of suicide in American youths fell between 1990 and 2003, the trend reversed itself in 2003 when the rate increased by 8%.[1458]

Suicide prevention is a complex and difficult task. In 2004, suicide experts from 15 different countries met in Austria to review the world medical literature on preventing suicide. They were able to identify only 2 interventions proven effective in lowering suicide rates. One was "means restriction", lessening access to firearms, jumping sites, and lethal substances and drugs. The other helpful intervention was increasing physician skill in the diagnosis and treatment of depression. [1459] Fortunately, there is no evidence of power to suggestion when it comes to medical assessments for suicide. Screening for depression and suicidal thought does not itself seem to increase the risk of suicide. In one study that addressed this concern, no increases in suicidal thoughts were found in adolescents after they were questioned about factors associated with suicide.[1460]

In the best of psychiatric hands, however, many suicides can simply not be predicted. Family arguments, break ups in romantic relationships, and other sudden stressful life events can precipitate suicidal thoughts and behavior in very short order. A small survey presented at a medical meeting in 2006 found that only 4% of adolescents who attempted suicide left notes beforehand. Few attempts appeared to be premeditated, and the researcher in that study suggested that suicide prevention programs should address "impulse control" as well as mood and depression.[1461]

It is unclear how to best treat depression. There is talk therapy, there is drug therapy, and there is controversy as to which works better. With regard to drug therapy, there is also great controversy as to whether or not the very medications used to treat depression increase the risk of suicide in children and adolescents.

In March of 2004, the United States Food and Drug Association issued an announcement publicizing data showing increased risks of suicidal behavior in children and adolescents treated with newer antidepressant drugs. A year later, they expanded their public health warning to include all antidepressant medications. This followed a re-examination by the FDA of pediatric trials of antidepressants. During those tests, suicidal thoughts, behavior, or attempts were seen in 4% of children and adolescents treated with antidepressant drugs, but in only 2% of those treated with fake, placebo pills.[1462]

Other data has yielded different conclusions. In Hungary,[1463] Sweden,[1464] Australia,[1465] and America,[1466] [1467] higher rates of antidepressant use have been associated with lower suicide rates. There are also studies showing lower rates of suicide attempts after the initiation of antidepressant medicines.[1468] A study that investigated the effectiveness of counseling therapy for adults with a history of recent suicide attempts found 50% fewer repeat attempts in those given special counseling compared to those given "usual" care.[1469] Similar therapy for adolescents was found effective in preventing depression in one study,[1470] but in another study talk therapy was most effective when combined with medication. In that study the combined therapy worked for 71% of children, whereas medication alone worked for 60%, and counseling worked for 43%. Untreated children got better on their own 35% of the time.[1471]

Overall, however, considering the effect of all types of therapies combined, we are not having much success preventing suicide, at least in adults. Between 1990 and 2001, the number of children and adolescents diagnosed with depression more than doubled.[1472] One study documented that over that same period, there was a dramatic increase in psychiatric treatment and counseling for adults. Yet that same study found no corresponding significant decrease in suicidal thoughts, plans, gestures, or attempts.[1473]

As a supplement to formal psychiatric care, there are many other ideas about how to help people suffering from depression:

1) **Work out to work it out**. Exercise has been known to improve mood. Ever heard of a "runner's high"? One study of overweight adolescents found that supervised exercise therapy was associated with improved measures of self-esteem.[1474] Another study of British adolescents found a correlation between vigorous physical activity and better "emotional wellbeing".[1475] A review of the evidence favoring the use of exercise in treating depression pointed out that it produced "a sense of mastery and control".[1476] [1477]

2) **Sleep on it**. Rest and relaxation can be therapeutic. Sleep problems are a well known symptom of depression, but there may also be an element of cause as well as effect. Data presented at the 2009 annual meeting of the professionals who research and treat sleep problems showed that teenagers who are allowed to stay up past midnight on school nights have higher rates of depression and suicidal thoughts [1478]

3) **Break bread, as a family**. The more frequently a family eats together, the lower the rates of depression, substance abuse, and suicidal behavior in their children.[1479] In a study at boarding schools, boys fed breakfast together in a dorm reported feeling "more positive" than those who waited till lunch to eat.[1480]

4) **Practice positive thinking**. "Don't worry, be happy" is a concept that has moved from the Reggae to the psychiatric world. In the United Kingdom, doctors concerned about the overuse of antidepressants have tried recommending instead "biblio-therapy", or self-help through reading. Their recommended book list includes titles like: *Mind Over Mood*, *Emotional Confidence*, and *How to Stop Worrying*. Reading lists are written on prescription pads and handed to patients. The books assigned focus on teaching self-help techniques, and mental health workers later meet with readers to discuss the books and reinforce their messages.[1481] In a similar

vein, researchers found an improvement in mood in adolescents who used an internet-based course focusing on behavior change and resiliency building.[1482] Harvard has a "Positive Psychology" class that was the most popular elective on campus in 2006, and there is a Positive Psychology Center at the University of Pennsylvania founded by a former president of the American Psychological Association.[1483] That center's "Resiliency Program" for children has demonstrated, through 17 studies involving almost 2500 middle school students, that it can prevent or lessen depressive symptoms for over a year. Schools in Australia and the United Kingdom are now also trying the program.[1484] Developed in the 1970s, Behavioral Activation therapy likewise focuses on the positive, emphasizing pleasurable conduct.

Multiple herbal remedies have also been used to treat depression.[1485] The best known are Ginkgo and St. John's wort. These substances are marketed as "dietary supplements" instead of as pharmaceuticals. Under American law they are thus exempt from the type of testing required for prescription drugs. St. John's wort is an herb that interacts with liver enzymes to speed the metabolism of many drugs, thereby decreasing their blood concentrations and impairing their effectiveness. Among the drugs rendered less effective by St. John's wort are birth control pills.[1486 1487] Studies testing St. John's wort for the treatment of depression have reported response rates ranging from 35%[1488] to 75%.[1489] As another herbal alternative, Ginkgo leaves are generally considered safe, although they do increase the risks of bleeding and should not be used just prior to any surgery. Trials have not proven Ginkgo effective in treating psychiatric disease, and in one study it was no better than placebo for preventing seasonal depression.[1490]

When considering the use of "natural" remedies for depression, recall that over a quarter of prescription drugs have plant origins. The heart medicine digoxin is from the foxglove plant. Morphine is from the opium-producing poppy plant. Both of these drugs are potent and dangerous, though "natural". Tobacco, cocaine, lead, and arsenic are also "natural". "Herbal" remedies are drugs, and should be evaluated and regulated as such. If "herbal" remedies really work for depression, let's all hope that the companies that manufacture them will prove it and get them legitimately on the market. Until then, adolescent depression should be recognized as a serious enough disease to warrant evidence based care.

In assessing the mental health of adolescents, it is controversial whether "cutting", or "carving" is a marker for depression or an increased risk of suicide. This self-laceration, often in the shape of friend's initials, Christian crosses, or rock group symbols, is now very common in adolescents. In one study, 11% of 9th graders had performed deliberate self-harm within the previous year. One in 25 admitted to repetitive self-harm.[1491] Half of Goth subculture members and a quarter of Punk subculture youth self-harm.[1492] By college, a quarter of students report having harmed their own bodies.[1493] [1494] Self-inflicted burns often accompany cutting behavior, and a newer and emerging form of self-mutilation is the embedding of foreign objects into body tissues. Radiologists have recently reported the discovery of deliberately placed paper clips, glass, and staples in adolescent's arms, legs, hands, and feet.[1495] Self-injury is more common among girls than boys. It is also more common in adolescents with depression, anxiety, eating disorders especially bulimia, and in people with a history of sexual abuse. [1496]

Rituals involving self-mutilation date back to the Stone Age, when such practices often involved primitive religious or healing rites.[1497] In modern times, their significance is less clear. A small study of embedding adolescents has found them to have greatly increased rates of psychiatric problems, suicidal thought, and past abuse. "Cutters" are a more diverse group. They report a variety of different underlying motivations for their self-harm, ranging from simple peer imitation to expression of extreme inner turmoil.[1498] [1499]

One psychiatrist specialist on cutting attributes some of the rise in cutting to a desensitization to body alteration as also reflected in rising rates of body piercing. He quotes his patients as describing cutting as a way to "feel better", like "popping a balloon", to release anxiety. He also explains that some adolescents cut themselves as a way to cope with sexual abuse. The pain of self-injury relieves them of the disassociation with their body that most abuse victims feel. That expert describes cutting as the "opposite" of suicide.[1500] Cutters themselves have described their habit as addictive but mood stabilizing.[1501] "It makes them feel alive" one nurse who works with high risk adolescents declared.[1502] Another researcher who has published articles on cutting and self-injury deems the practice a "coping mechanism" that is considered a "friend" by many adolescents.[1503] That "friend" knows how to work a crowd. Cutting is now considered "epidemic" among our youngsters, and is labeled "contagious" by one expert who has seen many cases of cutting by middle school students who simply mimic what they've seen older siblings or friends do. [1504]

Such complacency with cutting is in opposition to the belief of many that self-injury is a marker for suicidal behavior. Almost all studies on the topic document increased rates of suicidal thoughts and attempts among self-injuring adolescents.[1505] [1506] [1507] Whether or not self-injury is in itself a suicidal gesture, adolescents who perform it should be carefully watched and monitored for suicidal thought or behavior.

Besides depression, the most common mental health issue diagnosed in adolescents is ADD (Attention-Deficit Disorder) or ADHD (Attention-Deficit and Hyperactivity Disorder). In the United States, 7.8% of our offspring between 4 and 17 years of age report having ADD or ADHD, and 4.3% of them take prescription drugs to treat it. Children most likely to be medicated are those who are Caucasian, English speaking at home, medically insured, and displaying "psychological difficulties".[1508] Americans use 90% of the world's Ritalin,[1509] and it is prescribed at different rates in different regions, with residents of some zip codes using as much as 20 times as much as other communities. Adjusting for population differences, some states use 6 times more Ritalin than others.[1510] [1511] Between 2000 and 2004, ADHD drug treatment of adults in the United States doubled, as well. In 2004 Americans spent $3.1 billion on ADHD medicines, up from $759 million in 2000.[1512]

Such variances in the treatment and diagnosis of ADD highlight the subjectivity of this issue. In a profession committed to evidence-based science, it is problematic to see such inconsistency. Diseases with definitive diagnostic tests do not usually exhibit such geographical differences unless there is a physical, environmental cause.

There is an organization named "Fight For Kids"[1513] that loudly protests the increasing use of psychiatric drugs in children. In response to parents' reports of feeling pressured by school staff to use ADHD drugs to make their children easier to manage in the classroom, there have been laws passed in several states aimed at preventing such coercion. In 2004, the United States Congress even passed into law an amendment to the Individuals with Disabilities in Education Act prohibiting "mandatory medication" in schools.[1514] [1515]

From another perspective, there are those who point to data showing that treatment for ADHD is associated with lower rates of substance abuse,[1516] [1517] lower rates of tobacco use,[1518] better driving habits,[1519] and better math and reading scores.[1520]

There are also those who dispute the existence of ADD as a disease. They consider it a behavioral response to our lifestyle. In one medical journal, an interesting commentary on ADD called it "an epidemic of modernity". The author of that article, a pediatrician in a practice who serves over 800 Amish families, points out that he has never had a single Amish child referred by a school for ADD type problems. The Amish culture uses no televisions or video games. He also noted a low ADD rate in Asian immigrants. He calls us "culturally addicted" to speed in electronic form, with less exposure to slow, patient activities like reading.[1521] Another physician has started a nonprofit institute named "All Kinds of Minds". He urges us pediatricians to individualize strategies for helping with children's strengths and weaknesses. He also reminds us that the same traits that cause problems in school can foster success in adulthood. He cautions us to "be careful whom we call normal and whom we call deviant."[1522] Echoing these thoughts, a psychologist and pediatrician have written an insightful and thought-provoking book named *The Diseasing of America's Children.*[1523]

Others challenge the way we treat ADD. They are developing, testing, and offering alternatives and adjuncts to drug therapy. There is now a book titled *Brain Exercises to Cure ADHD.*[1524] There is also an interactive computer program developed by researchers from Stockholm that has been found effective in training children with ADHD to have better working memory and fewer symptoms.[1525] An American company, Cogmed Working Memory Training,[1526] is now using a home-based computer program combined with a personal coach to implement such treatment for ADD. Still other researchers have had success in treating ADHD using biofeedback.[1527]

ADHD symptoms may also be tempered by addressing sleep problems. Many connections have been made between poor sleep and ADHD symptoms. In data presented at a 2009 meeting of sleep specialists, non-napping preschoolers had more ADHD symptoms.[1528] In another study published the same year, Finnish children with average sleep durations of less than 7.7 hours displayed significantly more ADHD symptoms than better-rested peers.[1529] Yet another study, from the United States, looked at children with both ADHD and sleep disorders due to snoring. A year after tonsillectomies and adenoidectomies to cure their sleep issues, half the children were no longer considered to have ADHD.[1530] Higher rates of asthma and eczema have also been noted in children with ADHD. Again, the connection is thought to be poor sleep from the itching or breathing problems.[1531]

The most common side effects of medications used to treat ADD are tics and decreased appetite. About 9% of children treated with stimulant medications for ADD get tics, usually transient. Less than 1% develops chronic tics.[1532]

Early data on the effects of ADD medications on growth left room for optimism. A study published in 1998 looked at 124 boys with ADHD. Temporary growth slowing through mid-adolescence in those boys was "not related" to the use of medications, and catch-up growth was seen in late adolescence. The authors of that early study theorized that the effect was caused by the ADHD itself and not its treatment.[1533] Later data was more definitive and less positive. A study published in 2003 showed "significant differences" in height percentiles between medicated children and siblings, over 2 years of treatment. These authors blamed the loss in height on the drug and not the disease. They concluded that "our findings suggest that the …growth suppressive effects" of Ritalin are "greater than previously suspected."[1534] Another study published in 2003 showed that within the first 6 months of treatment, 86% of children grew less than the average expected amount for height, and 76% actually lost weight. Children in that study lost about a half inch of expected height per year the first 2 years of treatment.[1535] The same author, publishing in 2005, reviewed 29 studies on the topic and reiterated that stimulant medications cause a loss of height of a half inch per year through the first 3 years of treatment.[1536] Large scale National Institute of Mental Health data published in 2004 also showed "continued, mild growth suppression" in children treated for 2 years.[1537] Preschoolers treated with stimulant medications were found to have growth rates 20% less than expected for height, and 55% less than expected for weight, in a study published in 2006.[1538] Children first treated later for ADHD, after already starting school, were found by the same researchers to be generally larger than expected for their age before treatment. After they were medicated, their growth rates fell and there was no make-up spurt to replace lost height.[1539]

Another area of concern involves the effect of ADHD medications on sleep. A study of 12 children in a hospital, where sleep could be closely monitored, found that a dose of Ritalin given near dinner time did not cause insomnia.[1540] Another small Israeli study found shorter total sleep durations in children treated with Ritalin, but the sleep pattern was consistent, and the amount of quiet sleep was unchanged for medicated children.[1541] A less direct reflection on the possible association between ADHD stimulant drugs and sleep problems may be the increase in prescription rates of clonidine, a medicine prescribed "off label" for children to counteract insomnia. Some believe that spikes in clonidine use are due in turn to sleep problems from increased ADHD medication use.[1542] A study that investigated this connection documented that 10% of people under 18 years of age who were prescribed stimulant drug treatment for ADHD were also given clonidine at some point. It was also found that when the ADHD medication was changed to a non-stimulant drug, the rate of clonidine use fell by over 36%.[1543]

Much less frequently, hallucinations and psychotic reactions have been associated with the use of ADHD medications. In over 90% of such cases reported to the FDA, there was no prior history of any such previous event or psychiatric condition expected to cause them. Hallucinations in children often involve sensations of the presence of insects, snakes, or worms on the child's body.[1544] Similar reactions to amphetamine drugs are well known, and Ritalin and Adderall are derivatives of them.[1545] [1546]

As stimulants, ADHD drugs affect not only the nervous system, but also the heart. Treatment with stimulant ADHD medications raises both blood pressure and pulse. Theoretically, they might also increase the risk for sudden death. In response to reports of 20 sudden deaths and 12 strokes in users of Adderall in that nation, Canada briefly took the drug off the market there in 2005, but soon thereafter they re-approved it for use. The United States FDA chose to change the labeling of stimulant ADHD medications to include a warning that they might increase cardiovascular risks in children with cardiac abnormalities. A review of the topic published by the American Academy of Pediatrics found that "there does not seem to be a higher risk of sudden death in stimulant-treated" people compared to the general population. They recommended respecting previous guidelines calling for extra cardiac monitoring or testing only in people with previous heart problems or symptoms including fainting, palpitations, chest pain, dizziness, problems with exercise, or in people with a family history of sudden death.[1547]

Whatever the consensus on the associations of ADHD treatment with growth, nervous system, and cardiac problems, there is one "side effect" of ADHD medications that is indisputable—in and of themselves, they are seriously addictive drugs with high rates of abuse. In 1996, The New York Times publicized reports of adolescents crushing and sniffing Ritalin like cocaine, or cooking and injecting it like heroin. It was revealed that a Virginia teenager had died while sniffing the drug.[1548] A newspaper for pediatricians also published an article headlined "Ritalin Abuse a Potential

Problem Among Teens". It told of a pediatrician who had been told by addiction workers that "some of what's being sold on the street as cocaine is actually Ritalin." It also warned doctors not to necessarily attribute missing medication to misuse by children. "There have been reports of adults abusing it", they divulged.[1549]

In 2001, another article directed at prescribers, published in the Journal of the American Medical Association, said it all in the title. "Pay attention: Ritalin acts much like cocaine" we doctors were warned. When injected, reported a psychiatrist and addiction expert, Ritalin produces a sensation "addicts like very much"… "They say it's like cocaine." Using brain scans and chemical tracers that are markers for the "dopamine" system that reflects our responses to reward and pleasure, researchers were "surprised as hell" by images of men given Ritalin. The scans showed Ritalin as more potent in its effects on the dopamine system than cocaine. "We didn't expect this", the lead researcher said. "…The notion that Ritalin is a weak stimulant is completely incorrect."[1550] By 2002, 11% of adolescents prescribed ADHD medications reported selling their drugs, and 22% reported misusing it themselves.[1551] Poison Control Centers noted increasing numbers of Ritalin overdose cases from abuse as early as 1993, and in most instances Ritalin was the only drug involved.[1552] In one 4 day period in 2009, eastern Iowa hospitals saw 7 people with reactions to abuse of ADHD drugs.[1553]

Leading the way for chronic abuse, students are now using ADHD drugs not only to get high, but also to get higher grades. Used as study aids, they are sometimes called "academic steroids". Up to 20% of college students are reported to be trying ADHD drugs, usually purchased from people who obtain it via legitimate prescription.[1554]

Perhaps the best evidence that ADHD drugs are being overprescribed is the sheer volume of them available for re-distribution. Most ADHD meds being sold on the street and abused are not being obtained by bands of armed adolescents breaking into pharmacies. They are obtained legally by prescription. If those prescriptions were so absolutely necessary, the medicines would be used by those whose names are at the top of the script. If doctors writing re-distributed prescriptions are being "fooled" by patients being dishonest about their symptoms, it only proves how subjective the entity of ADHD really is.

ADHD and depression are not the only psychiatric diagnoses on the rise in today's adolescents. In the United States, "bipolar", "conduct", and "anxiety" disorders are being diagnosed, and medicated, more than ever before, and at younger ages than ever before. In 2002, 6 times as many antipsychotic prescriptions were written for American children as were prescribed from 1993-1995.[1555] A study that followed 4100 children on antipsychotic medicines, comparing them to unmedicated peers, found the medicated children to have increased rates of type-2 diabetes, obesity, weight gain, increased cholesterol levels, and unstable blood pressure.[1556]

The soaring rate of "bipolar" diagnoses in children is particularly controversial. This used to be a disorder of adults, virtually unheard of in children. Its original name was "manic depression", and many of its features used to be considered normal in children and adolescents. This changed when popular books declared it "childhood's most misunderstood disorder", and when "Young and Bipolar"[1557] became a Time magazine cover story. In contrast, at a 2000 meeting of prominent psychiatrists gathered by the then director of the National Institute of Mental Health, doctors argued about whether the syndrome even really exists in children.[1558] As a Harvard Medical School professor pointed out, the increases in bipolar diagnoses seem similar to overdiagnoses of ADHD. [1559]

Increases in the diagnosis of anxiety disorders, including obsessive-compulsive disease, have been more modest. The rate of "conduct disorders" has also been more stable. Adolescents with conduct disorders used to be called "juvenile delinquents". The antisocial, aggressive, and defiant behaviors that define this syndrome are well known. Less recognized is the link between conduct disorders and suicide. Up to 7 years after diagnosis, adolescents with conduct disorders have increased rates of suicidal thoughts and attempts.[1560] Also little known regarding this problem is the hopeful efforts of many to treat it without drugs. Yale University, among others, has a Parenting Center and Child Conduct Clinic.[1561]

If there is truly an increased rate of psychiatric problems in our children, perhaps it reflects the stress they weather. Many of our offspring face great change and upheaval in their immediate families, while their extended families are further and further away. For starters, today's adolescents have been exposed to more divorces than any previous generation. By the time they leave for college, it is not unusual for children to have been through not only one but multiple divorces as their parents subsequently and unsuccessfully remarry. For a review of the literature on the effects of divorce on both adults and children, consider reading *The Case for Marriage*, by University of Chicago professor Linda J. Waite. A more recent study of "family breakup" found that after recent changes in family structure, adolescents had increased rates of many types of psychiatric disorders and higher rates of alcohol and substance abuse.[1562]

Along with divorce often come moves. Americans move from house to house, and from city to city, now more than ever. Residential mobility is a risk factor for increased rates of many problems including substance abuse,[1563] school dropout,[1564] teenage pregnancy, depression, suicidal thoughts, and behavioral and emotional disorders.[1565] Frequently-moving families have higher rates of other adverse family issues that also fan these flames, but after factoring them out, residential mobility still has negative associations for children and teens.[1566] Parents as well as children are stressed by moving. A long term study of women found increased rates of chronic poor health in women who had moved more often,[1567] and parental poor health, stress, and depression are whole family affairs. Offspring of depressed parents have more health problems, both physical and psychiatric.[1568] [1569]

Children in America don't even have to move homes to change schools. Within the same school district, children often attend one preschool, another kindergarten, another school for primary grades, another middle school, a different junior high, and then a separate high school. At some of those transitions, friendships are disrupted as previous cohorts of students are split up and fed into different subsequent schools. There are now some efforts at keeping children with the same teacher for 2 years instead of one grade only. This is called "looping". Perhaps physical continuity could also be added by keeping children in the same school building though 8th grade.

There are physical as well as emotional tolls to the stress our children face. In adults, chronic stress has been associated with poor immune system function, reflected objectively by lower blood antibody responses to flu shots, lower killing ability of some white blood cells, and less production of some other types of white blood cells. In one study, children exposed to chronic family stress had more illnesses than peers living in calmer environments.[1570] In children infected with HIV, who undergo careful immune system monitoring, stressful life events have been found to increase their risk of impaired immune functioning as reflected in blood test results.[1571] In the brain, animal studies have demonstrated an association between exposure to fear and stress and a one-third decrease in the proliferation of cells in the brain "dentate gyrus", an area involved in memory and possibly inhibition and self-regulation.[1572] [1573] [1574] [1575] Ongoing studies are underway to identify ways to help adolescents adapt or deflect stress.[1576] The American Academy of Pediatrics has developed a web site for teens and parents with positive advice on managing stress and building resiliency.[1577]

Emotional disorders and psychiatric issues cause great suffering in adolescents. One study found that mental illness seemed to have a greater association with adverse measures of quality of life 17 years later than did physical illness.[1578] Besides the human toll of suffering, there are real dollar costs to mental illness in children and adolescents. A report by the Institute of Medicine and the National Research Council released in 2009 called on the White House to create a new agency to coordinate efforts to prevent childhood psychiatric disease. The authors of that report calculated an annual cost of $247 billion from the effects and treatment of emotional and behavioral disorders. They also reported demonstrated benefits of about $11,000 per child from a $5000 investment in care directed towards preventing such problems. School based interventions as well as home visit programs have also yielded positive results.[1579]

Between 1992 and 2002, there was a 42% increase in the number of students seeking treatment at college counseling centers.[1580] Yet one study recently estimated that fewer than 25% of young adults with psychiatric disorders reach out for help. Least often treated are college students with drug or alcohol dependency.[1581] The stresses of college social life, combined with increasing levels of sleep deprivation and drug and alcohol use, are a recipe for depression.[1582] Since 1988, the number of college students diagnosed with depression has doubled. Their suicidal thoughts have tripled, and four times as many as before are sexually assaulted.[1583] Back in high school, increased numbers of students are feeling "disconnectedness", a new concept defined as a lack of perceived caring and closeness to the environment. Disconnectedness is a risk for unhealthy and dangerous behaviors in adolescents. It is associated with declining health status, increased school nurse visits, smoking, and less extracurricular involvement.[1584]

On the other hand, some of the increase in visits to mental health facilities by adolescents reflects a loss of the stigmatization previously associated with the use of such services. There is also dispute about the reported tripling of youth suicide rates since 1950. Some attribute it to a more accurate coroner certification of teen deaths. The rise in teen "suicides" parallels an equivalent "decline" in accidents.[1585] Single car crashes, for example, can often be classified either way. The suicide rates for high school-aged youths are actually about half the rate for adults.[1586] The rate of mental illness in adults and adolescents is "almost identical".[1587]

Whatever the controversies in teen suicide and mental illness rates, there is no disputing a skyrocketing in psychiatric drug prescriptions for children over the decades of my career. Between 2000 and 2003, spending on behavioral medicines for children and adolescents increased by 77%, exceeding spending for either antibiotics or asthma drugs.[1588] Not only did the overall use of psychiatric medicines increase, the use of new, atypical drugs rose even more. In 1998, 9% of health care expenditures for American children and adolescents were for psychiatric medicines.[1589] I am sincerely convinced that there is absolutely no child or adolescent with vital signs who some well-trained, well-meaning physician wouldn't medicate.

In extreme cases, psychiatric drugs can be life saving. Other times, it's a reminder to me of where the road paved with good intentions leads. I often think of the case from 1899 of an overweight 2-year-old with a misshapen head who was slow to speak and then displayed echolalia and some aggressive tendencies, throwing a small bowling ball at his sister and chasing a violin teacher with a chair. What cornucopia of drugs would we treat him with today? His name, by the way, was Albert Einstein.[1590]

Also filling prescriptions if he came back to the future would be Mark Twain. Regarding behavior that would now garner him a psychiatric diagnosis, he wrote that "My mother had a good deal of trouble with me...She had none with my brother Henry... The unbroken monotony of his goodness and truthfulness and obedience would have been a burden for her but for the relief and variety which I furnished in the other direction."[1591]

Watching the popular television series "Extreme Makeover: Home Edition", the mother of star Ty Pennington cries tears of joy. After being told her son was "unruly" and the "worst kid in his school", he now puts his energy into positive causes. Three other individuals said to suffer from ADHD include the founder of Kinko's, the man who developed electronic airline ticketing and started JetBlue, and the developer of the Kidstuff toy store chain. Their families, however, refused to consider their traits a form of impairment. A beautiful article in The Wall Street Journal by columnist Sue Shellenbarger details their successes.[1592]

There's a lot of overlap between normal and pathological in children and adolescents. Children are hyperactive compared to adults, and they have shorter attention spans. Adolescents have wider mood swings than adults, and they are sullen by nature. Looking at behavioral symptoms in girls, one study found no correlation between pubertal developmental stages and mood. However, when the girls were divided instead by hormonal staging based on blood estrogen levels, a trend was established. Significant associations were found between depressive mood, poor impulse control, psychiatric symptoms, and times of fast increases in hormone levels.[1593]

Whether hormonally-driven adolescent symptoms constitute an abnormality is a complex medical and philosophical issue. To compare and contrast, the rest of the world seems to be in way-better mental health than we Americans. When the World Health Organization and Harvard Medical School teamed up to study the issue, they found Americans suffering mental health problems more than people of any other nationality. Mexicans have half as much depression, and the lowest rate is seen in Nigeria.[1594] A British psychologist considers our high rates of depression a political issue. In *Depression and Globalization* Carl Walker blames deregulation and "ultra-capitalism" for our social problems and increasing rates of mental illness.[1595]

In 2006, there was an article in a scientific journal about a boy from northern Pakistan who had a genetic mutation rendering him unable to sense pain. Before researchers could examine him, he died on his 14th birthday after jumping off a roof.[1596] "If we only get sunshine, we only have deserts" is an old Arab proverb.

The Chicago Sun-Times once published a full page personal testimony by an 18-year-old who had been on psychiatric medications for 8 years. "The pills don't allow me to think," she wrote, "I'm just…there… Will we become a society run by pills that keep us from being unique and normal?"[1597] Sigmund Freud's stated goal was not to make people happy, but rather, in extreme cases, to transform "hysterical misery into ordinary unhappiness." Writer Andrew Solomon, in his memoir titled *The Noonday Demon; An Atlas of Depression* defines the opposite of depression not as happiness but rather as a "vital sense of purpose". He reflects that "to be creatures who love, we must be creatures who can despair".[1598]

In a magazine written by and for bereaved parents, there is an article by a man who had lost a child to leukemia. In it he describes his reaction to a movie named *Pleasantville*, the story of a perfectly nice town without problems. The writer agrees with the movie's main character, "who finds this world enjoyable at first, [but] soon realizes that it is all wrong. People need to experience love, anger, sorrow, depression, joy. People need colors, not black and white, to make life real,"[1599] the reviewer explains. We have a lot to learn from this perspective, articulated by, of all people, one who has suffered life's ultimate loss. Could we doing our adolescents a disservice when we deprive them of the color blue?

Physician Ronald W. Dworkin certainly thinks so. His book *Artificial Happiness; The Dark Side of the New Happy Class*[1600], is a stinging indictment of our medical profession's mass medication of unhappiness instead of true, severe depression. Another writer actually titled his book *Against Happiness: In Praise of Melancholy.*[1601]

Time might not heal all wounds, but it does pretty well for most bumps and bruises we all inevitably suffer along the way. In the Book of Exodus, Moses is given the recipe for the incense used in the Holy Temple in ancient Jerusalem. G-d tells him to include the foul smelling "galbanum" in with the other, sweet spices.[1602] The theory is that this represents the full variety of what we meet in life. "Sweet and sour" makes for rich food. How are our quickly-medicated children supposed to know this?

Enjoy your teenager's general good health and your joint lack of contact with pediatricians. Empathize with your adolescent's body preoccupations, hormonal roller coaster, and physical transformation. Today's teens will be out of our jurisdiction and under the care of internists in the blink of an eye…

CHAPTER 11

● ● ●

LET THE GOOD TEENS RULE

Enjoyable Aspect of Parenting Adolescents Number Ten: Adolescents are introspective and idealistic. They care deeply about social issues we've long since given up on. Could someone older in the same situation have written, as did Anne Frank, that people are really good at heart? Enjoy your adolescent's perspective and let it inspire you.

Let's reflect on some famous adolescents past. Probably the most famous is Anne Frank, whose diary has been translated into over 50 languages and sold to over 20 million people. Anne Frank's story has also been made into a Broadway play, a movie, and a choral production. The original diary is displayed in the annex where it was written, which is now a museum.

Anne Frank, as we all know, lived to see none of this. At 13, she went into hiding with her family at the back of her father's business office annex. Two years later, the Frank family was discovered and sent, via a Dutch camp and then Auschwitz, to the Bergen-Belsen concentration camp, where Anne died before her 16th birthday, just a few weeks prior to the liberation of the camp. Her diary reveals astonishing optimism and hope. "…if I look up into the heavens, I think that it will all come [out all] right,… and that peace and tranquility will return again" she wrote. "In spite of everything," she also declared, "I still believe people are good at heart."[1603] Mirroring that same optimism, a contemporary of Anne Frank who survived the Holocaust was recently reunited with a note she threw from an uncomfortable, jam-packed transport train taking her to Auschwitz. "Regards from the train from Mauthausen into Germany," wrote the then adolescent. "We are well…"[1604]

Yet another consummate adolescent optimist was little Agnes Gonxha Bojaxhiu, from Macedonia. She lost her father when she was only 8 years old, and her mother supported the family by sewing clothing. At the age of only 12 Agnes felt a calling and decided to devote her life to the betterment of humanity. She never wavered. She started her own International Religious Family and specialized in working with impoverished people, while living among them. She spoke some of my favorite quotes, like "If we really want to love we must learn how to forgive," and "If you judge people, you have no time to love them", and "Love is the fruit of all seasons at all times and is within the reach of every hand" and "We cannot all do great things, but we can do small things with great love" and "...in the end, it is between you and G-d". She summarized her feelings about modern life by writing "everybody today seems to be in such a terrible rush, anxious for greater developments and greater riches and so on, so that children have very little time for their parents. Parents have very little time for each other, and in the home begins the disruption of peace of the world." When the former Agnes Gonxha Bojaxhiu grew up, she was known the world over as Mother Teresa.

At Anne Frank's age, only 15, American slave Harriet Tubman deliberately placed herself in harm's way. She blocked the path of a plantation overseer who was chasing another slave trying to escape. The overseer was enraged, and hit the young Harriet in the head with an iron counterweight. It fractured her skull and left her with seizures. For months after the injury, Harriet Tubman lay very ill and almost died. She survived, and went on to be a famous conductor on the underground slave railroad, helping at least 300 slaves reach freedom as far away as Canada. During the Civil War she volunteered for the Union army, and afterwards she opened homes for the needy, using her war pension to help fund them.[1605]

Harriet Tubman's legacy of freedom fighting was sustained through the civil rights movement of the 1950s. While Rosa Parks was 42 years old at the time of her heroic bus ride, much credit is also due to younger members of her generation. When Mrs. Parks died in October, 2005, our nation mourned her loss and honored her accomplishments. As we re-opened the books on this tumultuous and painful time in our history, some unsung heroes came to light. Many of these leaders of the civil rights movement were young teenagers at the time. Author Jeffrey Zaslow wrote a beautiful and informative tribute to them, published in The Wall Street Journal. He told of Barbara Johns, a then 16-year-old from Farmville, Virginia who organized a 2-week boycott of her underfunded high school in protest of the contrast between it and neighboring, affluent, white schools. With help from the NAACP, the situation came under the review of the United States Supreme Court. When the court declared such segregation illegal in its 1954 landmark *Brown versus Board of Education* case, the Johns' family home was burned to the ground. As a child, now Professor Daureen Loury of Arcadia University took a swim in a community pool with her brother, tolerating chants against her from an exodus of white swimmers. At only 15 years of age, and 9 months before Mrs. Parks' refusal to surrender her seat, adolescent Claudette Colvin did the same. Dr. Clayborne Carson, director of the Martin Luther King Jr Research and Educational Institute at Stanford University, considers the civil rights movement "the story of a teenage revolt."[1606]

In 1957, when 9 African-American high school students attended a previously all white high school in Little Rock, Arkansas they had to be escorted in by National Guard troops. They tolerated a year of verbal and physical abuse. One of them later characterized it as "a hellish torture chamber." Their academic career there only lasted one year because the next year, to avoid integration, Little Rock closed its public schools.[1607] During the civil rights movement, grade school children were among those jailed. Older students pioneered non-violent sit-in protests, and were in turn subjected to not only arrest but assault with high-pressure water hosing by fire fighters. Three students, members of The Student Nonviolent Coordinating Committee, were beaten and shot to death by Ku Klux Klansmen. One of those murdered students, James Chaney, was African American, and the others, Michael Schwerner and Andrew Goodman, were Jewish.

During her conductor years, Harriet Tubman's nickname was "Moses". The original Moses also fought for slaves. As a young man, Moses saved a slave's life when he killed an overseer who was severely beating the worker. For the crime, Moses was arrested and almost executed. He then fled Egypt. The Bible tells us many other stories of adolescents gone right. Moses was alive to help that slave only because he was pulled from the river and rescued by young Egyptian Princess Basya, in defiance of her father Pharaoh's orders to kill all Jewish babies. Several generations later, Jonathan also defies his father to warn his friend David of King Saul's plan to kill him. David survives to leave us the inspiring legacy of his psalms. Before Moses' time, young Joseph resisted despair after being sold into slavery by his own siblings. He acts modestly and admirably in fending off the improper advances of Potiphar's wife, and later helps and forgives the brothers who threw him into the pit.

While the accomplishments of Moses, Harriet Tubman, Anne Frank, and Mother Teresa were well recorded, the contributions of most adolescents go unsung. Although 16- and 17-year-olds comprise only 2.8% of our population, they donate 8% of our blood supply. In doing so, they suffer more adverse reactions, especially bruising and fainting, than older donors.[1608] A Red Cross official once wrote that if teenagers were barred from donating blood, the effect would be a "considerable crisis in the blood supply."[1609] In my own medical practice, I am now seeing teenagers go a step further and donate bone marrow. One of my patients, over the objections of her parents, happily donated bone marrow to a social acquaintance. Another of my patients donated bone marrow to a total stranger. I am proud to know these adolescents, who put idealism into action.

Over the years, I have also seen a surge in teen volunteer activities. Every year, I fill out an ever-increasing number of medical clearance forms for service programs. My patients spend spring breaks and summers building homes, schools, and hospitals. During the rest of the year, they clean cages at animal rescue societies. In one formal program in my area, which my own daughter participates in, they befriend special needs children and spend time with them every weekend. They also fund raise. Every year, high school students in my community choose a charity and raise funds to support it. One year, the inspiration for the charity choice was a patient of mine, and the money collected went to further research on the medical issues she so bravely faces. At the time, however, she was not herself a student at the high school. Her adolescent brother lovingly made the nomination on her behalf. In 2007, high school students in my district raised $360,000 for their charitable cause. Students at a New York school raised $250,000 for research on a disease afflicting one of their teachers.[1610]

In Chicago, the YMCA sponsors an annual day when high school students take over the City Council. One year while in "power", they raised taxes to fund a lakefront shelter for the homeless. They've also seriously considered releasing county inmates if they want to join the military, and they agonize over ways to protect babies whose mothers suffer drug addiction. "They're raising more questions than we do" commented a real alderman on his return one year.[1611]

And maybe that's one of their reasons for being here. Adolescents raise our consciousness. They challenge and question, and teach while they learn. Life will yield them some bitter answers, but in the meantime, enjoy learning from them. Let their optimism and hopefulness inspire and improve us.

CHAPTER 12

• • •

BETEEN GENERATIONS

Enjoyable Aspect of Parenting Adolescents Number Eleven: Adolescents bridge generations and give great joy to their grandparents, who know that the difficult years are temporary. Adolescents are also dearly loved by their younger siblings, who look up to them no matter what their issues. And further from home, extended family and adolescents are often able to keep lines of communication open. Share in grandparents' wisdom of their vision of the forest through the trees, and enjoy your adolescent's potential in your family's future.

Imagine getting lost on a vacation tour, in a country whose language you do not speak. As you wander the streets, increasingly tense, you finally hear your mother tongue and warmly greet a former acquaintance. One you haven't seen in years. Someone you always found annoying, and frankly, never liked. He guides you back to the cruise boat and becomes your BFF.

Parenting adolescents is a journey like none other. It will take you places you never expected to be. It will unleash feelings you never knew you had. It will send you running for bridges you never thought you'd set foot on.

Years ago, one of my then adolescent children accompanied me to a family event, complete with a shocking blue streak of hair. Certain relatives and I have significantly different views on such issues. I side with the child psychiatrist I once met who said they could sum up their entire attitude towards adolescents by reassuring parents that "all hair grows out eventually." Personally opposed to piercing and tattoos for teenagers, I was happy to use hair, instead, as a peace offering for one of my children at our family negotiating table. After a deal was struck, I called a delighted purple-haired patient of mine for styling instructions and headed to the nearest beauty supply store to purchase a rainbow in hair dye from a visibly shocked sales lady. Most of my relatives would have handled the issue differently, and their discomfort with my choice was palpable. When I felt a tap on my arm from my sister in law's conservative, childless octogenarian Aunt Mary, I expected the worst. Instead, she looked at me with a smile, winked, and whispered "I think it's kinda cute!!!" It was a great act of kindness I will never forget.

What gave this remarkably thoughtful woman the ability to transcend our differences? Wisdom and age. And what brought it to the forefront? An adolescent.

One of the many great joys of a pediatric practice is meeting grandparents. I usually find their perspective more gentle and tolerant than ours. Their teachers were experience and adversity.

First and foremost, the generation up from ours did not suffer from "affluenza". "Working out" meant working. Children and adolescents didn't need running tracks and football fields to be physically fit. One-third of the founders of Plymouth were children, and after 6 years of age boys helped clear forests and farm the land.[1612] After the Civil War, one-third of the mill workers were aged 10 to 13 years.[1613] For most of history, child labor has been a redundant term.

While it was a positive advance to eliminate this form of child abuse in America, maybe the pendulum has swung too far. "If you eat the fruit of your labor, you will be happy," King David teaches us in his Psalms.[1614] And some have interpreted the Fourth Commandment to rest on the Sabbath as an equally binding order to work the remainder of the week. It starts, after all, with the words "Six days shall you work…"[1615] When we deprive our children of labor, replacing their effort with landscapers and cleaning help, we may not be doing them favors.

We particularly fail when we try to replace the deep satisfaction of real jobs well done with sports awards for minimal accomplishment. There is even now a "participation trophy" many teams distribute to all players. In 2005, The Wall Street Journal featured an article on "Trophy Overload".[1616]

Some researchers have linked increased physical activity with lowered rates of depression, and one study found less psychiatric disturbance and behavioral problems in children living in very large families, where helping out is a necessity instead of an option.[1617] The average family of our grandparents' day had more children than today's families. Combining the lack of modern appliances with an absence of restaurant food, children had actual chores, and developed self-esteem through work and the satisfaction of really helping households run.

Our predecessors also had continuity in their lives. Divorce was the exception rather than the norm. Families moved much less often. Schools were not divided into separate primary, middle, and junior high institutions, and children often stayed in the same classroom building from kindergarten through high school.

As for birth and death, they were frequent and first-hand experiences for our grandparents. Many of our children have never seen a human corpse. They are exposed to death only through television and movie imagery. This was tragically not the case for earlier generations. Losses were commonplace household events, and survival was the exception and not the rule for children past. In the 17th century, 40% of all deaths occurred in children under 2 years of age. There is a Charles Dickens poem named "Drooping Buds", referring to the time when a third of all coffins made in London were child-sized.[1618]

The awareness of death that our grandparents couldn't avoid gave them a perspective that could do us some good. The shadow of death can cast a clarifying light on life. This was certainly the case for Alfred B. Nobel, who opened his newspaper one morning to his own obituary, mistakenly published about him when his brother died. Reading it had a profound effect on the wealthy Swedish inventor of dynamite, and it motivated him to establish the Nobel Prize to honor excellence.[1619] If an unexamined life is not worth living, then the introspection that exposure to mortality breeds may be bitter but medicinal. Grandparents' familiarity with death gives them a life cycle awareness that renders them better equipped than us to deal with adolescents. I once met a young adult who, on his own, overcame a serious drug habit during early adolescence. Even with the best of medical care from an addiction specialist, this is no easy task. But for this admirable young man, there was a special motivating force–the sudden death of his mother. "It gave me a whole new view of life," he told me. "It forced me to face my own mortality and make better use of my time here."

Grandparents enjoy a well deserved credibility with teenagers, who for all their issues are pretty good at recognizing truth and sincerity. When I see adolescents with their grandparents, there is affection and honesty and often better behavior and more restraint. There is a country song featuring a beautifully and formally dressed Loretta Lynn performing with a long-haired, much younger man in jeans. Their contrasts are overcome by their obvious joy in simply singing together. They reflect the innate respect and an earned admiration our teenagers have for their predecessors. A study from Emory University, published in 2006, found higher self-esteem, especially in girls, in families where there was shared reminiscing about past family history.[1620] Our children are hungry for perspective, and who better to provide it than grandparents? In 2009, there was an article on fashion in Newsweek magazine subtitled "Why Grandpa's clothes are suddenly chic." Evidently, they suddenly are. Boys who grew up wearing cutting-edge gear are now sporting sensible coats and comfortable shoes. I do not consider this a simple fashion statement, but rather something much deeper, an "ache for authenticity" as the fashion writer dubbed it.[1621] In America, we are not just what we wear, we are what we drive. Here, too, seniors are setting a trend. The Wall Street Journal recently ran a front page article on the new popularity of "Grandma" and "Grandpa" cars. Termed "donks" or "scraypers", the cars are being eagerly purchased from retirees who can no longer drive.[1622]

Grandparents purchase 1 of every 4 toys sold in the United States.[1623] They are famous for doting on our offspring. But overall, our children's grandparents are less materialistic than we are, and less likely to define themselves by their previous work or careers. When I ask, adolescents often can't tell me what their grandparents did for a living. This says a lot about both generations. Careers and income are one of my generation's false idols, and a source of too much of our perceived self-worth. When we define ourselves by our work we don the emperor's new clothes and miss out on the wisdom of our Aunt Marys everywhere.

Though many of our compromises are made on our families' behalf, we have taken it to a new extreme by failing to differentiate between necessities and luxuries. A recent magazine article regarding engagement rings was subtitled "for some, a one-carat diamond won't do." It relates that "young brides from Boulder to Boston are flashing rings twice the size of what their moms once wore."[1624] This is not progress. Children can have meaningful lives while sharing bedrooms and bathrooms, and they can be driven around in budget and used cars. Their future inheritances can be quietly saved instead of being spent on large mortgages.

Our children's grandparents likewise would never have fallen for differentiating our precious time with our children into "quality versus quantity", paving the way for guilt-free relinquishment of child-rearing to third parties. While children have an inherent sense of intent, and know our pain when we must leave them to support them, they also know when Nanny is there so we can play tennis or shop. And where did the term baby-"sitter" come from? We do not give birth to furniture to sit upon, but rather to precious souls that need our attention and time. A village helps, but its potential pales in comparison to the power of devoted parenting.

Teenagers also appreciate their grandparents as an often last vestige of ethnicity and faith. In our big "melting pot", the first thing that got fried, after ethnic identity, was faith. We are a much more secular generation than those before us. There is a parable I once read of a man making a long journey over tough terrain. His fellow travelers lighten their load by carrying only bare necessities, but this man drags with a violin. When asked why he tolerated the extra weight, he explains that for him, the violin was not a burden, but a way to ease his trek by playing beautiful music along the way. Our faith is that violin. It was a tool and life-line for our parents. We treat it as dead weight. Our children's souls are capable of hearing that music, and our parents are better than we are at playing it.

A high school in my area recently started a partnership with a local retirement home, matching its senior retirees with "teens in turmoil". The program is named "Partners to Success", and has been in place since 2005. "I always believe you can save them" said one mentor.[1625] I believe that if anyone can, it's our seniors. And history bears this out. Researchers from Finland studying 18th and 19th century population records found that having a grandmother in the family resulted in 2 extra grandchildren per decade that the matriarch survived past 50. Not only did families with grandmothers have more children, they had healthier offspring. Children with a grandmother alive at their birth had greater survival rates than those born into more isolated families.[1626] Over a century later, grandparents still make measurable medical differences in children's lives. A study published in 2008 found that children cared for by grandparents had significantly fewer injuries.[1627]

We are the only species to outlive childbearing years and participate in multigenerational childcare. Even primates continue to bear children throughout their entire lifespan, leaving no time for attention to skip a generation. An anthropologist researcher from the University of Michigan has credited this expanded lifespan as "critical…in the development of the human culture" and largely responsible for "population expansions and cultural innovations."[1628] [1629] There is anthropological evidence that this was appreciated by even primitive peoples. Researchers have unearthed an ancient skull, from around 1.77 million years ago, where the jawbone demonstrates a loss of all but one tooth several years before death. To survive toothless in an era of only raw food, this tribal elder had to have special family support.[1630] In more modern times, French Symbolist painter Emile Bernard showed his appreciation for his grandmother by immortalizing her on canvas in his famous *Portrait of Bernard's Grandmother*. Art lovers attribute Bernard's career to the influence of this beloved woman. The painter had a "difficult" childhood, and it was his grandmother who nurtured his artistic ambitions.[1631]

Our adolescents can be the glue between generations, in more than one direction. In "blended" families, I often see adolescents demonstrate great playfulness toward younger siblings from new step-parents, often with heavy hearts after bitter divorces. Only children can bridge such gaps.

One of my favorite characteristics of adolescents is their reluctance to judge others. They will defend their friends to the bitter end, and when push comes to shove, I find teenagers remarkably compassionate and willing to offer the benefit of the doubt. This is their idealism in action.

In the Jewish faith, there are prescribed blessings not only for food and drink, but for many other entities and events, as well. There is even a blessing to be recited at tragedies, which translates as an acknowledgement and reaffirmation of "The One True Judge". I have heard Rabbis declare this blessing after the final hours of far too many patients. When could we best be excused for judging others than during the ultimate tragedy of losing a child? Grief and anger often overlap, and bereaved parents' pain can take many forms and head many directions. If, during the depths of life's universal worst nightmare, grieving parents are reminded to let The Almighty do the judging, shouldn't we keep it in mind, too? As frustrating as it may be to watch our adolescents ignore their peer's shortcomings, admire their refusal to be judgmental.

Adversity and crisis can bring out the best in us. One of the most moving stories I have ever heard is that of the chaplains of the United States Army Transport Ship the Dorchester. On February 3, 1943, the ship was torpedoed by a German Nazi submarine. To allow more room in life-boats for others, the 4 chaplains refused to board them. Father John P. Washington, Reverend George L. Fox, Reverend Clark V. Poling, and Rabbi Alexander Goode remained on the ship, holding arms, and praying together as it sank. May their goodness inspire us all, and may their memory continue to be a blessing.

These 4 remarkable men knew Whom to call on. They turned to G-d, and to each other. And so should we, in the throes of parenting's toughest years.

Enjoy the challenges and insights our teenagers give us. Enjoy having a need for the experience and wisdom of grandparents. Look forward, G-d willing, to assuming the role of family elder and having wide-eyed little faces listen as we reminisce about cell phones the size of bricks.

If there is such a thing as a true "parenting expert" it's the quiet people on Medicare and not the wrinkle-free faces on talk shows. There's an old joke about how speeding taxi drivers are better than clergy at making people religious because more people pray in the back of taxis than anywhere else. On the bigger road of life, adolescents accomplish much the same thing. When parents of teenagers meet, ethnic and socioeconomic differences melt away. Enjoy this opportunity to explore your spiritual side, and savor the acquired taste of appreciating all generations of your extended family.

CHAPTER 13

• • •

ROUGHED AND HUMBLED
ANOTHER REDUNDANT CONCEPT:
THE HUMBLED PARENT

Enjoyable Aspect of Parenting Adolescents Number 12: Adolescents keep us humble. Inflated egos are not an occupational hazard for those of us who parent teenagers. We're way over the thrill of out-bragging the newer moms in playgroup. We're just grateful if our offspring lack parole officers and are unfamiliar with the back seat of squad cars. Enjoy your adolescent as the ultimate antidote for arrogance.

Without ever entering a political race, I nonetheless hold elected office. I am the Mayor of Loserville. I have been nominated for Duke of Dorkdom, and I am assured I am fully qualified to serve as Governor of Goaway. I am the mother of a teenager.

One of my adolescent children once expressed dismay at me writing a book about their age range. "If you know so much about teenagers," I was asked, "how come you haven't figured out how not to be so annoying at home?"

Things aren't much more ego-boosting at the office. One of the (many) great joys of being a pediatrician is the excitement I share with families when I weigh and measure their growing babies and toddlers. Parents marvel at watching growth in progress, and often ask for predictions about their children's ultimate height. There are some formulas we pediatricians are taught to predict adult height, but I have long since abandoned their use. This is because my patients change their growth pattern and avert their genetic potentials starting the nanosecond I go on record with any predictions about their future size. They do this, I am convinced, to make their doctor look really stupid.

Occasionally, life imitates work, and my personal offspring need medical help. None of their ailments is fixable. Their afflictions include an array of aches, twitches, spasms, and spots whose only common denominator is that any and all treatments fail to cure them, especially when prescribed by an expensively-educated physician parent.

If I had to summarize doctoring and parenting in one word it would be "humbling".

Humility is not a trait our culture values. Our American idol is "self-esteem". According to current standards, here are the most common causes of lack of self-esteem in our children:

being awarded less than above-average grades
having less than above-average social skills
displaying less than above-average athletic skills
having a less desirable than above-average appearance

The problem with this standard is that it ignores the reality that it is average to be average. The majority of the bell curve occupies the area in the middle. Outside of that, there's just as must space below as above that average range. This is a fact of life. But in a single generation, we have redefined average as abnormal. We worry that children "afflicted" with being "less" than above average will lack self-esteem.

Though this might seem like a trivial, philosophical issue, it has profound implications in the medical care of adolescents. Over and over the "self-esteem" card tips the balance as parents wrestle with decisions about medicating children or allowing elective plastic surgery procedures. That marginally justifiable breast reduction that will ruin future breastfeeding is a done-deal when the surgical candidate's "self-esteem" is mentioned. Psychiatric drugs for children who "could do better" in school become a necessity when the negative effects of less than above-average grades on "self-esteem" are brought up.

There is a game children play by repeating a word over and over until it sounds foreign and loses its familiarity. That's where I'm at with "self-esteem". I've heard it so often, in so many contexts, that it has ceased to be meaningful. Our obsession with self-esteem is a values issue. It's about our standards for defining whom we adults hold in high esteem, not about children's inherent standards for self-worth.

If our children feel a lack of self-esteem from getting average grades, then we have failed to teach them the role of school in their lives, and the value of the knowledge and skills they possess. Good grades are not the end-all and be-all. They are not the only ticket to gainful employment and responsible adult life.

If our children feel a lack of self-esteem from being less than popular, then we have failed to teach them the importance of quality over quantity, and the value of true friendship. Social success is not a single dimension.

If our children feel a lack of self-esteem from having less than average athletic abilities, then we have failed to teach them the limitations of the human body, the enjoyment any game well played, and the value of knowing how to accept defeat with grace.

If our children feel a lack of self-esteem from having a less than above-average appearance, then we have failed to teach them the value of simple good health.

Our children's "self-esteem" issues are about us and not them. There's an old story about a schoolboy being chided by his father to study more. The father points out that when Abraham Lincoln was the same age as this son, he was reading several hours a day and walking miles to the library. The boy replies that when Abraham Lincoln was same age as this father, he was President. The standards we set for our children can be deflected back at us. If we accept only above-average performance from our children, then we must be ready for them to respect only the same from us. Do we all make above-average salaries? Do we all look and dress better than average? Are we all above-average in our social functioning? Are we less worthy of respect and esteem because of this?

It started as "grade inflation", pressure for schools to abandon the bell curve and give more above-average grades than warranted. In 2004, a survey conducted by Princeton University, involving 8 Ivy League colleges, Stanford, MIT, and the University of Chicago found that half the grades given in undergraduate courses were A's.[1632] When researchers surveyed students at the University of California, a third of students reported that they expected B's for simply attending lectures, and 40% said they deserved B's for completing required reading.[1633]

It has reached the point where The Wall Street Journal once featured a lead article on our "Trophy Overload" of rewards for children.[1634] Two years later it published an article on the challenges bosses face when the "The Most-Praised Generation Goes to Work".[1635] It was subtitled "Praise Inflation" and it detailed the challenges current-day supervisors face on the job. The article had a subsection titled "The Art of Constructive Compliments". When young employees are chronically late reporting for work, for example, bosses are told to focus on the positive if they start showing up on time, recognizing "improvement". While waiting for tardy employees, supervisors having trouble adjusting can use their time reading books written by a popular corporate consultant titled *1001 Ways to Reward Employees,* [1636] or *The 1001 Rewards and Recognition Fieldbook.*[1637]

On psychological tests, college students in 2006 were 30% more narcissistic than in 1982. Is this a surprise? There are a variety of versions of the Narcissus story, but none of them end well. In most of them, he dies at the river, staring at his own reflection. Likewise, our children may be drowning in praise. Higher social self-esteem in girls and higher athletic self-esteem in boys are associated with higher rates of teen alcohol use.[1638] As an antidote to our culture of praise, try reading Professor Jean M. Twenge's *Generation Me; Why Today's Young Americans Are More Confident, Assertive, Entitled—and Miserable Than Ever Before.*[1639] Could our emphasis on praise instead of self-improvement be part of the reason for our surging divorce rate? Are we giving our children the tools to transition from "me" to "we"?

Just as power corrupts, ego taints. The natural extension of pride that becomes hubris is the basis of Greek tragedy instead of success. Recall that among young adolescents, one study found bullies to be generally psychologically strong and in high social standing among peers. Making their actions even more shameful, their victims tended to be emotionally distressed and socially excluded.[1640] Also recall that in teenagers, higher social self-esteem in girls and higher athletic self-esteem in boys are associated with higher rates of alcohol use.[1641] Showering children with praise is neither emotionally healthy nor intellectually honest.

If we want our children to feel good about themselves, we are going to have to feel good about them first, but on reasonable terms. Sigmund Freud, when asked to define mental health, replied simply *"lieben und arbeiten"* meaning "love and work". If our children develop into loving and working adults, that's the end point of successful child-rearing. And getting there is better helped by humility and service than by ego and self-esteem.

By Biblical tradition, my faith tells us that there are four people who lived lives devoid of sin: Benjamin (Jacob's youngest son), Amram (Moses' father), Jesse (King David's father), and Kilav (King Solomon's brother). Yet on our Sabbath, these four are not at all whom we mention in a special prayer to bless our children. Instead, we bless our sons to be like Ephraim and Menashe, and our daughters to be like Sarah, Rebecca, Rachel, and Leah. Not perfect people, but real people. Not ones who never erred, but ones who struggled with human imperfection and overcame it to make their mark and leave our world a better place. These are our role models.

King David, in his timeless psalms, describes himself as a "worm".[1642] Abraham considers himself "but dust and ash".[1643] And why is it Moses that G-d honors and chooses to speak to "mouth to mouth," "in a clear vision"? Because Moses was "extremely humble, more so than any other person on the face of the earth." "In My entire house he is the trusted one," G-d declares.[1644] And Moses is presented with the Ten Commandments and the Bible where? Not on big old Mt. Everest, but on little Mt. Sinai, the "humblest" of all the mountains.[1645] I know of no faith that disapproves of modesty or humility. The Jewish Talmud advises us that "one who runs from honor—the honor will catch up with him." Mother Teresa, revered by millions of people, considered herself "a little pencil in the hand of a writing G-d".

Rediscover and celebrate average. It's our ultimate, human common ground. And admire humility. Enjoy the unpleasant truth that as our adolescents humble us, they only make us better.

CHAPTER 14

● ● ●

SEEING THE FOREST THROUGH THE TEENS

Enjoyable Aspect of Parenting Adolescents Number Thirteen: Adolescents need us. They need our love, our discipline, our monitoring, and our guidance, even and especially when they don't want it. Endless devotion is the essence of parenting. Having an adolescent to agonize over is a gift and a privilege (and it's never boring). Appreciate and enjoy it.

There is a story of an exhausted mother bird flying her baby birds to safety across an ocean. While hauling each one, she asks if they will care for her in her old age. When they answer "yes", she stops, drops them helplessly into the water, and flies back for another. Finally one tells her what she wants to hear—"I don't know if I'll be able to help you, Mama, but I will definitely take care of your grandchildren." Only that bird merits a whole trip across the ocean, to safe, dry land at the other end.

And that's the real "forest through the teens". Our adolescents are our only and every hope for a future. As they leave our nest, they ensure our survival.

In our quest to keep them happy, we give our adolescents a lot of room to spread their wings. No other culture or generation has ever allowed their children the autonomy we give suburban American teenagers. Consider the Brazilian Indian tribes of the Upper Xingu. A book published by the Harvard University Press describes how they handle adolescents. "When they reach puberty, boys and girls remain in seclusion inside the hut for prolonged periods, which can amount to 1 to 2 years for males…receiving a lot of food and being introduced to the handicrafts and oral traditions of the tribe. At the end of the period, when the adolescent comes back to the community life, his physical and muscular condition are remarkably improved."[1646]

Substance abuse and delinquent behavior are not problems in traditional Upper Xingu families. Compare and contrast this with how we treat our vulnerable, pubertal offspring. We give them cars, car insurance, cell phones, charge cards, cash, and privacy. More teens than ever in our suburbs have both their own bedrooms and bathrooms, which they often consider private and "off limits" to other family members. All this is fertile ground for trouble. The extra space we give our adolescents may be too much for them. They are best off when we fill the void with family. Instead of stuff, they need us.

The New England Journal of Medicine once published an article investigating what worries teenagers. At the top of the list for American adolescents, above concerns for their own death, illness, or disability, was a fear of their "mother or father dying". This is data to remember and be inspired by.[1647] Our children need us, and deep down they know it.

Congressional Speaker of the House Nancy Pelosi has wisely described her best job training as having had 5 children in 6 years. Harvard graduate Bracha Goetz describes being a parent and homemaker as "the most challenging intellectual pursuit I could ever envision."[1648] During the 2004 American presidential election, it was alleged that First Lady Laura Bush had never had a "real job". What an offensive inaccuracy! A Democratic party spokesperson soon issued a clarification that the charge was in error and that Mrs. Bush had, indeed, worked as a librarian. Wrong again! Nobody who raised twins lacked a "real job".

Our ultimate of "real jobs", parenting, is harder than any payroll position. Parenting violates every labor law ever conceived of. Its 24 hours a day, 7 days a week, 365 days a year. There's no sick time or "parental leave". From a medical perspective, infection control is nonexistent. Bombardment by germs from every body fluid and cavity is the norm, and physical illness is a constant, occupational hazard. From a political perspective, our children are the ultimate minority rule, mimicking both monarchs and dictators. From a job description perspective, parenting requires expertise in psychology, conflict resolution, medicine, education, nutrition, and economics. And that's not a "real" job?

By the time our children reach adolescence, we've put in a lot of time on that job, but we're not done. Much like laundry, parenting is never, ever finished. We sometimes feel temporarily caught up when the hamper is empty, but there's always more on the way. Cell phones and car keys in hand, our teenagers need us more than ever. They are at the most danger-ous time of their lives. Just as the end of labor in childbirth, the "transitional phase" is the hardest, so it is with growing up. The end of childhood, ado-lescence, is life's "transitional phase".

When they reach the end of their twigs, inchworms hurl themselves in the air, twisting and turning, seeking the next branch and journey. Our adolescents are likewise propelled helplessly into adulthood, their next climb.

In Hebrew, the root of the word for "womb" (rechem) is the same as the root for "compassion" (rachamim). Once that safety zone is exited, the Chinese designation for "mother love" is "teng ai" a combination of the symbols for "pain" and "love".[1649] Further along, the root word of one term for "young" in Hebrew is related to the same root as for "hidden".[1650] After a quarter-century of watching adolescents grow and develop, I agree with these word associations. The compassionate love and accompanying pain of parenting may seem as if it has propelled us to a dead end as our chil-dren hit adolescence. This is because our adolescents are indeed "hidden". They are hidden treasures. The loudest of thunder heralds the break of the harshest of droughts. The same bees that sting us also produce the sweet-est honey. And given time, love, and protection, our adolescents likewise yield us beautiful fruits for all our loving, painful labor.

There is a blessing in my faith that is to be recited "after seeing a close friend after a lapse of 30 days or more." It is not widely used in that con-text. With phones and e-mail, I have occasionally pondered whether it is still ever really relevant. Then one day, into my office came an adolescent who, despite tender, loving parenting, had gone through a particularly rough spell. But now her spirit was back. Her depression had lifted, and her spark had returned. She leaned against her mother with appreciation and affection. She asked me to take her off my prayer list and replace her spot, instead, with wishes for her grandfather to recover from cancer. Her beautiful soul was no longer "hidden". I found the re-union blessing in my prayer book and recited it with newfound meaning. As hidden and dark as our adolescents can seem, they come back. They are a blessing all along, though sometimes in disguise.

As researchers probe the "hidden" in our adolescents, recurrent themes emerge. Over and over again, good medical literature documents a teen-age vulnerability to addictions, and then establishes addiction as the common denominator in a wide variety of adolescent problems, from substance abuse to habitual gambling to internet use. A vast array of medical research also documents the vulnerability of adolescents to engage in high-risk behaviors, from dangerous driving to eating disorders to physical aggression to sexual conduct with infectious disease risks. And over and over again, studies then establish links between those activities and our unfortunate environmental influences.

That's the bad news. The good news is that we are not powerless. Our hold over our adolescent children is not over. Our attitudes and influences still make a difference. Our efforts still matter.

In 2004, researchers published an article correlating family meals with well-being in adolescents. The more often families eat together, the less their teenagers use tobacco, alcohol, and marijuana; the less depressed and suicidal they are; the lower their rate of eating disorders,[1651] and the higher their grades.[1652] Nearly half of teens surveyed in one study cited meal times or just afterward as the best time to talk to parents about important issues.[1653] Another study found that trying to eat less at meals, and wanting to be thinner, among adolescents, is associated with the perception that their weight is important to their mother.[1654] Sadly, but still underscoring our influence, other researchers have documented long-lasting effects of negative parental comments about eating in sensitive, body-conscious college students.[1655]

Parental influence extends beyond the dinner table. Adolescents whose parents have anti-smoking rules are less likely to use tobacco.[1656] Interventions that increase parental monitoring of adolescents decrease not only smoking, but also marijuana and other illicit drug use, as well. Parental monitoring likewise lessens the use of weapons, disciplinary suspensions from school, and the number of sexual contacts without condoms.[1657] Eleven- to 13-year-olds home alone after school are 2½ times more likely to initiate sexual intercourse than those supervised by an adult.[1658]

The physical home environments we parents create also matter. Access to guns is associated with higher rates of suicidal thoughts, and the presence of alcohol, cigarettes, and marijuana in households is associated with a greater use of them by adolescents who live there.[1659] In the community at large, public youth anti-tobacco campaigns have been shown to decrease smoking susceptibilities, and when funding falls and they are cut back, there have been documented subsequent increases in illegal cigarette sales to minors.[1660]

When a program aimed at preventing high-risk behaviors in inner city boys involved parents, there were significant improvements in those teen's violent behavior, drug use, sexual activity rates, and use of condoms.[1661] A study of urban girls found a link between higher levels of perceived parental supervision and lower rates of sexually transmitted diseases.[1662] In an American Academy of Pediatrics publication based on data from northern California high schools, it was suggested that "high levels of parental monitoring do in fact discourage both boys and girls from beginning to use drugs."[1663] For adolescents in Colombia, where illegal drugs are especially available, one study found that the single element that cancelled out other risk factors for marijuana use was "a close parent-child bond".[1664] Closer to home, a survey of adolescents from Georgia "demonstrated a consistent pattern of health risk behaviors...associated with less perceived parental monitoring." In that study, adolescents from homes with less parental monitoring had over double the rate of frequent marijuana use than peers from more supervised homes. They also demonstrated riskier sexual behaviors with greater numbers of sexual partners, increased alcohol use, and more arrests and violent behaviors.[1665]

A National Longitudinal Study on Adolescent Health that collected data on over 12,000 students in 7th through 12th grades likewise correlated "parent-family connectedness" with better functioning on multiple measures of well being involving sexual, emotional, and behavioral dimensions.[1666] Such results are echoed by numerous other studies. A paper published in 2001 reviewed the medical literature in this area and cited 39 different references. The authors concluded that there is a definite association between the amount of parental monitoring and interaction, and adolescent involvement in drug and alcohol use, high risk driving, and juvenile delinquency.[1667] Another report, authored by 33 researchers and sponsored by the Dartmouth Medical School, The Institute for American Values, and the American YMCA, was published in 2003. It is a "Report to the Nation from the Commission on Children at Risk" and makes fascinating reading. Its title, "Hardwired to Connect",[1668] summarizes the 109 studies it cites pretty accurately. Our adolescents want and need to connect with us.

The further good news here is that when we do connect, supervise, and help our children through their vulnerable adolescent years, we are not simply delaying inevitable addictions. Exposures to addictable activities or substances are less likely to lead to dependency for adults than for teenagers. Adolescents who drink before 15 years of age are 4 times more likely to become alcohol dependent than people who wait until age 20 to first try alcohol.[1669] Smokers who try cigarettes during adolescence are those most likely to become addicted. [1670] Eighty-two percent of tobacco addicts started smoking before age 18, but almost no smokers start over age 25.[1671] When tobacco chemical byproducts are measured in saliva, the levels associated with daily use, and addiction with craving, are lower in adolescent compared to adult smokers.[1672] While the overall rate of dependence for people who try marijuana is 9%[1673], for adolescents who try it before age 16 the rate is 21%.[1674]

There is a biological basis to our teenagers' susceptibilities, with demonstrated differences in brain MRI studies in adolescents versus adults. When offered monetary rewards, adolescents show less anticipatory stimulation than adults in the "ventral striatal" region of the brain, reflecting differences that may relate to motivational behavior.[1675] Compared to older counterparts, special scans of adolescents' central nervous systems also show less activity in the frontal lobe (the home of more rational, logical thought and action) and more activity in the amygdala (a part of the brain "limbic" system that involves more emotional reactions).[1676] Other research has shown continuous growth of a part of the brain called the "anterior cingulate gyrus" through about age 21.[1677] The anterior cyngulate gyrus is responsible for inhibition.[1678] Still other studies involve the "nucleus accumbens", the area of the brain which involves motivation and responsiveness to rewards. Brain scans of adolescents being paid to complete simple, mundane tasks show much less activation in that region compared to young adults.[1679] What did show stimulation of the nucleus accumbens area was another study that scanned adolescents' brains as they were shown beer and liquor advertisements.[1680] These findings support a theory of addiction called the "reward deficit" theory. The idea is that since adolescents get less pleasure from everyday tasks and accomplishments, they are more tempted to turn to drugs and alcohol.

Parenting is all of our most ultimate of jobs. It's harder, and more important, than anything we do in our careers as doctors, lawyers, business moguls, or politicians. The same Teddy Roosevelt whom I quoted in the introduction to this book admitting that he was unable to both govern the country and control his daughter, later also said that raising children "makes all other forms of success and achievement lose their importance by comparison."[1681]

There is an often quoted old African proverb that "it takes a village to raise a child." To me, this is only indirectly true. It takes parents to raise a child, and a village to support us parents.

After the tragic death of Princess Diana, I saw a British official interviewed on television, regarding memorials for her. He was asked if there would be any permanent exhibits dedicated to her. "Well," he sniffed, "that would be difficult because she left no tangible works, such as art or literature..." What a bloke! No parent lacks a tangible legacy. From the most dripping-of-diamonds royalty to the frumpiest of pediatricians, from the most liberal-left of Democrats to the furthest right of Republicans, this is our one common thread. We leave our children to the world. They are our "magnum opuses". And during adolescence they are a work in progress. Maybe they're a pretty rough draft, but a lot of love, sweat, and tears have gone into them. A decade-and-a-half later, our babies are still our babies, just as precious as the day we first brought them home.

Underneath it all, our adolescents are as fragile as they are defiant, and as confused as they are unpleasant. They are a gift from their Maker that is entrusted and not given to us. And though the days are long, the years are short. Those endless, newborn nights flow into college semesters in what seems like a heartbeat when it's all over. In heart-wrenching tribute to his adolescent son, artist and poet Fairfield Porter once wrote "I think how carelessly I have regarded him/ And have not listened to the pleasant wit/ That marks the shrewdness of his watching mind." [1682] This is a pain all parents share.

The bumps along the way make for a rough ride not just for us parents, but for all involved. Our adolescents travel at lightning speed through the previously-uncharted territory of cyberspace. They navigate roads darker than any we ever faced, clouded by easy illicit drug availability and sexual innuendo. They stumble awkwardly on a slippery slope leading to a "beauty" ideal that most of us with normal bodies simply can't reach. They do this while carrying with them the emotional baggage of more personal upheaval than any previous generation has ever been sacked with, excepting those caught in war or political strife. They do this further away from extended family than previous generations. And they do it largely without the roadmap of faith that guided less secular generations.

It is false comfort to believe that material wealth can or should cushion our adolescent's family free-fall. In his book *The Paradox of Choice; Why*

More is Less, Barry Schwartz points out that unlimited choice leads to real suffering and depression.[1683] Psychologist Madeline Levine, in her insightful book *The Price of Privilege* points out quite bluntly that "money doesn't buy mental health." [1684] On the contrary, affluence brings with unique pressures. It can be lonely at the top for children as well as for their parents. There is some research that shows affluence to be a risk factor for alcohol abuse, drug use, and depression in teens. [1685]

As I meet parents distraught over various aspects of their teenagers' lives, like mediocre grades, average ACT scores, or mild degrees of over-weight, I often think of the story of a mother whose child wanders into the water at a beach and nearly drowns. As paramedics work feverishly to resuscitate the child, the mother looks up and demands of G-d: "Give me my child back RIGHT NOW! Don't You DARE take my child!" Thunder rolls, lightening sparks, and the child comes back to life. Again the mother looks skyward. "He had a HAT!" she hisses.

Parents wanting better grades, higher test scores, and Hollywood-type bodies for their children, of course have their best interests at heart. But in physically healthy adolescents lacking drug addiction, eating disorders, and a parole officer, how often are we asking for that hat?

In my office, I have two toy dolls representing adolescents, one a girl and the other a boy. They came labeled "perfect teenagers" on the tag. When the string on their back is pulled, a tape plays comments like "You are the coolest parents ever" or "I took out all the trash, even from the bathrooms." Parents and I have a good laugh over these dolls, but we get quickly bored. We much prefer our real, complex, human adolescents to any teen equivalent of the "Stepford Wives". This is because we know that the only thing harder than having children, is not having children. As Robert Browning so accurately pointed out, parenthood is indeed "the place where all love begins and ends."

I opened this book with a story about my first mentor, the late Dr. Ira Rosenthal. Let me end it with a story about his successor. Our next Department Chairman was a brilliant hematologist with both M.D. and Ph.D. degrees. He was a thoughtful clinician and real intellectual, with an extensive list of publications, who made wonderful contributions to pe-diatric hematology during his career. There is even a hemoglobin variant named after him. After my chief residency, our Department Head made a generous and kind offer to let me stay on and specialize in public health.

I turned it down, and left academic medicine. Starting my own medical practice allowed me to keep my children at my side. They stayed with me at my office and accompanied me on house-calls when they were young. It was a trade-off I have never regretted, but it was not without a price. I published nothing, becoming the anonymous community physician that fresh interns disdain.

Twenty years later, I ran into my former mentor. I asked what he was up to, expecting to hear of cutting edge-medical research. "Mostly what I do", he said instead, "is eat birthday cake. My wife and I have many grandchildren, and one of them is always having a birthday." The smile on his face said it all. The Grandchild Birthday-of-the-Month Club is where it's really at. And our ticket in are those adolescents of ours. They are exasperating. They are exhausting. They are our greatest pride and our Achilles heel. They bring us to our knees, literally and figuratively. And in the end, they are worth it, because they are our greatest legacy and our only future.

So put your adolescents to bed tonight, after their favorite snack. Make sure they know how unspeakably much we love them, and how our greatest wish is only that they should outlive us. Then let them rest. They have miles to go before they sleep, and their stopping place in our culture is more like a sweltering jungle than any snowy woods. Pray to the One who entrusted them to us to help us keep them wholesome, healthy, and un-addicted. And appreciate them as the most important people in our lives—the parents, G-d willing, of our grandchildren...

REFERENCES CITED

1 Shulman, Stanford T. The Teen Years (Whew!). Pediatric Annals 2005 October; 34(10);756.

2 Jay, M. Susan. The pediatric subspecialty of adolescent medicine—Help wanted! J Peds 2007 Jan; 150(1):2A.

3 Althouse LA, Stockman JA III. Pediatric workforce: a look at adolescent medicine data from the American Board of Pediatrics. J Peds 2007 Jan; 150:100-2.

4 Jay, M. Susan. The pediatric subspecialty of adolescent medicine—Help wanted! J Peds 2007 Jan; 150(1):2A.

5 Althouse LA, Stockman JA III. Pediatric workforce: a look at adolescent medicine data from the American Board of Pediatrics. J Peds 2007 Jan; 150:100-2.

6 Jay, M. Susan. The pediatric subspecialty of adolescent medicine—Help wanted! J Peds 2007 Jan; 150(1):2A.

7 Reitman DS. Focus on adolescents: close-up and personal. Consultant for Pediatricians 2005 February:57.

8 Lenzer, J. The importance of smelly feet and stinky cheese. Brit Med J 2006 Oct 14; 333(7572):771.

9 Goldbloom, Richard B., ed. New stars in the medical research firmament—the IgNOBEL Awards. Pediatric Notes 2007 Jan 25; 31(4):1.

10 "Teddy Roosevelt". Kids Discover Magazine 2005 September; 15(9):9.

11 Shakespeare. The Winter's Tale, III, iii, lines 59-65.

12 Southgate MT. On the cover. JAMA 2004 June 16;291(23):2793.

13 Eder AF, Hillyer CD, Dy BA, Notari EP IV, Benjamin RJ. Adverse reactions to allogeneic whole blood donation by 16- and 17- years olds. JAMA 2008 May 21; 299(19):2279-86.

14 Eder AF, Hillyer CD, Banjamin RJ. Letter to the editor, JAMA 2008 Oct 15;300(15):1759-60.

15 Dickens, Charles. A Tale of Two Cities. Book 1, Chapter 1, Page 1.

16 Shakespeare, William. Macbeth 2:2.

17 Lyamin O, Pryaslova J, Kosenko P, Siegel J. Behavioral aspects of sleep in bottlenose dolphin mothers and their calves. Physiol Behav 2007 Nov 23;92(4):725-33.

18 Moreira Naila. "Sleepless in SeaWorld: Some newborns and moms forgo slumber". Science News 2005 July 2;168:3.

19 Centers for Disease Control and Prevention. Perceived Insufficient rest or sleep—Four states, 2006. MMWR 2008 Feb 29; 57(8):200-3.

20 National Sleep Foundation. 2005. Sleep in America poll: summary of findings. Available at http://www.kintera.org/atf/cf/%7bf6bf2668-a1b4-4fe8-8dla-a5d39340d9cb%7d/2005_summary_of_findings.pdf.

21 Saranow, Jennifer. Asleep at the wheel? Morning rush hour now starts at 5AM. The Wall Street Journal 2006 Oct 17:D1,6.

22 Jurgensen, John. When life begins at 5: a new wake-up call. Wall Street Journal 2006 March 25/6: Lifestyles Section:1,9.

23 Klinkenborg, Verlyn and Richardson, Jim. Our vanishing night. National Geographic 2008 November: 105-120.

24 "A little less light". Pediatrics 2008 December;122(6):1309.

25 Centers for Disease Control and Prevention. Perceived Insufficient rest or sleep—Four states, 2006. MMWR 2008 Feb 29; 57(8):200-3.

26 Sheldon, Stephen H; Spire, Jean-Paul; Levy, Howard B. Pediatric Sleep Medicine. Philadelphia, Pennsylvania. W.B. Saunders Company, 1992:26.

27 Sheldon, Stephen H; Spire, Jean-Paul; Levy, Howard B. Pediatric Sleep Medicine. Philadelphia, Pennsylvania. W.B. Saunders Company, 1992:25.

28 Johnson EO, Roth T, Schultz L, Breslau N. Epidemiology of DSM-IV insomnia in adolescence: lifetime prevalence, chronicity, and an emergent gender difference. Pediatrics 2006;117:e247-e256.

29 Wolfson AR, Carskadon MA. Sleep schedules and daytime functioning in adolescents. Child Dev 1998;69:875-87.

30   LeBourgeois MK, Giannotti F, Cortesi F, et al. The relationship between reported sleep quality and sleep hygiene in Italian and American adolescents. Pediatrics 2005 January;115(1):257-65.

31   Chang-Kook Y, Kim JK, Patel SR, Lee J-H. Age-related changes in sleep/wake patterns among Korean teenagers. Pediatrics 2005 January;115(1):250-6.

32   Jenni OG, O'Connor BB. Children's sleep: an interplay between culture and biology. Pediatrics 2005 January;115(1):204-16.

33   Andrade MM,Benedito-Silva AA, Domenice S, et al. Sleep characteristics of adolescents: a longitudinal study. J Adolesc Health 1993 Jul;14(5):401-6.

34   Knutson KL, Lauderdale DS. Sociodemographic and behavioral predictors of bed time and wake time among US adolescents aged 15 to 17 years. J Peds 2009 Mar;154:426-30.

35   Moore, Stephen. "Want to improve education? Let kids sleep." The Wall Street Journal 2006 Sept 1:W11.

36   Chaker, Anne Marie. "Schools get tough on tardy students." The Wall Street Journal 2005 Nov 17: D1,4.

37   Mitler MM, Miller JC, Lipsitz JJ, et al. The sleep of long-haul truck drivers. N Engl J Med 1997;337:755-61.

38   Shelton DL. "Sleep-deprived drivers linked to highway 'carnage'." AMA News 1995 July 17.

39   Hotz, Robert Lee. "Scientists are still searching in the dark for the secrets of sleep." The Wall Street Journal 2008 Jan 18;B1.

40   Sheehan, Charles. "Pilots first went to the wrong plane; air controller wasn't watching jet's takeoff." Chicago Tribune 2006 Aug 30:Sec 1:3.

41   Coren Stanley. *Sleep thieves; an eye opening exploration into the science and mysteries of sleep.* New York, New York. The Free Press, 1990:ix.

42   "Exxon may pay more for Valdez cleanup." The Wall Street Journal 2006 September 23:A6.

43   Weinger MB, Ancoli-Israel S. Sleep deprivation and clinical performance. JAMA 2002 February 27;287(8):955-7.

44   Gaba DM, Howard SK. Fatigue among clinicians and the safety of patients. N Engl J Med 2002 October 17;347(16):1249-54.

45   Lamberg Lynne. Impact of long working hours explored. JAMA 2004 July 7;292(1):25-6.

46   Sloan VS, Smith AP. Reducing sleepiness on the roads and on the wards. Letter to the editor and reply. JAMA 1999 January 13;281(2):134-5.

47   Sachs BP, Discussant. A 38-year-old woman with fetal loss and hysterectomy. JAMA 2005 Aug 17;294(7):833-40.

48   Taffinder NJ, McManus IC, Gul Y, et al. Efect of sleep deprivation on surgeons' dexterity on laparoscopy simulator. Lancet 1998;1191:382.

49   Landrigan CP, Rothschild JM, Cronin JW, et al. Effect of reducing interns' work hours on serious medical errors in intensive care units. N Engl IJ Med 2004;351:1838-48.

50   Wu AW, Cavannaugh TA, McPhee SJ, et al. To tell the truth—ethical and practical issues in disclosing medical mistakes to patients. J Gen Intern Med 2000;12:770-5.

51   Arnedt JT, Owens J, Crouch M, et al. Neurobehavioral performance of residents after heavy night call vs after alcohol ingestion. JAMA 2005 Sept 7;294(9):1025-33.

52   Ayas NT, Barger LK, Cade BE, et al. Extended work duration and the risk of self-reported percutaneous injuries in interns. JAMA 2006 Sept 6;296(9):1055-62.

53   Barger LK,Cade BE, Ayas NT, et al. Extended work shifts and the risk of motor vehicle crashes among interns. N Engl J Med 2005;352:125-34.

54   Hecht Jeff. Amazing talent of the bird that doesn't sleep. New Scientist 2004 July 17:10.

55   Mastrianni JA, Nixon R, Layzer R, et al. Prion protein conformation in a patient with sporadic fatal insomnia. N Engl J Med 1999 May 27;340 (21):1630-8.

56   Gambetti P, Parchi P. Insomnia in prion diseases: sporadic and familial. N Engl J Med 1999 May 27;340(21):1675-7.

57   Dawson D, Reid K. Fatigue, alcohol, and performance impairment. Nature 1997;388:235.

58   Coren Stanley. Letter to the editor. Daylight savings time and traffic accidents. N Engl J Med 1996 April 4;334(14):922-3.

59   Lyznicki JM, Doege TC, Davis RM, et al. Sleepiness, driving, and motor vehicle crashes. JAMA 1998 June 17;279(23):1908-13.

60   Dement WC. The perils of drowsy driving. N Engl J Med 1997 September 11;337(11):783-4.

61   Spencer, Jane. The Quest to banish fatigue. Wall Street Journal 2003 July 1:D1,D4.

62   Pack AI, Pack AM, Rodgman E, Cucchiara A, Dinges DF, Schwab CW. Characteristics of crashes attributed to the driver having fallen asleep. Accid Anal Prev 1995;27:769-75.

63   Coren Stanley. Sleep thieves; an eye opening exploration into the science and mysteries of sleep. New York, New York. The Free Press, 1990:50-1.

64   Osman, Oral. Letter to the editor, Newsweek 2004 August 23:19.

65   Ireland JL, Culpin V. The relationship between sleeping problems and aggression, anger, and impulsivity in a population of juvenile and young offenders. J Adolesc Health 2006 June;38(6): 649-55.

66   Haynes PL, Bootzin RR, Smith L, et al. Sleep and aggression in substance-abusing adolescents: results from an integrative behavioral sleep-treatment pilot program. Sleep 2006 April 1;29(4):512-20.

67   Fredriksen K, Rhodes J, Reddy, Way N. Sleepless in Chicago: tracking the effects of adolescent sleep loss during the middle school years. Child Dev 2004 Jan-Feb;75(1):84-95.

68   Brunk, Doug. "Survey finds 13% of teens have sleep problems." Pediatric News 2003 October:22.

69   Worcester, Sharon. "Adolescent insomnia may have psychological repercussions." Pediatric News 2006 Sept:30.

70   Drake CL, Roehrs T, Richardson G, et al. Shift work sleep disorder: prevalence and consequences beyond that of symptomatic day workers. Sleep 2004;27:1453-62.

71   Knutsson A. Health disorders of shift workers. Occup Med (Lond) 2003;53:103-8.

72   "Restoring normal sleep reduces teen depression." Pediatric News 1986 February.

73   Voelker, Rebecca. Stress, sleep loss, and substance abuse create potent recipe for college depression. JAMA 2004 May 12;291(18):2177-9.

74   Sheldon, Stephen H; Spire, Jean-Paul; Levy, Howard B. *Pediatric Sleep Medicine*. Philadelphia, Pennsylvania. W.B. Saunders Company, 1992:93.

75   Finn, Robert. "Sleep restriction leads to symptoms of ADHD." Pediatric News 2003 April;37(4).

76   Brunk, Doug. "Sleep restriction may be behind inattention." Pediatric News 2000 September;34(9):38.

77   Fallone G, Acebo C, Seifer R, Carskadon MA. Experimental restriction of sleep opportunity in children: effects on teacher ratings. Sleep 2005;28(12):1561-7.

78   Hvolby A, Jorgensen J, Bilenberg N. Actigraphic and parental reports of sleep difficulties in children with attention-deficit/hyperactivity disorder. Arch Pediatr Adolesc Med 2008 Apr;162(4):323-9.

79   Sung V, Hiscock H, Sciberras E, et al. Sleep problems in children with attention-deficit/hyperactivity disorder. Arch Pediatr Adolesc Med 2008 Apr;162(4):336-42.

80   Blunden S, Lushington K, Lorenzen B, et al. Neuropsychological and psychosocial function in children with a history of snoring or behavioral sleep problems. J Peds 2005 June;146:780-6.

81   Blunden S, Lushington K, Lorenzen B, et al. Neuropsychological and psychosocial function in children with a history of snoring or behavioral sleep problems. J Peds 2005 June;146:780-6.

82   Ali NJ, Pitson D, Stradling JR. Sleep disordered breathing: effects of adenotonsillectomy on behaviour and psychological functioning. Eur J Pediatr 1996;155:56-62.

83   Huang YS, Guilleminault C, Li HY, et al. Attention-deficit/hyperactivity disorder with obstructive sleep apnea: a treatment outcome study. Sleep 2007 Jan;8(1):18-30.

84   Alfano CA, Ginsburg GS, Kingery JN. Sleep-related problems among children and adolescents with anxiety disorders. J Am Acad Child Adolesc Psychiatry 2007 Feb;46(2):224-32.

85   Lamberg, Lynne. Biological clock may be as crucial as stopwatch in deciding athletic contests. JAMA 1996 July 17;276(3):180-1.

86   Valent F, Brusaferro S, Barbone F. A case-crossover study of sleep and childhood injury. Pediatrics 2001 Feb;107(2):e23.

87   LeBourgeois MK, Giannotti F, Cortesi F, et al. The relationship between reported sleep quality and sleep hygiene in Italian and American adolescents. Pediatrics 2005 January;115(1):257-65.

88   d'Arcy H, Gillespie B, Foxman B. Respiratory symptoms in mothers of young children. Pediatrics 2000 November;106(5):1013-6.

89   Supplement to the Tufts University Health and Nutrition Letter. And to all a good night: how sleep deprivation may lead to chronic disease. 2004 October;22(8).

90   Spiegel K, Sheridan JF, VanCauter E. Research Letter: Effect of sleep deprivation on response to immunization. JAMA 2002 September 25; 288(12):1471-2.

91   Supplement to the Tufts University Health and Nutrition Letter. And to all a good night: how sleep deprivation may lead to chronic disease. 2004 October;22(8).

92   Zheng H, Patel M, Hryniewicz K, et al. Research Letter: association of extended work shifts, vascular function, and inflammatory markers in internal medicine residents: a randomized crossover trial. JAMA 2006 Sept 6;296(9):1049-50.

93   King CR, Knutson KL, Rathouz PJ, et al. Short sleep duration and incident coronary artery calcification. JAMA 2008 Dec 24/31;300(24):2859-66.

94   Janszky, I, Ljung R. Shifts to and from daylight saving time and incidence of myocardial infarction. Letter to the editor, N Engl J Med 2008 Oct 30;359(18):1966-8.

95   Vichayavilas P, Kelly, C. Relationship between sleep duration and incident coronary artery calcification. JAMA 2009 May 13;301(18):1879.

96   Gangwisch JE, Heymsfield SB, Boden-Albala B, et al. Short sleep duration as a risk factor for hypertension: analysis of the first National Health and Nutrition Examination Survey. Hypertension 2006 May;47(5):833-9.

97   Egan, BM. Sleep and hypertension: burning the candle at both ends really is hazardous to your health. Hypertension 2006 May;47(5):816-7.

98   DeRoos ST, Chillag KL, Keeler M, Gilbert DL. Effects of sleep deprivation on the pediatric electroencephalogram. Pediatrics 2009 Feb;123(2):703-8.

99   Finn, Robert. "Headache, disturbed sleep often are comorbid." Pediatric News 2006 April;40(4):60.

100 Supplement to the Tufts University Health and Nutrition Letter. And to all a good night: how sleep deprivation may lead to chronic disease. 2004 October;22(8).

101 Knutson KL, Ryden AM, Mander BA, et al. Role of sleep duration and quality in the risk and severity of type 2 diabetes mellitus. Ann Int Med 2006;166:1768-74.

102 Flint J, Kothare SV, Zihlif M, et al. Association between inadequate sleep and insulin resistance in obese children. J Pediatr 2007;150:364-9.

103 Hansen, Johnni. Increased breast cancer risk among women who work predominantly at night. Epidemiology 2001;12:74-7.

104 "Is night shift tied to cancer? Research finds rate of disease is higher for late workers." The Wall Street Journal 2007 Dec 3:B6.

105 Supplement to the Tufts University Health and Nutrition Letter. And to all a good night: how sleep deprivation may lead to chronic disease. 2004 October;22(8).

106 "You snooze, you lose? Looking for links between sleep, appetite, and obesity." Tufts University Health and Nutrition Letter 2005 April;23(2):6.

107 Kohatsu ND, Tsai R, Young T, et al. Sleep duration and body mass index in a rural population. Arch Int Med 2006;166:1701-5.

108 Landhuis CE, Poulton R, Welch D, Hancox RJ. Childhood sleep time and long-term risk for obesity: a 32-year prospective birth cohort study. Pediatrics 2008 Nov;122(5):955-60.

109 Carskadon MA. "Verbatim". Pediatric News 2004 October:19.

110 Yang C-K, Kim JK, Patel SR, et al. Age-related changes in sleep/wake patterns among Korean teenagers. Pediatrics 2005 January;115(1):250-6.

111 Sheldon, Dr. Stephen H, as quoted by Bates, Betsy. "Chronic fatigue may really be sleep deprivation." Pediatric News 1999 July:32.

112 Carskadon MA, Wolfson AR, Acebo C, Tzischinsky O, Seifer R. Adolescent sleep patterns, circadian timing, and sleepiness at a transition too early school days. Sleep 1998 Dec;21(8):871-81.

113 Carskadon MA, Harvey K, Kuke P, Anders TF, Litt IF, Dement WC. Pubertal changes in daytime sleepiness. Sleep 1980;2(4):453-60.

114 Carskadon MA, Acebo C. Regulation of sleepiness in adolescents: update, insights, and speculation. Sleep 2002 Sept 15;25(6):606-14.

115 Lamberg, Lynne. "Teens aren't lying—they really need to sleep later." American Medical News 1994 December 5.

116 Capri, John. "Let a sleeping teen lie—doctor's orders. Mood swings and poor grades tied to lack of shut-eye." Chicago Tribune 1997 October 6.

117 Wolfson AR, Carskadon MA. Understanding adolescents' sleep patterns and school performance: a critical appraisal. Sleep Med Rev 2003 Dec;7(6):491-506.

118 Epstein L, Mardon S. "Homeroom zombies." Newsweek 2007 Sept 17:64-5.

119 Danner F, Phillips B. Adolescent sleep, school start times, and teen motor crashes. J Clin Sleep Med 2008 Dec 15;4(6):533-5.

120 Inanenko, Anna, editor. Sleep and psychiatric disorders in children and adolescents. New York, NY, Informa Healthcare, 2008. ISBN 978-1-4200-4807-0.

121 Lamberg, Lynne. High schools find later start time helps students' health and performance. JAMA 2009 June 3;301(21):2200-1.

122 Bennett, Sara, and Kalish, Nancy. The Case Against Homework; How Homework is Hurting our Children and What We Can Do About It. New York, NY, Crown Books, 2006.

123 Kohn, Alfie. The Homework Myth: Why our Kids Get Too Much of a Bad Thing. New York, NY, Lifelong Books, 2004.

124 Buell, John. Closing the Book on Homework: Enhancing Public Education and Freeing Family Time. Philadelphia, PA, Temple University Press, 2004.

125 Lamberg, Lynn. Work schedules' role in sleep disorders stressed. Pediatric News 1990 October.

126 Naska A, Oikonomou E, Trichopoulou A, et al. Siesta in healthy adults and coronary mortality in the general population. Arch Intern Med 2007 Feb;167(3):296-301.

127 Praskakis E, Hitas M, Ntouros T, et al. Siesta and sleep habits of adolescents in Greece. Abstracts of the 25th International Congress of Pediatrics, August 25-30, 2007, Athens, Greece, published in Pediatrics 2008 Jan;121(suppl 2):590.

128 Centers for Disease Control and Prevention. Drowsy driving prevention week—November 5-11, 2007. MMWR 2007 Nov 2;56(43):1141.

129 Johnson JG, Cohen P, Kasen S, et al. Association between television viewing and sleep problems during adolescence and early adulthood. Arch Pediatr Adolesc Med 2004 June;158:562.

130 Dworak M, Schierl T, Bruns T, Struder HK. Impact of singular excessive computer game and television exposure on sleep patterns and memory performance of school-aged children. Pediatrics 2007 Nov;120(5):978-85.

131 Paavonen IJ, Pennonen M, Roine M, et al. TV exposure associated with sleep disturbances in 5- to 6-year-old children. J Sleep Res 2006;15;15:154-61.

132 Pollak CP, Bright D. Caffeine consumption and weekly sleep patterns in US seventh-, eighth-, and ninth-graders. Pediatrics 2003 January;111(1):42-6.

133 Orbeta RL, et al. High caffeine intake in adolescents: associations with sleep difficulties and feeling tired in the morning. J Adolesc Health 2006 Apr;38:451-3.

134 Lee KA, McEnany G, Weekes D. Gender differences in sleep patterns for early adolescents. Adolescent Health 1999;24:16-20.

135 Stewart, Elizabeth A. Exploring Twins; Towards a Social Analysis of Twinship. New York, NY. Palgrave Macmillan, 2001:92.

136 Eisenberg ME, Olson RE, Newmark-Sztainer D, et al. Correlations between family meals and psychosocial well-being among adolescents. Arch Pediatr Adolesc Med 2004 Aug;158:792-6.

137 Fulkerson JA, Story M, Leffert N, et al. Family dinner meal frequency and adolescent development: relationships with developmental assets and high-risk behaviors. J Adolesc Health 2006 Sept;39(3):337-45.

138 Fisher LB, Miles IW, Austin B, et al. Predictors of initiation of alcohol use among US adolescents. Arch Pediatr Adolesc Med 2007 Oct;161(10):959-66.

139 National Center on Addiction and Substance Abuse at Colombia University, sponsored by The Safeway Foundation. The Importance of Family Dinners IV. 2007 Sept. Available at www.casa-**columbia**.org/absolutenm/articlefiles/380-ImportanceofFamilyDinnersIV.pdf.

140 Eisenberg ME, Neumark-Sztainer D, Fulkerson JA, Story M. Family meals and substance abuse: is there a long-term protective association? J Adolesc Health 2008 Aug;43(2):151-6.

141 Neumark-Sztainer D, Eisenberg ME, Fulkerson JA, Story M, Larson NI. Family meals and disordered eating in adolescents. Arch Pediatr Adolesc Med 2008 Jan;162(1):17-22.

142 Widenhorn-Muller K, Hille K, Klenk J, Weiland U. Influence of having breakfast on cognitive performance and mood in 13- to 20-year-old high school students: results of a crossover trial. Pediatrics 2008 Aug;122(2):279-84.

143 Forni PM. The Civility Solution; What to Do When People are Rude. New York, NY, St. Martin's Press, 2008.

144 Stracher, Cameron. "Much Depends on Dinner." The Wall Street Journal 2005 July 29:W13.

145 Rapp, Alicia S. "Dinner for eight". Newsweek 2008 Nov 24:19.

146 Halterman JS, Kaczorowski JM, Aligne A, et al. Iron deficiency and cognitive achievement among school-aged children and adolescents in the United States. Pediatrics 2001 June;107(6):1381-6.

147 Nead KG, Halterman JS, Kaczorowski JM, et al. Overweight children and adolescents: a risk group for iron deficiency. Pediatrics 2004 July;114(1):104-8.

148 Halterman JS, Kaczorowski JM, Aligne A, et al. Iron deficiency and cognitive achievement among school-aged children and adolescents in the United States. Pediatrics 2001 June;107(6):1381-6.

149 Weijmer MC, Neering H, Welten C. Preliminary report: furunculosis and hypoferraemia. Lancet 1990;336(8713):464-6.

150 Daoud AS, Batieha A, Abu-Eksteish F, et al. Iron status: a possible risk factor for the first febrile seizure. Epilepsia 2002;43:740-3.

151 Konofal E, Lecendreux M, Arnulf I, Mouren MC. Iron deficiency in children with attention-deficit/hyperactivity disorder. Arch Pediatr Adolesc Med 2004 December;158(12):1113-5.

152 Bruner AB, Joffe A, Duggan AK, et al. Randomised study of cognitive effects of iron supplementation in non-anaemic iron-deficient adolescent girls. Lancet 1996 October 12;348(9033):992-6.

153 Ballin A, Berar M, Rubenstein U, et al. Am J Dis Child 1992;146:803-5.

154 Konofal E, Cortese S, Lecendreux M, et al. Effectiveness of iron supplementation in a young child with attention-deficit/hyperactivity disorder. Pediatrics 2005;116:e732-4.

155 Abrahams SA, et al. Pediatr Research 1996 Jan;39:171-5.

156 Shah M, Griffin IJ, Lifschitz CH, Abrams SA. Effect of orange and apple juices on iron absorption in children. Arch Pediatr Adolesc Med 2003 December;157:1232-6.

157 Merhav H, Amitai Y, Palti H, Godfrey S. Tea drinking and microcytic anemia in infants. Am J Clin Nutr 1985 June;41(6):1210-3.

158 Das G, Crocombe S, McGrath M, et al. Hypovitaminosis D among healthy adolescent girls attending an inner city school. Arch Dis Child 2006 Jul;91(7)569-72.

159 Greer FR, Krebs NF, and the Committee on Nutrition. Optimizing bone health and calcium intakes of infants, children, and adolescents. Pediatrics 2006 Feb;117(2):578-85.

160 MacReady Norra. "Vitamin D deficiency may be widespread in teens; two studies share similar findings." Pediatric News 2003 November;37(11):28.

161 MacReady Norra. "Vitamin D deficiency may be widespread in teens; two studies share similar findings." Pediatric News 2003 November;37(11):28.

162 Perry CL, McGuire MT, Neumark-Sztainer D, Story M. Adolescent vegetarians; how well do their dietary patterns meet the Healthy People 2010 objectives. Arch Pediatr Adolesc Med 2002 May;156:431-7.

163 Zlotkin S. Adolescent vegetarians; how well do their dietary patterns meet the Healthy People 2010 objectives. Arch Pediatr Adolesc Med 2002 May;156:426-7.

164 Das G, Crocombe S, McGrath M, et al. Hypovitaminosis D among healthy adolescent girls attending an inner city school. Arch Dis Child 2006 Jul;91(7)569-72.

165 Schnadower D, Agarwal C, Oberfield SE, et al. Hypocalcemic seizures and secondary bilateral femoral fractures in an adolescent with primary vitamin D deficiency. Pediatrics 2006 Nov;118(5):2226-30.

166 Greer FR, Krebs NF, and the Committee on Nutrition. Optimizing bone health and calcium intakes of infants, children, and adolescents. Pediatrics 2006 Feb;117(2):578-85.

167 Carakushansky M, O'Brien KO, Levine MA. Vitamin D and calcium: strong bones for life through better nutrition. Contemporary Pediatrics2003 March;20(3):37-53.

168 Ward KA, et al, University of Manchester, Manchester, UK. A Randomized, controlled study of calcium supplementation in pre-pubertal gymnasts vs. controls. Paper presented at the 9th Spring Meeting, Royal College of Paediatrics and Child Health, York, UK 2005 Apr 18-21 as abstracted in Pediatric Notes, Goldbloom RB, ed, 2005 July 21;29(29).

169 DeBar LL, Ritenbaugh C, Aickin M, et al. A health plan-based lifestyle intervention increases bone mineral density in adolescent girls. Arch Pediatr Adol Med 2006 Dec;160:1269-76.

170 Fonesca V, Houlder S, Thomas M, et al. Osteopenia in women with anorexia nervosa. Letter to the editor, N Engl J Med 1985 August 1;313(5).

171 Fonseca A, Agnew J, Dandona P. Secondary hyperparathyroidism and bone density. Br Med J 1985;290:555-6.

172 Pereyra LC, Schneider M. Adolescent Health Update: Vegetarianism. American Academy of Pediatrics, Section on Adolescent Health Vol. 17(1):2004 October.

173 Pereyra LC, Schneider M. Adolescent Health Update: Vegetarianism. American Academy of Pediatrics, Section on Adolescent Health Vol. 17(1):2004 October.

174 Perry CL, McGuire MT, Neumark-Sztainer D, Story M. Adolescent vegetarians; how well do their dietary patterns meet the Healthy People 2010 objectives. Arch Pediatr Adolesc Med 2002 May;156:431-7.

175 Zlotkin S. Adolescent vegetarians; how well do their dietary patterns meet the Healthy People 2010 objectives. Arch Pediatr Adolesc Med 2002 May;156:426-7.

176 Neumark-Sztainer D, Story M, Resnick MD, Story M. Adolescent vegetarians; a behavioral profile of a school-based population in Minnesota. Arch Pediatr Adolesc Med 1997 August;151:833-8.

177 Adolescent Health Update Editorial Board, American Academy of Pediatrics. True eating disorders sometimes masked by vegetarian diet. American Academy of Pediatric News 2004 October;25(4):175.

178 Pereyra LC, Schneider M. Adolescent Health Update: Vegetarianism. American Academy of Pediatrics, Section on Adolescent Health Vol. 17(1):2004 October.

179 Pereyra LC, Schneider M. Adolescent Health Update: Vegetarianism. American Academy of Pediatrics, Section on Adolescent Health Vol. 17(1):2004 October.

180 Pereyra LC, Schneider M. Adolescent Health Update: Vegetarianism. American Academy of Pediatrics, Section on Adolescent Health Vol. 17(1):2004 October.

181 Lindenbaum J, Healton EB, Savage DG, et al. Neuropsychiatric disorders caused by cobalamin deficiency in the absence of anemia or macrocytosis. N Engl J Med 1988;318:1720-8.

182 Sklar Ronald. Nutritional vitamin B-12 deficiency in a breast-fed infant of vegan-diet mother. Clinical Pediatrics;1986 April.

183 Renault F, Verstichel P, Ploussard JP, Costil J. Neuropathy in two cobalamin-deficient breast-fed infants of vegetarian mothers. Muscle Nerve 1999;22:252-4.

184 Codazzi D, Sala F, Parini R, Langer M. Coma and respiratory failure in a child with severe vitamin B12 deficiency. Pediatr Crit Care Med 2005; 6(4):483-5.

185 Milea D, Cassoux N, LeHoang P. Blindness in a strict vegan. Letter to the editor, N Engl J Med 2000;342:897-8.

186 Li K, McKay G. Ischemic retinopathy caused by severe megaloblastic anemia. N Engl J Med 1000;342:342:860.

187 Chandra RK. Effect of vitamin and trace-element supplementation on immune responses and infection in elderly subjects. Lancet 1992 Nov 7;340(8828):1124-7.

188 Kin I, Williamson DF, Byers T, Koplan JP. Vitamin and mineral supplement use and mortality in a US cohort. Am J Publ Health 1993 Apr;83(4):546-50.

189 Naismith DJ, Nelson M, Burley VJ, Gatenby SJ. Can children's intelligence be increased by vitamin and mineral supplements? Lancet 1988 Aug 6;2(8606):335.

190 Bjelakovic G, Nikolova D, Gluud LL, et al. Mortality in randomized trials of antioxidant supplements for primary and secondary prevention; systemic review and meta-analysis. JAMA 2007 Feb 28;297(8):842-57.

191 Braganza SF, Ozuah PO. What's the evidence on treating disease with vitamin C and megavitamins. Contemporary Pediatrics 2006 June;23(6):81-90.

192 Foxhall, K. Panel slams lack of science behind vitamin and mineral supplementation. Contemporary Pediatrics 2006 August;23(8):12,98.

193 Goh YI, Bollano E, Einarson TR, Koren G. Prenatal multivitamin supplementation and rates of pediatric cancers: a meta-analysis. Clin Pharmacol Ther 2007 May;81(5):685-91.

194 Oakley GP. Eat right and take a multivitamin. The N Engl J Med 1998 April 9;338(15):1060-1.

195 Fairfield KM, Fletcher RH. Vitamins for chronic disease prevention in adults; a scientific review. JAMA 2002 June 19;287(23):3116-26.

196 Fletcher RH, Fairfield KM. Vitamins for chronic disease prevention in adults; clinical applications. JAMA 2002 June 19;287(23):3127-9.

197 Willett WC, Stampfer MJ. What vitamins should I be taking, doctor? N Engl J Med 2001 December;345(25):1819-24.

198 Pearson HA, Ehrenkranz RA, Rinder HM, Riely CA. Hemosiderosis in a normal child secondary to oral iron medication. Pediatrics 2000:429.

199 Lippe B, Nensen I. Mendoza G, et al. Chronic vitamin A intoxication. Am J Dis Child 1981 July;135:634-6.

200 Patel P, et al. Can Med Assoc J 1988 Oct 15;139:755-6.

201 "Vitamin Supplements". The Medical Letter 1998 July 31;40(#1032).

202 Wahl Richard. Nutrition in the adolescent. Pediatric Annals 1999 February;28(2):107-11.

203 Lloyd T, Chinchilli VM, Eggli DF, et al. Body composition development of adolescent white females. Arch Pediatr Adolesc Med 1998 Oct;152:998-1002.

204 Dietz WH. Overweight in childhood and adolescence. N Engl J Med 2004 Feb 26;359(9):855-8.

205 Lissau I, Overpeck MD, Ruan J, et al. Body mass index and overweight in adolescents in 13 European Countries, Israel, and the United States. Arch Pediatr Adolesc Med 2004 January;158:27-33.

206 Friedrich MJ. Epidemic of obesity expands its spread to developing countries. JAMA 2002 March 20;287(11):1382-6.

207 Heymsfield S, Allison DB. Book Review on *Nutrition, Genetics, and Obesity*. New Engl J Med 2000 March 9;342(10):747-8.

208 Gortmaker SL, Dietz WH, Sobol AM, Wehler CA. Increasing pediatric obesity in the United States; AJDC 1987 May;141:535-540.

209 Swallen KC, Reither EN, Haas SA, Meier AM. Overweight, obesity, and health-related quality of life among adolescents: the National Longitudinal Study of adolescent Health. Pediatrics 2005 February;115(2):340-7.

210 Stunkard AJ, Sorensen TIA, Hanis C, et al. An adoption study of human obesity. N Engl J Med 1986 January 23;314(4):193-8.

211 Stunkard AJ, Fock TT, Hrubec Z. A twin study of human obesity. JAMA 1986;256(1):51-4.

212 Stunkard AJ, Harris JR, Pedersen NL, et al. The body-mass index of twins who have been reared apart. N Engl J Med 1990;322:1483-7.

213 Bouchard C, Tremblay A, Despres J-P, et al. The response to long-term overfeeding in identical twins. N Engl J Med 1990 May 24;322:1477-82.

214 Sims EAH. Destiny rides again as twins overeat. The New Engl J Med 1990 May 24;322(21):1522-3.

215 Farooqu IS, Wannensteen T, Collins S, et al. Clinical and molecular genetic spectrum of congenital deficiency of the leptin receptor. N Engl J Med 2007 Jan 18;356(3):237-47.

216 Heymsfield SB, Reitman ML. Book review, *Obesity: Genomics and Postgenomics*. New York, NY; Informa Healthcare, 2008.

217 Christakis NA, Fowler JH. The spread of obesity in a large social network over 32 years. N Engl J Med 2007 July 26;357(4):370-9.

218 St. John, W. "On the final journey, one size doesn't fit all." The New York Times 2003 September 28.

219 Must A, Spadano J, Coakley EH, et al. The disease burden associated with overweight and obesity. JAMA 1999 October 27;282(16):1523-9.

220 Calle EE, Rodriguez C, Walker-Thurmond K, Thum MJ. Overweight, obesity, and mortality from cancer in a prospectively studied cohort of U.S. adults. N Engl J Med 2003 April 24;348(17):1625-38.

221 Timm NL, Grupp-Phelan J, Ho ML. Chronic ankle morbidity in obese children following an acute ankle injury. Arch Pediatr Adolesc Med 2005 January;159:33-6.

222 Manson JE, Willett WC, Stampfer MJ, et al. Body weight and mortality among women. The N Engl J Med 1995 September 14; 333(11):677-85.

223 Byers T. Body weight and mortality. N Engl J Med 1995 September 14;333(11):723-4.

224 Stevens J, Cai J, Pamuk E, et al. The effect of age on the association between body-mass index and mortality. N Engl J Med 1998 January 1;338(1):1-7.

225 HaJee S, Sull JW, Jungyong P, et al. Body-mass index and mortality in Korean men and women. N Engl J Med 2006 Aug 24;355(8):779-87.

226 Adams KF, Schatzkin A, Harris TB, et al. Overweight, obesity, and mortality in a large prospective cohort of persons 50 to 71 years old. N Engl J Med 2006 Aug 24;355(8):763-8.

227 Fontaine KR, Redden DT, Wang C, Westfall AO, Allison DB. Years of life lost due to obesity. JAMA 2003;289:187-93.

228 Allison DB, Fonaine KR, Manson JoAnn. Annual deaths attributable to obesity in the United States. JAMA 1999 October 27;282(16):1530-8.

229 Waller DK, Shaw GM, Rasmussen SA, et al. Prepregnancy obesity as a risk factor for structural birth defects. Arch Pediatr Adolesc Med 2007;161(8):745-50.

230 Cedergren M, Kallen B. Maternal obesity and the risk for orofacial clefts in the offspring. Cleft Palate Craniofac J 2005 Jul;42(4):367-71.

231 Wolf AM, Colditz GA. Social and economic effects of body weight in the United States. Am J Clin Nutr 1996;63(supl 3):466S-469S.

232 Kuczmarski RJ, Flegal KM, Campbell SM, Johnson CL. Increasing prevalence of overweight among US adults. JAMA 1994 July 20;272(3):205-11.

233 Yanovski SZ, Yanovski JA. Obesity. N Engl J Med 2002 February 21;591-600.

234 Schneider MB, Brill SR. Obesity in children and adolescents. Pediatrics in Review 2005 May;26(5):155-62.

235 Davis, Matthew M presenting at the 2006 AcademyHealth Annual Meeting as abstracted in Kirn, Timothy F. Obesity costs $49 billion for every 4 million born in U.S. Pediatric News 2006 Dec;40(12):60.

236 Crosnoe R. Gender, obesity, and education. Sociology of Education 2007;80:241-60.

237 Robinson S. Victimization of obese adolescents. J School Nursing 2006 Nov;22(4):201-6.

238 Franklin J, Gareth D, Steinbeck KS, et al. Obesity and risk of low self-esteem: a statewide survey of Australian children. Pediatrics 2006 Dec;118(6):2481-7.

239 Fallon EM, Tanofsky-Kraff M, Normal A-C, et al. Health-related quality of life in overweight and nonoverweight black and white adolescents. J Pediatr 2005;147:443-50.

240 Thomas C, Hypponen E, Power C. Obesity and type 2 diabetes risk in mid adult life: the role of childhood adversity. Pediatrics 2008 May;121(5):e1240-9.

241 Leim ET, Sauer PJ, Oldehinkel AJ, et al. Association between depressive symptoms in childhood and adolescence and overweight in later life. Arch Pediatr Adolesc Med 2008 Oct;162(10):981-8.

242 Anderson SE, Cohen P, Naumova E, Must A. Association of depression and anxiety disorders with weight change in a prospective community-based study of children followed up into adulthood. Arch Pediatr Adolesc Med 2006 Mar;160:285-91.

243 Lemeshow AR, Fisher L, Goodman E, et al. Subjective social status in the school and change in adiposity in female adolescents. Arch Pediatr Adol Med 2008 Jan;162(1):2308.

244 Dansinger ML, Gleason JA, Griffith JL, et al. Comparison of the Atkins, Ornish, Weight Watchers, and Zone Diets for Weight Loss and Heart Disease Risk Reduction. JAMA 2005 January 5;293(1):45-53.

245 Kassirer JP, Angell MA. Losing weight—an ill-fated new year's resolution. N Engl J Med 1998 Jan 1:52-4.

246 Field AE, Austin SB, Taylor CB, et al. Relation between dieting and weight change among pre-adolescents and adolescents. Pediatrics 2003;112(4):900-6.

247 Williamson DF. The prevention of obesity. N Engl J Med 1999 October 7;341(15):1140-1.

248 Goldbloom R. Pediatric Notes 2003;27:187.

249 The Medical Letter, Inc. Diet, drugs and surgery for weight loss. Treatment Guidelines. Treatment Guidelines from The Medical Letter 2003 December;1(16):101-6.

250 Bouchard C. Is weight fluctuation a risk factor? N Engl J Med 1991 June 27;324(26):1887-8.

251 Manson JE, Colditz GA, Stampfer MJ. Parity, ponderosity, and the paradox of a weight-preoccupied society. JAMA 1994 June 8;271(22):1788-90.

252 Leibel RL, Rosenbaum M, Hirsch J. Changes in energy expenditure resulting from altered body weight. The New Engl J Med 1995 March 9;332(10):621-8.

253 Frank Arthur. Futility and avoidance; medical professionals in the treatment of obesity. JAMA 1993 28;269(16):2132-3.

254 Yanovski JA, Yanovski SZ. Recent advances in basic obesity research. JAMA 1999 October 27;282(16):1504-7.

255 Kassirer JP, Angell MA. Losing weight—an ill-fated new year's resolution. N Engl J Med 1998 Jan 1:52-4.

256 Denke MA. Book reviewer for *Obesity: Epidemiology, Pathophysiology, and Prevention*. New Engl J Med 2007 Dec 13;357(24):2526-7.

257 Livingstone MBE, Rennie KL in Childhood Obesity: Contemporary Issues. Boca Raton, FL, CRC Press, 2006.

258 Collins CE, Warren J, Neve M, et al. Measuring effectiveness of dietetic interventions in child obesity. Arch Pediatr Adolesc Med 2006 Sept;160:906-22.

259 Caballero B, Clay T, Davis SM, et al. Pathways: a school-based, randomized controlled trial for the prevention of obesity in American Indian schoolchildren. Am J Clin Nutr 2003 Nov;78(5)1030-8.

260 Webber LS, Osganian SK, Feldman HA, et al. Cardiovascular risk factors among children after a 2-1/2 year intervention-The CATCH study. Prev Med 1996 Jul-Aug;25(4):432-41.

261 Wake, Melissa as quoted by Bates, Betsy, in "Talk therapy fails overweight kids". Pediatric News 2008 Aug;42(8):44.

262 Singh AS, Paw MJMCA, Brug J, van Mechelen W. Short-term effects of school-based weight gain prevention among adolescents. Arch Pediatr Adol Med 2007 June;161:565-71.

263 Paineau DL, Beaufils F, Boulie A, et al. Family dietary coaching to improve nutritional intakes and body weight control. Arch Pediatr Adol Med 2008 Jan;162(1):34-43.

264 Carrel AL, Clark R, Peterson S, et al. School-based fitness changes are lost during the summer vacation. Arch Pediatr Adol Med 2007 June;161:561-4.

265 Rosenbaum M, Nonas C, Weil R, et al. School-based intervention acutely improves insulin sensitivity and decreases inflammatory markers and body fatness in junior high school students. J Clin Endocrinol Metab 2007;92:504-8.

266 Livingstone MBE, Rennie KL in *Childhood Obesity: Contemporary Issues*. Boca Raton, FL, CRC Press, 2006.

267 Stock S, Miranda C, Evans S, et al. Healthy buddies: a novel, peer-led health promotion program for the prevention of obesity and eating disorders in children in elementary school. Pediatrics 2007 Oct;120(4):e1059-68.

268 Wing RR, Tate DF, Gorin AA, et al. A self-regulation program for maintenance of weight loss. N Engl J Med 2006 Oct 12;355(15):1563-71.

269 Bristol, Nellie. "Group visits help teens shed weight." Pediatr News 2006 Dec;40(12):1.

270 Sacks FM, Bray GA, Carey VJ, et al. Comparison of weight-loss diets with different compositions of fat, protein, and carbohydrates. N Engl J Med 2009 Feb 26;360(9):859-73.

271 Ives N. "A report on childhood obesity." The New York Times 2004 February 25.

272 Dennison BA, Erb TA, Jenkins PL. Television viewing and television in bedroom associated with overweight risk among low-income preschool children. Pediatrics 2002 June; 109(6):1028-35.

273 Andersen RE, Crespo CJ, Bartlett SJ, et al. Relationship of physical activity and television watching with body weight and level of fatness among children. JAMA 1998 March 25;279(12):938-42.

274 Robinson TN. Does television cause childhood obesity? JAMA 1998 March 25;279(12):959-60.

275 Matheson DM, Killen JD, Wang Y, et al. Children's food consumption during television watching. Am J Clin Nutr 2004 June;79(6):1088-94.

276 Hu FB, Li TY, Colditz GA, et al. Television watching and other sedentary behaviors in relation to risk of obesity and type 2 diabetes mellitus in women. JAMA 2003 April 9;289(14):1785-91.

277 Davidson KK, Marshall SJ, Birch LL. Cross-sectional and longitudinal associations between TV viewing and girls' body mass index, overweight status, and percentage of body fat. J Pediatr 2006;149:32-7.

278 Viner, RM, Cole TJ. Television viewing in early childhood predicts adult body mass. J Peds 2005;147:429-35.

279 Lumeng JC, Rahnama S, Appugliese D, et al. Television exposure and overweight risk in preschoolers. Arch Pediatr Adolesc Med 2006;160:417-22.

280 Gortmaker SL, Must A, Sobol AM, et al. Television viewing as a cause of increasing obesity among children in the United States, 1986-1990. Arch Pediatr Adolesc Med 1996 Apr;150:356-62.

281 Wiecha FL, Peterson KE, Ludwig DS, et al. When children eat what they watch. Arch Pediatr Adol Med 2006 Apr;160:436-42.

282 McMillan JA. Getting England into shape: is there a lesson for the States? Contemporary Pediatrics 2005 January;22(1):8.

283 "Why Kraft decided to ban some food ads to children." Excerpted from the Wall Street Journal 2005 Oct 31 in Pediatrics 2006 Jan;117(1):138.

284 Faith MS, Berman N, Heo M, et al. Effects of contingent television on physical activity and television viewing in obese children. Pediatrics 2001 May;107(5):1043-8.

285 Robinson TN. Reducing children's television viewing to prevent obesity. JAMA 1999 October 27;282(16):1561-7.

286 Gortmaker SL, Peterson K, Wiecha J, et al. Reducing obesity via a school-based interdisciplinary intervention among youth. Arch Pediatr Adolesc Med 1999;153:409-18.

287 Mellecker RR, McManus AM. Energy expenditure and cardiovascular responses to seated and active gaming in children. Arch Pediatr Adolesc Med 2008;162(9):886-91.

288 Lanningham-Foster L, Jensen TB, Foster RC, et al. Energy expenditure of sedentary screen time compared with active screen time for children. Pediatrics 2006;118:e1831-5.

289 Maffeis C, Zaffanello M, Schutz Y. Relationship between physical inactivity and adiposity in prepubertal boys. J Pediatr 1997;131:288-92.

290 Levin S, Lowry R, Brown DR, Dietz WH. Physical activity and body mass index among U.S. Adolescents; youth risk behavior survey, 1999. Arch Pediatr Adolesc Med;2003 August;157: 816-20.

291 Epstein LH, Paluch RA, Gordy CC, Dorn J. Decreasing sedentary behaviors in treating pediatric obesity. Arch Pediatr Adolesc Med 2000 March;154:220-6.

292 Wang YC, Gortmaker SL, Sobel AM. Estimating the energy gap among US children: a counter-factual approach. Pediatr 2006;118:e1739-44.

293 Howard, Philip K. "Why safe kids are becoming fat kids." The Wall Street Journal 2008 August 18:A15.

294 Ludwig DS, Peterson KE, Gortmaker SL. Relation between consumption of sugar-sweetened drinks and obesity: a prospective, observational analysis. Lancet 2001 Feb 17;357:505-8.

295 Giammettei J, Blix G, Marchak HH, et al. Television watching and soft drink consumption. Arch Pediatr Adolesc Med 2003 September;157:882-6.

296 Apovian CM. Sugar-sweetened soft drinks, obesity, and type 2 diabetes. JAMA 2004 August 25;292(8):978-9.

297 James J, Thomas P, Cavan D. Preventing childhood obesity by reducing consumption of carbonated drinks; cluster randomized controlled trial. Brit Med J 2004;328:1237-42.

298 American Academy of Pediatrics Committee on School Health. Soft drinks in schools. Pediatrics 2004 Jan;113(1Pt1):152-4.

299 Ebbeling CB, Feldman HA, Osgoanian SK, et al. Effects of decreasing sugar-sweetened beverage consumption on body weight in adolescents: a randomized, controlled pilot study. Pediatrics 2006 Mar;117(3):673-80.

300 "Restaurant meals have about 60% more calories than meals made at home." Univ of California Wellness Letter 2007 Feb;23(5):1.

301 Critser, Greg. *Fat Land: How Americans Became the Fattest People in the World.* Boston, MA, Houghton Mifflin, 2003.

302 Brownell KD. Fast food and obesity in children. Pediatrics 2004:132.

303 Ebbeling CB, Sinclair KB, Pereira MA, et al. Compensation for energy intake from fast food among overweight and lean adolescents. JAMA 2004 June 16;291(23):2828-33.

304 Bowman SA, Gortmaker SL, Ebbeling CB, et al. Effects of fast-food consumption on energy intake and diet quality among children in a national household survey. Pediatrics 2003;113:112-8.

305 Maddock J. Am J Health Promotion 2004 November/December;19:137-43.

306 Timlin, MT, Pereira MA, Story M, Neumark-Sztainer D. Breakfast eating and weight change in a 5-year prospective analysis of adolescents: project EAT (Eating Among Teens). Pediatrics 2008;121:e638-45.

307 "Dining halls lose the trays in hopes of reducing waste." Wall Street Journal 2008 Jan 31;B8.

308 "Beware big bowls." Nutrition Action Healthletter 2006 Nov:8.

309 Parker-Pope, Tara. Latest weight-loss advice: slow down and pay attention. The Wall Street Journal 2007 Jan 16;D1.

310 Landhuis CE, Poulton R, Welch D, Hancox RJ. Childhood sleep time and long-term risk for obesity: a 32-year prospective birth cohort study. Pediatrics 2008 Nov;122(5):955-60.

311 Jiang F, Zhu S, Yan C, et al. Sleep and obesity in preschool children. J Pediatr 2009 June;154:814-8.

312 Davison KK, Francis LA, Birch LL. Links between parents' and girls' television viewing behaviors: a longitudinal examination. Pediatr 2005;147:436-42.

313 Lee Y, Mitchell DC, Smicklas-Wright H, Birch LL. Diet quality, nutrient intake, weight status, and feeding environments of girls meeting or exceeding recommendations for total dietary fat of the American Academy of Pediatrics. Pediatrics 2001 Jun;107(6):e95.

314 Von Kries R, Koletzko B, Sauerwald T, et al. Breast feeding and obesity: cross sectional study. British Med J 1999 Jul 17;319(7203):147-50.

315 Butte NF. The role of breastfeeding in obesity. Pediatr Clin N America 2001;48:189-98.

316 Gillman MW, Rifas-Shiman SI, Camargo CA, et al. Risk of overweight among adolescents who were breastfed as infants. JAMA 2001;285:2461-7.

317 Hediger MI, Overpeck MD, Kuczmarski RJ, Ruan WJ. Association between infant breastfeeding and overweight in young children. JAMA 2001;285:2453-60.

318 Toschke AM, Vignerova J, Lhotska L, Osancova K, et al. Overweight and obesity in 6- to 14-year old Czech children in 1991:protective effect of breast-feeding. J Pediatr 2002;141:764-9.

319 Grummer-Strawn LM, Mei Z, Centers for Disease Control and Prevention Pediatric Nutrition Surveillance System. Does breastfeeding protect against pediatric overweight? Analysis of longitudinal data from the Centers for Disease Control and Prevention Pediatric Nutrition Surveillance System. Pediatrics 2004 Feb;113(2):e81-6.

320 Harder T, Bergmann R, Kallischnigg G, Plagemann A. Longer duration of breastfeeding and risk of overweight: a meta-analysis. Am J Epidemiol 2006;162(5):397-403.

321 Owen CG, Martin RM, Whincup PH, et al. Effect of infant feeding on the risk of obesity across the life course: a quantitative review of published evidence. Pediatrics 2005 May;115:1367-77.

322 "Infant feeding and the risk of later obesity." Pediatric Alert 2005 May 12:54.

323 Von Kries R, et al. Maternal smoking during pregnancy and childhood obesity. Am J Epid 2002;156:954-61.

324 Wansink B, Payne C, Werle C. Consequences of belonging to the "Clean Plate Club". Arch Pediatr Adol Med 2008 Oct;162(10):994.

325 Burdette HL, Whitaker RC, Hall WC, et al. Maternal infant-feeding style and children's adiposity at 5 years of age. Arch Pediatr Adol Med 2006 May;160:513-20.

326 Spruijt-Metz D, Li C, Cohen E, et al. Longitudinal influence of mother's child-feeding practices on adiposity in children. J Pediatr 2006;148:314-20.

327 Lumeng JC, Burke LM. Maternal prompts to eat, child compliance, and mother and child weight status. J Pediatr 2006;149:330-5.

328 Wright CM, Parkinson DN, Drewett, RF. How does maternal and child feeding behavior relate to weight gain and failure to thrive? Data from a prospective birth cohort. Pediatr 2006 Apr;117(4):1262-9.

329 "Health's holy grail: a vaccine to prevent obesity." NewsMax 2006 Nov:94.

330 Xanthakos SA, Inge TH. Extreme pediatric obesity: weighing the health dangers. J Pediatr 2007;150:3-5.

331 Davis MM, Slish K, Chao C, et al. National trends in bariatric surgery, 1996-2002. Arch Surg 2006;141:71-4.

332 Spencer J. Emergence of alcoholism after weight-loss surgery offers clues to roots of dependency. Wall Street Journal 2006 July 18.

333 Katz DL, O'Connell MO, Yeh, M-C, et al. Public health strategies for preventing and controlling overweight and obesity in school and worksite settings; a report on recommendations of the task force on community preventive services. MMWR 2005 Oct 7;54(RR-10)1-12.

334 Katz DL, O'Connell MO, Yeh, M-C, et al. Public health strategies for preventing and controlling overweight and obesity in school and worksite settings; a report on recommendations of the task force on community preventive services. MMWR 2005 Oct 7;54(RR-10)1-12.

335 Field AE, Austin SB, Taylor CB, et al. Relation between dieting and weight change among pre-adolescents and adolescents. Pediatrics 2003;112(4):900-6.

336 Fisher JO, Birch LL. Restricting access to foods and children's eating. Appetite 1999;32:405-19.

337 "Children are 'programmed' to reject most new foods. Pediatric News" 1999 February;33(2).

338 Birch LL, Fisher JO. Am J Clin Nutr 2000;71:1054-61.

339 Faith MS, Heshka S, Keller KL, et al. Maternal-child feeding patterns and child body weight. Arch Pediatr Adolesc Med 2003 September;157:926-32.

340 National Task Force on the Prevention and Treatment of Obesity. Weight Cycling. JAMA 1994 October 19;272(15):1196-1202.

341 Lissner L, Odell PM, D'Agostino RB, et al. Variability of body weight and health outcomes in the Framingham population. N Engl J Med 1991 June 27;324(26):1839-44.

342 Ernsberger P, Kiletsky RJ. Letter to the editor, weight cycling and mortality: support from animal studies. N Engl J Med 1993 March 3;269(9):1116.

343 Bouchard C. Is weight fluctuation a risk factor? N Engl J Med 1991 June 27;324(26):1887-8.

344 Wadden TA, Van Itallie TB, Blackburn GL. Responsible and irresponsible use of very-low-calorie diets in the treatment of obesity. JAMA 1990 January 5;263(1):83-5.

345 "Panel recommends approval of new anti-obesity drug." American Medical News 1995 December 11:43.

346 Khan MA, Herzog CA, St. Peter JV, et al. The prevalence of cardiac valvular insufficiency assessed by transthoracic echocardiography in obese patients treated with appetite-suppressant drugs. The N Engl J Med 1998 September 10;339(11):713-8.
347 National Task Force on the Prevention and Treatment of Obesity. Weight Cycling. JAMA 1994 October 19;272(15):1196-1202.
348 Khan MA, Herzog CA, St. Peter JV, et al. The prevalence of cardiac valvular insufficiency assessed by transthoracic echocardiography in obese patients treated with appetite-suppressant drugs. The N Engl J Med 1998 September 10;339(11):713-8.
349 Weissman NJ, Tighe JF, Gottdiener JS, et al. An assessment of heart-valve abnormalities in obese patients taking dexfenfluramine, sustained-release dexfenfluramine, or placebo. N Engl J Med 1998 September 10;339(11):725-32.
350 Devereux RB. Appetite suppressants and valvular heart disease. N Engl J Med 1998 September 10;339(11):765-6.
351 Curfman GD. Diet pills redux. N Engl J Med 1997 August 28;337(9):629-30.
352 Mark EJ, Patalas ED, Chang HT, et al. Fatal pulmonary hypertension associated with short-term use of fenfluramine and phentermine. N Engl J Med 1997 August 28;337(9):600-1.
353 Marinella MA, Berrettoni BA. Digital necrosis associated with dexfenfluramine. Letter to the editor, N Engl J Med 1997 December 11;337(24):1775-6.
354 McCann UD, Seiden LS, Rubin LJ, et al. Brain serotonin neurotoxicity and primary pulmonary hypertension from fenfluramine and dexfenfluramine. JAMA 1997 August 27;278(8): 666-72.
355 The Medical Letter. Performance-enhancing drugs 2004 July 19;46(Issue 1187):57-9.
356 Matthews AW, Munoz, SS. Judge overturns ban on ephedra, roils FDA policy. Wall Street Journal 2005 April 15:A3,7.
357 Yanovski SZ, Yanovski JA. Obesity. N Engl J Med 2002 February 21;346(8):591-600.
358 Hampton T. More scrutiny for dietary supplements? JAMA 2005 January 5;293(1):27-8.
359 Yanovski SZ, Yanovski JA. Obesity. N Engl J Med 2002 February 21;346(8):591-600.
360 "Herbal Fen-Phen Warning". FDA Consumer 1998 January-February:2.
361 Haller CA, Benowitz NL. Adverse cardiovascular and central nervous system events associated with dietary supplements containing ephedra alkaloids. N Engl J Med 2000;343:1833-8.
362 Sullivan PF. Mortality in anorexia nervosa. Am J Psychiatry 1995;152:1073-4.
363 Becker AE, Grinspoon SK, Klibanski A, Herzig DB. Eating disorders. N Engl J Med 1999April 8;340(14):1092-8.
364 Anderson AE. Anorexia nervosa and bulimia in adolescent males. Pediatric Annals 1984 December;13(12):901-7.
365 Golden N, Sacker IM. An overview of the etiology, diagnosis, and management of anorexia nervosa. Clinical Pediatrics 1984 April;23(4):209-14.
366 Silber T. Anorexia nervosa: morbidity and mortality. Pediatric Annals 1984 November;13(11):851-8.
367 Foreyt JP, Poston WSC, Goodrick GK. Future directions in obesity and eating disorders. Addict Behav 1996;21:767-8.
368 Brown NW. Anorexia nervosa visited and revisited: weight is the issue. J Am Med Women's Assn 1993;48(1):23-6.
369 Campo-Flores A. "The legacy of Terri Schiavo." Newsweek 2005 April 4:22-8.
370 Herzog DB, Copeland PM. Medical progress: eating disorders. N Engl J Med 1985 August 1;313(5):295-302.
371 Miller KK, Grinspoon SK, Ciampa J, et al. Medical findings in outpatients with anorexia nervosa. Arch Int Med 2005;165:561-6.
372 Modan-Moses D, Yaroslavsky A, Novikov I, et al. Stunting of growth as a major feature of anorexia nervosa in male adolescents. Pediatrics 2003 February;111(2):270-6.
373 Nussbaum M, Baird D, Sonenblick M, et al. J Adolesc Health Care 1985;6:453-5.
374 Andersen Arnold E. Anorexia nervosa and bulimia in adolescent males. Pediatric Annals 1984 December;13(12):901-7.
375 Siegel JH, et al. Medical complications in male adolescents with anorexia nervosa. J Adolesc Health1995;16:448-53.
376 Katzman DK, Lambe EK, Mikulis DJ, et al. Cerebral gray matter and white matter volume deficits in adolescent girls with anorexia nervosa. J Peds 1996 December;129(6):794-803.

377 Golden NH, Ashtari M, Kohn MR, et al. Reversibility of cerebral ventricular enlargement in anorexia nervosa, demonstrated by quantitative magnetic resonance imaging. J Peds 1996 February;128(2):296-301.

378 Katzman DK, Christensen B, Young AR, Zipursky RB. Starving the brain: structural abnormalities and cognitive impairment in adolescents with anorexia nervosa. Semin Clin Neuropsychiatry 2001 Apr;6(2):146-52.

379 Katzman DK, Zipursky RB, Lambe EK, Mikulis DJ. A longitudinal magnetic resonance imaging study of brain changes in adolescents with anorexia nervosa. Arch Pediatr Adolesc Med 1997 August;151:793-7.

380 Rigotti NA, Nussbaum SR, Herzog DB, Neer RM. Osteoporosis in women with anorexia nervosa. N Engl J Med 1984 December 20;311(25):1601-6.

381 Misra M, Aggarwal A, Miller KK, et al. Effects of anorexia nervosa on clinical, hematologic, biochemical, and bone density parameters in community-dwelling adolescent girls. Pediatrics 2004 December;114(6):1574-83.

382 Szmukler GI, Brown SW, Parsons V, Darby A. Premature loss of bone in chronic anorexia nervosa. Br Med J 1985;290:26-7.

383 Raymond CA. Long-term sequelae pondered in anorexia nervosa. JAMA 1987 June 26;257(24):3324-5.

384 Golden NH, presenting at an American Academy of Pediatrics Meeting, reviewed in "Osteopenia is grave anorexia complication" by Sherman, Carl; in Pediatric News 1997; January;31(1).

385 Galetta F, Franzoni F, Cupisti A, et al. QT interval dispersion in young women with anorexia nervosa. J Pediatr 2002 April;140(4):456-60.

386 Franzoni F, Galetta F, Cupisti A, et al. Ultrasonic tissue characterization of the myocardium in anorexia nervosa. Acta Paediatr 2003;92(3):297-300.

387 De Simone G, Scalfi L, Galderisi M, et al. Cardiac abnormalities in young women with anorexia nervosa. Br Heart J 1994;71(3):287-92.

388 Palla B, Litt IF. Medical complications of eating disorders in adolescents. Pediatrics 1988 May 5;81(5):613-23.

389 Vande Berg, BC, et al. Anorexia nervosa: correlation between MR appearance of bone marrow and severity of disease. Radiology 1994;193:859-64.

390 Misra M, Aggarwas A, Miller KK, et al. Effects of anorexia nervosa on clinical, hematologic, biochemical, and bone density parameters in community-dwelling adolescent girls. Pediatrics 2004 December 6;114(6):1574-83.

391 Silber T. Anorexia nervosa: morbidity and mortality. Pediatric Annals 1984;13(11):851-8.

392 Gavish D, Eisenerg S, Berry EM, et al. An underlying behavioral disorder in hyperlipidemic pancreatitis: a prospective multidisciplinary approach. Archives of Internal Medicine 1987 April; 147(4):705-8.

393 Fong H-F, DiVasta AD, DiFabio D, et al. Prevalence and predictors of abnormal liver enzymes in young women with anorexia nervosa. J Pediatr 2008;153:247-53.

394 Silber T. Anorexia nervosa: morbidity and mortality. Pediatric Annals 1984;13(11):851-8.

395 Silber T. Anorexia nervosa: morbidity and mortality. Pediatric Annals 1984;13(11):851-8.

396 Beumont PJV, Large M. Hypophosphataemia, delirium, and cardiac arrhythmia in anorexia nervosa. Med J Aust 1991;155:519-22.

397 Katz RL, Keen CL, Litt IF. Zinc deficiency in anorexia nervosa. J Adolescent Health Care 1987 Sept;(8):400-6.

398 Quirk CM, Seykora J, Wingate BJ, Cotsarelis G. Acrodermatitis enteropathica associated with anorexia nervosa. JAMA 2002 December 4;288(21):2655-6.

399 Stewart DE, Robinson E, Goldbloom DS, Wright C. Infertility and eating disorders. Am J Obstet Gynecol 1990 Oct;163:1196-9.

400 Overby KJ, Litt IF. Mediastinal emphysema in an adolescent with anorexia nervosa and self-induced emesis. Pediatrics 1988 January;81(1):134-6.

401 Kirk AD, Bowers BA, Moylan JA, Meyers WC. Toothbrush swallowing. Arch Surg 1988;123:382-4.

402 Wilcox DT, Karamanoukian HL, Blick PL. Toothbrush ingestion by bulimics may require laparotomy. J Pediatr Surg 1994(29):1596.

403 Faust J, Schreiner O. A swallowed toothbrush. Lancet 2001;357:1012.

404 Silber T. Anorexia nervosa: morbidity and mortality. Pediatric Annals 1984;13(11):851-8.

405 Miller KK, Grinspoon SK, Ciampa J, et al. Medical findings in outpatients with anorexia nervosa. Arch Int Med 2005;165:561-6.

406 Rosenberg, Sarina. "On campus: addicted to exercise." Newsweek 2007 Apr 23:10.

407 Brown Myda Williams. Anorexia nervosa visited and revisited: weight is the issue. J Am Med Womens Assn 1993 January/February;48(1):23-6.

408 Golden N, Sacker IM. An overview of the etiology, diagnosis, and management of anorexia nervosa. Clinical Pediatrics 1984 April;23(4):209-14.

409 Golden N, Sacker IM. An overview of the etiology, diagnosis, and management of anorexia nervosa. Clinical Pediatrics 1984 April;23(4):209-14.

410 Andersen Arnold E. Anorexia nervosa and bulimia in adolescent males. Pediatric Annals 1984 December;13(12):901-7.

411 Czajka-Narins DM, Parham ES. Fear of fat: attitudes toward obesity; the thinning of America. Nutrition Today 1990 Jan/Feb;25(1):26-32.

412 Rubinstein S, Caballero B. Is Miss America an undernourished role model? JAMA 2000 March 22/29;283(12):1569.

413 Devlin MJ, Zhu A. Body image in the balance. JAMA 2001 November 7;286(17):2159.

414 Becker AE. *Body, Self, and Society: The View from Fiji*. Philadelphia, PA: University of Philadelphia Press; 1995.

415 Field AE, et al Arch Pediatr Adolesc Med 1999 November;153:1184-9.

416 Field AE, Cheung L, Wolf A, et al. Exposure to the mass media and weight concerns among girls. Pediatrics 1999 March;103(3)e36.

417 Martinez-Gonzalez, MA, Gual P, Lahortiga F, et al. Parental factors, mass media influences, and the onset of eating disorders in a prospective population-based cohort. Pediatrics 2003 February;111(2):315-20.

418 Brownell KD, Napolitano MA. Distorting reality for children: body size proportions of Barbie and Ken dolls. Int J Eat Disord 1995;18:295-8.

419 Focus and Opinion in Pediatrics 1996 May/June;2(3):241.

420 Graham, Judith. "Web sites fuel teen desire to be anorexic." Chicago Tribune 2001 August 5;Section 1:6.

421 Gomez JE. ATHENA (Athletes Targeting Healthy Exercise and Nutrition Alternatives);Arch Pediatr Adolesc Med 2004 Nov;158:1084-5.

422 Vaisman, Voet H, Akivis A, Sive-Ner I. Weight perception of adolescent dancing school students. Arch Pediatr Adolesc Med 1996 Feb;150(187-90).

423 Pediatric News 1989 March;23(3):7.

424 Oppliger RA, Landry GL, Foster SW, Lambrecht AC. Bulimic behaviors among interscholastic wrestlers: a statewide survey. Pediatrics 1993;91:826-31.

425 Stiene HA. A comparison of weight-loss methods in high school and collegiate wrestlers. Clin J Sport Med 1993;3:95-100.

426 Rosen LW, McKeag DB, Hough DO, Curley V. Pathogenic weight-control behavior in female athletes. Physician Sportmed 1986;14:79-84.

427 Rosen LW, Gough DO. Pathogenic weight-control behaviors of female college gymnasts. Physician Sportsmed 1988;16:141-4.

428 Nattiv A, Agostini R, Drinkwater B, et al. The female athlete triad: the interrelatedness of disordered eating, amenorrhea, and osteoporosis. Clin Sports Med 1994;13:405.

429 Stashwick Carole. When you suspect an eating disorder. Contemporary Pediatrics 1996 November;13(11):124-53.

430 Martinez-Gonzalez MA, Gual P, Lahortiga F, et al. Parental factors, mass media influences, and the onset of eating disorders in a prospective population-based cohort. Pediatrics 2003 February;111(2):315-20.

431 Comerci GD. Eating disorders in adolescents. Pediatr Rev 1988 Aug;10(2):37-47.

432 DuPont RL. Bulimia: a modern epidemic among adolescents. Pediatr Ann 1984 Dec;13(12):908-15.

433 Killen JD, Taylor B, Telch MJ, Saylor KE, Maron DJ, Robinson, TN. Self induced vomiting and laxative and diuretic use among teenagers. JAMA 1986 Mar;255(11):1447-9.

434 Neumark-Sztainer D, Hannan PJ. Weight-related behaviors among adolescent girls and boys. Arch Pediatr Adolesc Med 2000 June;154:569-77.

435 Body weight perceptions and selected weight-management goals and practices of high school students–United States, 1990. MMWR 1991 Nov 1;40(43):746-50.

436 Moore DC. Body image and eating behavior in adolescent boys. Am J Dis Child 1990 Apr;144(4):475-9.

437 Casper RC, Offer D. Weight and dieting concerns in adolescents; fashion or symptom? Pediatrics 1990 Sept;86(3):384-90.

438 Progress toward achieving the 1990 National Health Objectives for Improved Nutrition. MMWR 1991 July 12;40(27):459-63.

439 "Did you know that..." Tufts University Diet and Nutrition Letter 1990 July;8(5):3.

440 Neumark-Sztainer D, Story M, Hannan PJ, et al. Weight-related concerns and behaviors among overweight and nonoverweight adolescents. Arch Pediatr Adolesc Med 2002 Feb;156: 171-8.

441 Strauss RS. Self reported weight status and dieting in a cross-sectional sample of young adolescents. Arch Pediatr Adolesc Med 1999 July;153:741-7.

442 Moses N, Banilivy M-M, Lifshitz F. Fear of obesity among adolescent girls. Pediatrics 1989 March;83(3):393-8.

443 Maloney MJ, McGuire J, Daniels SR, Specker B. Dieting behavior and eating attitudes in children. Pediatrics 1989 Sept;84(3):482-9.

444 Pediatric News 1997 January;31(1).

445 Schreiber GB, Robins M, Striegel-Moore R, et al. Weight modification efforts reported by black and white preadolescent girls: National Heart, Lung, and Blood Institute Growth and Health Study. Pediatrics 1996 July;98:63-70.

446 Saarilehto S, Lapinleimu H, Keskinen S, et al. Body satisfaction in 8-year-old children after long-term dietary counseling in a prospective randomized atherosclerosis prevention trial. Arch Pediatr Adolesc Med 2003 August;157:753-8.

447 Maloney MJ, McGuire J, Daniels SR, Specker B. Dieting behavior and eating attitudes in children. Pediatrics 1989 Sept;84(3):482-9.

448 Bostic JQ, Muriel AC, Hack S, et al. Anorexia nervosa in a 7-year-old girl. J Dev Behav Pediatr 1997 Oct;18(5):331-3.

449 Parker SG. Psychological signs help identify eating disorders. Pediatric News 1998 July;32(7):42.

450 Martinez-Gonzalez MA, Gual P, Lahortiga F, et al. Parental factors, mass media influences, and the onset of eating disorders in a prospective population-based cohort. Pediatrics 2003 February;111(2):315-20.

451 Lilenfeld LR, et al. A controlled family study of anorexia nervosa and bulimia nervosa: psychiatric disorders in first-degree relatives and effects of proband comorbidity. Arch of Gen Psych 1998;55:603-10.

452 Stashwick, Carole. When you suspect an eating disorder. Contemporary Pediatrics 1996 November;13(11):124-153.

453 Committee on Sports Medicine and Fitness. Promotion of healthy weight-control practices in young athletes. Pediatrics 1996;97(5):752-3.

454 "Eating Disorders May Be Twice as Common in Type I Diabetic Girls". Pediatric News 1986 January.

455 Field AE, Austin B, Striegel-Moore R, et al. Weight concerns and weight control behaviors of adolescents and their mothers. Arch Pediatr Adolesc Med 2005 Dec;159:1121-6.

456 Keery H, Boutelle K, van den Beg P, Thompson JK. The impact of appearance-related teasing by family members. J Adol Health 2005 Aug;37(2):120-7.

457 Taylor CB, Bryson S, Doyle AC, et al. The adverse effect of negative comments about weight and shape from family and siblings on women at high risk for eating disorders. Pediatrics 2006 August;118(2):731-8.

458 Haines J, Neumark-Sztainer D, Eisenberg ME. Weight teasing and disordered eating behaviors in adolescents: longitudinal findings from project EAT (Eating Among Teens). Pediatrics 2006 Feb;117(2):e209-15.

459 Mehler PS. Bulimia Nervosa. New Engl J Med 2003 August 28;349(9):875-80.

460 Martinez-Gonzalez MA, Gual P, Lahortiga F, et al. Parental factors, mass media influences, and the onset of eating disorders in a prospective population-based cohort. Pediatrics 2003 February;111(2):315-20.

461 Freund KM, Graham SM, Lesky LG, Moscowitz MA. Detection of bulimia in a primary care setting. J Gen Intern Med 1993 May;8(5):236-42.

462 Cotton MA, Ball C, Robinson P. Four simple questions can help screen for eating disorders. J Gen Internal Med 2003;18:53-6.

463 Neumark-Sztainer D, Story M, French SA. Covariations of unhealthy weight loss behaviors and other high-risk behaviors among adolescents. Arch Pediatr Adolesc Med 1996 March;150:304-8.

464 Vastag, Brian. What's the connection? No easy answers for people with eating disorders and drug use. JAMA 2001 February 28;285(8):1006-7.

465 Yanovski JA, Yanovski SZ. Recent advances in basic obesity research. JAMA 1999 October 27;282(16):1504-7.

466 Dietz WH. Overweight in childhood and adolescence. N Engl J Med 2004 February 26;350(9):855-8.

467 Mayo Clinic Clinical Update. Family-based therapy for anorexia nervosa. Mayo Clinic 2005;21(2):1.

468 Schreiber GB, Robins M, Striegel-Moore R, et al. Weight modification efforts reported by black and white preadolescent girls: National Heart, Lung, and Blood Institute Growth and Health Study. Pediatrics 1996;98(1):63-70.

469 Saarilehto S, Lapinleimu H, Keskinen S, et al. Body satisfaction in 8-year-old children after long-term dietary counseling in a prospective randomized atherosclerosis prevention trial. Arch Pediatr Adolesc Med 2003 August;157:753-8.

470 National Association of Anorexia Nervosa and Associated Disorders. "ANAD Position Statement" 2004 Summer.

471 Saarilehto S, Lapinleimu H, Keskinen S, et al. Body satisfaction in 8-year-old children after long-term dietary counseling in a prospective randomized atherosclerosis prevention trial. Arch Pediatr Adolesc Med 2003 August;157:753-8.

472 Austin SB, Field AE, Wiecha J, et al. The impact of a school-based obesity prevention trial on disordered weight-control behaviors in early adolescent girls. Arch Pediatr Adolesc med 2005 March;159:225-30.

473 Austin SB, Kin J, Wiecha J, et al. School-based overweight preventive intervention lowers incidence of disordered weight-control behaviors in early adolescent girls. Arch Pediatr Adol Med 2007 Sept;161(9):865-9.

474 Taylor CB, Bryson S, Luce KH, et al Prevention of eating disorders in at-risk college-age women. Arch Gen Psych 2006 Aug;63(8):881-8.

475 Neumark-Sztainer Dianne. Addressing obesity and other weight-related problems in youth. Arch Pediatr and Adolesc Med 2005 March;159:290-1.

476 Eaton DK, Lowry R, Brener ND, et al. Associations of body mass index and perceived weight with suicide ideation and suicide attempts among US high school students. Arch Pediatr Adol Med 2005 June;159:513-9.

477 Eisenberg ME, Olson RE, Neumark-Sztainer D, Story M, Bearinger LH. Correlations between family meals and psychosocial well-being among adolescents. Arch Pediatr Adolesc Med 2004 August;158:792-6.

478 Milton, John. "On His Blindness", line 14.C

479 MacMillan, Julia A. Editorial: Puppies and children: some similarities. Contemporary Pediatr 2008 Mar;25(3).

480 Fisher, Roger; Ury, William. *Getting to Yes*. New York, NY; Penguin Books, 1981.

481 Mike Smith, Las Vegas Sun, 1998.

482 "The Principal's Office First". Editorial, New York Times 2009 Jan 4.

483 Weland, Ross. "Obnoxious parents win out over kids." Chicago Tribune 2006 Sept 17;Sec 13:8.

484 *Tanach; the Torah/Prophets/Writings: the twenty-four books of the Bible*. Brooklyn, NY; The ArtScroll Series, Stone Edition, 1996:1730-49.

485 Ladd, Less as quoted by Jeffrey Zaslow in "Out of line: why we're reluctant to reprimand other people's children." The Wall Street Journal 2006 July 27:D1.

486 Murphy, Sean. "Mom: my way or the highway." Chicago Tribune 2005 Nov 17:sec 1 p1.

487 Roese, Neal. *If Only; How to Turn Regret into Opportunity*. New York, NY; Broadway Books, 2005.

488 Zaslow, Jeffrey. The "guilted age': how to convert guilt into a productive emotion. Wall Street Journal 2006 Apr 6:D1.

489 Twitchell JB. *Lead Us Into Temptation*. New York, NY; Columbia University Press, 1999.

490 "Malls place curfews on teens but miss their pocket money." The Wall Street Journal 2007 June 29:B6.

491 "A cure for spiritual deficiency syndrome." Orthodox Union Department of Public Relations 2003 May .

492 Mason, Michael. "The energy-drink buzz is unmistakable." The health impact is unknown. The New York Times 2006 Dec 12.

493 Frye, Stephen H. Is the drug was working or worse than the disease. Letter to the editor, The Wall Street Journal 2008 Dec 13/14.

494 "Prescription abuse high". JAMA 2008 Jan 30;299(4):99.

495 McCabe SE. Screening for drug abuse among medical and nonmedical users of prescription drugs in a probability sample of college students. Arch Pediatr Adolesc Med 2008 March;162(3):225-1.

496 "Psychiatry". The Prescriber's Letter 2005 Jan:4.

497 Boyd CJ, McCabe SE, Cranford JA, Young A. Prescription drug abuse and diversion among adolescents in a southeast Michigan school district. Arch Pediatr Adol Med 2007 Mar;161:276-81.

498 Friedman Richard A. The changing face of teenage drug abuse—the trend toward prescription drugs. N Engl Med 2006 Apr 6;354(14):1448-50.

499 Jernigan DH, Ostroff J, Ross C, O'Hara JA III. Sex differences in adolescent exposure to alcohol advertising in magazines. Arch Pediatr Adolesc Med 2004 July;158:629-34.

500 McClure AC, Stoolmiller M, Tanski SE, et al. Alcohol-branded merchandise and its association with drinking attitudes and outcomes in US adolescents. Arch Pediatr Adolesc Med 2009 Mar;163(3):211-7.

501 Foster SE, Vaughan RD, Foster WH, Califano JA, Jr. Estimate of the commercial value of underage drinking and adult abusive and dependent drinking to the alcohol industry. Arch Pediatr Adolesc Med 2006 May;160:473-8.

502 Newsweek 2004 May 3:37.

503 Department of Health and Human Services, Centers for Disease Control and Prevention. Youth Risk Behavior Surveillance—United States, 2003. MMWR 2004 May 21;53(SS-2).

504 Department of Health and Human Services, Centers for Disease Control and Prevention. Youth Risk Behavior Surveillance—United States, 2003. MMWR 2004 May 21;53(SS-2).

505 Boyer EW, Shannon M, Hibberd PL. The internet and psychoactive substance use among innovative drug users. Pediatrics 2005 February;115(2):302-5.

506 Sullivan G. Raving on the Internet. CMAJ 2000;162(13):1864.

507 McColgan MD, Giardino AP. Internet poses multiple risks to children and adolescents. Pediatric Annals 2005 May;34(5):404-14.

508 Capitol Health Call: Drug Abuse "propaganda". JAMA 2005 February 9;293(6).

509 Jancin, Bruce. Ecstasy linked to permanent neurotoxicity: can emerge years later. Pediatric News 37(10);October, 2003:24.

510 Helmuth, Laura. Beyond the pleasure principle. Science 294;November 2, 2001:983-4.

511 Ungless, Mark. Nature; May 31, 2001.

512 Bada HS, Das A, Rauer CR, et al. Impact of prenatal cocaine exposure on child behavior problems through school age. Pediatrics 2007 Feb;119(2):e348-59.

513 Vogel G. Cocaine wreaks subtle damage on developing brains. Science 1997 Oct 3;278:38-9.

514 Singer LT, Nelson S, Short E, et al. Prenatal cocaine exposure: drug and environmental effects at 9 years. J Peds 2008 July;153:105-11.

515 Warner TD, Behnke M, Eler FD, et al. Diffusion tensor imaging of frontal white matter and executive functioning in cocaine-exposed children. Pediatrics 2006 Nov;118(5):2014-24.

516 Rivkin MJ, Davis PE, Lemaster JL, et al. volumetric MRI study of brain in children with intrauterine exposure to cocaine, alcohol, tobacco, and marijuana. Pediatrics 2008 pr;121(4):741-50.

517 Behnke M, Eyler FD, Warner TD, et al. Outcome from a prospective, longitudinal study of prenatal cocaine use: preschool development at 3 years of age; J Pediatr Psychol 2005 Apr 12;doi:10.1093/jpepsy/jsj027.

518 Richardson GA, Goldschmidt L, Larkby. Effects of prenatal cocaine exposure on growth: a longitudinal analysis. Pediatrics 2006 Oct;120:e1017-7.

519 De Moraes Barros MC, Ruinsburg R, De Araujo Pees, C, et al. Exposure to marijuana during pregnancy alters neurobehavior in the early neonatal period. J Pediatr 2006;149;781-7.

520 Dahl RE, Scher MS, Williamson DE, et al. A longitudinal study of prenatal marijuana use. Arch Pediatr Adolesc Med 1995 Feb;149:145-50.

521 Bada HS, Reynolds EW, Hansen WF. Marijuana use, adolescent pregnancy, and alteration in newborn behavior: how complex can it get? J Peds 2006 Dec;149:742-5.

522 Klonoff-Cohen H, Lam-Kruglick P. Maternal and paternal recreational drug use and sudden infant death syndrome. Arch Pediatr Adolesc Med 2001 July;155:765-70.

523 Masten AS, Faden VB, Zucker RA, Spear LP. Underage drinking: a developmental framework. Pediatrics 2008 Apr;121(4):S235-51.

524 Siqueira, Lorena M, as quoted by McNamara, Damian. "Straight talk can help dry up teen alcohol abuse." Pediatric News 2005 July:30.

525 Wilson W, Matthew R, Turkington T, Hawk T, Coleman RE, Provenzale J. Brain morphological changes and early marijuana use: a magnetic resonance and positron emission tomography study. J Addict Dis 2000;19(1):1-22.

526 Schilt T, de Win MML, Koeter M, et al. Cognition in novice ecstasy users with minimal exposure to other drugs: a prospective cohort study. Arch Gen Psych 2007;64:728-36.

527 Geis GL, DiGiulio G. Substernal chest pain with an abnormal electrocardiogram in an adolescent male presenting to a pediatric emergency department. Clin Ped Emerg Med 2005;6:257-62.

528 Hsue, Priscilla, as quoted by Boschert, Sherry in "Suspect cocaine use in patients with chest pain." Pediatric News 2007 Feb;41(2):41.

529 Williams JF, Storch M, and the Committee on Substance Abuse and the committee on Native American Child Health. Inhalant abuse. Pediatrics 2007 May;119(5):1009-17.

530 Crocetti M. Inhalants. Pediatrics in Review 2008 Jan;29(1):33-4.

531 Lypka MA, Urata MM. Cocaine-induced palatal perforation. N Engl J Med 2007 Nov 8;357(19):1956.

532 Stover MC, Perrone J. Vascular occlusion after intra-arterial cocaine injection. N Engl J Med 2006 Nov 9;355(19);2021.

533 Hurley, Chuck, CEO of Mothers Against Drunk Driving, as quoted by Kantrowitz B, Underwood A in "The teen drinking dilemma." Newsweek 2007 June 25:36.

534 Fernandez J, Lozano M. Cocaine-induced acute hepatitis and thrombotic microangiopathy. Letter to the editor, N Engl J Med 2005 June 8;293(22):2715.

535 Eldridge DL, Hillebrand K. Hallucinogens. Pediatrics in Review 2006 August;27(8):314-5.

536 Centers for Disease Control and Prevention. Unintentional poisoning deaths—United States, 1999-2004. MMWR 2007 Feb 9;56(5):94-6.

537 Centers for Disease Control and Prevention. Atypical reactions associated with heroin use—five states, January-April 2005. MMWR 2005 August 19;54(32):793-6.

538 Yong RL, Holmes DT, Sreenivasan GM. Aluminum toxicity due to intravenous injection of boiled methadone. Letter to the editor, N Engl J Med 2006 Mar 16;354(11):1210-1.

539 Ring, Priscilla. Pediatricians discuss meth's youngest victims. AAP News 2006 May:4.

540 Adolescent medicine—substance abuse. Pediatrics in Review 23(3);March, 2002.

541 Arendt M, Mortensen PB, Rosenberg R, et al. Familial predisposition for psychiatric disorder: comparison of subjects treated for cannabis-induced psychosis and schizophrenia. Arch Gen Psych 2008;65(11):1269-74.

542 Moore TH, Zammit S, Lingford-Hughes A, et al. Cannabis use and risk of psychotic or affective mental health outcomes: a systematic review. Lancet 2007 Jul 28;370(9584):319-28.

543 Zammit S, Allelbeck P, Andreasson S, et al. Self reported cannabis use as a risk factor for schizophrenia in Swedish conscripts of 1969: historical cohort study. British Med J 2002 Nov 23;325(7374):1199-2001.

544 Arsenault L, Cannon M, Poulton R, et al. Cannabis use in adolescence and risk for adult psychosis: longitudinal prospective study. British Med J 2002 Nov 23;325(7374):1212-13.

545 Boutros NN, Bowers MB Jr. Chronic substance-induced psychotic disorders: state of the literature. J Neuropsychiatry Clin Neuroscience 1996 Summer; 8(3):262-9.

546 Patton, GC, Coffey C, Carlin JB, et al. Cannabis use and mental health in young people: cohort study. British Med J 2002 November 23;325(7374):1195-8.

547 Silverman, Jennifer. "Depression and marijuana use." Pediatric News 2005 June;39(6):48.

548 Hayatbakhsh MR, Najman JM, Jamrozik K, et al. Cannabis and anxiety and depression in young adults: a large prospective study. J Am Acad Child Adolesc Psych 2007 March;46(3):408-17.

549 American Academy of Pediatrics, Committee on Substance Abuse. Marijuana—a continuing concern for pediatricians. Pediatrics104(4); October 4, 1999:982-5.

550 Lynskey MT, Heath AC, Bucholz KK, et al. Escalation of drug use in early-onset cannabis users versus co-twin controls. JAMA 2003 Jan 22/29;289(4):427-33.

551 Herman-Stahl MA, Krebs CP, Kroutil LA, Heller DC. Risk and protective factor for nonmedical use of prescription stimulants and methamphetamine among adolescents. J Adolesc Health 2006 Sept;39(3):374-80.

552 Compton WM, Grant BF, Colliver JD, Glantz MD, Stinson FS. Prevalence of marijuana use disorders in the United States. JAMA 2004 May 5;291(17):2114-21.

553 Hilliker Kevin. "As marijuana use rises, more people are seeking treatment for addiction." The Wall Street Journal 2006 May 2:D1.

554 Lynskey M, Hall W. The effects of adolescent cannabis use on educational attainment: a review. Addiction 2000;95:1621-30.

555 Lehman WE, Simpson DD. Employee substance abuse and on-the-job behaviors. J Appl Psychol 1992;77:309-21.

556 National Highway Traffic Safety Administration. *Traffic Safety Facts 2001.* Washington DC: national Highway Traffic Safety Administration; 2001.

557 Bolla KI, Brown K, Eldreth D, et al. Dose-related neurocognitive effects of marijuana use. Neurology 2002 Nov 12;59(9):1337-43.

558 Khalsa, Jag H, as quoted by McNamara, Damian in "Federal researcher: marijuana use prevention should start at age 8." Pediatric News 2007 Sept:32.

559 Mittleman MA, Lewis RA, Maclure M, Sherwood JB, Muller JE. Triggering myocardial infarction by marijuana. Circulation 2001;103:2805-9.

560 Tashkin DP. Pulmonary complications of smoked substance abuse. West J Med 1990;152:525-30.

561 Zhang ZF, Morgenstern H, Spitz MR, et al. Marijuana use and increased risk of squamous cell carcinoma of the head and neck. Cancer Epid Biomarkers Prev 1999;8:1071-8.

562 Compton WM, Grant BF, Colliver JD, Glantz MD, Stinson FS. Prevalence of marijuana use disorders in the United States. JAMA 2004 May 5;291(17):2114-21.

563 Wu T-C, Tashkin DP, Djahed B, Rose JE. Pulmonary hazards of smoking marijuana as compared to tobacco. N Engl J Med 1988 Feb 11;318(6):47-51.

564 Ferguson RP, Hasson J, Walker S. Metastatic lung cancer in a young marijuana smoker. JAMA 1989 Jan 6;261(1):41-2.

565 Geller T, Loftis L, Brink DS. Cerebellar infarction in adolescent males associated with acute marijuana use. Pediatrics 2004;113:e360-4

566 Kagen SL. *Aspergillus*: an inhalable contaminant of marijuana. N Engl J Med 1981;304:483-4.

567 Schwartz IS. Marijuana and fungal infection. Am J Clin Pathol 1985;84:256.

568 Kurup VP, Resnick A, Kagan SL, et al. Allergenic fungi and actinomycetes in smoking materials and their health implications. Mycopathologia 1983;82:61-8.

569 Kagan SL, Kurup VP, Sohnle PG, et al. Marijuana smoking and fungal sensitization. J Allergy Clin Immunol 1983;71:389-93.

570 Thomson WM, Poulton R, Broadbent JM, et al. Cannabis smoking and periodontal disease among young adults. JAMA 2008 Feb;299(5):525-31.

571 Harrison LH, Kreiner CJ, Shutt KA, et al. Risk factors for meningococcal disease in students grades 9-12. Pediatr Inf Dis J 2008 Mar;27(3):193-9.

572 Pacifici, Roberta, et al. Research letter: modulation of the immune system in cannabis users. JAMA 289(15);April 16, 2003:1929-31.

573 Centers for Disease Control and Prevention. Heterosexual transmission of HIV—29 states. MMWR 2004 Feb 20;53(6):125-9.

574 Semple SJ, Patterson TL, Grant I. Motivations associated with methamphetamine use among HIV+ men who have sex with men. J Subst Abuse Treat 2002 Apr;22(3):149-56.

575 Urbina A, Jones K. Crystal methamphetamine, its analogues, and HIV infection: medical and psychiatric aspects of a new epidemic. Clin Infect Dis 2004 Mar;38(6):890-4.

576 The Medical Letter. Methamphetamine abuse. The Medical Letter 2004 August 2;46(Issue 1188):62.

577 Khalsa, Jag H, as quoted by McNamara, Damian. Federal researcher: marijuana use prevention should start at age 8. Pediatric News 2007 Sept:32.

578 Hingsten, R, Heeren T, Winter MR, Wechsler H. early age of first drunkenness as a factor in college students' unplanned and unprotected sex attributable to drinking. Pediatrics 2003 May;111:34-41..

579 Committee on Pediatric AIDS. Reducing the risk of HIV infection associated with illicit drug use. Pediatrics 2006;117;566-71.

580 Ellickson, DL, Tucker JS, Klein DJ. Ten-year prospective study of public health problems associated with early drinking. Pediatrics 2003 May;111(5Pt1):949-54.

581 Centers for Disease Control and Prevention. Alcohol use among adolescents and adults—New Hampshire, 1991-2003. MMWR 53(8):174-5.

582 Brewer RD, Swahn MH. Binge drinking and violence. JAMA 2005 Aug 3;294(5):616-8.

583 Centers for Disease Control and Prevention. Alcohol-attributable deaths and years of potential life lost—United States, 2001. 2004 Sept 24;53(37):866-70.

584 Hingson R, Heeren T, Winter M, Wechsler H. Magnitude of alcohol-related mortality and morbidity among US college students ages 18-24: changes from 1998-2001. Ann Rev Publ Health 2005;26:259-79.

585 "College: a time to booze and get high." Contemporary Pediatrics 2007 Apr;24(4):15.

586 Cole, TB. Rape at US colleges often fueled by alcohol. JAMA 2006 August;296(5):504-5.

587 Worcester, Sharon. Energy drink sales hit $3billion—at what health cost; millions of teens go for their buzz. Pediatric News 2007 Feb;41(2):1,4.

588 O'Brien MC, McCoy TP, Rhodes SD, Wagoner A, Wolfson M. Caffeinated cocktails: energy drink consumption, high-risk drinking, and alcohol-related consequences among college students. Acad Emerg Med 2008 May;15(5):453-60.

589 McGinn CG. Close calls with club drugs. N Engl J Med 2005 June 30;352(26):2671-2.

590 Brown SA, McGue , Maggs J, et al. A developmental perspective on alcohol and youths 16 to 20 years of age. Pediatrics 2008 Apr;121, Suppl 4:S290-310.

591 Leirer VO, et al. Marijuana carry-over effects on aircraft pilot performance. Aviat Space Environ Med 1991;62:221-7.

592 Zador PL, Krawchuk SA, Voas RB. Alcohol-related relative risk of driver fatalities and driver involvement in fatal crashes in relation to driver age and gender: an update using 1996 data. J Stud Alcohol 2000;61(3):387-95.

593 Warren, Susan. "Spring break is a legal specialty for Ben Bollinger; Florida lawyer enjoys a spike in his business; defendants in flip-flops." The Wall Street Journal 2007 Mar 17;A1,10.

594 "Very tough love". People 2006 Oct 2:90.

595 Busse F, Omidi L, Windgassen M, Kluge E. Lead poisoning due to adulterated marijuana. Letter to the editor, N Engl J Med 2008 Apr 10;358(15):1641-2.

596 Sanchez, Jaun; Lilac, Laura; Holt, Richard W. Gunshot wounds to legs in drug runners. NEJM April 20, 1989.

597 Rothstein SG; Gittelman, Paul; Persky, Mark. Crack smiles. JAMA 265(12); March 27, 1991.

598 Luhnow D, deCordoba, J. "Hit men kill Mexican hero's family". The Wall Street Journal 2009 Dec 23:A1,12.

599 Benuck Irwin, Jurtarte Jennifer. Polls show many teens get alcohol from parents. Illinois Pediatrician 2005 Fall;23(3):15.

600 "Adults most common source of alcohol for teens, according to poll of teens 13-18." Press release; Chicago IL; American Medical Association 2005 August 8.

601 "Underage drinking prevention course." Infectious Diseases in Children 2006 October.

602 Swahn MH, Bossarte RM, Sullivant EE 3rd. Age of alcohol use initiation, suicidal behavior, and peer and dating violence victimization and perpetration among high-risk, seventh-grade adolescents. Pediatrics 2008;121(2):297-305.

603 Hingson RW, Heeren T, Jamanka A, Howland J. Age of drinking onset and unintentional injury involvement after drinking. JAMA 2000 September 27;284(12):1527-33.

604 McCarty CA, Ebel BE, Garrison MM, et al. Continuity of binge and harmful drinking from late adolescence to early adulthood. Pediatrics 2004 September;114(3):714-9.

605 Hingson RW, Heeren T, Winter MR. Age at drinking onset and alcohol dependence; age at onset, duration, and severity. Arch Pediatr Adolesc Med 2006 July;160:739-46.

606 McCarty CA, Ebel BE, Garrison MM, et al. Continuity of binge and harmful drinking from late adolescence to early adulthood. Pediatrics 2004 Sept;114(3):714-9.

607 Hingson R, Kenkel D. Social, health and economic consequences of underage drinking. In: Bonnie R, ed. *Reducing Underage Drinking: A Collective Responsibility*. Washington, DC; National Academies Press, 2004:351-82.

608 Donovan, John E. Estimated blood alcohol concentrations for child and adolescent drinking and their implications for screening instruments. Pediatrics 2009;123:e975-81.

609 Swahn MH, Bossarte RM. Gender, early alcohol use, and suicide ideation and attempts: findings from the 2005 youth risk behavior survey. J Adolesc Health 2007 August;41(2):175-81.

610 Swahn MH, Bossarte RM, Sullivent EE. Eage of alcohol use initiation, suicidal behavior, and peer and dating violence victimization and perpetration among high-risk, seventh-grade adolescents. Pediatrics 2008 Feb;121(2):297-305.

611 Deardorff J, Gonzales NA, Christopher S, et al. Early puberty and adolescent pregnancy: the influence of alcohol. Pediatrics 2005 Dec;116(6):1451-6.

612 Miller JW, Naimi TS, Brewer RD, Jones SE. Binge drinking and associated health risk behaviors among high school students. Pediatrics 2007 Jan;119(1):76-85.

613 Benuck I, Hurtarte J. Polls show many teens get alcohol from parents. Illinois Pediatrician 2005 Fall:15.

614 Adults most common source of alcohol for teens, according to poll of teens 13-18 (press release). Chicago: American Medical Association 2005 Aug 8.

615 "Ups and down in the picture of teenage substance abuse". Contemporary Pediatrics 2006 Oct;23(10):10.

616 Zailackas, Koren. Smashed; Story of a Drunken Girlhood. New York, NY; Viking Penguin Group, 2005.

617 Grant BF, Dawson DA. Age at onset of alcohol use and its association with DSM IV alcohol abuse and dependence: results from the National Longitudinal Alcohol Epidemiological Survey. J Substance Abuse 9:1997:103-10.

618 United States Department of HHS. Preventing tobacco use among young people: a report of the Surgeon General. Washington DC: US Dept. of HHS, 1994.

619 Marijuana and medicine: assessing the science base. Washington, DC: National Academies Press, 1999.

620 Fergusson DM, et al. Early reactions to cannabis predict later dependence. Arch of Gen Psych 60;2003:1033-9.

621 Marijuana and medicine: assessing the science base. Washington, DC: National Academies Press, 1999.

622 "Study: one in 10 Scottish teens using cocaine." Contemporary Pediatrics 2008 March;25(3):23.

623 Lawson, Kim. MRI finds teens have less frontal cortex function than adults. Pediatric News 34(5);May, 2000.

624 Vastag, Brian. Nora Volkow MD; NIDA's new leader: from rejection to direction. JAMA 290(20);November 26, 2003:2647-52.

625 Vastag, Brian. Nora Volkow MD; NIDA's new leader: from rejection to direction. JAMA 290(20);November 26, 2003:2647-52.

626 Vastag, Brian. Brain sabotages sobriety, right on cue. JAMA 291(9);March 3,2004:1053-5.

627 Tapert, Susan. Arch Gen Psychiatry, volume 60; 2003: 727-35.

628 Anderson MR, Leroux BG, Bricker JB, Rajan KB, Peterson AV. Antismoking parenting practices are associated with reduced rates of adolescent smoking. Arch Pediatr Adolesc Med 2004 April;158:348-52.

629 Albers AB, Biener L, Siegel M, et al. Household smoking bans and adolescent antismoking attitudes and smoking initiation: findings from a longitudinal study of Massachusetts youth cohort. Am J Publ Health 2008;98(10):1886-93.

630 Dalton MA, Adachi-Mejia AM, Longacre MR, et al. Parental rules and monitoring of children's movie viewing associated with children's risk for smoking and drinking. Pediatrics 2006 Nov;118(5):1932-42.

631 Stanton B, Cole M, Galbraith J, et al. Randomized trial of a parent intervention. Arch Pediatr Adolesc Med 2004 October;158:947-55.

632 Flay BR, Graumlich S, Segawa E, et al. Effects of 2 prevention programs on high-risk behaviors among African American youth. Arch Pediatr Adolesc Med 2004 April;158:377-84.

633 Spoth RL, Clair S, Shin C, Redmond C. Long-term effects of universal preventive interventions on methamphetamine use among adolescents. Arch Pediatr Adolesc Med 2006;160:876-82.

634 Steinberg, Lawrence. Parental monitoring and peer influence on alcohol and substance use. Pediatrics 93(6);June, 1994:1060-72.

635 Brook JS, et al. The role of parents in protecting Colombian adolescents from delinquency and marijuana use. Arch Pediatr and Adolesc Med 153;May, 1999:457-64.

636 DiClemete RJ, et al. Parental monitoring: associated with adolescents' risk behavior. Pediatrics 107(6);June, 2001:1363-6.

637 DiClemete RJ, Wingood GM, Crosby R, et al. Parental monitoring: associated with adolescents' risk behavior. Pediatrics 2001 June; 107(6):1363-6.

638 Chen C-Y, Storr CL, Anthony JC. Influences of parenting practices on the risk of having a chance to try cannabis. Pediatrics 2005 June;115(6):1631-9.

639 Hindelang RL. Adolescent risk-taking behavior: a review of the role of parental involvement. Current problems in pediatrics; March, 2001:67-82.

640 Centers for Disease Control and Prevention. Youth Risk Behavior Surveillance—United States, 2007. MMWR 2008 June 6;57(SS-4).

641 Barnett TA, Gauvin L, Lambert M, et al. The influence of school smoking policies on student tobacco use. Arch Pediatr Adolesc Med 2007 Sept;161(9):842-8.

642 Biederman J, Faraone SV, Monuteaux MC, Feighner JA. Patterns of alcohol and drug use in adolescents can be predicted by parental substance use disorders. Pediatrics 2000 Oct;106(4):792-7.

643 Hughes PH, Conard SE, Baldwin DC Jr, et al. Resident physician substance use in the United States. JAMA 1991 Apr 24;265(16):2069-73.

644 McAuliffe WE, Rohman M, Santangelo S, et al. Psychoactive drug use among practicing physicians and medical students. NEJM 1986 Sept 25;315(13):805-10.

645 Verghese, Abraham. Physicians and addiction. NEJM 346(20);May 16, 2002:1510-11.

646 Menk EJ, Baumgarten RK, Kingsley CP, et al. Success of re-entry into anesthesiology training programs by residents with a history of substance abuse. JAMA 1990 June 13;263(22):3060-2.

647 Schernhammer, Eva. Taking their own lives—the high rate of physician suicide. N Engl J Med 2005 June 16;352(24):2473-6.

648 National Center on Addiction and Substance Abuse (CASA) at Columbia University. Prescription drug diversion and abuse: final report. New York; CASA:2005.

649 Sung H, Richter L, Vaughan R, et al. Misuse of prescription opioids rising among teens. J Adolesc Health 2005;37:44-51.

650 Hall AJ, Logan JE, Toblin RL, et al. Patterns of abuse among unintentional pharmaceutical overdose fatalities. JAMA 2008 Dec 10;300(22):2613-20.

651 Substance Abuse and Mental Health Services Administration. Non-medical use of prescription-type drugs among youths and young adults, the NHSDA Report. Rockville, MD; SAMHSA, 2003.

652 Steinberg, Lawrence. Parental monitoring and peer influence on alcohol and substance use. Pediatrics 93(6);June, 1994:1060-72.

653 Kuntsche E, Simons-Morton B, Fotiou A, et al. Decrease in adolescent cannabis use from 2002 to 2006 and links to evenings out with friends in 31 European and North American countries and regions. Arch Pediatr Adol Med 2009 Feb;163(2):119-25.

654 Baruzzi, Roberto and Franco, Laercio. Western Diseases. Harvard University Press, 1981. Chapter 10, page 148.

655 "April is alcohol awareness and underage drinking prevention month." Illinois Chapter, American Academy of Pediatrics ICAAP-lets 2007 April:5.

656 Kantrowitz B, Underwood A. "The teen drinking dilemma." Newsweek 2007 June 25:36.

657 Rothman EF, Edwards EM, Heeren T, Hingson RW. Adverse childhood experiences predict earlier age of drinking onset: results from a representative of US sample of current or former drinkers. Pediatrics 2008 Aug;122(2):e298-304.

658 Modesto-Lowe, Vania. The conduct disorder-alcohol link: implications for prevention strategies. Letter to the editor, Pediatrics 2008 July;122(1):209.

659 Young SYN, Hansen J, Gibson RL, Ryan MAK. Risky alcohol use, age at onset of drinking, and adverse childhood experiences in young men entering the US Marine Corps. Arch Pediatr Adolesc Med 2006 Dec;160:1207-14.

660 Wu P, Bird HR, Fan B, et al. Childhood depressive symptoms and early onset of alcohol use. Pediatrics 2006 Nov;118(5):1907-15.

661 Hampton, Tracy. Interplay of genes and environment found in adolescents' alcohol use. JAMA 2006 Apr 19;295(15):1760-1.

662 Fisher LB, Miles IW, Austin B, et al. Predictors of initiation of alcohol use among US adolescents. Arch Pediatr Adolesc Med 2007 Oct;161(10):959-66.

663 Johnson C, Drgon T, Liu QR, et al. Pooled association genome scanning for alcohol dependence using 104,268 SNP's: validation and use to identify alcoholism vulnerability loci in unrelated individuals from the collaborative study on the genetics of alcoholism. Am J Med Genet B Neuropsychiatr Gen 2006 Dec 5;141B(8):844-53.

664 Fisher LB, Miles IW, Austin B, et al. Predictors of initiation of alcohol use among US adolescents. Arch Pediatr Adolesc Med 2007 Oct;161(10):959-66.

665 Wechsler H, Lee JE, Kuo M, et al. Trends in college binge drinking during a period of increased prevention efforts: findings from 4 Harvard School Public Health College Alcohol Study Surveys: 1993-2001. J Am Coll Health 2002;50:202-17.

666 Cole, Thomas B. Rape at US colleges often fueled by alcohol. JAMA 2006 Aug 2;296(5):504-5.

667 Knight JR, Schrier L, Bravender T, et al. A new brief screen for adolescent alcohol abuse. Arch Pediatr Adol Med 1999;153:591.

668 Splete, Heidi. Developmental factors play role in teen drinking. Pediatric News 2008 June:23.

669 Markowitz S, Grossman M. The effects of beer taxes on physical child abuse. J Health Econ 2000;19:271-82.

670 Brewer RD, Swahn MH. Binge Drinking and violence. JAMA 2005 Aug 3;295(5):616-8

671 Centers for Disease Control and Prevention. Enhanced enforcement of laws to prevent alcohol sales to underage persons—New Hampshire, 1999-2004. MMWR 2004;53:452-4.

672 McClure, Auden as quoted by Kilgore, Christine. Alcohol promotional items raise risk of Drinking. Pediatric News 2005 July:31.

673 Young SYN, Hansen J, Gibson RL, Ryan MAK. Risky alcohol use, age at onset of drinking, and adverse childhood experiences in young men entering the US Marine Corps. Arch Pediatr Adolesc Med 2006 Dec;160:1207-14.

674 Wu P, Bird HR, Fan B, et al. Childhood depressive symptoms and early onset of alcohol use. Pediatrics 2006 Nov;118(5):1907-15.

675 Hampton, Tracy. Interplay of genes and environment found in adolescents' alcohol use. JAMA 2006 Apr 19;295(15):1760-1.

676 Eisenberg ME, Neumark-Sztainer D, Fulkerson JA, Story M. Family meals and substance use: is there a long-term protective association? J Adolesc Health 2008 Aug;43(2):151-6.

677 Fisher LB, Miles IW, Austin B, et al. Predictors of initiation of alcohol use among US adolescents. Arch Pediatr Adolesc Med 2007 Oct;161(10):959-66.

678 Hanewinkel R, Tanski S, Sargent JD. Exposure to alcohol in motion pictures and teen drinking in Germany. Presentation at the Pediatric Academic Societies' Annual Meeting, 2007 May 5-8; Toronto, Canada.

679 Centers for Disease Control and Prevention. Youth exposure to alcohol advertising on radio—United States, June-August, 2004. MMWR 2006 Sept 1;55(34):937-40.

680 Centers for Disease Control and Prevention. Youth exposure to alcohol advertising in magazines—United States, 2001-5. MMWR 2007 Aug 3;56(30):763-7.

681 "Mass. To add a recovery high school." Pediatric News 2006 May;40(5):56.

682 "A cure for spiritual deficiency syndrome." Orthodox Union Department of Public Relations 2003 May .

683 Tompkins, Ptolemy. Father Sam; How a humble priest is changing the world, one life at a time. Guideposts 2005 Oct;18-22.

684 Hansen, Helena. Faith-based treatment for addiction in Puerto Rico. JAMA 2004 June 16;291(23):2882.

685 Southgate M Therese. The Cover. JAMA 2007 Jan 3;297(1):11.

686 Koepsell, Thomas D. Rembrandt Peale (1778-1860). Arch Pediatr Adolesc Med 2005 Dec;159:1100.

687 Centers for Disease Control and Prevention. Youth Risk Behavior Surveillance—United States, 2007. MMWR 2008 June 6;57(SS-4).

688 Halpern-Felsher BL, Cornell JL, Kropp RY, Tschann JM. Oral versus vaginal sex among adolescents: perceptions, attitudes, and behavior. Pediatrics 2005 April;115(4):845-51.

689 Centers for Disease Control and Prevention. Trends in sexual risk behaviors among high school students: United States, 1991-2001. MMWR 2002;51:856-9.

690 Centers for Disease Control and Prevention. Youth Risk Behavior Surveillance—United States, 2007. MMWR 2008 June 6;57(SS-4).

691 Department of Health and Human Services, Centers for Disease Control and Prevention. Youth Risk Behavior Surveillance—United States, 2003. MMWR 2004 May 21;53(SS-2).

692 McGinn, Daniel. "Mating Behavior 101." Newsweek 2004 October 4:44-5.

693 "Together Time: Home Remedies for Great Sex" Parents 2005 April:98.

694 "Sex, Romance & the New Dad." Child 2005 June-July.

695 Smart Solutions; One Mom Asks: "I wish my husband and I had sex as much as we used to. What can we do?" Parenting 2005 June:47.

696 Brashares, Ann. The Sisterhood of the Traveling Pants. New York, NY; Delacorte Press, 2001.

697 Geller, Mark. My Life in the 7th Grade. New York, NY; Harper & Row, Publishers, 1986.

698 Collins RL, Elliott MN, Berry SH, et al. Watching sex on television predicts adolescent initiation of sexual behavior. Pediatrics 2004;114:e280-9.

699 Cope-Farrar KM, Kunkel D. Sexual messages in teens' favorite prime-time television programs. In: Brown JD, Steele JR, Walsh-Childers K, editors. Sexual Teens, Sexual Media: Investigating Media's Influence on Adolescent Sexuality. Mahwah, NJ: Lawrence Erlbaum;2002:59-78.

700 Kunkel D, Biely E, Eyal K. Cope-Farrar K, Donnerstein E, Fandrich R. Sex on TV 3: a biennial report to the Kaiser Family Foundation, 2003. Available at www.kff.org/entmedia/loader.cfm?url=/commonspot/security/getfile.cfm&PageID-14209. as accessed 2005 Jan 27.

701 Escobar-Chaves SL, ed. Impact of the media on adolescent sexual attitudes and behaviors. Pediatrics 2005 July;116(1)Suppl:297-331.

702 Committee on Public Education, American Academy of Pediatrics. Sexuality, contraception, and the media. Pediatrics 2001;107(1):191-3

703 Collins RL, Elliott MN, Berry SH, et al. Watching sex on television predicts adolescent initiation of sexual behavior. Pediatrics 2004;114:e280-9.

704 Chandra A, Martino SC, Collins RL, et al. Does watching sex on television predict teen pregnancy? Findings from a national longitudinal survey of youth. Pediatrics 2008 Nov;122(5):1047-54.

705 Collins RL, Elliott MN, Berry SH, et al. Watching sex on television predicts adolescent initiation of sexual behavior. Pediatrics 2004;114:e280-9.

706 Ashby SL, Arcari CM, Edmonson B. Television viewing and risk of sexual initiation by young adolescents. Arch Pediatr Adolesc Med 2006 Apr;160:375-80.

707 Wingood, GM, DiClemente RJ, Harrington K, et al. Exposure to X-rated movies and adolescents' sexual and contraceptive-related attitudes and behaviors. Pediatrics 2001 May;107(5):1166-9.

708 Martino SC, Collins RL, Elliott MN, et al. Exposure to degrading versus nondegrading music lyrics and sexual behavior among youth. Pediatrics 2006 August;118(2):e430-41.

709 Adam MB, McGuire JK, Walsh M, Basta J, LeCroy C. Acculturation as a predictor of the onset of sexual intercourse among Hispanic and white teens. Arch Pediatr Adolesc Med 2005 March;159:261-5.

710 Hoadland, Brother Kenneth, and Eichner, Reverend Philip. "Too much of a good thing: the party's over." Chicago Tribune 2005 Oct 23.

711 Sieving RE, McNeely CS, Blum RW. Maternal expectations, mother-child connectedness, and adolescent sexual debut. Arch Pediatr Adolesc Med 2000 August;154:809-16.

712 Romer D, Stanton B, Galbraith J, Feigelman S, Black MM, Li X. Parental influence on adolescent sexual behavior in high-poverty settings. Arch Pediatr Adolesc Med 1999 October;153:1055-62.

713 Ashby SL, Arcari CM, Edmonson B. Television viewing and risk of sexual initiation by young adolescents. Arch Pediatr Adolesc Med 2006 Apr;160:375-80.

714 Ford CA, Pence BW, Miller WC, et al. Predicting adolescents' longitudinal risk for sexually transmitted infection: results from the National Longitudinal Study of Adolescent Health. Arch Pediatr Adolesc Med 2005;159:657-64.

715 Resnick MD, Bearman PS, Blum RW, et al. Protecting adolescents from harm. Findings from the National Longitudinal Study on Adolescent Health. JAMA 1997 Sept 10;278(10):823-32.

716 Ford CA, Pence BW, Miller WC, et al. Predicting adolescents' longitudinal risk for sexually transmitted infection: results from the National Longitudinal Study of Adolescent Health. Arch Pediatr Adolesc Med 2005 July;159:657-64.

717 Ford CA, Pence BW, Miller WC, et al. Predicting adolescents' longitudinal risk for sexually transmitted infection: results from the National Longitudinal Study of Adolescent Health. Arch Pediatr Adolesc Med 2005 July;159:657-64.

718　Gold, Melanie, as quoted by Mahoney, Diana in "Religiosity may stem risky sexual behavior in girls." Pediatric News 2007 September;41(9):22.

719　Splete, Heidi. "Help guide patients to healthy adult sexuality". Pediatric News 2004 August;38(8):39.

720　Roche KM, Ellen J, Astone NM. Effects of out-of-school care on sex initiation among young adolescents in low-income central city neighborhoods. Arch Pediatr Adolesc Med 2005 January;159:68-73.

721　Crosby RA, DiClemente FJ, Wingood GM. Infrequent parental monitoring predicts sexually-transmitted infections among low-income African American female adolescents. Arch Pediatr Med 2003;157:169-73.

722　DiClemente RJ, Wingood GM, Crosby Ra, et al. Parental monitoring and its association with a spectrum of adolescent health risk behaviors. Pediatrics 2001;107:1363-8.

723　Bettinger JA, Celentano DD, Curriero FC, Adler NE, Millstein SG, Ellen JM. Does parental involvement predict new sexually transmitted diseases in female adolescents. Arch Pediatr Adolesc Med 2004 July;158:666.

724　Crosby RA, DiClemente FJ, Wingood GM. Infrequent parental monitoring predicts sexually-transmitted infections among low-income African American female adolescents. Arch Pediatr Med 2003;157:169-73.

725　Ford CA, Pence BW, Miller WC, et al. Predicting adolescents' longitudinal risk for sexually transmitted infection: results from the National Longitudinal Study of Adolescent Health. Arch Pediatr Adolesc Med 2005 July;159:657-64.

726　Cohen DA, Farley TA, Taylor SN, et al. When are where do youths have sex? The potential role of adult supervision. Pediatrics 2002;110(6):e66.

727　Sieverding JA, Adler N, Witt S, Ellen J. The influence of parental monitoring on adolescent sexual initiation. Arch Pediatr Adolesc Med 2005 Aug;159:724-9.

728　Wight D. Parental influences on young people's sexual behaviour: a longitudinal analysis. J Adolesc 2006;29(4):473-94.

729　Rai AA, Stanton B, Wu Y, et al. Relative influences of perceived parental monitoring and perceived peer involvement on adolescent risk behaviors: an analysis of six cross-sectional data sets. J Adolesc Health 2003;33(2):108-18.

730　Romer D, Stanton B, Galbraith S, et al. Parental monitoring and communications as influences on adolescent sexual behavior in high-risk urban settings. Arch Pediatr Adolesc Med 1999;153(10):1055-62.

731　Steinberg L, Fletcher D. Parental monitoring and peer influences on adolescent substance use. Pediatrics 1994;93(6 pt 2):1060-4.

732　Cheung CK, Liu SC, Lee TY. Parents, teachers, and peers and early adolescent runaway in Hong Kong. Adolescence 2005;40(158):403-24.

733　Shek DT, Lee TY. Perceived parental control processes in Chinese adolescents: implications for positive youth development programs in Hong Kong. Int J Adolesc Med Health 2006;18(3):505-19.

734　Steinberg L, Dornbusch SM, Brown BB. Ethnic differences in adolescent achievement: an ecological perspective. Am Psychol 1992;47(6):723-9.

735　Chewning B, Douglas J, Kokotailo PK, et al. Protective factors associated with American Indian adolescents' safer sexual patterns. Matern Child Health J 2001;5(4):273-80.

736　Piko BF, Fitzpatrick KM, Wright DR. A risk and protective factors framework for understanding youth's externalizing problem behavior in two different cultural settings. Eur Child Adolesc Psychiatry 2005;14(2):95-103.

737　Deveaux L, Stanton B, Lunn S, et al. Reduction in Human Immunodeficiency Virus risk among youth in developing countries. Arch Pediatr Adolesc Med 2007 Dec;161(12):1130-9.

738　Wolf, Tom, as quoted in "Sex on Campus; Hanging Out and Hooking Up; Connect and forget it" Chicago Sun Times 2005 March 18:29-31.

739　Freitas, Donna. "Sex Education". The Wall Street Journal 2008 Apr 4:W11.

740　Freitas, Donna. *Sex and the Soul: Juggling Sexuality, Spirituality, Romance & Religion on America's College Campuses.* New York, NY; Oxford University Press, 2008.

741　Kosunen E, Kaltaila-Heino R, Rimpela M, Laippala P. Risk-taking sexual behaviour and self-reported depression in middle adolescence—a school-based survey. Child Care Health Dev 2003 Sept;29(5):337-44.

742 Shrier LA, Harris SK, Beardslee WR. Temporal associations between depressive symptoms and self-reported sexually transmitted disease among adolescents. Arch Pediatr Adolesc Med 2002 June;156(6):559-606.

743 Orr DP, Beiter M, Ingersoll G. Premature sexual activity as an indicator of psychosocial risk. Pediatrics 1991 Feb;87(2):141-7.

744 Hallfos DD, Waller MW, Ford CA, et al. Adolescent depression and suicide risk: association with sex and drug behavior. Am J Prev Med 2004 Oct;27(3):224-31.

745 Kosunen E, Kaltaila-Heino R, Rimpela M, Laippala P. Risk-taking sexual behaviour and self-reported depression in middle adolescence—a school-based survey. Child Care Health Dev 2003 Sept;29(5):337-44.

746 Hallfos DD, Waller MW, Ford CA, et al. Adolescent depression and suicide risk: association with sex and drug behavior. Am J Prev Med 2004 Oct;27(3):224-31.

747 Block, SL. Clinical practice primer. Infectious Diseases in Children. 2005 March;18(3):16.

748 Spencer JM, Zimet GD, Analsma MC, Orr DP. Self-esteem as a predictor in initiation of coitis in early adolescents. Pediatrics 2002 April;109(4):581-4.

749 Kaestle CE, Halpern CT. Sexual activity among adolescents in romantic relationships with friends, acquaintances, or strangers. Arch Pediatr Adolesc Med 2005 Sept;159:849-853.

750 Sullivan MG. "Teens often overestimate sex partner's monogamy." Pediatric News 2004;38(5):14.

751 Block, SL. Clinical practice primer. Infectious Diseases in Children. 2005 March;18(3):16.

752 Department of Health and Human Services, Centers for Disease Control and Prevention. Youth Risk Behavior Surveillance—United States, 2003. MMWR 2004 May 21;53(SS-2).

753 Blythe MJ, Fortenberry D, Temkit M'H, et al. Incidence and correlates of unwanted sex in relationships of middle and late adolescent women. Arch Pediatr Adolesc Med 2006 June;160:591-5.

754 Kellogg ND, Huston RL. Unwanted sexual experiences in adolescents. Clinical Pediatrics 1995 June:306.

755 Rickert VI, Wiemann CM, Vaughan RD, White JW. Rates and risk factors for sexual violence among an ethnically diverse sample of adolescents. Arch Pediatr Adolesc Med 2004 Dec;158:1132-9.

756 Forke CM, Myers RK, Catallozzi M, Schwarz DF. Relationship violence among female and male college undergraduate students. Arch Pediatr Adolesc Med 2008;162(7):634-41.

757 Silverman JG, Raj A, Clements K. Dating violence and associated sexual risk and pregnancy among adolescent girls in the United States. Pediatrics 2004;114:e220-5.

758 Kogan SM. Disclosing unwanted sexual experiences: results from a national sample of adolescent women. Child Abuse Negl 2004 Feb;28(2):147-65.

759 Kellogg ND, Huston RL. Unwanted sexual experiences in adolescents. Clinical Pediatrics 1995 June:306.

760 Forke CM, Myers RK, Catallozzi M, Schwarz DF. Relationship violence among female and male college undergraduate students. Arch Pediatr Adolesc Med 2008;162(7):634-41.

761 Kellogg ND, Huston RL. Unwanted sexual experiences in adolescents. Clinical Pediatrics 1995 June:306.

762 Munoz-Rivas MJ, Grana JL, O'Leary KD, Gonzalez MP. Aggression in adolescent dating relationships: prevalence, justification, and health consequences. J Adolesc Health 2007 Apr;40(4):295-7.

763 Forke CM, Myers RK, Catallozzi M, Schwarz DF. Relationship violence among female and male college undergraduate students. Arch Pediatr Adolesc Med 2008;162(7):634-41.

764 Forke CM, Myers RK, Catallozzi M, Schwarz DF. Relationship violence among female and male college undergraduate students. Arch Pediatr Adolesc Med 2008;162(7):634-41.

765 Gibbs, Bonnie. In "Babysitters: what parents need to know." Good Housekeeping 2006 June:90, quoting statistics from: 1) FBI national incident-based reporting system; US Dept of Justice Programs, Office of Juvenile Justice and Delinquencies Prevention, 2001 Sept and 2) Finkelhor, David and Ormrod, Richard. Crimes Against Children by Babysitters. The Juvenile Justice Bulletin 2001 Sept.

766 Centers for Disease Control and Prevention. Unintentional strangulation deaths from the "choking game" among youths aged 6-19 years in the United States, 1995-2007;2008 Feb 15;57(6):141-4.

767 Olshen E, McVeigh KH, Wunsch-Hitzig RA, Rickert VI. Dating violence, sexual assault, and suicide attempts among urban teenagers. Arch Pediatr Adolesc Med 2007 June ;161:539-45.

768 Bonomi AE, Kelleher K. Dating violence, sexual assault, and suicide attempts among minority adolescents; ending the silence. Editorial, Arch Pediatr Adolesc Med 2007 June;161:609-10.

769 Blythe MJ, Fortenberry D, Temkit M'H, et al. Incidence and correlates of unwanted sex in relationships of middle and late adolescent women. Arch Pediatr Adolesc Med 2006 June;160:591-5.

770 Decker MR, Silverman JG, Raj A. Dating violence and sexually transmitted disease/HIV testing and diagnosis among adolescent females. Pediatrics 2005;116:e272-6.

771 Ackard DM, Eisenberg ME, Neumark-Sztainer D. Long-term impact of adolescent dating violence on the behavioral and psychological health of male and female youth. J Pediatr 2007;151:476-81.

772 Sanci L, Coffey C, Olsson C, et al. Childhood sexual abuse and eating disorders in females. Arch Pediatr Adolesc Med 2008 Mar;162(3):261-7.

773 Sandfort TG, Orr M, Hirsch JS, Santelli J. Long-term health correlates of timing of sexual debut: results from a national US study. Am J Publ Health 2008 Jan;98(1):155-61.

774 Shrier LA, Pierce JD, Emans J, DuRant RH. Gender differences in risk behaviors associated with forced or pressured sex. Arch Pediatr Adolesc Med 1998 Jan;152:57-63.

775 Roberts TA, Klein JD, Fisher S. Longitudinal effect of intimate partner abuse on high-risk behavior among adolescents. Arch Pediatr Adolesc Med 2003 Sept;157:875-81.

776 Eisenberg ME, Achard DM, Resnick MD. Protective factors and suicide risk in adolescents with a history of sexual abuse. J Pediatr 2007;151:482-7.

777 Cavenar JO Jr, Maltbie AA, Sullivan JL. Aftermath of abortion. Anniversary depression and abdominal pain. Bull Menninger Clin 1978 Sept;42(5):433-8.

778 Tishler CL. Adolescent suicide attempts following elective abortion: a special case of anniversary reaction. Pediatrics 1981 November;68(5):670-1.

779 Benute GR, Nomura RM, Pereira PP, et al. Spontaneous and induced abortion: anxiety, depression and guilt. Rev Assoc Med Bras 2009 May-Jun;55(3):322-7.

780 Cougle JR, Reardon DC, Coleman PK. Depression associated with abortion and childbirth: a long-term analysis of the NLSY cohort. Med Sci Monit 2003 Apr;9(4):CR105-12.

781 Kumar r, Robson K. Previous induced abortion and ante-natal depression in primiparae: preliminary report of a survey of mental health in pregnancy. Psychol Med 1978 Nov;8(4):711-5.

782 Centers for Disease and Control. National STD Awareness Month—April, 2005. MMWR 2005 April 22;54(15).

783 Institute of Medicine. *The Hidden Epidemic: Confronting Sexually Transmitted Diseases.* Washington, DC: National Academy Press; 1997.

784 Cates W Jr. Estimates of the incidence and prevalence of sexually transmitted diseases in the United States: American Social Health Association Panel. Sex Transm Dis 1999;26(suppl):S2-7.

785 Centers for Disease Control and Prevention. *Sexually Transmitted Diseases Survey 2000.* Atlanta, GA: US Department of Health and Human Services, Centers for Disease Control and Prevention; 2001 Sept.

786 Centers for Disease Control and Prevention. Sexual and reproductive health of persons aged 10-24 years—United States, 2002-2007. MMWR 2009 July 17;58(SS-6):1-60.

787 Koyle P, Jensen L, Olsen J. Comparison of sexual behaviors among adolescents having an early, middle and late first intercourse experience. Youth Soc 1989;20:461-76.

788 Shrier LA, Bowman FP, Crowley-Nowick PA. Mucosal immunity of the adolescent female genital tract. Presented at the 2001 annual meeting of the Society for Adolescent Medicine, 2001 March 21-25, San Diego CA.

789 Kronemyer, Bob. "Teens particularly vulnerable to HIV." Infectious Diseases in Children 2004 September;17(9):78-9.

790 Fleming PL, Wortley PM, Karon JM, DeCock KM, Janssen RS. Tracking the HIV epidemic: current issues, future challenges. Am J Public Health 2000;90:1037-41.

791 Centers for Disease Control and Prevention. HIV prevalence estimates—United States, 2006. MMWR 2008 Oct 3;57(39):1073-6.

792 "CDC: Almost 50% of HIV-positive young people are unaware of status". American Academy of Pediatrics Smart Brief 2009 June 26.

793 Lubin, Katlyne as quoted by Goldman, Erik in "Many in cohort surviving HIV-infected heritage". Pediatric News 2006 June; 40(6):20.

794 Marston C, King E. Factors that shape young people's sexual behaviour: a systematic review. Lancet 2006 Nov 4;368(9547):1581-6.

795 Westrom L, Eschenbach D. Pelvic inflammatory disease: in Holmes KK, Sparling PF, Mardh P-A, eds._Sexually Transmitted Diseases: 3ʳᵈ ed. New York, NY: McGraw-Hill Co;1999.

796 Stamm WE, Holmes KK. Chlamydia trachomatis infections in the adult. In: Holmes KK, Mardh PA, Sparling PF, et al, eds. Sexually Transmitted Diseases, 2ⁿᵈ ed. New York, NY: McGraw-Hill, Inc, 1990:181-93.

797 Zimmerman HL, Potterat JJ, Dukes RL, et al. Epidemiologic differences between Chlamydia and gonorrhea. Am J Public Health 1990:80:1338-42.

798 American College of Obstetricians and Gynecologists Committee Opinion "Sexually Transmitted Diseases in Adolescents" No. 301; 2004 Oct;892-3.

799 Bates, Betsy. "Free home Chlamydia tests net high return." Pediatric News 2009 May;43(5):14.

800 Fang J, Husman C, DeSilva L, et al. Evaluation of self collected vaginal swab, first void urine, and endocervical swab specimens for the detection of Chlamydia trachomatis and Neisseria gonorrhoeae in adolescent females. J Pediatr Adolesc Gynecol 2008 Dec;21(6):355-60.

801 Cook RL, Hutchison SL, Ostergaard L, et al. Systemic review: noninvasive testing for Chlamydia trachomatis and Neisseria gonorrhoeae. Ann Int Med 2005 June 7;142(11):914-25.

802 Rock EM, Ireland M, Resnick MD, McNeely CA. A rose by any other name? Objective knowledge, perceived knowledge, and adolescent male condom use. Pediatrics 2005 March;115(3): 677-72.

803 Department of Health and Human Services, Centers for Disease Control and Prevention. Youth Risk Behavior Surveillance—United States, 2003. MMWR 2004 May 21;53(SS-2).

804 Centers for Disease Control and Prevention. Youth Risk Behavior Surveillance—United States, 2007; 2008 June 6;57(SS-4).

805 Paz-Bailey G, Koumans EH, Sternberg M, et al. The effect of correct and consistent condom use on Chlamydial and gonococcal infection among urban adolescents. Arch Pediatr Adolesc Med 2005 June;159:536-42.

806 Abe K, Inchauspe G. Transmission of hepatitis C by saliva. Lancet 1991 Jan 26;337(8735):248.

807 Abe K, Kurata T, Shikata T, et al. Experimental transmission of non-A, non-B hepatitis by saliva. J Infect Dis 1987 May;155(5):1078-9.

808 Halpern-Felsher BL, Cornell JL, Kropp RY, Tschann JM. Oral versus vaginal sex among adolescents: perceptions, attitudes, and behavior. Pediatrics 2005 April;115(4):845-51.

809 Stephenson,, Joan. "HIV risk from oral sex higher than many realize". JAMA 2000 March 8;283(10):1279.

810 Xu F, Sternberg MR, Kottiri BJ, et al. Trends in herpes simplex virus type 1 and type 2 seroprevalence in the United States. JAMA 2006 August 23-30;296(8):964-73.

811 Psyrri A, DiMaio D. Human papillomavirus in cervical and head-and-neck cancer. Nat Clin Pract Oncol 2008 Jan;5(1):24-31.

812 Williams H, Higgins CD, Crawford DH. Human papillomavirus and oropharyngeal cancer. N Engl J Med 2007 Sept 13;357(11):1157.

813 Healy, Bernadine. "Clueless about risks of oral sex." US News & World Report 2008 Mar 10:60.

814 Brady SS, Halpern-Felsher BL. Adolescents' reported consequences of having oral sex versus vaginal sex. Pediatrics 2007 Feb;119(2):229-36.

815 Report by the National Institutes of Health Scientific Evidence on Condom Effectiveness for STD prevention panel. www.niaid.nih.gov/dmid/stds/condomreport.pdf.

816 Steiner MJ, Cates W. Condoms and sexually-transmitted infections. N Engl J Med 2006 June 22;354(25):2642-3.

817 Fitch JT, Stine C, Hager WD, et al. Condom effectiveness: factors that influence risk reduction. Sex Transm Dis 2002;29(12):811-7.

818 Davis KR, Weller SC. The effectiveness of condoms in reducing heterosexual transmission of HIV. Fam Plann Perspect 1999 Nov-Dec;31(6):272-9.

819 Weller, Susan as quoted by Orange, Lisa M. Condom appears to be a rather poor HIV barrier. Pediatric News 1993 Nov:44.

820 Rose, E, DiClemente RJ, Wingood GM, McDermott Sales J, et al. The validity of teens' and young adults' self-reported condom use. Arch Pediatr & Adolesc Med 2009;163(1):61-4.

821 www.plannedparenthood.org, accessed 8-6-09.

822 Fitch, J Thomas. "Keep Sexual Risk Info Flowing." Pediatric News 2004 Feb;38(2). Also Fitch JT. Are condoms effective in reducing the risk of sexually transmitted disease? Ann Pharmacother 2001 Sept;35(9):113-8.

823 Centers for Disease Control and Prevention. Sexual risk behaviors of STD clinic patients before and after Earvin "Magic" Johnson's HIV-infection announcement—Maryland, 1991-1992. MMWR 1993 January 29;42(3):45-8.

824 Brown JD, L-Engle KL, Pardun CJ, et al. Sexy media matter: exposure to sexual content in music, movies, television, and magazines predicts black and white adolescents' sexual behavior. Pediatrics 2006 Apr 4;117(4):1018-27.

825 Freitas, Donna. "Sex Education". The Wall Street Journal 2008 Apr 4:W11.

826 Fanos JH, Little GA, Edwards WH. Candles in the snow: ritual and memory for siblings of infants who died in the Intensive Care Nursery. J Pediatr 2009 June;154:849-53.

827 Sulloway FJ. *Born to Rebel: Birth Order, Family Dynamics, and Creative Lives.* New York, NY: Pantheon Books;1996, as quoted in Pediatrics 1997 March;99(3):357.

828 Mintz, Jessica. "Sibling Rivalries." The Wall Street Journal 2006 May 8;R3.

829 Trevisan M, Krough V, Klimowski L, Bland S, Winkelstein W. Absence of siblings—a risk factor for hypertension? Letter to the editor, N Engl J Med 1991 May 2;324:1285.

830 Whincup P, Cook D, Papacosta O, Shaper G, Walker M. Relation of blood pressure to number of siblings. Letter to the editor, N Engl J Med 1991 Sept 9;325(12):891.

831 Ball TM, Castro-Rodriguez JA, Griffith DA, et al. Siblings, day-care attendance, and the risk of asthma and wheezing during childhood. N Engl J Med 2000 Aug 24;343(8):538-43.

832 Ponsonby AL, van der Mie I, Dwyer T, et al. Exposure to infant siblings during early life and risk of multiple sclerosis. JAMA 2005 Jan 26;293(4):463-9.

833 Ponsonby AL, van der Mie I, Dwyer T, et al. Exposure to infant siblings during early life and risk of multiple sclerosis. JAMA 2005 Jan 26;293(4):463-9.

834 Kinra S, Davey Smith G, Jeffreys M, et al. Association between sibship size and allergic diseases in the Glasgow Alumni Study. Thorax 2006 Jan;61(1):48-53.

835 Cullinan P. Editorial, Thorax 2006 Jan;61(1):3-5.

836 Douwes J, van Strien R, Doekes G, et al. Does early indoor microbial exposure reduce the risk of asthma? The Prevention and Incidence of Asthma and Mite Allergy birth cohort study. J Allerg Clin Immunol 2006 May;117(5):1067-73.

837 Claudy JG. The only child as a young adult: results from Project Talent. In: Falbo T, editor. *The Single-Child Family.* New York, NY: Guilford Press, 1984:211-52.

838 Falbo T, ed. Only children: a review. In: *The Single Child Family.* New York, NY: Guilford Press, 1984:1-24.

839 Taanila A, Ebeling H, Kotimaa A, Moilanen I, Jarvelin MR. Is a large family a protective factor against behavioural and emotional problems at the age of 8 years? Acta Pediatr 2004 Apr;93(4):508-17.

840 Sack, Susan, as quoted by Cline, Paula in "Sibling rivalry not all bad—therapist". Northbrook Life 1983 March 10;10(11):1.

841 Genesis 25:22.

842 Taanila A, Ebeling H, Kotimaa A, et al. Is a large family a protective factor against behavioural and emotional problems at the age of 8 years? Acta Paediatr 2004 Apr;93(4):508-17.

843 Ponsonby A-L, van der Mie, I, Dwyer, et al. Exposure to infant siblings during early life and risk of multiple sclerosis. JAMA 2005 January 26;293(4):463-9.

844 Benn CS, Melbye M, Wohlfahrt J, et al. Cohort study of sibling effect, infectious diseases, and risk of atopic dermatitis during first 18 months of life. Brit Med J 2004 May 22;328(7450):1223-7.

845 Kinra S, Davey Smith G, Jeffreys M, et al. Association between sibship size and allergic diseases in the Glasgow Alumni Study. Thorax 2006 Jan;61(1):48-53.

846 Cullinan P. Editorial, Thorax 2006 Jan;61(1):3-5.

847 "Sada and Emily Jacobson: Fighting to Win" Self Magazine, 2004 August.

848 As quoted in "Breeding Evil? Defending Video Games" The Economist 2005 August 6;376:9.

849 Eisenberg, Azriel L. Children and radio programs. Am J Psychiatr 1936;93:493-4.

850 Jellinek, MS. Behavioral Consult; Web Strategy for Adolescents. Pediatric News 2004 August;38(8):39.

851 Fowler, Geoffrey A. "Chinese censors of internet face 'hacktivists' in the US". The Wall Street Journal 2006 Feb 12:A1,9.

852 Stecklow, Steve. "Repro man". The Wall Street Journal 2005 Oct 15-16:A1,8.

853 Virtually Home Alone. Pediatrics 2005;115:1324.

854 Christakis DA, Zimmerman FJ. Children and television; a primer for pediatricians. Contemporary Pediatrics 2007 Mar;24(3):31-45.
855 Elliott C. Better than Well. Norton, 2003; as quoted in Pediatrics 2004 February:113(2):237.
856 Strasburger VC, Donnerstein E. Review Article: Children, adolescents, and the media: issues and solutions. Pediatrics 1999 January;103(1):129-39.
857 Nielsen Media Research data as reported by Associated Press in the New York Times 2006 Nov 22.
858 Fosarelli PD. Television and children: a review. Developmental and Behavioral Pediatrics 1984 February;5(1):30-6.
859 American Automobile Association, Foundation for Traffic Safety data from 1987 as quoted by Borsch, Barbara in "How Madison Avenue Seduces Children"; Pediatric Management 1991 March:14-24.
860 Ozmert E, Toyran M, Yurdakok K. Behavioral correlates of television viewing in primary school children evaluated by the child behavior checklist. Arch Pediatr Adolesc Med 2002 Sept;156(9):910-4.
861 Goldbloom R. Pediatric Notes 2002 October 3:26(40):159.
862 Cao F, Su L. Internet addiction among Chinese adolescents: prevalence and psychological features. Child Care Health Dev 2007;33:275-8.
863 Center for the Digital Future, Annenberg School for Communication, University of South Carolina, Annual Internet Survey, 2009 accessed online 2009 July 19.
864 Boynton-Jarrett R, Thomas TN, Peterson KE, et al. Impact of television viewing patterns on fruit and vegetable consumption among adolescents. Pediatrics 2003;112(6):1321-6.
865 Crespo CJ, Smit E, Troiano RP, et al. Television watching, energy intake, and obesity in US children. Arch Pediatr Adolesc Med 2001 March;155:360-5.
866 Wiecha JL, Peterson KE, Ludwig DS, et al. When children eat what they watch: impact of television viewing on dietary intake in youth. JAMA 2006;160:436-42.
867 Dietz WH, Gortmaker SL. Do we fatten our children at the television set? Obesity and television viewing in children and adolescents. Pediatrics 1985;;75(5):807-12.
868 Institute of Medicine. Food marketing to children and youth: threat or opportunity? www.iom.edu accessed 1-5-06.
869 Connor SM. Food-related advertising on preschool television: building brand recognition in young viewers. Pediatrics 2006 Oct;118(4):1478-87.
870 Wosje KS, Khoury PR, Claytor RP, et al. Adiposity and TV viewing are related to less bone accrual in young children. J Pediatr 2009Jan;154:79-85.
871 Tazawa Y, Soukalo AV, Okada K, Takada G. Excessive playing of home computer games by children presenting unexplained symptoms. J Pediatr 1997 Jun;130(6):1010-1.
872 Levinbook WS, Mallet J, Grant-Kels JM. Laptop computer-associated erythema ab igne. Cutis 2007;80:319-20.
873 "There's SpongeBob, prancing in the produce aisle!" Contemporary Pediatrics 2006 Sept;23(9):14.
874 Lanningham-Foster L, Foster RC, McCrady SK, et al. Activity-promoting video games and increased energy expenditure. J Pediatr 2009;154;819-23.
875 Christakis DA, Zimmerman FJ, DeGiuseppe DL, McCarty CA. Early television exposure and subsequent attentional problems in children. Pediatrics 2004 April;113(4):708-13.
876 Johnson JG, Cohen P, Kasen S, Brook JS. Extensive television viewing and the development of attention and learning difficulties during adolescence. Arch Pediatr Adolesc Med 2007 May;161:480-6.
877 Landhuis CE, Poulton R, Welch D, Hancox RJ. Does childhood television viewing lead to attention problems in adolescence? Results from a prospective, longtitudinal study. Pediatrics 2007 Sept;120(3):532-7.
878 Zimmerman FJ, Christakis DA. Associations between content types of early media exposure and subsequent attentional problems. Pediatrics 2007 Nov;120(5):986-92.
879 Stevens T, Mulsow M. There is no meaningful relationship between television exposure and symptoms of attention-deficit/hyperactivity disorder. Pediatrics 2006 Mar;117(3):665-72.
880 Christakis DA, Gilkerson J, Richards JA, et al. Audible television and decreased adult words, infant vocalizations, and conversational turns. Arch Pediatr Adol Med 2009 June;163(6):554-8.

881 Zimmerman FJ, Christakis DA. Children's television viewing and cognitive outcomes. Arch Pediatr Adolesc Med 2005 July;159:619-25.

882 Borzekowski DLG, Robinson TN. The remote, the mouse, and the number 2 pencil. Arch Pediatr Adolesc Med 2005 July;159:607-13.

883 Barr-Anderson DJ, van den Berg P, Neumark-Sztainer D, Story M. Characteristics associated with older adolescents who have a television in their bedrooms. Pediatrics 2008 Apr;121(4):718-24.

884 Sharif I, Sargent JD. Association between television, movie, and video game exposure and school performance. Pediatrics 2006 Oct;118(4):e1061-70.

885 Hancox RJ, Milne BJ, Poulton R. Association of television viewing during childhood with poor educational achievement. Arch Pediatr Adolesc Med 2005 July;159:614-8.

886 Cummings HM, Vandewater EA. Relation of adolescent video game play to time spent in other activities. Arch Pediatr Adolesc Med 2007 July;161(7):684-9.

887 The Internet: It's the New TV. Pediatrics 2005 May;115(5):1377.

888 Tomopoulos S, Valdez P, Dreyer B, et al. Is exposure to media intended for preschool children associated with less parent-child shared reading aloud and teaching activities? Ambul Pediatr 2007;7:18-24.

889 "TV habit begins early, takes place of reading". Infectious Diseases in Children 1996 June;9(6).

890 Bayard, Peirre. *How to Talk About Books You Haven't' Read*. London, England; Bloombury Books, 2007.

891 Kronman, Anthony T. *Education's End; Why Our Colleges and Universities Have Given Up on the Meaning of Life*. New Haven, CT; Yale University Press, 2007.

892 Marshall, Tom. "Young, old readers happy to get carded." Chicago Tribune 2006 Dec 13:3.

893 Uberos DJ, Gomez A, Munoz A, et al. Television and childhood injuries: is there a connection? Arch Pediatr Adolesc Med 1998 July;152:713-4.

894 Daven F, O'Conner J, Briggs R. The consequences of imitative behavior in children: the "Evel Knievel syndrome". Pediatrics 1976;57:418-19.

895 Arch Pediatr Adolesc Med 2000;154(3):283-6.

896 Cowan JA, Dubosh N, Hadley C. Seatbelt and helmet depiction on the big screen: blockbuster injury prevention messages? J Trauma 2009;66(3):912-7.

897 McArthur DL, Peek-Asa C. Western J Med 2000 Sept;173:164-8.

898 Moreno MA, Parks MR, Zimmerman FJ, et al. Display of health risk behaviors on MySpace by adolescents. Arch Pediatr Adolesc Med 2009 Jan;163(1):27-34.

899 Moreno MA, VanderStoep A, Parks MR, et al. Reducing at-risk adolescents' display of risk behavior on a social networking web site. Arch Pediatr Adolesc Med 2009 Jan;163(1):35-41.

900 Johnson JG, Cohen P, Kasen S, et al. Association between television viewing and sleep problems during adolescence and early adulthood. Arch Pediatr Adolesc Med 2004 June;158:562.

901 Owens J, Maxim R, McGuinn M, et al. Television-viewing habits and sleep disturbance in school children. Pediatrics 1999 Sept;104(3):e27.

902 Calamaro CJ, Mason TB, Ratcliffe SJ. Adolescents living the 24/7 lifestyle: effects of caffeine and technology on sleep duration and daytime functioning. Pediatrics 2009;123;e1005-10.

903 Owens J, Maxim R, McGuinn M, et al. Television-viewing habits and sleep disturbance in school children. Pediatrics 1999 Sept;104(3):e27.

904 Committee on Public Education, American Academy of Pediatrics. Children, adolescents, and television. Pediatrics 2001;107(2):423-6.

905 Singer MI, Slovak K, Frierson T, York P. Viewing preferences, symptoms of psychological trauma, and violent behaviors among children who watch television. J Am Acad Child Adolesc Psychiatry 1998 Oct;37(10):1041-8.

906 Cantor Joanne. Does your patient have sleep problems? Ask about TV first. AAP News 2000 May;17(3):124.

907 Hamer M, Stamatakis E, Mishra G. Psychological distress, television viewing, and physical activity in children aged 4 to 12 years. Pediatrics 2009 May;123(5):1263-8.

908 Primack BA, Swanier B, Georgiopoulos AM, Land SR, et al. Association between media use in adolescence and depression in young adulthood: a longitudinal study. Arch Gen Psych 2009;66(2):181-8.

909 Yokata F, Thompson KM. Violence in G-rated animated films. JAMA 2000;283:2716-20.

910 Center for Communication and Social Policy. National Television Violence Study, Vol. 3. Santa Barbara: University of California, 1998.

911 Jenkins L, Webb T, Browne N, Afife AA, Draus J. An evaluation of the Motion Picture Association of America's treatment of violence in PG-, PG-13, and R-rated films. Pediatrics 2005;115:e512-7.
912 Burnstine R. Violence in the media. Illinois Pediatrician 1999/2000 Winter;17(4):9. (Referring to data from the US Senate Judiciary report on Children, Violence, and the Media, 1999 September.
913 "Television Violence". JAMA 1993 December 15;270(23):2870.
914 Rich M, Woods E, Goodman E. Aggressors or victims: gender and race in music video violence. Pediatrics 1988 April;101(4):669-74.
915 Anderson Charles R. Television commercial violence during nonviolent programming: the 1998 Major League Baseball Playoffs. Pediatrics 2000 October;106(4):819.
916 Rideout VJ. Generation Rx.com: How young people use the internet for health information. Washington, DC: the Henry J Kaiser Foundation; 2001.
917 Bellieni CB, Cordelli DM, Raffaelli M, et al. Analgesic effect of watching TV during venipuncture. Arch Dis Child 2006 Dec 9;91(12):1015-7.
918 Zimmerman FJ, Glew GM, Christakis DA, Katon W. Early cognitive stimulation, emotional support, and television watching as predictors of subsequent bullying among grade-school children. Arch Pediatr Adolesc Med 2005 Apr;159:384-8.
919 Singer DG. Children, Adolescents, and Television—1989: I. Television Violence: A Critique. Pediatrics 1989 March;83(3):445-6.
920 Williams TB (ed): *The Impact of Television: A Natural Experiment in Three Communities.* New York, NY; Academic Press, 1986.
921 Anderson CA, Sakamoto A, Gentile DA, et al. Longitudinal effects of violent video games on aggression in Japan and the United States. Pediatrics 2008;122:e1067-72.
922 Committee on Public Education, American Academy of Pediatrics. Media Education. Pediatrics 1999;104(2):341-3.
923 Zimmerman FJ, Glew GM, Christakis DA, Katon W. Early cognitive stimulation, emotional support, and television watching as predictors of subsequent bullying among grade-school children. Arch Pediatr Adolesc Med 2005 Apr;159(4):384-8.
924 Garbarino, James. *See Jane Hit: Why Girls Are Growing More Violent and What We Can Do About It.* New York NY, Penguin Books, 2006.
925 Zaslow, Jeffrey. "Moving On: Email can make divorce worse." The Wall Street Journal 2005 Dec 15;D4.
926 Kowalski RM, Limber SP. Electronic bullying among middle school students. J Adolesc Health 2007 Dec;41(6 Suppl):S22-30.
927 Ybarra ML, Mitchell KJ, Wolak J, Finkelhor D. Examining characteristics and associated distress related to internet harassment: findings from the second youth internet safety survey. Pediatrics 2006 Oct;118(4):e1169-77.
928 Sontag, Lisa M, as quoted by Dixon, Bruce in "Cyberbullying appears common, psychologically damaging." Pediatric News 2008;42(6):16.
929 Wendling, Patrice. "Violent video games affect brain, MRIs show." Summary of paper by Dr. Vincent Mathews presented at 2007 Radiological Society of N America Meeting, 2006 in Chicago. Pediatric News 2007 Jan;41(1):34.
930 Mathews VP, Kronenberger WG, Wang Y, et al. Media violence exposure and frontal lobe activation measured by functional magnetic resonance imaging in aggressive and nonaggressive adolescents. J Comp Assist Tomogr 2005 May-June;29(3):287-92.
931 Robinson TN, Wilde ML, Navracruz LC, Haydel KF, Varady A. Effects of reducing children's television and video game use on aggressive behavior. Arch Pediatr Adolesc Med 2001 Jan;155:17-23.
932 Rosser JC, Lynch PJ, Cuddihy L, et al. The impact of video games on training surgeons in the 21st century. Arch Surg 2007;142:181-6.
933 Green CS, Vavelier D. Effect of vide games on the special distribution of visuospatial attention. J Exp Psychol Hum Percept Perform 2006 Dec;32(7):1465-78.
934 Johnson, Steven. *Everything Bad Is Good for You; How Today's Popular Culture is Actually Making Us Smarter.* New York, NY; Penguin Books, 2005.
935 Collins RL, Elliott MN, Berry SH, et al. Watching sex on television predicts adolescent initiation of sexual behavior. Pediatrics 2004;114:e280-9.

936   Committee on Public Education, American Academy of Pediatrics. Sexuality, contraception, and the media. Pediatrics 2001;107(1):191-3

937   Collins RL, Elliott MN, Berry SH, et al. Watching sex on television predicts adolescent initiation of sexual behavior. Pediatrics 2004;114:e280-9.

938   Ashby SL, Arcari CM, Edmonson B. Television viewing and risk of sexual initiation by young adolescents. Arch Pediatr Adolesc Med 2006 Apr;160:375-80.

939   Data from the National Institute of Child Health and Human Development published in J Adol Health 33:60-70; J Adol Health 31:153-70; J Sex Res 39:1,22-26; and J Adol Health 33:108-18 as quoted in Prevention,2005 February:44.

940   Chandra A, Martino SC, Collins RL, et al. Does watching sex on television predict teen pregnancy? Findings from a national longitudinal survey of youth. Pediatrics 2008 Nov;122(5): 1047-54.

941   Data from the National Institute of Child Health and Human Development published in J Adol Health 33:60-70; J Adol Health 31:153-70; J Sex Res 39:1,22-26; and J Adol Health 33:108-18 as quoted in Prevention,2005 February:44.

942   Bryan-Low, Cassall; Pringle David. "Sex Cells." The Wall Street Journal 2005 May;B1-2.

943   Wolak J, Mitchell K, Finkelhor D. Unwanted and wanted exposure to online pornography in a national sample of youth internet users. Pediatrics 2007 Feb;119(2):247-57.

944   Tanski SE, Stoolmiller M, Cin SD, et al. Movie character smoking and adolescent smoking: who matters more, good guys or bad guys. Pediatrics 2009 July;124(1):135-43.

945   Centers for Disease Control and Prevention. Effect of ending an antitobacco youth campaign on adolescent susceptibility to cigarette smoking—Minnesota, 2002-2003. MMWR 2004 April 16;53(14):301-3.

946   Department of Health and Human Services, Centers for Disease Control and Prevention. Tobacco use, access, and exposure to tobacco in media among middle and high school students—United States, 2004. MMWR 2005 April 1;54(12):297-301.

947   Gidwani PP, Sobol A, DeJong W, et al. Television viewing and initiation of smoking among youth. Pediatrics 2002 September;110(3):505-8.

948   "Drugs in Entertainment". Pediatric News 1999 June;33(6).

949   Primach BA, Dalton MA, Carroll MV, et al. Content analysis of tobacco, alcohol, and other drugs in popular music. Arch Pediatr Adolesc Med 2008;162(2):169-75.

950   Primach BA, Dalton MA, Carroll MV, et al. Content analysis of tobacco, alcohol, and other drugs in popular music. Arch Pediatr Adolesc Med 2008;162(2):169-75.

951   Strasburger VC, Donnerstein E. Children, adolescents, and the media in the 21st century. Adolesc Med: State of the Art Rev 2000;11:51-68.

952   Strasburger VC. Prevention of adolescent drug abuse: why 'Just Say No' just won't work. J Pediatr 1989;114:676-81.

953   Center for Science in the Public Interest. "Kids are as aware of booze as President, survey finds. Washington, DC; Center for Science in the Public Interest, 1988 September 4.

954   Dietz WH, Strasburber VC. Children, adolescents, and television. Current Problems in Pediatrics 1991 January:8-31.

955   Robinson TN, Chen HL, Killen JD. Television and music video exposure and risk of adolescent alcohol use. Pediatrics 1988;102(5):e54.

956   Keeshan, Robert. Television: parents can cure kids' TV viewing ills. American Academy of Pediatrics Medical/Science Writer's Conference, New York, NY; 1988 July 19.

957   Klein JD, Havens CG, Carlson EJ. Evaluation of an adolescent smoking-cessation media campaign: GottaQuit.com. Pediatrics 2005 Oct;116(4):950-6.

958   Parker-Pope, Tara. "Role models: how images of smoking may affect kids." The Wall Street Journals 2007 May 15:D1.

959   Mumme DL, et al. Child Dev 2003;74:221.

960   Chamberlain LJ, Wang Y, Robinson TN. Does children's screen time predict requests for advertised products? Arch Pediatr Adolesc Med 2006 Apr;160:363-8.

961   American Psychological Association. Television advertising leads to unhealthy habits in children; says APA Task Force. APA Online, 2004 Task Force Press Release accessed at www.apa.org/releases/childrensads.html on 7-19-09.

962   American Academy of Pediatrics Committee on Communications. Policy Statement: Children, adolescents, and advertising. Pediatrics 2006 Dec;118(6):2563-9.

963 Lewis, Jay. "Experts recommend advertising restrictions to help curb childhood obesity." Infectious Diseases in Children 2006 May;32-3.

964 Lewis, Jay. "Experts recommend advertising restrictions to help curb childhood obesity." Infectious Diseases in Children 2006 May;32-3.

965 Saranow, Jennifer. " 'This is the car we want, Mommy'; car makers direct more ads at kids (and their parents); a 5 year old's toy Hummer." The Wall Street Journal 2006 Nov 9:D1.

966 Steel, Emily. "TV networks launch bit campus push; new Nielsen system makes college students coveted-ratings draw." The Wall Street Journal 2007 Mar 5:B3.

967 Hogan MJ, Strasburger VC. Body image, eating disorders, and the media. Adolescent Med State Art Rev 2008;19(3):521-46.

968 Becker AE, Burwell RA, Gilman SE, et al. Eating behaviours and attitudes following prolonged exposure to television among ethnic Fijian adolescent girls Br J Psychiatry 2002;180:509-14.

969 Cao F, Su L. Internet addiction among Chinese adolescents: prevalence and psychological features. Child Care Health Dev 2007;33:275-8.

970 Zhang L, Amos C, McDowell WC. A comparative study of internet addiction between the United States and China. Cyberpsychol Behav 2008 Dec;11(6):727-9.

971 Reuters. The New York Times 2007 Jan 18 as abstracted in "China: 2 million teenagers addicted to internet. Pediatrics 2007 March;119(3):508.

972 National Public Radio, August 28, 2007, "China takes steps to curb addiction to videogames". The Wall Street Journal 2007 August 30:B6.

973 Shaw M, Black DW. Internet addiction: definition, assessment, epidemiology and clinical management. CNS Drugs 2008;22(5):353-65.

974 Verkler, Erin. "Upping the ante". American Academy of Pediatrics News 2005 May;26(5):1,11.

975 Mitka, Mike. "Win or lose, internet gambling stakes are high." JAMA 2001 Feb;285(8):1005.

976 Ybarra ML, Mitchell KJ, Finkelhor D, Wolak J. Internet prevention messages; targeting the right online behaviors. Arch Pediatr Adolesc Med 2007 Feb;161:138-45.

977 Fefe CE, Smith LA, Maus EA, et al. Dying to play video games: carbon monoxide poisoning from electrical generators used after hurricane Ike. Pediatrics 2009;123:e1035-8.

978 Bickham DS, Rich M. Is television viewing associated with social isolation? Arch Pediatr Adolesc Med 2006 Apr;160:387-92.

979 Cummings HM, Vandewater EA. Relation of adolescent video game play to time spent in other activities. Arch Pediatr Adolesc Med 2007;161(7):684-9.

980 Vandewater EA, Bickham DS, Lee JH. Time well spent? Relating television use to children's free-time activities. Pediatrics 2006;117:e181-91.

981 Center for the Digital Future, Annenberg School for Communication, University of South Carolina, Annual Internet Survey, 2009 accessed online 2009 July 19.

982 Center for the Digital Future, Annenberg School for Communication, University of South Carolina, Annual Internet Survey, 2008 accessed online 2009 July 19.

983 Ybarra ML, Mitchell KJ, Finkelhor D, Wolak J. Internet prevention messages; targeting the right online behaviors. Arch Pediatr Adolesc Med 2007 Feb;161:138-45.

984 Idriss SZ, Kvedar JC, Watson AJ. The role of online support communities: benefits of expanded social networks to patients with psoriasis. Arch Derm 2009;145(1):46-51.

985 Burdette HL, Whitaker RC. A national study of neighborhood safety, outdoor play, television viewing, and obesity in preschool children. Pediatrics 2005 Sept;116(3):657-62.

986 Finkelhor D, Mitchell KJ, Wolak J. Online Victimization: A Report on the Nation's Youth. Alexandra VA: National Center for Missing and Exploited Children. Crimes Against Children Research Center 2000.

987 Ybarra ML, Mitchell KJ. How risky are social networking sites? A comparison of places online where youth sexual solicitation and harassment occurs. Pediatrics 2008;121:e350-7.

988 Mitchell KJ, Finkelhor D, Wolak J. Risk factors for and impact of online sexual solicitation of youth. JAMA 2001;285(23):3011-4.

989 Finkelhor D, Mitchell KJ, Wolak J. Online Victimization: A Report on the Nation's Youth. Alexandra VA: National Center for Missing and Exploited Children. Crimes Against Children Research Center 2000.

990 Ybarra ML, Mitchell KJ, Finkelhor D, Wolak J. Internet prevention messages; targeting the right online behaviors. Arch Pediatr Adolesc Med 2007 Feb;161:138-45.

991 Bryan-Low, Cassall; Pringle David. "Sex Cells." The Wall Street Journal 2005 May;B1-2.

992   Kirn, Timothy F. Internet access fuels child sexual predation. Pediatric News 2007 Apr;41(4):38.

993   Finkelhor D, Mitchell KJ, Wolak J. Online Victimization: A Report on the Nation's Youth. Alexandra VA: National Center for Missing and Exploited Children. Crimes Against Children Research Center 2000.

994   Boyer EW, Shannon M, Hibberd PL. The internet and psychoactive substance use among innovative drug users. Pediatrics 2005 February;115(2):302-5.

995   Sullivan G. Raving on the Internet. CMAJ 2000;162(13):1864.

996   McColgan MD, Giardino AP. Internet poses multiple risks to children and adolescents. Pediatric Annals 2005 May;34(5):404-14.

997   McColgan MD, Giardino AP. Internet poses multiple risks to children and adolescents. Pediatric Annals 2005 May;34(5):404-14.

998   Lawson, Kim. MRI finds teens have less frontal cortex function than adults. Pediatric News 34(5);May, 2000.

999   Vastag, Brian. Nora Volkow MD; NIDA's new leader: from rejection to direction. JAMA 290(20);November 26, 2003:2647-52.

1000 Vastag, Brian. "Brain sabotages sobriety, right on cue." JAMA 291(9);March 3,2004:1053-5.

1001 Tapert SF, Cheung EH, Brown GG, et al. Neural response to alcohol stimuli in adolescents with alcohol use disorder. Arch Gen Psychiatry 2003 Jul;60(7):727-35.

1002 Jancin Bruce. "Teen Addiction to Cybersex Pervasive". Pediatric News 2005 April;39(4):24.

1003 Barr-Anderson DJ, van den Berg P, Neumark-Sztainer D, Story M. Characteristics associated with older adolescents who have a television in their bedrooms. Pediatrics 2008 Apr;121(4):718-24.

1004 Davison KK, Francis LA, Birch LL. Links between parents' and girls' television viewing behaviors: a longitudinal examination. J Pediatrics 2005 Oct;147(4):436-42.

1005 Barradas DT, Fulton JE, Blanck HM, Huhman M. Parental influences on youth television advertising. J Pediatr 2007 Oct;151(4):334-6.

1006 Mistry KB, Minkovitz CS, Strobino DM, Borzekowski DLG. Children's television exposure and behavioral and social outcomes at 5.5 years: does timing of exposure matter? Pediatrics 2007 Oct;762-9.

1007 Barkin S, Ip E, Richardson I, et al. Parental mediation styles for children aged 2 to 11 years. Arch Pediatr Adolesc Med 2006 Apr;160:395-401.

1008 Christakis, Dimitri and Zimmerman, Frederick J. *The Elephant in the Living Room: Make Television Work for Your Kids.* New York, NY; Rodale Books, 2006.

1009 Akst, Daniel. "Fun for the Whole Family, Really." The Wall Street Journal 2006 Apr 14:W11.

1010 Kim, Jane J. Internet, financial firms join nonprofit to fight child porn. 2006 Mar 16:D4.

1011 Chaker, Anne Marie. "Schools act to short-circuit spread of 'cyberbullying'". The Wall Street Journal 2007 Jan 24:D1.

1012 Associated Press. "Young adults learn downside of an online life". The Wall Street Journal 2007 Jan 2:B8.

1013 Weir, William. "Pop music ignores wedded bliss, misery." Chicago Tribune 2007 Feb 20;5:1,9.

1014 Gamble JH, Ormerod JO, Freeneaux MP. Exercise can be effective therapy for depression. Practitioner 2008 Sept;252(1710):19-20,23-4.

1015 Mellion MB. Exercise therapy for anxiety and depression. 1. Does the evidence justify its recommendation? Postgrad Med 1985 Feb;77(3):59-62,66.

1016 Brosnahan J, Steffen LM, Lytle L, et al. The relation between physical activity and mental health among Hispanic and non-Hispanic white adolescents. Arch Pediatr Adolesc Med 2004 Aug;158:818-23.

1017 Steptoe A, Butler N. Sports participation and emotional wellbeing in adolescents. Lancet 1996 Jun 29;347(9018):1789-92.

1018 Martin CK, Church TS, Thompson AM, Earnest CP, et al. Exercise dose and quality of life: a randomized controlled trial. Arch Internal Med 2009;169(3):269-78.

1019 Escobedo LG, Marcus SE, Holtzman D, Giovino GA. Sports participation, age at smoking initiation, and the risk of smoking among US high school students. JAMA 1993 Mar 17;269(11):1391-5.

1020 Audrain-McGovern J, Rodriguez D, Wileyto EP, et al. Effect of team sport participation on genetic predisposition to adolescent smoking progression. JAMA 2006 June 28;295(24):433-41.

1021 Nelson MC, Gordon-Larsen P. Physical activity and sedentary behavior patterns are associated with selected adolescent health risk behaviors. Pediatrics 2006;117(4):1281-90.

1022 Eaton DK, Kann L, Kinchen S, et al. Youth risk behavior surveillance—United States, 2007. MMWR 2008 June 6;57(SS-4).

1023 Hoyert DL, Mathews MS, Menacher F, et al. Annual Summary of Vital Statistics: 2004. Pediatrics 2006 Jan;117(1):168-82.

1024 Committee on Injury, Violence, and Poison Prevention, Committee on Adolescence. The Teen Driver. Pediatrics 2006 Dec;118(6):2570-81.

1025 Gutgesell, ME, Payne N. Issues of adolescent psychological development in the 21st century. Pediatrics in Review 2004 March;25(3):79-84.

1026 Committee on Injury and Poison Prevention and Committee on Adolescence. The teenage driver. Pediatrics 1996;98(5):987.

1027 American Academy of Pediatrics, Section on Adolescent Health. Teenagers and Driving; A Guide for Parents. Adolescent Health Update 1991 February.

1028 Committee on Injury and Poison Prevention and Committee on Adolescence. The teenage driver. Pediatrics 1996;98(5):987.

1029 Winston FK, Kallen MJ, Senserrick TM, Elliott MR. Risk factors for death among older child and teenaged motor vehicle passengers. Arch Pediatr Adolesc Med 2008 Mar;162(3):253-60.

1030 American Academy of Pediatrics, Section on Adolescent Health. Teenagers and Driving; A Guide for Parents. Adolescent Health Update 1991 February.

1031 Gardner R, Smith GA, Chany AM, et al. Factors associated with hospital length of stay and hospital charges of motor vehicle crash related hospitalizations among children in the United States. Arch Pediatr Med 2007 Sept;161(9):889-95.

1032 Centers for Disease Control. Update: alcohol-related traffic crashes and fatalities among youth and young adults—United States, 1982-1994. MMWR 1995 December 1;44(47):869-74.

1033 Ginsburg DR, Winston FK, Senserrick TM, et al. National young-driver survey: teen perspective and experience with factors that affect driving. Pediatrics 2008 May;121(5):e1391-403.

1034 Chen, L-H, Baker SP, Braver ER, Li G. Carrying passengers as a risk factor for crashes fatal to 16- and 17-year-old drivers. JAMA 2000 March 22/29;283(12):1578-82.

1035 Preusser DF, Ferguson SA, Willliams AF. The effect of teenage passengers on the fatal crash risk of teenage drivers. Accid Annal Prev 1998;30(2):217.

1036 McKay MP, Curtis L. Children in cars—keeping them safe at every age. Contemporary Pediatrics 2003 September;29(9):65-78.

1037 McKay MP, Curtis L. Children in cars—keeping them safe at every age. Contemporary Pediatrics 2003 September;29(9):65-78.

1038 Department of Health and Human Services, Centers for Disease Control and Prevention. Youth Risk Behavior Surveillance—United States, 2003. MMWR 2004 May 21;53(SS-2).

1039 Gonzales MM, Dickinson LM, DiGuiseppi C, Lowenstein SR. Student drivers: a study of fatal motor vehicle crashes involving 16-year-old drivers. Ann Emerg Med 2005 Feb;45(2):140-6.

1040 "Wake-Up Call". American Medical News 1995 Jan 16:13-14.

1041 Smart RG, Stoduto G, Adlaf EM, et al. Road rage victimization among adolescents. J Adolesc Health 2007 Sept;41(3):277-82.

1042 Trebilcock, Bob. "Daredevil driving: #1 teen killer". Good Housekeeping 1997 May:169.

1043 www.aap.org/policy/mgrad.html

1044 Centers for Disease Control and Prevention. Involvement by young drivers in fatal motor-vehicle crashes—United States, 1988-1995. MMWR 1996 December 6;45(48):1049-53.

1045 Shope JT, Molnar LJ, Elliott MR, Waller PF. Graduated driver licensing in Michigan; early impact on motor vehicle crashes among 16-year-old drivers. JAMA 2001 October 3;286(13):1593-8.

1046 Foss RD, Feaganes JR, Rodgman EA. Initial effects of graduated driver licensing on 16-year-old driver crashes in North Carolina. JAMA 2001 October 3;286(13):1588-92.

1047 Chen L-H, Baker SP, Li G. Graduated driver licensing programs and fatal crashes of 16-year-old drivers: a national evaluation. Pediatrics 2006 July;118(1):56-62.

1048 Higgins, Michelle. "A back-seat driver for your teen's car." The Wall Street Journal 2005 February 23.

1049 Pediatric Notes 2000 November; 34(10).

1050 National Highway and Transportation Safety Administration data as quoted by Tolchin, Deborah in "Saving lives on the highway". Pediatric News 2007 Apr;41(4):31.

1051   Nicholson M, Hoye R. Reducing adolescents' exposure to alcohol advertising and promotion during televised sports. JAMA 2009 Apr 8;301(14):1479-82.

1052   Tucker, Miriam E. "Helping to keep teens out of car accidents." Pediatric News 1998 June;32(6):45.

1053   Evans, Leonard. *Traffic Safety*. Bloomfield Hills, Mich; Science Serving Society, 2004.

1054   Hatfield J, Fernandes R. The role of risk-propensity in the risky driving of younger drivers. Accid Anal Prev 2009;41(1):25-35.

1055   Valadez-Meltzer A, Silber TJ, Meltzer AA, K'Angelo LJ. Will I be alive in 2005? Adolescent level of involvement in risk behaviors and belief in near-future death. Pediatrics 2005 July;116(1): 24-31.

1056   Winfield, Nicole, Associated Press. "Pope's rules of the road" released 2007 June 19.

1057   Cole, Thomas B. Global road safety crisis remedy sought. JAMA 2004 June 2;291(21):2531-2.

1058   Macias AE, Munoz JM, Galvan A, et al. Nosocomial bacteremia in neonates related to poor standards of care. The Pediatr Infect Dis J 2005 Aug;24(8):713-6.

1059   Peters CJ. Marburg and Ebola—arming ourselves against deadly filoviruses. N Engl J Med 2005 June 23:2571-3.

1060   DeCock KM, Bunnell R, Mermin J. Unfinished business-expanding HIV testing in developing countries. N Engl J Med 2006 Feb 2;354(5):440-2.

1061   Visco-Comandin U, Longo B, Perinelli P, et al. Research letter: Possible child-to-mother transmission of HIV by breastfeeding. JAMA 2005 Nov 9;294(18):2301-2.

1062   Bishai DM, Baker T. Illness in returned travelers. N Engl J Med 2006 Apr 27;354(17):1851.

1063   Hargarten SW, Baker SP. Fatalities in the Peace Corps: a retrospective study: 1962 through 1983. JAMA 1985:254:1326-9.

1064   Efrati, Amir. "Bolivia sees marked rise in tourist abductions." The Wall Street Journal 2006 Aug 29:D6.

1065   Gould, Jodie. "Kids gone crazy; what really happens on spring break." Family Circle 2003 March 4:137-41.

1066   Jones, Tamara. "Will your teen be safe on a party trip?" Good Housekeeping 2006 Feb:102-9.

1067   Slutske WS. Alcohol use disorders among US college students and their non-college-attending peers. Arch Gen Psychiatry 2005;62:321-7.

1068   Kadison Richard; Digeronimo, Theresa Foy. *College of the Overwhelmed: The Campus Mental Health Crisis and What to Do About It*. San Francisco, California; Jossey-Bass, 2004.

1069   Healy PO. New York Times 2005 March 3.

1070   Oler, MJ, Mainous AG 3rd, Martin CA, et al. Depression, suicidal ideation, and substance use among adolescents: are athletes at less risk? Arch Fam Med 1994 Sept; 3(9):781-5.

1071   Kulig K, Brener ND, McManus T. Sexual activity and substance use among adolescents by category of physical activity plus team sports participation. Arch Pediatr Adolesc Med 2003 September;157:905-12.

1072   Pate RR, Trost SG, Levin S, Dowda M. Sports participation and health-related behaviors among US youth. Arch Pediatr Adolesc Med 2000;154:904-11.

1073   Brosnahan J, Steffen LM, Lytle L, Patterson J, Boostrom A. The relation between physical activity and mental health among Hispanic and non-Hispanic white adolescents. Arch Pediatr Adolesc Med 2004 August;158:818-23.

1074   Elliot DL, Goldberg L, Moe EL, et al. Preventing substance use and disordered eating. Arch Pediatr Adolesc Med 2004 November;158:1043-9.

1075   Kimm SYS, Glynn NW, Kriska AM, et al. Decline in physical activity in black girls and white girls during

1076   Department of Health and Human Services, Centers for Disease Control and Prevention. Youth Risk Behavior Surveillance—United States, 2003. MMWR 2004 May 21;53(SS-2).

1077   Aaron DJ, Storti KL, Robertson RJ, Kriska AM, LaPorte RE. Longitudinal study of the number and choice of leisure time physical activities from mid to late adolescence. Arch Pediatr Adolesc Med 2002 Nov;156:1075-80.

1078   Evenson KR, Huston SL, MiMillen BJ, et al. Statewide prevalence and correlates of walking and bicycling to school. Arch Pediatr Adolesc Med 2003 September;157:887-92.

1079   Kristof ND. "Should our schools be more like Japan's?" The New York Times 1995 July 18.

1080   Michaels, Daniel. "Is this any way to run a railroad? In Hungary, they put kids to work." The Wall Street Journal 2008 Aug 7:A1,9.

1081 Banco L, et al. Work-related injury among Connecticut minors. Pediatrics 1992;89:957-60.

1082 Centers for Disease Control and Prevention. Occupational burns among restaurant workers— Colorado and Minnesota. MMWR 1993 September 24;42(37):713-6.

1083 Woolf AD, Flynn E. Workplace toxic exposures involving adolescents aged 14 to 19 years. Arch Pediatr Adolesc Med 2000 Mar;154:234-9.

1084 Runyan CW, Dal Santo J, Schulman M, et al. Work hazards and workplace safety violations experienced by adolescent construction workers. Arch Pediatr Adolesc Med 2006 July;160:721-7.

1085 Runyan CW, Schulman M, Dal Santo J, et al. Work-related hazards and workplace safety of US adolescents employed in the retail and service sectors. Pediatrics 2007 March;119(3): 526-34.

1086 Belville R, Pollack SH, Goodbold JH, Landrigan PJ. Occupational injuries among working adolescents in New York State. JAMA 1993 June 2;269(21):2754-9.

1087 Shellenbarger, Sue. "Keeping teens safe on the job." The Wall Street Journal 2007 May 10:D1.

1088 Rauscher KJ. Workplace violence against adolescent workers in the U.S. Am J Ind Med 2008;51(7):539-44.

1089 "Many US children serve as caregivers for elderly, ill" Contemporary Pediatrics 2005 Oct;22(10):12.

1090 Anseberry, Clare. "Young caregivers: parents turn to their children for help; many juggle school with feeding tubes, IVs." The Wall Street Journal 2007 Jan 5;A1,10.

1091 Tofler IR, Stryer BK, Micheli LJ, Herman SR. Physical and emotional problems of elite female gymnasts. N Engl J Med 1996 July 25;335(4):281-3.

1092 De Coverley Veale DM. Exercise dependence. Br J Addict 1987 Jul;82(7):735-40.

1093 Fisher M, Juszczak L, Friedman S. Sports participation in an urban high school: academic and psychological correlates. J Adolesc Health 1996 May;18(5):329-34.

1094 Richter, Laurie A. *Put Me in Coach: A Parent's Guide to Winning the Game of College Recruiting.* Riverwoods, Illinois; Right Fit Press, 2009.

1095 Field AE, Austin SB, Camargo CA Jr, et al. Exposure to the mass media, body shape concerns, and use of supplements to improve weight and shape among male and female adolescents. Pediatrics 2005 Aug;116(2):e214-20.

1096 Schneider, Mary Ellen. "Performance-enhancing drug can be dangerous." Pediatric News 2004 April:23.

1097 Mofenson HC, Caraccio TR, et al. Substance Abuse in Sports. Pediatric Therapeutics and Toxicology/Supplement;1988 June:S5-8.

1098 The Medical Letter. Performance-enhancing drugs. 2004 July 19;46(Issue 1187):57-9.

1099 Koch, Jason J. Performance-enhancing substances and their use among adolescent athletes. Pediatrics in Review 2002 September;23(9):310-16.

1100 The Medical Letter. Dehydroepiandrosterone (DHEA). The Medical Letter 2005 May 9;47(Issue 1208):37-8

1101 Chorley JN. Dietary supplements as ergogenic aids. Adolescent Health Update 2000 October;13(1):1-8.

1102 The Medical Letter. Creatine and androstenedione—two "dietary supplements". The Medical Letter 1998 November 6;40(Issue 1039):105-6.

1103 Mack, Ronald B. Mucking the stalls without the help of creatine. Contemporary Pediatrics 1999 January:97-105.

1104 Griesemer, Bernard A. Ergogenic Aids. Pediatric Annals 2003 November;32(11):733-8.

1105 Council on Scientific Affairs. Drug abuse in athletes; anabolic steroids and human growth hormone. JAMA 1988 March 18;259(11):1703-5.

1106 Nanda Sharmila, Konnur Neelam. Adolescent drug & alcohol use in the 21st century. Pediatric Annals 2006 Mar 35(3):193-9.

1107 Koch, Jason J. Performance-enhancing substances and their use among adolescent athletes. Pediatrics in Review 2002 September;23(9):310-16.

1108 Elliot DL, Cheong J, Moe EL, et al. Cross-sectional study of female students reporting anabolic steroid use. Arch Pediatr Adolesc Med 2007;161:572-77.

1109 Van den Berg P, Neumark-Sztainer D, Cafri G, Wall M. Steroid use among adolescents: longitudinal findings from Project EAT. Pediatrics 2007 Mar;119(3):476-86.

1110 Metzl JD. Anabolic steroids and the pediatric community. Commentary, Pediatrics 2005 Dec;116(6):1542.

1111   Gautschi OP, Zellweger R. Methicillin-resistant staphylococcus aureus abscess after intramuscular steroid injection. N Engl J Med 2006 Aug 17;355(7):713.

1112   Millman RB, Ross EJ. Steroid and nutritional supplement use in professional athletes. Am J Addict 2003;12(suppl 2):48.

1113   Smith DV, McCambridge TM. Performance-enhancing substances in teens. Contemporary Pediatr 2009 Feb;26(2):36-45.

1114   Grimes JM, Ricci LA, Melloni RH Jr. Plasticity in anterior hypothalamic vasopressin correlates with aggression during anabolic-androgenic steroid withdrawal in hamsters. Behav Neurosci 2006 Feb;120(1):115-24.

1115   McConnell, Greg. "Getting an edge?" AAP News 2005 April:11.

1116   Lombardo JA. Supplements and athletes. South Med J 2004;39:879.

1117   Smith DV, McCambridge TM. Performance-enhancing substances in teens. Contemporary Pediatr 2009 Feb;26(2):36-45.

1118   Scott WC. The abuse of erythropoietin to enhance athletic performance. Letter to the editor, JAMA 1990 October 3.

1119   Stockman, JA III. Journal Club Newsletter, Children's Memorial Hospital 1991 September;6(4):1-2.

1120   Klein, Harvey G. Blood transfusions and athletics; games people play. N Engl J Med 1985 March 28;312(13):854-6.

1121   Rickert VI, Pawlak-Morello C, Sheppart IV, Jay MS. Human growth hormone: a new substance of abuse among adolescents? Clin Pediatr 1992 Dec;31(12):723-6.

1122   Study of substance use habits of college student-athletes;2001. www.ncaa.org/library/ research.#html#substance_use_habits.pdf as accessed 2009 Jan.

1123   Smith DV, McCambridge TM. Performance-enhancing substances in teens. Contemporary Pediatr 2009 Feb;26(2):36-45.

1124   Lui H, Bravata DM, Olkin I, et al. Systematic review: the effects of growth hormone on athletic performance. Ann Intern Med 2008;5:200.

1125   Bartke A. A word of caution: can growth hormone accelerate aging? J Anti Aging Med 2001;4:301-9.

1126   Perls TT, Reisman NR, Olshansky SJ. Provision or distribution of growth hormone for "anti-aging": clinical and legal issues. JAMA 2005;294:2086-90.

1127   Hoffman RJ, Hoffman RS, Freyberg CL, et al. Clenbuterol ingestion causing prolonged tachycardia, hypokalemia, and hypophosphatemia with confirmation by quantitative levels. J Toxicol Clin Toxicol 2001;39(4):339-44.

1128   Snead OC III, Gibson KM. Gamma-Hydroxybutyric Acid. N Engl J Med 2005 June 30;352(26): 2721-32.

1129   Delach, Anthony. Weight-loss efforts endanger young athletes. AAP News 1995 November;11(11):20-21.

1130   Walsh, Nancy. "Closer regulation due for dietary supplements." Pediatric News 2007 Feb;41:6.

1131   Waninger KD, Harcke HT. Determination of safe return to play for athletes recovering from infectious mononucleosis: a review of the literature. Clin J Sport Med 2005;15:410-6.

1132   Auwaeter PG. Infectious mononucleosis: return to play. Clinics in Sports Medicine 2004;23: 485-97.

1133   Van Camp S, Bloor C, Mueller R, Cantu R, Olson H. Non-traumatic sports death in high school and college athletes. Med Sci Sports Exerc 1995;27:641-7.

1134   Wood, Debra. "Taking simple steps to prevent sudden death." Pediatric News 2004 September:28.

1135   Maron BJ, Shirani J, Poliac LC, et al. Sudden death in young competitive athletes: clinical, demographic, and pathological profile. JAMA 1996;276:199-204.

1136   Cantwell JD, Fontanarosa PB. Aspirations and ideals in the Olympic Games. JAMA 1996 July 17;276(3):247-9.

1137   Curfman GD. Fatal impact—concussion of the heart. N Engl J Med 1998 June 18;338(25):1841-3.

1138   Link MS, Wang PJ, Pandian NG, et al. An experimental model of sudden death due to low-energy chest-wall impact (commotio cordis). N Engl J Med 1998 June 18;338(25):1805-11.

1139 Weinstock J, Maron BJ, Song C, et al. Failure of commercially available chest protectors to prevent sudden cardiac death induced by chest wall blows in an experimental model of commotion cordis. Pediatrics 2006;117:e656-62.

1140 Cuzick J, Terry G, Ho L, et al. HPV in cervical smears. Lancet 1992 Jul 11;340(8811):112-3.

1141 Huston TP, Puffer JC, Rodney WM. The athletic heart syndrome. The N Engl J Med 1995 July 4;313:24-30.

1142 Cantwell JD, Fontanarosa PB. Aspirations and ideals in the Olympic Games. JAMA 1996 July 17;276(3):247-9.

1143 Rowland, Thomas. Sudden unexpected death in young athletes: reconsidering "hypertrophic cardiomyopathy". Pediatrics 2009 Apr;123(4):1217-22.

1144 Corrado D, Basso C, Pavei A. Trends in sudden cardiovascular death in young competitive athletes after implementation of a preparticipation screening program. JAMA 2006 Oct 4;296(13):1593-601.

1145 Achar, Suraj as quoted by Wendling, Patrice in "Use B-type natriuretic peptide test in preparticipation exam." Pediatric News 2007 Feb;41(2):40.

1146 Simpson RK, Grossman RG. Seizures after jogging. Letter to the editor, N Engl J Med 1989 September 21;321(12):835.

1147 Chen SP, Fuh JL, Lu SR, Wang SJ. Exertional headache—a survey of 1963 adolescents Cephalgia 2009 Apr;29(4):401-7.

1148 Steinberg, Irving, as quoted by Rosenthal, Marie in "CA-MRSA becoming fact of life for some athletes involved in contact sports." Infectious Diseases in Children 2005 Nov;52-3.

1149 Shukla AY, Green JB. Bowling plexopathy. Letter to the editor, New Engl J Med 1991 March28;324(13):928.

1150 Mavrelis PG, Wylie RR. Water-ski colon. Letter to the editor, New Engl J Med 1984 October 25;311(17).

1151 Spindler KP, Wright RW. Anterior cruciate ligament tear. N Engl J Med 2008 Nov 13;359(20): 2135-42.

1152 Ganley, Theodore J, as quoted by Kirn, Timothy F in "Short, light training helps prevent ACL injuries in girls". Pediatric News 2007 May;41(5):52.

1153 Goldberg B. Injury patterns in youth sports. Phys Sports Med 1989;17:175-85.

1154 Ni H, Barnes P, Hardy AM. Recreational injury and its relation to socioeconomic status among school aged children in the US. Injury Prevention 2002;8:60-5.

1155 Smith AM, Milliner EK. Injured athletes and the risk of suicide. J Athl Train 1994 Dec;29(4): 337-41.

1156 Chen JK, Johnston KM, Petrides M. Neural substrates of symptoms of depression following concussion in male athletes with persistent postconcussion symptoms. Arch Gen Psych 2008;65(1):81-9.

1157 Garrick, James G as quoted by Little, Linda in "Childhood dancers are the forgotten athletes". Pediatric News 2005 Aug;39(8):37.

1158 McCambridge, Teri as quoted by Tanzola, Melinda in "Ther harder the stunt, the harder they may fall". Pediatric News 2006 Nov:46.

1159 Shields BJ, Smith GA. Cheerleading-related injuries to children 5 to 18 years of age: United States, 1990-2002. Pediatrics 2006 Jan;117(1):122-9.

1160 Centers for Disease Control and Prevention. Football-related spinal cord injuries among high school players—Louisiana, 1989;MMWR 39(34):586-7.

1161 "Wrestling said to cause most injuries of any sport". Pediatric News 1989 March;23(3):65.

1162 Mueller FO, Cantu RC. Catastrophic injuries and fatalities in high school and college sports, fall 1982-spring 1988. Med Science in Sports and Exercises 1990 December;22(6):737-41.

1163 Xiang H, Stallones L, Smith GA. Downhill skiing injury fatalities among children. Inj Prev 2004;10:99-102.

1164 Centers for Disease Control and Prevention. Injuries associated with horseback riding—United States, 1987 and 1988. MMWR 1990 May 25;39(20):329-32.

1165 Schultz MR, Marshall SW, Mueller FO, et al. Incidence and risk factors for concussion in high school athletes, North Carolina, 1996-1999. Am J Epid 2004 Nov 15;160(10):937-44.

1166 Schultz MR, Marshall SW, Mueller FO, et al. Incidence and risk factors for concussion in high school athletes, North Carolina, 1996-1999. Am J Epid 2004 Nov 15;160(10):937-44.

1167   Cole, Thomas B. Can sports-minded kids have too many helmets? JAMA 1996 May 8;275(18):1391.

1168   Weiss J, Okun M, Quay N. Predicting bicycle helmet stage-of-change among middle school, high school, and college cyclists from demographic, cognitive, and motivational variables. J Pediatr 2004;145:360-4.

1169   Quan L, Cummings P. Characteristics of drowning by different age groups. Inj Prev 2003;9:163-8.

1170   Powell JW, Barber-Foss KD. Traumatic brain injury in high school athletes. JAMA 1999 September 8;282(10):958-63.

1171   Powell JW, Barber-Foss KD. Traumatic brain injury in high school athletes. JAMA 1999 Sept 8;282(10):958-63.

1172   Meehan WP III, Bachur RG. Sport-related concussion. Pediatrics 2009 Jan;123(1):114-23.

1173   Powell JW, Barber-Foss KD. Traumatic brain injury in high school athletes. JAMA 1999 Sept 8;282(10):958-63.

1174   McCrea M, Hammeke T, Olsen G, et al. Unreported concussion in high school football players: implications for prevention. Clin J Sport Med 2004;14:13-17.

1175   Delaney JS, Lacroix MJ, Leclerc S, Johnston KM. concussions during the 1997 Canadian Football League season. Clin J Sport Med 2000;10(1):9-14.

1176   McCrory PR, Berkovic SF. Second impact syndrome. Neurology 1998 Mar;50(3):677-83.

1177   Vastag, Brian. "Football brain injuries draw increased scrutiny." JAMA 2002 January 23/30;287(4):437-9.

1178   Guskiewicz KM, McCrea M, Marshall SW, et al. Cumulative effects associated with recurrent concussion in collegiate football players: the NCAA Concussion Study. JAMA 2003;290(19):2459-55.

1179   Delaney JS, Lacroix MJ, Leclerc S, Johnston KM. concussions during the 1997 Canadian Football League season. Clin J Sport Med 2000;10(1):9-14.

1180   Ropper AH, Gorson KC. Concussion. N Engl J Med 2007 Jan 11;356(2):166-72.

1181   Meehan WP III, Bachur RG. Sport-related concussion. Pediatrics 2009 Jan;123(1):114-23.

1182   Centers for Disease and Control Sports-related recurrent brain injuries—United States. MMWR 1997 March 14;46(10):224-7.

1183   Collins MW, Grindel SH, Lovell, MR, et al. Relationship between concussion and neuropsychological performance in college football players. JAMA 1999 September 8;282(10):964-70.

1184   Matser EJT, Kessels AG, Lezak MD, et al. Neuropsychological impairment in amateur soccer players. JAMA 1999;282:971-3.

1185   Kelly, James P. Traumatic brain injury and concussion in sports. JAMA 1999 September 8;282(10):989-91.

1186   Omalu BI, DeKosky ST, Minster RL, et al. Chronic traumatic encephalopathy in a National Football League player. Neurosurgery 2005;57:128-34.

1187   Omalu BI, DeKosky ST, Hamilton RL, et al. Chronic traumatic encephalopathy in a national football league player: part II. Neurosurgery 2006;59(5):1086-93.

1188   Saunders RL, Harbaugh RE. The second impact in catastrophic contact-sports head trauma. JAMA 1984;252:538-9.

1189   Kelly JP, Nichols JS, Filley CM, Lillihei KO, Rubinstein D, Kleinschmidt-DeMasters BK. Concussion in sports: guidelines for the prevention of catastrophic outcome. JAMA 1991;266:2867-9.

1190   Cantu RC, Voy R. Second impact syndrome: a risk in any contact sport. Physician and Medicine 1995;23:27-34.

1191   Boden BP, Tacchetti RL, Cantu RC, et al. Catastrophic head injuries in high school and college football players. Am J Sports Med 2007;35(7):1075-81.

1192   Hong, Eugene, as quoted by Sullivan, Michele G. "Ill-fitted helmets leave school athletes at risk for concussion." Pediatric News 2006 Oct:54.

1193   Zarda, Brett. "Burn notice; a football helmet tells the sideline when players are dangerously overheated." Popular Science 2009 June:34.

1194   Football and its dangers. JAMA 1905 Nov 25;45:1656-7 as reprinted in "JAMA 100 years ago". JAMA 2005 Nov 23/30;294(20):2645.

1195   Rozin, Skip. "The brutal truth about college sports." The Wall Street Journal 2005 Sept 19:D7.

1196   Rozin, Skip. "A weak policeman talks tough when tackling sports and its critics." The Wall Street Journal 2006 Nov 1:D10.

1197 Murray TM, Livingston LA. Hockey helmets, face masks, and injurious behavior. Pediatrics 1995 March;95(3):419-21.

1198 Murray TM, Livingston LA. Hockey helmets, face masks, and injurious behavior. Pediatrics 1995 March;95(3):419-21.

1199 Goldberg JN. The big technological tennis upset. Invention and Technology. 1997 Spring, as reprinted in Pediatrics 1997 July;100(1):38.

1200 Reid SR, Losek JD. Factors associated with significant injuries in youth ice hockey players. Pediatric Emergency care 1999;15(5):310-13.

1201 Batoosingh, Karen A. About 1 in 3 boys who play hockey sustain injury. Pediatric News 1993 January;27(1):10.

1202 Nansel JR, Overpech M, Pilla RS, et al. Bullying behaviors among US youth. JAMA 2001 Apr 25;285(16):2194-200.

1203 Storch EA, Milsom VA, Debraganza N, et al. Peer victimization, psychosocial adjustment, and physical activity in overweight and at-risk-for-overweight youth. J Pediatr Psychol 2007 Jan-Feb;32(1):80-9.

1204 Storch EA, Heidgerken AD, Geffken GR, et al. Bullying, regimen self-management, and metabolic control in youth with type I diabetes. J Pediatr 2006 June;148:784-7.

1205 Gini G, Pozzoli T. Association between bullying and psychosomatic problems: a meta-analysis. Pediatrics 2009 Mar;123(3):1059-65.

1206 Juvonen J, Graham S, Schuster MA. Bullying among young adolescents: the strong, the weak, and the troubled. Pediatrics 2003 Dec;112(6):1231-7.

1207 Olweus D. Bully/victim problems among school children in Rubin K, Pepler D, editors. *The Development and Treatment of Childhood Aggression.* Hillsdale, NJ; Erlbaum, 1991:411-48.

1208 Hazler R, Hoover J, Oliver R. Student perceptions of victimization by bullies in school J Humanist Educ Dev 1991;29:143.

1209 Suarez, Mariann as quoted by Brunk, Doug in "NIMH data flag girlish aggression. Pediatric News 2005 Dec:27.

1210 Olweus D. Bully/victim problems among school children in Rubin K, Pepler D, editors. *The Development and Treatment of Childhood Aggression.* Hillsdale, NJ; Erlbaum, 1991:411-48.

1211 Garrity C, Baris MA. Bullies and victims: a guide for pediatricians. Contemporary Pediatr 1996 Feb;13(2):90-116.

1212 Vreeman RC, Carroll AE. A systemic review of school-based interventions to prevent bullying. Arch Pediatr Adolesc Med 2007 Jan;161:78-88.

1213 Jekkes M, Pijpers FIM, Verloove-Vanhorick P. Effects of antibullying school program on bullying and health complaints. Arch Pediatr Adolesc Med 2006 June;160:638-44.

1214 Centers for Disease Control and Prevention. Physical dating violence among high school students—United States, 2003. MMWR 2006 May 19;55(19):532-6.

1215 Lehrer JA, Buka S, Gortmaker S, Shrier LA. Depressive symptomatology as a predictor of exposure to intimate partner violence among US female adolescents and young adults. Arch Pediatr Adolesc Med 2006 Mar;160:270-6.

1216 Glow, Kimberly M. Teen dating violence: know the facts, work for solutions. Illinois Pediatrician 2006 Spring;24(1):10-1.

1217 Centers for Disease Control and Prevention. Youth violence facts at a glance. Accessed at http://www.cdc.gov/ncipc/dvp/YV_DataSheet.pdf. 6-1-07.

1218 Ginsburg, Kenneth R. Guiding adolescents away from violence. Contemporary Pediatrics 1997 Nov;101-11.

1219 Song L-u, Singer MI, Anglin TM. Violence exposure and emotional trauma as contributors to adolescents' violent behaviors. Arch Pediatr Adolesc Med 1998 June;152:531-6.

1220 Dahlberg L. Youth violence: developmental pathways and prevention challenges. Am J Prev Med 2001;20(suppl 1):3-14.

1221 Song L-u, Singer MI, Anglin TM. Violence exposure and emotional trauma as contributors to adolescents' violent behaviors. Arch Pediatr Adolesc Med 1998 June;152:531-6.

1222 Lamberg, Lynne. Younger children, more girls commit acts of violence. JAMA 2002 Aug 7;288(5):566-8.

1223 Endresen IM, Olweus D. Participation in power sports and antisocial involvement in preadolescent and adolescent boys. J Child Psychol Psychiatry 2005 May;46(5):468-78.

1224 DuRant RH, Treiber F, Goodman E, Woods ER. Intentions to use violence among young adolescents. Pediatrics 1996 Dec;98(6):1104-8.

1225 Molnar BE, Browne A, Cerda M, Buka SL. Violent behavior by girls reporting violent victimization; a prospective study. Arch Pediatr Adolesc Med 2005 Aug;159:731-9.

1226 Mollen CJ, Fein JA, Localio R, Durbin DR. Characterization of interpersonal violence events involving young adolescent girls vs events involving young adolescent boys. Arch Pediatr Adolesc Med 2004 June;158:545-50.

1227 Borowsky IW, Ireland M. Predictors of future fight-related injury among adolescents. Pediatrics 2004 March;113(3):530-6.

1228 Malek MK, Chang BH, Davis TC. Self-reported characterization of 7th grade students' fights. J Adolesc Health 1998;23:103-9.

1229 DuRant RH, et al. Weapon carrying on school property among middle schools students. Arch Pediatr Adolesc Med 1999 Jan;153:21-6.

1230 Centers for Disease Control and Prevention. Violence-related behaviors among high school students—United States, 1991-2003. MMWR 2004 July 30;53(29):651-5.

1231 Boynton-Jarrett R, Ryan LM, Berkman LF, Wright RJ. Cumulative violence exposure and self-rated health: longitudinal study of adolescents in the United States. Pediatrics 2008;122(5):961-70.

1232 Campbell C, Schwarz DF. Prevalence and impact of exposure to interpersonal violence among suburban and urban middle school students. Pediatrics 1996 Sept;98(3):396-402.

1233 Song L-y, Singer MI, Anglin TM. Violence exposure and emotional trauma as contributors to adolescents' violent behaviors. Arch Pediatr Adolesc Med 1998 June;152:531-6.

1234 Cheng TL, Haynie D, Brenner R, et al. Effectiveness of a mentor-implemented, violence prevention intervention for assault-injured youths presenting to the emergency department: results of a randomized trial. Pediatrics 2008 Nov 122(5):938-46.

1235 Walton M, Cunningham R, Xue Y, et al. Internet referrals for adolescent violence prevention: an innovative mechanism for inner-city emergency departments. J Adolesc Health 2008 Sept;43(3):309-12.

1236 Barnes, Vernon A, as quoted by Worcester, Sharon in "School-based intervention improves teens' anger control." Pediatric News 2009 Jan;43(1):15.

1237 Borowsky IW, Mozayeny S, Stuenkel K, Ireland M. Effects of a primary care-based intervention on violent behavior and injury in children. Pediatrics 2004;114:e392-9.

1238 Ohene, S-A, Ireland M, McNeely C, Borowsky IW. Parental expectations physical punishment, and violence among adolescents who score positive on a psychosocial screening test in primary care. Pediatrics 2006;117(2):441-7.

1239 http://consensus.nih.gov

1240 www.ahrq.gov/clinic/epcsums/adolvisum.htm

1241 Centers for Disease Control and Prevention, Task Force on Community Preventive Services. Therapeutic foster care for the prevention of violence. MMWR 2004 June 25;53(RR-9):1-9.

1242 Ziv A, Boulet JR, Slap GB. Utilization of physician offices by adolescents in the United States. Pediatrics 1999 July;104(1):35-42.

1243 Wellbery C. A Mutual Anxiety. JAMA 2003 July 16;290(3):305.

1244 American Academy of Pediatrics. In Brief: Nutrition in Adolescence. Pediatrics in Review 2000 January;21(1):32.

1245 Gold MA, Friedman SB. Conversion reactions in adolescents. Pediatric Annals 1995 June;24(6).

1246 Poikolainen K, Kanerva R, Lonnqvist J. Life events and other risk factors for somatic symptoms in adolescence. Pediatrics 1995 July;96(1):59-63.

1247 Ghandour RM, Overpeck MD, Huang ZJ, Kogan MD, Scheidt PC. Headache, stomachache, backache, morning fatigue among adolescent girls in the United States. Arch Pediatr Adolesc Med 2004 August;158:797-803.

1248 Rimes KA, Goodman R, Hotopf M, et al. Incidence, prognosis, and risk factors for fatigue and chronic fatigue syndrome in adolescents. Pediatrics 2007;119:e603-9.

1249 ter Wolbeek M van Doornen LJP, Kavelaars A, Heijnen C. Severe fatigue in adolescents: a common phenomenon? Pediatrics 2006;117:e1078-86.

1250 Wang SJ, Fuh JL, Lu SR, Juang KD. Chronic daily headache in adolescents: prevalence, impact, and medication overuse. Neurology 2006 Jan 24;66(2):193-7.

1251 Chambers CT, et al. Self administration of over-the-counter medication for pain among adolescents. Arch Pediatr Adolesc Med 1997;151:449-55.

1252 Jancin, Bruce. "Tall order: predicting a child's adult height." Pediatric News 1995 February;29(2).

1253 Freedman DS, Khan LK, Serdula MK, Srinivasan SS, Berenson GS. Secular trends in height among children during 2 decades. Arch Pediatr Adolesc Med 2000 Feb;154:155-61.

1254 Schumacher LB, Pawson IG, Kretchmer N. Growth of immigrant children in the newcomer schools of San Francisco. Pediatrics 1987 Dec;80(6):861-8.

1255 Boller PF. *The Presidents*. New York, NY; Oxford University Press, 1984.

1256 Stockman, James A III. "Clinical Facts and Curios". Clinical Problems in Pediatrics 1992 December.

1257 Klein, Nora J. "Notes from Readers: on thirty thousand children in France who are below the first percentile for height." Pediatric Notes 1991 September 24;15(39):156.

1258 Albanes, Demetrius, Jones DY, Schatzkin A, et al. Adult stature and risk of cancer. Cancer Res 1988 Mar 15;48(6):1658-62.

1259 Zimet GD, Owens R, Dahms W, Cutler M, Litvene M, Cuttler L. Psychosocial outcome of children evaluated for short stature. Arch Pediatr Adolesc Med 1997 October;151:1017-23.

1260 Voss LD, et al. Short stature and school performance—the Wessex Growth Study. Acta Paediatr Scand 1991;377(Suppl):20-7.

1261 Sandberg DE, Bukowski WM, Fung CM, Noll RB. Height and social adjustment: are extremes a cause for concern and action? Pediatrics 2004 September;114(3):744-50.

1262 Cuttler, Leona, as quoted in "Children better able to cope with being short than parents fear." Pediatric News 1990 July:1,13.

1263 Voss LD, Mulligan J. Bullying in school: are short pupils at risk? Questionnaire study in a cohort. Brit Med J 2000;320:612-3.

1264 The Medical Letter on Drugs and Therapeutics. Growth hormone for normal short children. The Medical Letter 2003 November 10;45(Issue 1169):89-90.

1265 Stockman James A III. "Clinical Facts and Curios." Current Problems in Pediatrics, 1989.

1266 Lee JM, Davis MM, Clark SJ, et al. Estimated cost-effectiveness of growth hormone therapy for idiopathic short stature. Arch Pediatr Adolesc Med 2006 Mar;160(3):263-9.

1267 Lee, Mary M. Idiopathic short stature. N Engl J Med 2006 June 15;354(24):2576-82.

1268 Rowan-Legg, Anne MD. Comment regarding "The rise and fall of estrogen therapy to attenuate growth in very tall girls." Pediatric Notes 2007 Jan 4;31(1):2.

1269 Rieser, Patricia; Underwood, Louis E. Growing Children: a Parents' Guide, second edition. South San Francisco, CA. Genentech , Inc., 1991.

1270 Silventoinen K, Haukka J, Dunkel L, et al. Genetics of pubertal timing and its associations with relative weight in childhood and adult height: the Swedish young male twins study. Pediatrics 2008 Apr;121(4):e885-91.

1271 Kaplowitz PB. Precocious puberty: making the distinction between common normal variants and more serious problems. Contemporary Pediatrics 2006 Aug;23(8):55-61.

1272 Schindler, Alan M. *Too Tall? Too short? Too Fat? Too Thin? A Guide to the Growth and Sexual Development of Children*. New York, NY; Agathon Press, 1989.

1273 Prose CC, Ford CA, Lovely LP. Evaluating amenorrhea: the pediatrician's role. Contemporary Pediatrics 1998 October;15(10):83-110.

1274 Kaplowitz PB, Oberfeld SE. Reexamination of the age limit for defining when puberty is precocious in girls in the United States: implications for evaluation and treatment. Pediatrics 1999;104:936-41.

1275 Tiwary CM. Premature sexual development in children following the use of estrogen- or placenta- containing hair products. Clinical Pediatrics 1998;37(12):733-40.

1276 Johansson T, Ritzen EM. Very long-term follow-up of girls with early and late menarche. Endocr Dev 2005;8:126-36.

1277 Burt SA, McGue M, DeMarte JA, et al. Timing of menarche and the origins of conduct disorder. Arch Gen Psych 2006;63:890-6.

1278 Campbell MA, McGrath PJ. Use of medication by adolescents for the management of menstrual discomfort. Arch Pediatr and Adolesc Med 1997 September;151:905-13.

1279 American Academy of Pediatrics, Committee on Adolescence; American College of Obstetricians and Gynecologists, Committee on Adolescent Health Care. Menstruation in girls and adolescents: using the menstrual cycle as a vital sign. Pediatrics 2006 Nov;118(5):2245-50.

1280 Weller A, Weller L. Menstrual synchrony between mothers and daughters and between roommates. Physiology and Behavior 1993 May;53(5):943-9.

1281 McClintock MK. Menstrual synchrony and suppression. Nature 1971;229(5282):244-5.

1282 Legro RS. A 27-year-old woman with a diagnosis of polycystic ovary syndrome. JAMA 2007 Feb 7;297(5):509-19.

1283 Fleischman A, Mansfield J. Diagnosis and treatment of polycystic ovarian syndrome and insulin resistance. Pediatric Annals 2005 Sept;34(9):733-42.

1284 Halac I, Zimmerman D. Evaluating short stature in children. Pediatric Annals 2004 March;33(3):170-7.

1285 Schindler, Alan M. *Too Tall? Too short? Too Fat? Too Thin? A Guide to the Growth and Sexual Development of Children.* New York, NY; Agathon Press, 1989.

1286 Kaplowitz PB, Oberfeld SE. Reexamination of the age limit for defining when puberty is precocious in girls in the United States: implications for evaluation and treatment. Pediatrics 1999;104:936-41.

1287 Albanese A, Stanhope R. Predictive factors in the determination of final height in boys with constitutional delay of growth and puberty. J Pediatr 1995;126:545-50.

1288 Schindler, Alan M. *Too Tall? Too short? Too Fat? Too Thin? A Guide to the Growth and Sexual Development of Children.* New York, NY; Agathon Press, 1989.

1289 Sher ES, Migeon CJ, Berkovitz GD. Evaluation of boys with marked breast development at puberty. Clinical Pediatrics 1998 June;;37(6):367-72.

1290 Henley DV, Lipson N, Korach KS, Bloch CA. Prepubertal gynecomastia linked to lavender and tea tree oils. N Engl J Med 2007 Feb 1;356(5):479-85.

1291 Nasrallah PF, et al. Male self health awareness. Abstracted in Pediatric Primary Care 1999:48.

1292 Cordain L, Lindeberg S, Hurtado M, et al. acne vulgaris: a disease of Western civilization. Arch Dermatol 2002 Dec;138(12):1584-90.

1293 "Feeling the Scars of Acne". JAMA 1995 January 4;273(1):10.

1294 James, William D. Acne. New Engl J Med 2005 April 7;352(14):1463-72.

1295 Gilman, Alfred Goodman. *The Pharmacological Basis of Therapeutics, 8th ed.* Maxwell House, Fairview Park, Elmsford New York; Pergamon Press, Inc., 1990.

1296 Kristal L, Silverberg N. Acne: simplifying a complex disorder. Contemporary Pediatrics 1998 August;Supplement:1-10.

1297 The Medical Letter. Azelaic Acid—A New Topical Drug for Acne. The Medical Letter 1996 June 7;38(Issue 976):52-3.

1298 The Medical Letter. Adapalene for Acne. The Medical Letter 1997 February 28; 29(Issue 995): 19-20.

1299 Haider A, Shaw JC. Treatment of Acne Vulgaris. JAMA 2004 August 11;292(6):726-35.

1300 James, William D. Acne. New Engl J Med 2005 April 7;352(14):1463-72.

1301 The Medical Letter. Tazarotene (Tazorac) for Acne. The Medical Letter 2002 June 10;44(Issue 1132):52-3.

1302 Beard, LM. "Beyond Chicken Soup; Acne." Pediatric News 2004 January;38(1).

1303 Orringer JS, Kang S, Hamilton T, et al. Treatment of acne vulgaris with a pulsed dye laser. JAMA 2004 June 16;291(23):2834-9.

1304 The Medical Letter. Blue Light (Clearlight) for acne vulgaris. The Medical Letter 2003 June 23;45(Issue 1159):50-1.

1305 DiGiovanna JJ, Langman CB, Tschen EH, et al. Effect of a single course of isotretinoin therapy on bone mineral density in adolescent patients with severe, recalcitrant, nodular acne. J Am Acad Dermatol 2004;51:709-17.

1306 The Medical Letter. Is Accutane really dangerous? The Medical Letter 2002 September 16;44(Issue 1139):82.

1307 Titelbaum JE, Perez-Atayde AR, Cohen M, et al. Minocycline-related autoimmune hepatitis. Arch Pediatr Adolesc Med 1998 November;152:1132-6.

1308 El-Hallak, Moussa; Giani T; Sozeri B, et al. Chronic minocycline-induced autoimmunity in children. J Peds 2008;153:314-9.

1309 Chia CY, Lane W, Chibnall J, et al. Isotretinoin therapy and mood changes in adolescents with moderate to severe acne: a cohort study. Arch Derm 2005;141:557-60.

1310 Seukeran DC, Cunliffe WJ. The treatment of acne fulminans: a review of 25 cases. Br J Dermatol 1999 Aug;141(2):307-9.

1311 Choi JM, Lew VK, Kimball AB. A single-blinded, randomized, controlled clinical trial evaluating the effect of face washing on acne vulgaris. Pediatr Dermatol 2006 Sept-Oct;23(5):421-7.

1312 Fulton JE, Plewig G, Dligman AM. Effect of chocolate on acne vulgaris. JAMA 1969 Dec 15; 210(11):2071-4.

1313 Adebamowo CA, Spiegelman D, Berkey CS, et al. Milk consumption and acne in teenaged boys. J Am Acad Dermatol 2008;59(5):787-93.

1314 Adabmowo CA, Spiegelman, D, Danby FW, et al. High school dietary intake and teenage acne. J Am Acad Dermatol 2005;52(2):207-14.

1315 Cordain L, Lindeberg S, Hurtado M, et al. Acne vulgaris: a disease of western civilization. Arch Derm 2002;138(12):1584-90.

1316 Galobardes B, Davey Smith G, Jeffreys M, et al. Acne in adolescence and cause-specific mortality: lower coronary heart disease and higher prostate cancer mortality: the Glasgow Alumni Cohort Study. Am J Epidemiology 2005 June 15;161(12):1094-101.

1317 Peter J, Ray G. Infectious Mononucleosis. Pediatrics in Review 1998 August;19(8):276.

1318 Harrison CJ. "ID Consult; Understanding the Enigma that is Mononucleosis." Pediatric News 2001 September;35(9).

1319 Chan CW, Chiang AKS, Chan KH, Lau ASY. Epstein-Barr virus-associated infectious mononucleosis in Chinese children. Pediatr Infect Dis J 2003;22(11):974-8.

1320 Higgins CD, Swerdlow AJ, Macsween KF, et al. A study of risk factors for acquisition of Epstein-Barr virus and its subtypes. J Infect Dis 2007 Feb 15;195(4):474-82.

1321 Peter J, Ray G. Infectious Mononucleosis. Pediatrics in Review 1998 August;19(8):276.

1322 Cameron B, Bharadwaj M, Burrows J, et al. Prolonged illness after infectious mononucleosis is associated with altered immunity but not with increased viral load. J Infect Dis 2006 Mar 1;193(5):664-71.

1323 Miller JP, Amin NM. Young woman with sore throat and extreme fatigue. Consultant for Pediatricians 2004 October;451-3.

1324 Krugman, Saul; Katz, Samuel L; Gershon Anne A; Wilfert Catherine M. *Infectious Diseases of Children*. St. Louis, Missouri; Mosby-Year Book, 1992.

1325 Jancin, Bruce. "Infectious mono management in athletes varies widely." Pediatric News 1997 August;31(8).

1326 Roy M, Bailey B, Amre DK, et al. Dexamethasone for the treatment of sore throat in children with suspected infectious mononucleosis. Arch Pediatr Adolesc Med 2004 March;158:250-4.

1327 Thompson SK, Doerr TD, Hengerer AS. Infectious mononucleosis and corticosteroids: management practices and outcomes. Arch Otolaryngol-Head and Neck Surg 2005;131:900-4.

1328 Van der Horst C, Joncas J, Ahronheim G, et al. Lack of effect of peroral acyclovir for the treatment of acute infectious mononucleosis. J Infect Dis 1991 Oct;164(4):788-92.

1329 Balfour HH Jr, Hokanson KM, Schacherer RM, et al. A virologic pilot study of valacyclovir in infectious mononucleosis. J Clin Virol 2007 May;39(1):16-21.

1330 DeLorenze GN, Munger KL, Lennette ET, et al. Epstein-Barr virus and multiple sclerosis: evidence of association from a prospective study with long-term follow-up. Arch Neurol 2006;63:63: 839-44.

1331 Nielsen TR, Rostgaard K, Nielsen NM, et al. Multiple sclerosis after infectious mononucleosis. Arch Neurol 2007;64:72-5.

1332 Levin LI, Munger KL, Rubertone MV, et al. Temporal relationship between elevation of Epstein-Barr virus antibody titers and initial onset of neurological symptoms in multiple sclerosis. JAMA 2005 May 25;293(20):2496-500.

1333 Harrison CJ. "ID Consult; Understanding the Enigma that is Mononucleosis." Pediatric News 2001 September;35(9).

1334 Schmitt, Barton D. When your child has mononucleosis. Contemporary Pediatrics 1996 April;13(4):66-7.

1335 "What's your diagnosis?" Infectious Diseases in Children 1998 March;11(3):44,60.

1336 Peter J, Ray G. Infectious Mononucleosis. Pediatrics in Review 1998 August;19(8):276.

1337   Krugman, Saul; Katz, Samuel L; Gershon Anne A; Wilfert Catherine M. *Infectious Diseases of Children*. St. Louis, Missouri; Mosby-Year Book, 1992.

1338   Laumann AE, Derick AJ. Tattoos and body piercings in the United States: a national data set. J Am Acad Dermatol 2006 Sept;55(3):413-21.

1339   Mayers LB, Judelson DA, Moriarty BW, Rundell KW. Prevalence of body art (body piercing and tattooing) in university undergraduates and incidence of medical complications. Mayo Clinic Proc 2002 January;77(1):29-34.

1340   Boardman R, Smith RA. Dental implications of oral piercing. J Calif Dent Assoc 1997 Mar;25(3):200-7.

1341   Gold MA, Schorzman CM, Murray PJ, et al. Body piercing practices and attitudes among urban adolescents. J Adolesc Health 2005 Apr;36(4):352.e17-24.

1342   Hellard M, et al. Investigation of infection control practices and knowledge of hepatitis C among body-piercing practitioners. Am J Infection Control 2003;31:215-20.

1343   More DR, et al. Ear-piercing techniques as a cause of auricular chondritis. Pediatr Emerg Care 1999;15:189-94.

1344   Long, Rickman. Clin Infect Dis 1994;18:610.

1345   Ronge, Laura. Pediatricians' piercing insight can help teens get the point. AAP News 1997 January;13(1):1,10-ll.

1346   Dyce O, Bruno JR, Hong d, et al. Tongue piercing. The new "rusty nail"? Head Neck 2000 Oct;22(7):728-32.

1347   Centers for Disease Control and Prevention. Methicillin-resistant *staphylococcus aureus* skin infections among tattoo recipients—Ohio, Kentucky, and Vermont, 2004-2005. MMWR 2006 June 26;55(24):677-9.

1348   Haley RW, Fischer RP. Commercial tattooing as a potentially important source of hepatitis C infection. Clinical epidemiology of 626 consecutive patients unaware of their hepatitis C serological status. Medicine (Baltimore) 2001 Mar;80(2):134-51.

1349   Samuel MC, Bultreys M, Jenison S, Doherty P. Tattoos, incarnation and hepatitis B and C among street-recruited injection drug users in New Mexico, USA: update. Epidemiol Infect 2005 Dec;133(6):1146-8.

1350   FDA. Tattoos. FDA Medical Bulletin 1994 May:8.

1351   Antonovich DD, Callen JP. Development of sarcoidosis in cosmetic tattoos. Arch Derm 2005;141:869-72.

1352   Daniel AR, Sheha T. "Transmission of hepatitis C through swapping body jewelry." Letter to the Editor, Pediatrics 2005 Nov;116(5).

1353   Boardman R, Smith RA. Dental implications of oral piercing. J Calif Dent Assoc 1997 Mar;25(3):200-7.

1354   Richardson, James D as quoted by Wang, Jennifer M in "Tongue bolt leads to invasive invasive *N. meningitis*." Pediatric News 2000 Dec;34(12)

1355   Gazzeri R, Mercuri S. Atypical trigeminal neuralgia associated with tongue piercing. Research letter JAMA 2006 October 18;296(15):1840-2.

1356   More DR, Seidel JS, Bryan PA. Ear-piercing techniques as a cause of auricular chondritis. Pediatr Emergency Care 1999;15(3):189-92.

1357   Keene WE, Markum AC, Samadpour M. Outbreak of Pseudomonas aeruginosa infections caused by commercial piercing of upper ear cartilage. JAMA 2004 February 25;291(8):981-5.

1358   Donohue, Maureen. "Only 10% to 15% of body piercings get infected." Pediatric News 2000 March;34(3):18-19.

1359   Staley R, Fitzgibbon JJ, Anderson C. Auricular infections caused by high ear piercing in adolescents. Pediatrics 1997 April;99(4):610-11.

1360   Bykowski Mike. "Body piercing: infectious agents differ by site." Pediatric News 1997 October;31(10):22.

1361   "Piercing cartilage riskier than ear lobe." Infectious Diseases in Children 2002 December;15(12): 29-30.

1362   Mayers L, Chiffriller S. Sequential survey of body piercing and tattooing prevalence and medical complication incidence among college students. Pediatric Forum, Arch Pediatr Adolesc Med 2007 Dec;161(12):1219-20.

1363   Laumann AE, Derick AJ. Tattoos and body piercings in the United States: a national data set. J Am Acad Dermatol 2006 Sept;55(3):413-21.

1364 The Medical Letter. Removable permanent tattoo ink. The Medical Letter 2007 Sept 10;49;Issue 1269:75-6.

1365 Jacob SE, Zapolanski T, Chayavichitsilp P, et al. p-Phenylenediamine in black henna tattoos. Arch Pediatr Adolesc Med 2008 Aug;162(8):790-2.

1366 The Medical Letter. Removable permanent tattoo ink. The Medical Letter 2007 Sept 10;49;Issue 1269:75-6.

1367 Carroll ST, Riffenburgh RH, Roberts TA, Myhre EB. Tattoos and body piercings as indicators of adolescent risk-taking behaviors. Pediatrics 2002 June;109(6):1021-7.

1368 Roberts TA, Ryan SA. Tattooing and high-risk behavior in adolescents. Pediatrics 2002 Dec;110(6):1058-63.

1369 Pearl A, Weston J. Attitudes of adolescents about cosmetic surgery. Ann Plastic Surg 2003 June;50(6):628-30.

1370 Corcoran JF. "Physicians should guide teens considering cosmetic surgery." AAP News 2005 Dec;26(12):14.

1371 Inge TH, Zeller MH, Lawson L, Daniels, SR. A critical appraisal of evidence supporting a bariatric surgical approach to weight management for adolescents. J Pediatr 2005 July;147:10-9.

1372 Ramsay DT, Kent JC, Hartmann RA, Hartmann PE. Anatomy of the lactating human breast redefined with ultrasound imaging. J Anat 2005 June;206(6):525-34.

1373 Geller AC, Colditz G, Oliveria S, et al. Use of sunscreen, sunburning rates, and tanning bed use among more than 10,000 US children and adolescents. Pediatrics 2002 June;109(6): 1009-14.

1374 Demko CA, Borawski EA, Debanne SM, et al. Use of indoor tanning facilities by white adolescents in the United States. Arch Pediatr Adolesc Med 2003;157:854-60.

1375 Knight JM, et al. Awareness of the risks of tanning lamps does not influence behavior among college students. Arch Derm 2002;138:1311-5.

1376 "WHO recommends people younger than 18 should avoid using tanning devices." Infectious Diseases in Children 2005 April;18(4):38.

1377 Centers for Disease Control. Injuries associated with ultraviolet tanning devices—Wisconsin. MMWR 1989 May 19;38(19):333-5.

1378 Culley CA, Mayer JA, Eckhardt L, et al. Compliance with federal and state legislation by indoor tanning facilities in San Diego. J Am Acad Dermatol 2001 Jan;44(1):53-60.

1379 Zeller S, Lazovich D, Forester J, et al. Do adolescent indoor tanners exhibit dependency? J Am Acad Dermatol 2006;54:589-96.

1380 Warthan MM, Uchida T, Wagner RF. UV light tanning as a type of substance-related disorder. Arch Dermatol 2005 Aug;141(8):963-6.

1381 Freeman S, Francis S, Lundahl K, et al. UV tanning advertisements in high school newspapers. Arch Dermatol 2006;142:460-2.

1382 Hester EJ, Heilig LF, D'Ambrosia R, et al. Compliance with youth access regulations for indoor UV tanning. Arch Dermatol 2005;141:959-62.

1383 Cokkinides V, Weinstock M, Lazovich D, et al. State regulations have not decreased indoor tanning by adolescents. Cancer 2009;115(1):190-8.

1384 Hoerster KD, Mayer JA, Woodruff SI, et al. The influence of parents and peers on adolescent indoor tanning behavior: findings from a multi-city sample. J Am Acad Dermatol 2007 Dec;57(6):990-7.

1385 Cokkinides V, Weinstock M, Lazovich D, et al. Indoor tanning use among adolescents in the US, 1998 to 2004. Cancer 209;115(1):190-8.

1386 Cokkinides VE, Weinstock MA, O'Connell MC, Thun MJ. Use of indoor tanning sunlamps by US youth, ages 11-18 years, and by their parent or guardian caregivers: prevalence and correlates. Pediatrics 2002 June;109(6):1124-30.

1387 Sargent JD, Dalton M. Does parental disapproval of smoking prevent adolescents from becoming established smokers? Pediatrics 2001 Dec;108(6):1256-62.

1388 Eisenberg ME, Neumark-Sztainer D, Fulkerson JA, Story M. Family meals and substance use: is there a long-term protective association? J Adolesc Health 2008;43:151-6.

1389 Siegel M, Albers AB, Cheng DM, et al. Local restaurant smoking regulations and the adolescent smoking initiation process. Arch Pediatr Adolesc Med 2008 May;162(5):477-83.

1390 Patton GC, Coffey C, Carlin JB, et al. Teen smokers reach their mid twenties. J Adolesc Health 2006 Aug;39(2):214-20.

1391 Escobedo LG, Marcus SE, Holtzman D, Giovino GA. Sports participation, age at smoking initiation, and the risk of smoking among US high school students. JAMA 1993 March 17;269(11):1391-5.

1392 Winkleby MA, Feighery E, Dunn M, et al. Effects of an advocacy intervention to reduce smoking among teenagers. Arch Pediatr Adolesc Med 2004 Mar;158:269-75.

1393 Gilman SE, Rende R, Boergers J, et al. Parental smoking and adolescent smoking initiation: an intergenerational perspective on tobacco control. Pediatrics 2009;123:e274-81.

1394 Hill KG, Hawking SJ, Catalano RF, et al. Family influences on the risk of daily smoking initiation. J Adolesc Health 2005 Sept;37(3):202-10.

1395 Collins CC, Lippmann BM, Lo SJ, Moolchan ET. Time spent with smoking parents and smoking topography in adolescents. Addict Behav 2008 Dec;33(12):1594-7.

1396 Brooks JS, Pahl K, Ning Y. Peer and parental influences on longitudinal trajectories of smoking among African Americans and Peurto Ricans. Nicotine Tob Res 2006;8(5):639-51.

1397 Federal Trade Commission. Federal Trade Commission cigarette report for 2003. Washington, DC: Federal Trade Commission; 2005.

1398 Sargent JD, Beach ML, Adachi-Mejia AM, et al. Exposure to movie smoking: its relation to smoking initiation among US adolescents. Pediatrics 2005 Nov;116(5):1183-91.

1399 Healton CG, Watson-Stryker ES, Allen JA, et al. Televised movie trailers: undermining restrictions on advertising tobacco to youth. Arch Pediatr Adolesc Med 2006 Sept;160(9):885-8.

1400 Sargent JD, Beach ML, Adachi-Mejia AM, et al. Exposure to movie smoking: its relation to smoking initiation among US adolescents. Pediatrics 2005 Nov;116(5):1183-91.

1401 Wellman RJ, Sugarman DB, DiFranza JR, et al. The extent to which tobacco marketing and tobacco use in films contribute to children's use of tobacco. Arch Pediatr Adolesc Med 2006 Dec;160:1285-96.

1402 Hanewinkel R, Sargent JD. Exposure to smoking in internationally distributed American movies and youth smoking in Germany: a cross-cultural cohort study. Pediatrics 2008;121:e108-17.

1403 Titus-Ernstoff L, Dalton MA, Adachi-Mejia AM, et al. Longitudinal study of viewing smoking in movies and initiation of smoking by children. Pediatrics 2008 Jan;121(1):15-21.

1404 Charlesworth A, Glantz SA. Smoking in the movies increases adolescent smoking: a review. Pediatrics 2005 Dec;116(6):1516-28.

1405 Tanski SE, Stoolmiller M, Cin SD, et al. Movie character smoking and adolescent smoking: who matters more, good guys or bad guys? Pediatrics 2009 July;124(1):135-43.

1406 Centers for Disease Control and Prevention. Tobacco use, access, and exposure to tobacco media among middle and high school students—United States, 2004. MMWR 2005;54(12):297-301.

1407 Centers for Disease Control and Prevention. Racial/Ethnic differences among youths in cigarette smoking and susceptibility to start smoking—United States, 2002-2004. MMWR 2006 Dec 1;55(47):1275-7.

1408 Centers for Disease Control and Prevention. Cigarette use among high school students—United States, 1991-2007. MMWR 2008 June 27;57(25):686-8.

1409 Rigotti NA, Lee FE, Wechsler H. US college students' use of tobacco products; results of a national survey. JAMA 2000 Aug 9;284(6):699-705.

1410 O'Connell, Vanessa. "Rx from Marlboro Man: device that delivers drugs, not smoke". The Wall Street Journal 2005 Oct 27:A1,11.

1411 Sloan FA, Ostermann J, Picone G, et al. *The Price of Smoking*. Cambridge, Mass; MIT Press, 2004.

1412 Centers for Disease Control and Prevention. Smoking-attributable mortality, years of potential life lost, and productivity losses—United States, 2000-2004. MMWR 2008;57:1226-8.

1413 McKay, Betsy. "Global fight against tobacco intensifies." Wall Street Journal 2008 Feb 8:B4.

1414 Centers and Disease Control and Prevention. Comparative causes of annual deaths in the United States. http://www.cdc.gov/tobacco/research_data/health_consequences/and ths. htm as accessed on 2005 Jan 12.

1415 Doll R, Peto R, Boreham J, Sutherland I. Mortality in relation to smoking: 50 years' observations on male British doctors. Brit Med J 2004;328:1519.

1416 Jha P, Jacob B, Gajalakshmi V, et al. A nationally representative case-control study of smoking and death in India. N Engl J Med 2008 March 13;358(11):1137-47.

1417 Kreslake JM, Wayne GH, Alpert HR, et al. Tobacco industry control of menthol in cigarettes and targeting of adolescents and young adults. Am J Publ Health 2008 Sept;98(9):1685-92.

1418 Contemporary Pediatrics 2006 Oct;23(10):18.

1419 DiFranza JR, Savageau JA, Fletcher K, et al. Symptoms of tobacco dependence after brief, intermittent use. Arch Pediatr Adolesc Med 2007 July;161(7):704-710.

1420 US Department of Health and Human Services. *Preventing Tobacco Use Among Young People: A Report of the Surgeon General.* Washington, DC; US Dept of Health and Human Services, 1994.

1421 Taioli E, Wynder EL. Effect of the age at which smoking begins on the frequency of smoking in adulthood. N Engl J Med 1991 Sept 26;325(13):968-9.

1422 Bush T, Curry SJ, Hollis J, et al. Preteen attitudes about smoking and parental factors associated with favorable attitudes. Am J Health Promot 2005 Jul-Aug;19(6):410-7.

1423 Eissenberg T, Ward KD, Smith-Simone S, Maziak W. Waterpipe tobacco smoking on a US college campus: prevalence and correlates. J Adolesc Health 2008 May;42(5):526-9.

1424 Primack BA, Walsh M, Bryce C, Eissenberg T. Water-pipe tobacco smoking among middle and high school students in Arizona. Pediatrics 2009;123:e282-8.

1425 Knishkowy B, Amitai Y. Water-pipe (narghile) smoking: an emerging health risk behavior. Pediatrics 2005;116:e113-9.

1426 Boffetta P, Hecht S, Gray N, et al. Smokeless tobacco and cancer. Lancet Oncol 2008 Jul;9(7): 667-75.

1427 Ribisl KM, Williams RS, Kim AE. Internet sales of cigarettes to minors. JAMA 2003 Sept 10;290(10);1356-9.

1428 Jensen JA, Hickman NJ III, Landrine H, Klonoff EA, Availability of tobacco to youth via the internet. JAMA 2004 Apr 21;291(15):1837.

1429 Williams RS. Internet cigarette vendors' lack of compliance with a California state law designed to prevent tobacco sales to minors. Arch Pediatr Adolesc Med 2006 Sept;160:988-9.

1430 Clark PI, Natanblut SL, Schmitt CL, et al. Factors associated with tobacco sales to minors: lessons learned from the FDA compliance checks. JAMA 2000;284:729-34.

1431 Schwartz RH, O'Donnell R, Mann L, et al. Adolescents who smoke cigarettes: criteria for addiction, health concerns, and readiness to quit. Presentation at American Pediatrics Association Meeting 1993 May 5-7, abstracted in Am J Dis Ch 1993 April;147.

1432 Centers for Disease Control and Prevention. Use of cessation methods among smokers aged 16-24 years—United States, 2003. MMWR 2006 Dec 22;55(50):1351-4.

1433 Bearer CF, Stefanak MA. Looking ahead to a tobacco-free generation. J Peds 2009 Jan;154:5-7.

1434 "ISEA petitions OSHA to improve hearing protection regulations." Business Wire 2007 Mar 9.

1435 Opperman DA, Reifman W, Schlauch R, Levine S. Incidence of spontaneous hearing threshold shifts during modern concert performances. Otolaryngol Head Neck Surg 2006 Apr;134(4): 667-73.

1436 Vogel I, Brug J, Hosu EJ, et al. MP3 players and hearing loss: adolescents' perceptions of loud music and hearing conversation. J Pediatr 2008;152:400-4.

1437 Spencer, Jane. "Behind the music: IPods and hearing loss." The Wall Street Journal 2006 Jan 10:D1.

1438 "Cut the Noise". JAMA 2008 Nov 26;300(20):2359.

1439 James, Frank. Is music to their ears a threat to hearing? Chicago Tribune 2006 Mar 15: Sec 1, page 3.

1440 Vogel I, Brug J, van der Pleog CPB, Raat H. Strategies for the prevention of MP3-induced hearing loss among adolescents: expert opinions from a Delphi study. Pediatrics 2009 May;123(5): 1257-62.

1441 Kuehn BM. Panel: government must work harder to prevent mental illness in young people. JAMA 2009 Apr 8;301(14):1424-5.

1442 American College Health Association. American College Health Association-National College Health Assessment (ACHA-NCHA) Web Summary. Updated 2007 August. Accessed at www. acha-ncha.org/data_highlights.html accessed 8-11-09.

1443 Lamberg, Lynne. Experts work to prevent college suicides. JAMA 2006 Aug 2;296(5):502-3.

1444 Anderson RN, Smith BL. Deaths: leading causes for 2002. National Vital Statistics Reports. 2005;53(17):1-89.

1445 Pfeffer CR. Spotting the red flags for adolescent suicide. Contemporary Pediatrics 1989 February:59-70.

1446 Males, Mike A. "Expert debunks top 10 myths about teens. AAP News 1997 July:11.

1447 Brezo J, Barker ED, Paris J, et al. childhood trajectories of anxiousness and disruptiveness as predictors of suicide attempts. Arch Pediatr Adol Med 2008 Nov;162(11):1015-21.

1448 Foley DL, Goldston DB, Costello EJ, Angold A. Proximal psychiatric risk factors for suicidality in youth: the Great Smoky Mountains Study. Arch Gen Psychiatry 2006 Sept;63(9): 1017-24.

1449 Mann JJ, Apter A, Bertolote J, et al. Suicide prevention strategies; a systematic review. JAMA 2005 Oct 26;294(16):2064-74.

1450 Sourander A, Klomek AB, Niemela S, et al. Childhood predictors of completed and severe suicide attempts. Arch Gen Psych 2009 Apr;66(4):398-406.

1451 Remafedi G, French S, Story M, Resnick MD, Blum R. The relationship between suicide risk and sexual orientation: results of a population-based study. Am J Publ Health 1998; 88:57-60.

1452 Centers for Disease Control and Prevention. Youth risk behavior surveillance: United States, 2003. MMWR 2004;43(2):1-96.

1453 Centers for Disease Control and Prevention. Suicide trends among youths and young adults aged 10-24 years—United States, 1990-2004. MMWR 2007 Sept 7;56(35):905-8.

1454 American Academy of Pediatrics, Committee on Injury and Poison Prevention. Firearm injuries affecting the pediatric population. Pediatrics 1992;89:788-90.

1455 Brent DA, Perper JA, Allman CJ, Moritz GM, et al. The presence and accessibility of firearms in the home of adolescent suicides: a case-control study. JAMA 1991;266:2989-95.

1456 Gould MS, Greenberg T, Velting DM, Shaffer D. Youth suicide risk and preventive interventions: a review of the past 10 years. J Am Acad Child Adolesc Psychiatry 2003;42:386-405.

1457 Prinstein MJ. Moderators of peer contagion: a longitudinal examination of depression socialization between adolescents and their best friends. J Clin Child Adolesc Psychol 2007 Apr-June;36(2):159-70.

1458 Centers for Disease Control and Prevention. Suicide trends among youths and young adults aged 10-24 years—United States, 1990-2004. MMWR 2007 Sept 7;56(35):905-8.

1459 Mann JJ, Apter A, Bertolote J, et al. Suicide prevention strategies; a systematic review. JAMA 2005 Oct 26;294(16):2064-74.

1460 Gould MS, Marrocco FA, Kleinman M, et al. Evaluating latrogenic risk of youth suicide screening programs. JAMA 2005 April 6;293(13):1635-43.

1461 Fiore, Kelly as quoted by MacNeil, Jane Salodof in "Impulsivity drives adolescent suicide attempts, study shows." Pediatric News 2006 Apr;40(4):30.

1462 Hammad TA, Laughren T, Racoosin J. Suicidality in pediatric patients treated with antidepressant drugs. Arch Gen Psychiatry 2006;63:332-9.

1463 Rihmer Z, Belso N, Kalmar S. Antidepressants and suicide prevention in Hungary. Acta Psychiatr Scand 2001;103:238-9.

1464 Carlston A, Waern M, Ededahl A, Ranstam J. Antidepressant medication and suicide in Sweden. Pharmacoepidemiol Drug Safety 2001;10:525-30.

1465 Hall WD, Mant A, Mitchell PB, Rendle VA, Hickie IB, McManus P. Association between antidepressant prescribing and suicide in Australia, 1991-2000: trend analysis. Brit Med J 2003;326:1008.

1466 Gibbons RD, Hur K, Bhaumik DK, Mann JJ. The relationship between antidepressant medication use and rate of suicide. Arch Gen Psychiatry 2005;65:165-72.

1467 Gibbons RD, Hur K, Bhaumik DK, Mann JJ. The relationship between antidepressant prescription rates and rate of early adolescent suicide. Am J Psychiatry 2006;163:1898-904.

1468 Simon GE, Savarino J, Operskalski B, Wang PS. Suicide risk during antidepressant treatments. Am J Psychiatry 2006;163:41-7.

1469 Brown GK, Ten Have T, Henriques GR, et al. Cognitive therapy for the prevention of suicide attempts. JAMA 2005 Aug 3;294(5):563-70.

1470 Garber J, Clarke GN, Weersing VR, et al. Prevention of depression in at-risk adolescents. JAMA 2009 June 3;301(21):2215-24.

1471 March J, Silva S, Petrycki S, et al. Fluoxetine, cognitive-behavioral therapy, and their combination for adolescents with depression: Treatment for Adolescents With Depression Study (TADS) randomized controlled trial. JAMA Aug 18;292(7):807-20.

1472 Robison, Linda M presenting at a poster session of the American Academy of Child and Adolescent Psychiatry, as quoted by Brunk, Doug in "Diagnoses of depression doubled in decade". Pediatric News 2006 Dec;40(12):29.

1473 Kessler RC, Berglund P, Borges G, et al. Trends in suicide ideation, plans, gestures, and attempts in the United States, 1990-1992 to 2001-2003. JAMA 2005 May 25;293(20):2487-95.

1474 Daley AJ, Copeland RJ, Wright NP, et al. Exercise therapy as a treatment for psychopathologic conditions in obese and morbidly obese adolescents: a randomized, controlled trial. Pediatrics 2006 Nov;118(5):2126-34.

1475 Steptoe A, Butler N. Sports participation and emotional wellbeing in adolescents. Lancet 1996 June 29;347(9018):1789-92.

1476 Mellion MB. Exercise therapy for anxiety and depression: 1. Does the evidence justify its recommendation? Postgrad Med 1085 Feb 15;77(3):59-62,66.

1477 Gamble JH, Ormerod JO, Frenneaux MP. Exercise can be effective therapy for depression. Practitioner 2008 Sept;252(1710):19-20,23-4.

1478 Gangwisch, James, presenter at the 2009 annual meeting of the Associated Professional Sleep Societies, Seattle, WA, as reported by USA Today 2009 June 6.

1479 Eisenberg ME, Olson RE, Neumark-Sztainer D, et al. Correlations between family meals and psychosocial well-being among adolescents. Arch Pediatr Adolesc Med 2004 Aug;158:792-6.

1480 Widenhorn-Muller K, Hille K, Klenk J, Weiland U. Influence of having breakfast on cognitive performance and mood in 13- to 20-year-old high school students: results of a crossover trial. Pediatrics 2008;122(2):279-84.

1481 Whalen, Jeanne. "For mild depression, some U.K. doctors prescribe reading." The Wall Street Journal 2005 Aug 9;B1.

1482 Van Voorhees BW, Fogel J, Reinecke MA, et al. Randomized clinical trial of an internet-based depression prevention program for adolescents (Project CATCH-IT) in primary care: 12-week outcomes. J Dev Behav Pediatr 2009 Feb;30(1):23-37.

1483 Bernstein, Elizabeth. "Therapy that keeps on the sunny side of life." The Wall Street Journal 2006 Sept 26:D1,4.

1484 Lyon, Lindsay. "Positive psychology for kids: teaching resilience with positive education." US News and World Report health.usnews.com accessed 2009 June 25.

1485 Gardiner Paula, Kemper KJ. "Natural" remedies for depression: are they safe? Do they work? Contemporary Pediatrics 2006 Sept;23(9):58-72.

1486 Williamson EM. Drug interactions between herbal and prescription medications. Drug Safety 2003;26:1075.

1487 Murphy PA, Kern SE, Stanczyk FZ, et al. Interaction of St. John's wort with oral contraceptives. Effects on the pharmacokinetics of norethindrone and ethinyl estradiol, ovarian activity and breakthrough bleeding. Contraception 2005;71:402.

1488 Horrigan FP, Sikich L, courveisie HE, et al. Alternative therapies in the child psychiatric clinic. J Child Adolesc Psychopharmacol 1998;8:249.

1489 Findling RL, McNamara NK, O'Riordan MA, et al. An open-label pilot study of St. John's wort in juvenile depression. Jam Acad Child & Adolesc Psychiatry 2003;42:908.

1490 Lingaerde O, Foreland AR, Magnusson A. Can winter depression be prevented by Ginkgo biloba extract? A placebo-controlled trial. Acta Psychiatr Scand 1999;100:62.

1491 Brunner R, Parzer P, Haffner J, et al. Prevalence and psychological correlates of occasional and repetitive self harm in adolescents. Arch Pediatr Adolesc Med 2007 July;161(7):641-9.

1492 Young R, Sweeting H, West P. Prevalence of deliberate self harm and attempted suicide within contemporary Goth youth subculture: longitudinal cohort study. Brit Med J 2006;332:1058-61.

1493 Whitlock J, Knox KL. The relationship between self-injurious behavior and suicide in a young adult population. Arch Pediatr Adolesc Med 2007 July;161(7):634-40.

1494 Whitlock J, Eckenrode J, Silverman D. Self-injurious behaviors in a college population. Pediatrics 2006 June;117(6):1939-48.

1495 Shiels, William II MD, speaking at the Radiological Society of North America Meeting, as quoted by Birk, Susan, "Abused adolescents are embedding objects." Pediatric News 2009 Feb;43(2):14.

1496 Rosen DS. 'Cutting' more common among youths, difficult to extinguish. AAP News 2005 July:15.

1497 Favazza AR. Self-injurious behavior in college students. Commentary in Pediatrics 2006 June;117(6):2283-4.

1498 Schwartz RH, et al. Clin Pediatr 1989 August;28:340-6.

1499 Jellinek, Michael S. Behavioral Consult; 'Cutting' pain more than skin deep. Pediatric News 2005:21.

1500 Favazza, Armando as quoted by Johnson, Deborah in "Copycat cutters; some adolescents experimenting with self-mutilation to bond with others." AAP News 2005 Dec:37.

1501 Rosen DS. 'Cutting' more common among youths, difficult to extinguish. AAP News 2005 July:15.

1502 Cordoni, Allyson as quoted by Kirn, Timothy F in "Kids and self-injury: 'Pain makes them feel alive". Pediatric News 2007 April:36.

1503 Whitlock, Janis as quoted by Blazek, Nicole in "Self-injurious behaviors often undetected in adolescents. Infectious Dis in Children 2008 Sept;121(9):50.

1504 Whitlock, Janis as quoted by Blazek, Nicole in "Self-injurious behaviors often undetected in adolescents. Infectious Dis in Children 2008 Sept;121(9):50.

1505 Whitlock J, Knox KL. The relationship between self-injurious behavior and suicide in a young adult population. Arch Pediatr Adolesc Med 2007 July;161(7):634-40.

1506 Young R, Sweeting H, West P. Prevalence of deliberate self harm and attempted suicide within contemporary Goth youth subculture: longitudinal cohort study. Brit Med J 2006;332: 1058-61.

1507 Brunner R, Parzer P, Haffner J, et al. Prevalence and psychological correlates of occasional and repetitive deliberate self-harm in adolescents. Arch Pediatr Adolesc Med 2007 July;161(7):641-9.

1508 Visser SN, Sesesne CA, Perou R. National estimates and factors associated with medication treatment for childhood attention-deficit/hyperactivity disorder. Pediatrics 2007 Feb;119 Suppl 1:S99-106.

1509 UN International Narcotics Control Board. Report of the UN International Narcotics Control Board, 1994. New York: UN Publications, 1995.

1510 Spanos B. Quotas, ARCOS, UN report and statistics. Conference report: stimulant use in the treatment of ADHD. Washington, DC: Drug Enforcement Administration, December 1996.

1511 Diller, Lawrence H. Attention-Deficit-Hyperactivity Disorder. Letter to the editor, N Engl J Med 1999 June 3;340(22):1766.

1512 Associated Press. "ADHD drug use among adults doubles in 4 years." The Wall Street Journal 2005 Sept 15;D2.

1513 www.fightforkids.org

1514 United States Federal Public Law 108-446.

1515 "Eye on Washington" Contemporary Pediatrics 2005 Dec;22(12):14.

1516 Biederman J, Wilens T, Mick E, et al. Pharmacotherapy of attention deficit/hyperactivity disorder reduces risk for substance use disorder. Pediatrics 1999;104(2):e20.

1517 Wilens TE, Faraone SV, Biederman J, Gunawardene S. Does stimulant therapy of attention-deficit/hyperactivity disorder beget later substance abuse? A meta-analytic review of the literature. Pediatrics 2003 Jan;111(1):179-85.

1518 Wilens, TE, Adamson J, Monuteaux MC, et al. Effect of prior stimulant treatment for attention-deficit/hyperactivity disorder on subsequent risk for cigarette smoking and alcohol and drug use disorders in adolescents. Arch Pediatr Adolesc Med 2008 Oct;162(10):916-21.

1519 Cox DJ, Mikami AY, Cox BS, et al. Effect of long-acting OROS methylphenidate on routine driving in young adults with attention-deficit/hyperactivity disorder. Arch Pediatr Adol Med 2008 Aug;162(8):793-4.

1520 Scheffler RM, Brown TT, Fulton BD, et al. Positive association between attention-deficit/hyperactivity disorder medication use and academic achievement during elementary school. Pediatrics 2009 May;123(5):1273-9.

1521 Ruff ME. Attention deficit disorder and stimulant use: an epidemic of modernity. Clin Pediatr 2005 Sept;44(7):557-63.

1522 Levine, Melvin D as quoted by MacNeil, Jane in "Reject psychiatric view of attention disorders." In Pediatric News 2006 April;40(4):28-9.

1523 Rosemond John, and Ravenel Bose. *The Diseasing of America's Children*. Nashville, Tennessee. Thomas Nelson Publishers, 2008.

1524 Gimpel, Amnon. *Brain Exercises to Cure ADHD*. North Charleston, South Carolina, Book Surge Publishers, 2007.

1525 Klingberg t, Fernell E, Olesen PJ, et al. Computerized training of working memory in children with ADHD—a randomized, controlled trial. J Am Acad Child Psych 2005 Feb;44(2):177-86.

1526 Cogmed Working Memory Training. 888-748-3828 or www.cogmed.com.

1527 Strehl U, Leins U, Goth G, et al. Self-regulation of slow cortical potentials: a new treatment for children with attention-deficit/hyperactivity disorder. Pediatrics 2006;118:e1530-40.

1528 Crosby, Brian. Presentation at the Associated Professional Sleep Societies annual meeting 2009 June 8, Seattle WA.

1529 Paavonen EJ, Raikkonen K, Lahti J, et al. Short sleep duration and behavioral symptoms of attention-deficit/hyperactivity disorder in healthy 7- to 8-year-old children. Pediatrics 2009 May;123(5):e857-64.

1530 Chervin RD, Ruzicka DL, Giordani BJ, et al. Sleep-disordered breathing, behavior, and cognition in children before and after adenotonsillectomy. Pediatrics 2006 Apr;117(4):e769-78.

1531 Schmitt J, Romanos M, Schmitt NM, et al. Atopic eczema and attention-deficit/hyperactivity disorder in a population-based sample of children and adolescents. Research letter, JAMA 2009 Feb 18;301(7):724-6.

1532 Lipkin PH, Goldstein IJ, Adesman AR. Tics and dyskinesias associated with stimulant treatment in attention-deficit hyperactivity disorder. Arch Pediatr Adolesc Med 1994 Aug;148:859-61.

1533 Spencer T, Biederman J, Wilens T. Growth deficits in children with attention deficit hyperactivity disorder. Pediatrics 1998;102(supplement):S501-6.

1534 Lisska MC, Rivkees SA. Daily methylphenidate use slows the growth of children: a community based study. J Pediatr Endocrinol Metab 2003 June;16(5):711-8.

1535 Poulton A, Cowell CT. Slowing of growth in height and weight on stimulants: a characteristic pattern. J Paediatr Child Health 2003 Apr;39(3):180-5.

1536 Poulton A. Growth on stimulant medication; clarifying the confusion: a review. Arch Dis Child 2005 Aug;90(8):801-6.

1537 MTA Cooperative Group. National Institute of Mental Health Multimodal Treatment Study of ADHD follow-up: changes in effectiveness and growth after the end of treatment. Pediatrics 2004 Apr;113(4):762-9.

1538 Swanson J, Greenhill L, Wigal T, et al. Stimulant-related reductions on growth rates in PATS. J Am Acad Child Adolesc Psych 2006 Nov;45(11):1304-13.

1539 Swanson JM, Elliott GR, Greenhill LL, et al. Effects of stimulant medication on growth rates across 3 years in the MTA follow-up. J Am Acad Child Adolesc Psychiatr 2007 Aug;46(8):1015-27.

1540 Kent JD, Blader JC, Koplewicz HS, et al. Effects of late-afternoon methylphenidate administration on behavior and sleep in attention-deficit hyperactivity disorder. Pediatrics 1995 August;96(2):320-5.

1541 Tirosh Emanuel, et al. Effects of methylphenidate on sleep in children with attention-deficit hyperactivity disorder: an activity monitor study. Am J Dis Children 1993;147:1313-5.

1542 "Psychotropics". Pediatric News 2000 April;34(4):5.

1543 Johnston JA, Ye w, Van Brunt DL, et al. Decreased use of clonidine following treatment with atomoxetine in children with ADHD. J Clin Psychopharmacol 2006 Aug;26(4):389-95.

1544 Mosholder AD, Gelperin K, Hammad TA, et al. Hallucinations and other psychotic symptoms associated with the use of attention-deficit/hyperactivity disorder drugs in children. Pediatrics 2009 Feb;123(2):611-6.

1545 Calello DP. Acute psychosis associated with therapeutic use of dextroamphetamine. Letter to the editor, Pediatrics 2004 May;113(5):1466.

1546 Iversen, Leslie. *Speed, Ecstasy, Ritalin: The Science of Amphetamines*. New York, NY, Oxford University Press, 2006.

1547 Wilens TE, Prince JB, Spencer TJ, Biederman J. Stimulants and sudden death: what is a physician to do? Pediatrics 2006 Sept;118(3):1215-19.

1548 Associated Press. "Ritalin maker opens drive to end abuse." The New York Times 1996 March 28:A20.

1549 Maurer, Katherine. "Ritalin abuse a potential problem among teens." Pediatric News 1996 Apr;30(4):16.

1550 Volkow, Nora, as quoted by Vastag, Brian in "Pay attention: Ritalin acts much like cocaine." JAMA 2001 August 22/29;286(8):905-6.

1551 Wilens TE, Gignac M, Swezey A, et al. Characteristics of adolescents and young adults with ADHD who divert or misuse their prescribed medications. J Am Acad Child Adolesc Psychiatr;2006 Apr;45(4):408-14.

1552 Klein-Schwartz W, McGrath J. Poison centers' experience with methylphenidate abuse in pre-teens and adolescents. J Am Acad Child Adolesc Psychiatr 2003 Mar;42(3):288-94.

1553 Associated Press. "Apparent increase of ADHD drug abuse in Iowa." Chicago Tribune 2009 June 22.

1554 Prescribers Letter 2005 Jan;12(1):4.

1555 Olfson M, Blanco C, Liu L, et al. National trends in the outpatient treatment of children and adolescents with antipsychotic drugs. Arch Gen Psychiatr 2006;63:679-85.

1556 McIntyre RS, Jerrell JM. Metabolic and cardiovascular adverse events associated with antipsychotic treatment in children and adolescents. Arch Pediatr Adolesc Med 2008 Oct;162(10):929-35.

1557 Kluger, Jeffrey. "Young and Bipolar" Time 2002 Aug 19.

1558 Groopman, Jerome. "What's Normal?" The New Yorker 2007 Apr 9;28.

1559 Groopman, Jerome. "What's Normal?" The New Yorker 2007 Apr 9;28.

1560 Thompson MP, Ho CH, Kingree JB. Prospective associations between delinquency and suicidal behaviors in a nationally representative sample. J Adolesc Health 2007 Mar;40(3):232-7.

1561 Abboud, Leila. "A pragmatic approach for troubled kids." The Wall Street Journal 2005 Nov 1;D1,3.

1562 Roustit C, Chaix B, Chauvin P. Family breakup and adolescents' psychosocial maladjustment: public health implications of family disruptions. Pediatrics 2007;120:e984-91.

1563 Lee D. Residential mobility and gateway drug use among Hispanic adolescents in the U.S.: evidence from a national survey. Am J Drug Alcohol Abuse 2007;33(6):799-806.

1564 Astone NM, McLanahan SS. Family structure, residential mobility, and school dropout: a research note. Demography 1994;31(4):575-84.

1565 Jelleyman T, Spencer N. Residential mobility in childhood and health outcomes: a systematic review. J Epidemiol Community Health 2008 July;62(7):584-92.

1566 Dong M, Anda RF, Felitti VJ, et al. Childhood residential mobility and multiple health risks during adolescence and adulthood: the hidden role of adverse childhood experiences. Arch Pediatr Adol 2005;159:1104-10.

1567 Larson A, Bell M, Young AF. Clarifying the relationships between health and residential mobility. Soc Sci Med 2004 Nov;59(10):2149-60.

1568 Olfson M, Marcus SC, Druss B, et al. Parental depression, child mental health problems, and health care utilization. Med Care 2003 June;41(6):702-5.

1569 Sills MR, Shetterly S, Xu s, et al. Association between parental depression and children's health care use. Pediatrics 2007 Apr;119(4):e829-36.

1570 Wyman PA, Moynihan J, Eberly S, et al. Association of family stress with natural killer cell activity and frequency of illnesses in children. Arch Pediatr Adolesc Med 2007;161:228-34.

1571 Howland LC, Gortmaker SL, Mofenson LM, et al. Effects of negative life events on immune suppression in children and youth infected with Human Immunodeficiency Virus type 1. Pediatrics 2000;106;3:540-6.

1572 Pham E, McEwen BS, Ledoux JE, Nader K. Fear learning impairs hippocampal cell proliferation. Neuroscience 2005;130(1):17-24.

1573 Compas BE. Psychobiological processes of stress and coping: implications for resilience in children and adolescents—comments on the papers of Romeo & McEwen and Fisher et al. Ann N Y Acad Sci 2006 Dec;1094:226-34.

1574 McEwen BS. Stressed or stressed out: what is the difference? J Psychiatr Neurosci 2005 Sept;30(5):315-8.

1575 Roozendaal B, McEwen BS, Chattarji S. Stress, memory and the amygdale. Nat Rev Neurosci 2009 June;10(6):423-33.

1576 Hampton, Tracy. Effects of stress on children examined. JAMA 2006 Apr 26;295(16):1888.

1577 www.aap.org/stress

1578 Chen H, Cohen P, Kasen S, et al. Impact of adolescent mental disorders and physical illness on quality of life 17 years later. Arch Pediatr Adol Med. 2006;160:93-9.

1579 Kuehn, Bridget M. Panel: Government must work harder to prevent mental illness in young people. JAMA 2009 Apr 8;301(14):1424-5.

1580 Voelker, Rebecca. Mounting student depression taxing campus mental health services. JAMA 2003 April 23/30;289(16):2055-6.

1581 Blanco C, Okuda M, Wright C, Hasin DS, et al. Mental health of college students and their non-college-attending peers: results from the National Epidemiologic Study on Alcohol and Related Conditions. Arch Gen Psych 2008;65(12):1429-37.

1582 Voelker, Rebecca. Stress, sleep loss, and substance abuse create potent recipe for college depression. JAMA 2004 May 12;291(18):2177-9.

1583 Kadison, Richard; Foy, Theresa. *College of the Overwhelmed: the campus mental health crisis and what to do about it.* San Francisco, California; Jossey-Bass, 2004.

1584 Bonny AE, Britto MT, Klostermann BK, Hornung RW, Slap GB. School disconnectedness: identifying adolescents at risk. Pediatrics 2000 November;106(5):1017-21.

1585 Males, Mike A. "Expert debunks top 10 myths about teens. AAP News 1997 July:11.

1586 Males, Mike A. "Expert debunks top 10 myths about teens. AAP News 1997 July:11.

1587 Offer, Daniel; Ostrov, Eric; Howard Kenneth I. Adolescence; what is normal? Am J Dis Child 1989 June;143:731-6.

1588 Annual Drug Trend Report, Medco Health Solutions, Inc., Orlando, Florida, as quoted in "Pediatric Behavioral Drugs" Pediatric News 2004 June.

1589 Martin A, Leslie D. Trends in psychotropic medication costs for children and adolescents, 1997-2000. Arch Pediatr Adolesc Med 2003 October;157:997-1004.

1590 Overbye D. New York Times 2005 March 10.

1591 "Beside the 'river of stories': Exploring Hannibal, Missouri". LifeTimes 2006 May;8-9.

1592 Shellenbarger Sue. "The creative energy behind ADHD." The Wall Street Journal 2008 Apr 17:D1.

1593 Warren MP, Brooks-Gunn J, et al. Mood and behavior at adolescence: evidence for hormonal factors. J Clin Endocrine Metabol 1989;69:77-83.

1594 Stephens, Bret. "Richest country, saddest people—any coincidence?" The Wall Street Journal 2007 Mar 9;W11.

1595 Walker, Carl. *Depression and Globalization: The Politics of Mental Health in the Twenty-First Century.* New York, NY; Springer, 2007.

1596 Cox JJ, Reimann F, Nicholas AK, et al. An SCN9A channelopathy causes congenital inability to experience pain. Nature 2006 Dec 14;444(7121):894-8.

1597 Smidebush, Amber. "The Downside of Happy Pills". The Chicago Sun-Times 2006 Jan 15;5B.

1598 Solomon, Andrew. *The Noonday Demon: An Atlas of Depression.* New York, NY; Touchstone Books, 2001.

1599 Sowers, Bill. "We Can Never Return to *Pleasantville*". We Need Not Walk Alone. 2004/2005 Winter:5.

1600 Dworkin Ronald W. *Artificial Happiness; The Dark Side of the New Happy Class.* New York, NY; Carroll & Graff Publishers, 2006.

1601 Wilson, Eric G. Against Happiness: In Praise of Melancholy. New York, NY; Farrar, Straus & Giroux, 2008.

1602 Exodus; Chapter 30: Verse 34.

1603 Slater Elinor, Slater Robert. *Great Jewish Women.* Middle Village, New York. Jonathan David Publishers, 2001:87-9.

1604 Spritzer Dinah. Holocaust survivor's rescued note reminds town of victims' humanity. Chicago Jewish News 2005 April 1-7:27-8.

1605 Johnson AD. The *Value of Helping; the Story of Harriet Tubman.* LaJolla, California, Value Communications, Inc., 1979.

1606 Zaslow, Jeffrey. "Kids on the bus: the overlooked role of teenagers in the civil-rights era." The Wall Street Journal 2005 Nov 11:D1.

1607 "Civil Rights". Kids Discover 2006 Jan;16(1):7.

1608 Eder AF, Hillyer CD, Dy BA, Notari EP IV, Benjamin RJ. Adverse reactions to allogeneic whole blood donation by 16- and 17- year olds. JAMA 2008 May 21; 299(19):2279-86.

1609 Eder AF, Hillyer CD, Banjamin RJ. Letter to the editor, JAMA 2008 Oct 15;300(15):1759-60.

1610 Merrick, Amy. "These benefactors do homework as charities fawn." The Wall Street Journal 2008 March 4:A1.

1611 Spielman, Fran. Students rate high marks in city rule. Chicago Sun Times 1991 March 2:1,11.

1612   Bloch, Harry. Circumstantiality and child rearing in colonial and early American society. Clinical Pediatrics 1985 July;24(7):397-9.

1613   Martensen, Robert L. The emergence of the science of childhood. JAMA 1996 February 28;275(8):649.

1614   Psalms, 128:2.

1615   Exodus 20:8-9.

1616   "Trophy Overload". The Wall Street Journal 2005 March 11.

1617   Taanila A, Ebeling H, Kotimaa A, et al. Is a large family a protective factor against behavioural and emotional problems at the age of 8 years? Acta Paediatr 2004 Apr;93(4):508-17.

1618   Kevill-Davies, Sally. *Yesterday's Children*. Woodbridge, Suffolk; the Antique Collectors' Club Ltd., 1991.

1619   Greenberg, Dov. Reading your obituary. L'Chaim Northbrook, 2005 May;2(5).

1620   Bohanek JG, Marin KA, Fivush R, Duke MP. Family narrative interaction and children's sense of self. Fam Process 2006 March;45(1):39-54.

1621   Romano, Andrew. "Authentic Americana: why Grandpa's clothes are suddenly chic." Newsweek 2009 Feb 9:61.

1622   Saranow, Jennifer. "Hip to be square: why young buyers covet 'grandpa' cars; old models are tricked out as fashion statements; the less-stodgy LeSabre." The Wall Street Journal 2006 May 9;A1.

1623   "Finding the perfect gift for your grandchild." The Erickson Tribune 2005 Dec:1.

1624   Kuchment, Anna. "The new bling rings." Newsweek 2005 May 2:57.

1625   Streit, Meghan. "Surrogate 'grandparents' for teens in turmoil." The Erikson Tribune 2008 Jan:3.

1626   Lahdenpera M, Lummae V, Helle S, Tremblay M, Russell AF. Fitness benefits of prolonged post-reproductive lifespan in women. Nature 2004 Mar 11;428(6979):178-81.

1627   Bishai D, Trevitt JL, Zhang Y, et al. Risk factors for unintentional injuries in children: are grandparents protective? Pediatrics 2008;122:e980-7.

1628   Caspari R, Lee SH. Older age becomes common late in human evolution. Proc Natl Acad Sci USA 2004 Jul 27;101(30):10895-900.

1629   Schmidt, Margaret Anne. "Thanks, Grandma & Grandpa." LifeTimes 2006 Sept:10.

1630   Lordkipanidze D, Vekua A, Ferring R, et al. The earliest toothless hominin skull. Nature 2005 Apr 7;434(7034):717-8.

1631   M. Therese Southgate. The cover. JAMA 2008 Jan 2;299(1):13.

1632   Arenson KW. "Fewer A's, and Princeton calls it progress." New York Times 2005 Sept 20 as reprinted in Pediatrics 2005 Nov;116(5):1133.

1633   Greenberger, Ellen. Self-entitled college students: contributions of personality, parenting, and motivational factors. J Youth and Adolesc 2008 as excerpted in Pediatrics 2009 June;123(6):1515.

1634   Jeffrey, Nancy Ann. "Trophy Overload." The Wall Street Journal 2005 March 11: W1,12.

1635   Zaslow, Jeffrey. "The most-praised generation goes to work". The Wall Street Journal 2007 April 20:W1,7.

1636   Nelson, Bob. *1001 Ways to Reward Employees*. New York NY; Workman Publishing Co, Inc, 2005.

1637   Nelson, Bob. The *1001 Rewards and Recognition Fieldbook*. . New York NY; Workman Publishing Co, Inc, 2003.

1638   Fisher LB, Miles IW, Austin B, et al. Predictors of initiation of alcohol use among US adolescents. Arch Pediatr Adolesc Med 2007 Oct;161(10):959-66.

1639   Twenge, Jean M, PhD. *Generation Me; Why Today's Young Americans Are More Confident, Assertive, Entitled—and Miserable Than Ever Before*. New York, NY; Free Press, Simon & Schuster, 2006.

1640   Juvonen J, Graham S, Schuster MA. Bullying among young adolescents: the strong, the weak, and the troubled. Pediatrics 2003 Dec;112(6):1231-7.

1641   Fisher LB, Miles IW, Austin B, et al. Predictors of initiation of alcohol use among US adolescents. Arch Pediatr Adolesc Med 2007 Oct;161(10):959-66.

1642   Psalms 22:7.

1643   Genesis 18:27.

1644   Numbers 12:1-8.

1645 Rubin, Rabbi Israel. "Mountain Climbing". L'Chaim Northbrook;2005 May;2(5):1.

1646 Baruzzi, Roberto and Franco, Laercio. Western Diseases. Harvard University Press, 1981. Chapter 10, page 148.

1647 Chivian E, Robinson JP, Tudge JRH, Popov NP, Andreyenkov VG. American and Soviet teenagers' concerns about nuclear war and the future. N Engl J Med 1988 Aug 18;319(7):407-13.

1648 Goetz, Bracha. From Harvard to Homemaking. Chabad.org The Jewish Woman, accessed 2009 May 10.

1649 Rubinstein, Nechama. From a curse to a blessing. Chabad.org. Parenting. Accessed 2008 Nov 12.

1650 Etymological insight per linguist/ attorney/ master proof-reader Martin A. Blumenthal.

1651 Neumark-Sztainer D, Eisenberg ME, Fulkerson JA et al. Family meals and disordered eating in adolescents; longitudinal findings from Project Eat. Arch Pediatr Adolesc Med 2008 Jan;162(1):17-22.

1652 Eisenberg ME, Olson RE, Nuemark-Sztainer D, Story M, Bearinger LH. Correlations between family meals and psychosocial well-being among adolescents. Arch Pediatr Adolesc Med 2004 August;158:792-6.

1653 Califano, Joseph A. Jr. Data from the National Center on Addiction and Substance Abuse (CASA) at Columbia University, 4th Annual Report, 2007 as excerpted Goldbloom, Richard in Pediatric Notes 2007 Nov 15;31(46):184.

1654 Field AE, Austin B, Striegel-Moore R, et al. Weight concerns and weight control behaviors of adolescents and their mothers. Arch Pediatr Adolesc Med 2005 Dec;159:1121-6.

1655 Taylor CB, Bryson S, Celio Doyle AA, et al. The adverse effect of negative comments about weight and shape from family and siblings on women at high risk for eating disorders. Pediatrics 2006 Aug;118(2):731-8.

1656 Anderson MR, Leroux BG, Bricker JB, Rajan KB, Peterson AV. Antismoking parenting practices are associated with reduced rates of adolescent smoking. Arch Pediatr Adolesc Med 2004 April;158:348-52.

1657 Stanton B, Cole M, Galbraith J, et al. Randomized trial of a parent intervention. Arch Pediatr Adolesc Med 2004 October;158:947-55.

1658 Roche KM, Ellen J, Astone M. Effects of out-of-school care on sex initiation among young adolescents in low-income central city neighborhoods. Arch Pediatr Adolesc Med 2005 January;159:68-73.

1659 Resnick MD, Bearman PS, Blum RW, et al. Protecting adolescents from harm; findings from the National Longitudinal Study on Adolescent Health. JAMA 1997 September 10;278(10): 823-32.

1660 Centers for Disease Control and Prevention. Effect of ending an antitobacco youth campaign on adolescent susceptibility to cigarette smoking—Minnesota, 2002-2003. MMWR 2004 April 16;53(14).

1661 Flay BR, Graumlich S, Segawa E, et al. Effects of 2 prevention programs on high-risk behaviors among African American youth. Arch Pediatr Adolesc Med 2004 April;158:377-84.

1662 Bettinger JA, Celentano DD, Curriero FC, et al. Does parental involvement predict new sexually transmitted diseases in female adolescents? Arch Pediatr Adol Med 2004 July;158:666-70.

1663 Steinberg, Lawrence. Parental monitoring and peer influence on alcohol and substance use. Pediatrics 93(6);June, 1994:1060-72.

1664 Brook JS, et al. The role of parents in protecting Colombian adolescents from delinquency and marijuana use. Arch Pediatr and Adolesc Med 153;May, 1999:457-64.

1665 DiClemete RJ, Wingood GM, Crosby R, et al. Parental monitoring: association with adolescents' risk behaviors. Pediatrics 2001 June;107(6):1363-8.

1666 Resnick MD, Bearman PS, Blum RW, et al. Protecting adolescents from harm; findings from the National Longitudinal Study on Adolescent Health. JAMA 1997 September 10;278(10): 823-32.

1667 Hindelang RL, Dwyer WO, Leeming FC. Adolescent risk-taking behavior: a review of the role of parental involvement. Current problems in pediatrics; March, 2001:67-82.

1668 YMCA of the USA, Dartmouth Medical School, Institute for American Values. Hardwired to Connect; The new Scientific Case for Authoritative Communities. Published by the Institute for American Values, 1841 Broadway Suite 211, New York NY 10023; 2003.

1669 Grant B, Dawson D. Age of onset of alcohol use and its association with DSM-IV alcohol abuse and dependence. Results from the National Longitudinal Alcohol Epidemiologic Survey. J Sub Abuse 1997;9:103-10.

1670 Centers for Disease Control and Prevention. Effect of ending an antitobacco youth campaign on adolescent susceptibility to cigarette smoking—Minnesota, 2002-2003. MMWR 2004 April 16;53(14).

1671 United States Department of HHS. Preventing tobacco use among young people: a report of the Surgeon General. Washington DC: US Dept. of HHS, 1994.

1672 Kim, Timothy F. "Tobacco addiction: teens more susceptible." Pediatric News 2005 June;39(6):6 referring to a presentation by Dr. Mark Rubenstein at the annual meeting of the Society for Adolescent Medicine.

1673 *Marijuana and Medicine: Assessing the Science Base*. Washington, DC: National Academies Press, 1999.

1674 Fergusson DM, et al. Early reactions to cannabis predict later dependence. Arch of Gen Psych 60;2003:1033-9.

1675 Bjork JM, Knutson B, Fong GW, et al. incentive-elicited brain activation in adolescents: similarities and differences from young adults. Neurosci 2004 Feb 25;24(8):1793-802.

1676 Lawson, Kim. "MRI finds teens have less frontal cortex function than adults." Pediatric News 34(5);May, 2000.

1677 Vastag, Brian. "Nora Volkow MD; NIDA's new leader: from rejection to direction." JAMA 290(20);November 26, 2003:2647-52.

1678 Vastag, Brian. "Nora Volkow MD; NIDA's new leader: from rejection to direction." JAMA 290(20);November 26, 2003:2647-52.

1679 Vastag, Brian. "Brain sabotages sobriety, right on cue." JAMA 291(9);March 3,2004:1053-5.

1680 Tapert SF, Cheung EH, Brown GG, et al. Neural response to alcohol stimuli in adolescents with alcohol use disorder. Arch Gen Psychiatry 2003 Jul;60(7):727-35.

1681 "Teddy Roosevelt". Kids Discover 2005 Sept;15(9):3.

1682 Porter, Fairfield, as quoted by Cole, Thomas B in JAMA 2009 June 3;301(21):2189.

1683 Schwartz, Barry. *The Paradox of Choice; Why More is Less*. New York, NY; HarperCollins, 2004.

1684 Levine, Madeline. *The Price of Privilege*. New York, NY; HarperCollins, 2006.

1685 Mesic, Penelope. "Privileged." North Shore Magazine 2008 Nov:69-75.

Made in the USA
Lexington, KY
16 January 2015